Power BI in the Workplace Part 1a

HR Attendance and Absence Reporting

Grant Gamble

Contents

Introduction

There are many ways to learn Power BI, but very few of them mirror the way people actually use Power BI at work. Most courses serve up a familiar diet: sample sales data, fictional companies, and stylised dashboards that look great but bear little resemblance to the reporting challenges faced in real organisations.

This book takes a different path.

Power BI in the Workplace Part 1a HR Attendance and Absence Reporting is the first in a series designed for those who want to go beyond generic examples and start working with realistic, internal-facing data. Here, you'll build HR reports that feel like the kind you'd be expected to deliver in a real company—whether you work in HR, support HR reporting as an analyst, or simply want to broaden your Power BI experience with datasets that aren't just about products, sales, and profit margins.

This introduction is not here to rehash what Chapter 1 already covers. You've likely already seen how this series sets itself apart by focusing on workplace realism and practical structure. Instead, this introduction is about helping you understand the why behind the content, the who it's really for, and what kind of thinking is encouraged as you work through the chapters.

Why HR? Why Attendance and Absence?

In every organisation, people data matters—but it's often the most underreported. Unlike finance or sales reporting, which typically benefits from years of embedded systems and clear KPIs, HR data tends to be fragmented. Attendance logs, absence reports, leave summaries, and overtime tracking may all sit in separate spreadsheets, SharePoint folders, or cloud-based exports from different systems.

This creates a perfect challenge for Power BI—and a perfect opportunity to teach it. Working with this kind of data means handling messy formats, inconsistent entries, evolving metrics, and changing organisational structures. That's exactly what makes it such a rich foundation for learning Power BI in a way that's genuinely useful.

By focusing on absence and attendance, we ground our learning in one of the most common—and often most scrutinised—reporting areas in HR. Executives want absence costs; managers want team-level insights; HR needs to monitor patterns and spot early warning signs. In this book, we build a solution that supports all those needs.

Who This Book Is For

This book is written for Power BI users who are beyond the beginner stage—but not necessarily experts. Maybe you've built a few reports. Maybe you've taken a course or two. Maybe you've been asked to "tidy up this Excel file and make something visual from it." If you understand the basics of loading data, adding visuals, and writing simple measures, then this book will give you the next step: working with more complex scenarios while developing a real-world solution from start to finish.

This book is also ideal for:

- HR professionals looking to gain Power BI skills using data that actually reflects their day-to-day work
- Analysts supporting HR departments
- IT or business intelligence staff building internal reports
- Trainers or team leads tasked with onboarding Power BI users using meaningful examples

Even if HR isn't your focus, the techniques and report design patterns you'll learn—cleaning data from multiple sources, structuring navigation, building dynamic visuals, publishing and sharing securely—will apply across industries and use cases.

How This Series Is Structured

This first volume builds gradually but deliberately. You start with a lightweight report from a staff survey, and by the end of the book, you'll have built a fully functional attendance and absence report—styled, parameterised, drillable, and shareable.

Each chapter introduces a practical objective and walks you through a realistic task: connecting to shared folders, dealing with hidden sheets, constructing custom measures, building field parameter toggles, formatting responsive layouts, and managing report distribution.

But you'll also be encouraged to think like a report developer: to question what the report user needs, to consider what makes a visual clear or confusing, and to develop habits that support sustainability—like using templates, creating metadata indicators, and planning navigation from the start.

The Bigger Picture

Power BI is not just about visuals. It's about communication. It's about helping others understand what the data is saying—and being confident that the story the data tells is accurate, current, and useful.

This book equips you to do that, using the kind of data you're more likely to encounter in real life than in a sales textbook. But it also encourages a mindset: one that values clarity, simplicity, and professional polish over flashy features that rarely get used after the report is published.

You're not just learning how to use Power BI. You're learning how to build reporting solutions that people trust and rely on.

What Comes Next

Future volumes in this series will expand into other HR themes—such as employee turnover, compensation analysis, DEI reporting, and training evaluation. Each will layer on new techniques while reinforcing the core principle that good reporting is grounded in real work, not canned examples.

Chapter 1: Getting Started

1.1: Welcome

Are you learning Power BI but finding yourself weary of the same old sales-oriented demo data that turns up in course after course, regardless of the concept being taught: Microsoft's AdventureWorks, Contoso Sales, even the old Northwind Traders. It can feel like every example is drawn from a generic product sales spreadsheet. If this resonates with you, then the approach you'll find in Power BI in the Workplace offers a refreshing and much-needed change of direction.

Power BI in the Workplace is a practical series designed to help you build reports that genuinely reflect the kind of internal data you encounter in real organisations. It focuses entirely on business-ready reporting, grounded in realistic workplace scenarios. This volume is centred on one of the most common internal reporting needs across many organisations: HR attendance and absence reporting.

This book is intended for users who are already familiar with the basics of Power BI—those who can comfortably load data, create visuals, and understand simple DAX. That said, because this is the first volume in the series, we begin from first principles to ensure that even readers who are slightly rusty or self-taught can follow along with confidence.

You'll start by learning how to create reports that don't just display data but look and feel professional. This includes applying basic branding principles, building a report start page, designing clear navigation bars, and adding useful dynamic elements such as titles that update according to filters and automatic refresh date indicators.

We then introduce the HR absence dataset. This is a realistic and structured set of data that reflects genuine HR scenarios. You'll learn how to import data not just from Excel, but from SharePoint Online—a platform commonly used in real businesses. We'll show you how to locate data stored in tables and even extract information from hidden sheets—ensuring nothing is overlooked during the reporting process.

After importing the data, the next step is to prepare it for use. That means cleaning and transforming it in Power Query to turn messy or inconsistent files into structured tables that Power BI can work with efficiently. These skills are essential for any real-world Power BI developer.

Once the data is ready, you'll move on to building robust DAX measures. Rather than simplistic summaries, we focus on meaningful business metrics such as attendance rates, absence costs, and total working time lost. These measures form the foundation of the insights that HR and management teams actually care about.

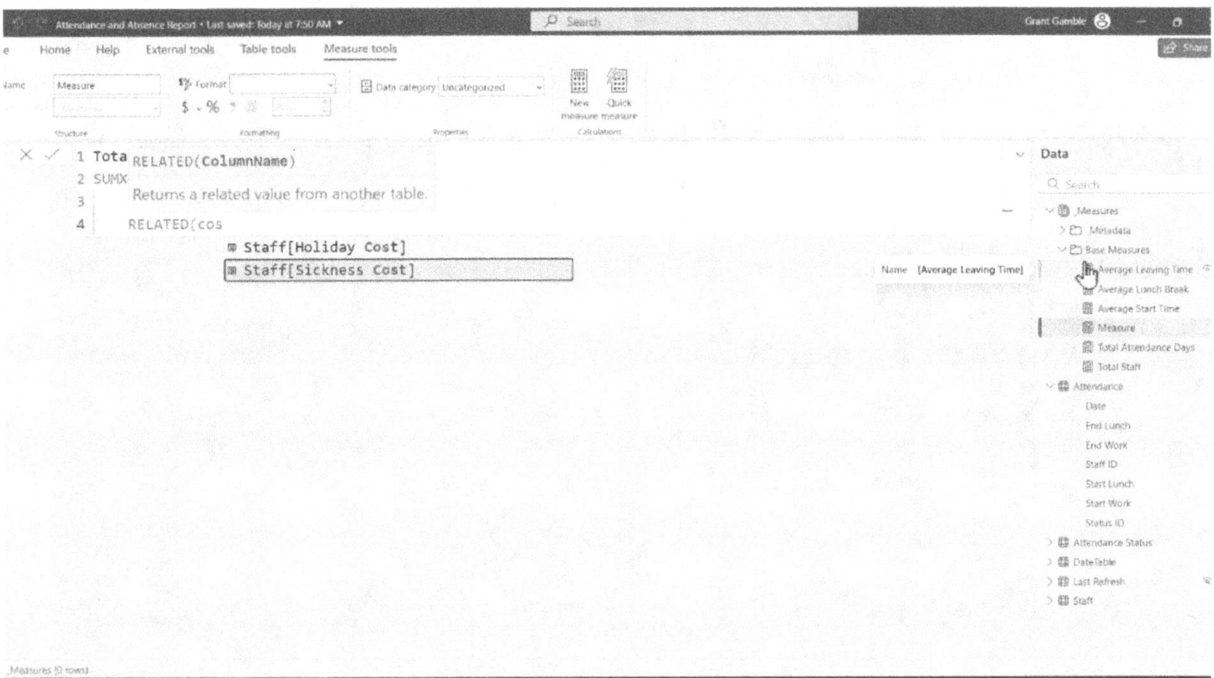

The report you'll build is more than just a set of charts. You'll apply a range of powerful features including field parameters to allow user-controlled metric switching, dropdown slicers for filtering, synchronised slicers across pages for consistent analysis, and card grids for displaying KPIs in a clean, modern layout. You'll also construct hierarchies and drill-down paths so users can explore the data naturally, from the big picture down to individual records.

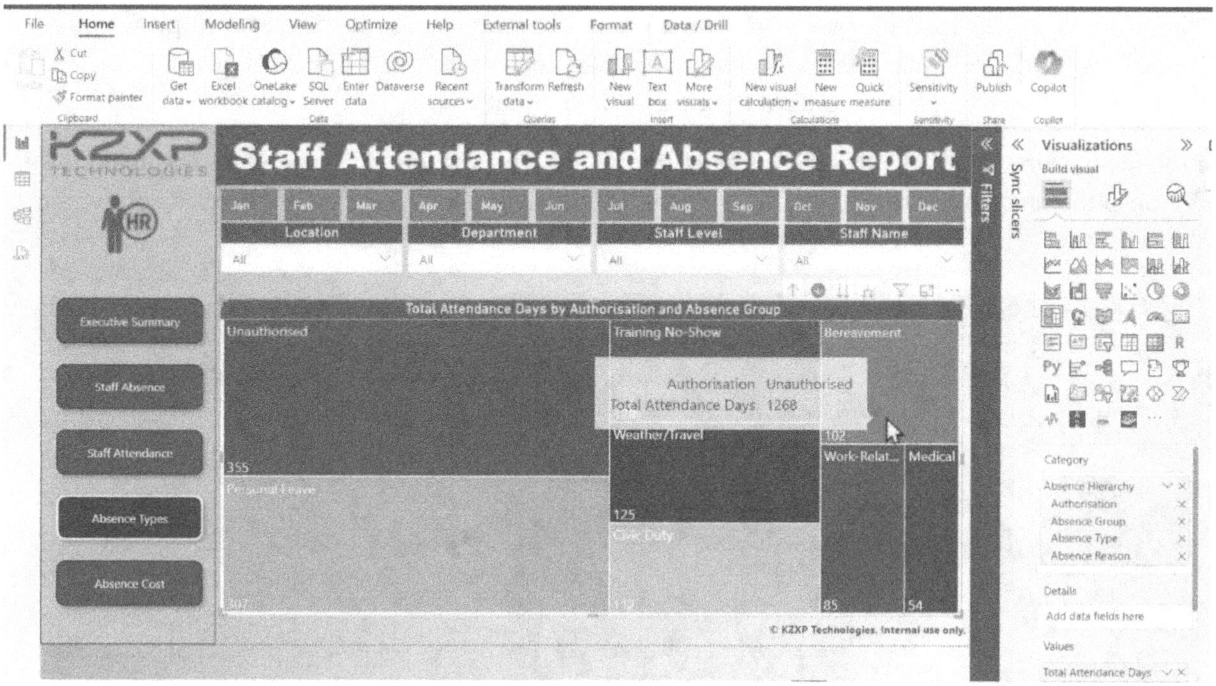

And finally, you'll learn how to publish your report to the Power BI Service. From there, we'll show you how to create dashboards, manage access, and wrap the entire solution into a polished Power BI app—ready to be rolled out to HR, management or any team who needs it.

This book is about building solutions that work. It's about making reports that are functional, insightful, and professional—tools that can be used with confidence in the workplace.

1.2: Downloading the Course Files

Before beginning any practical work in Power BI, it's important to have the correct resources downloaded and ready. These files provide the foundation for the HR reporting scenarios that will be explored throughout this book. In this section, we'll walk through the process of locating, downloading, and preparing the course files that accompany this guide.

You can download the exercise files used in this book from our website:

Primary download link:

https://gcomsolutions.co.uk/powerbi/pbiwp1a

Direct AWS download link (ZIP file):

https://powerbitraining.s3.eu-west-2.amazonaws.com/pbiw-1a-hr-attendance-and-absence.zip

If you're unable to access the website due to a workplace firewall or security restrictions, try using the AWS direct download link above. Still having trouble? Contact our support team at:

Email: support@gcomsolutions.co.uk

You'll be prompted to choose a location on your computer to save the ZIP file. Select your preferred folder and click Save. Depending on your browser settings, the file may automatically begin downloading, or you may need to confirm the download manually.

Once the file has downloaded, navigate to the folder where it was saved. This next step is critical: make sure to unzip the file. Do not simply double-click the ZIP archive to look inside it—this does not extract the files properly.

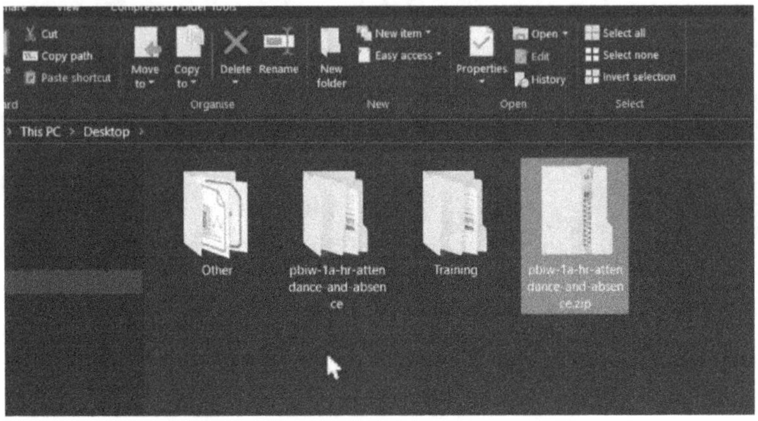

You won't need any additional software to do this. Just right-click the ZIP file and choose Extract All, then click the Extract button in the dialogue box that appears. This will create a new folder in the same location, containing the full set of course materials.

Inside the extracted folder, the content is structured to match the layout of this book and is divided into three key sections:

- Section 2 – This is where you will build the Quick Staff Survey Report.
- Section 3 – Here, you'll construct a Reusable Report Template.
- Section 4 – This section focuses on building the Main Attendance and Absence Report.

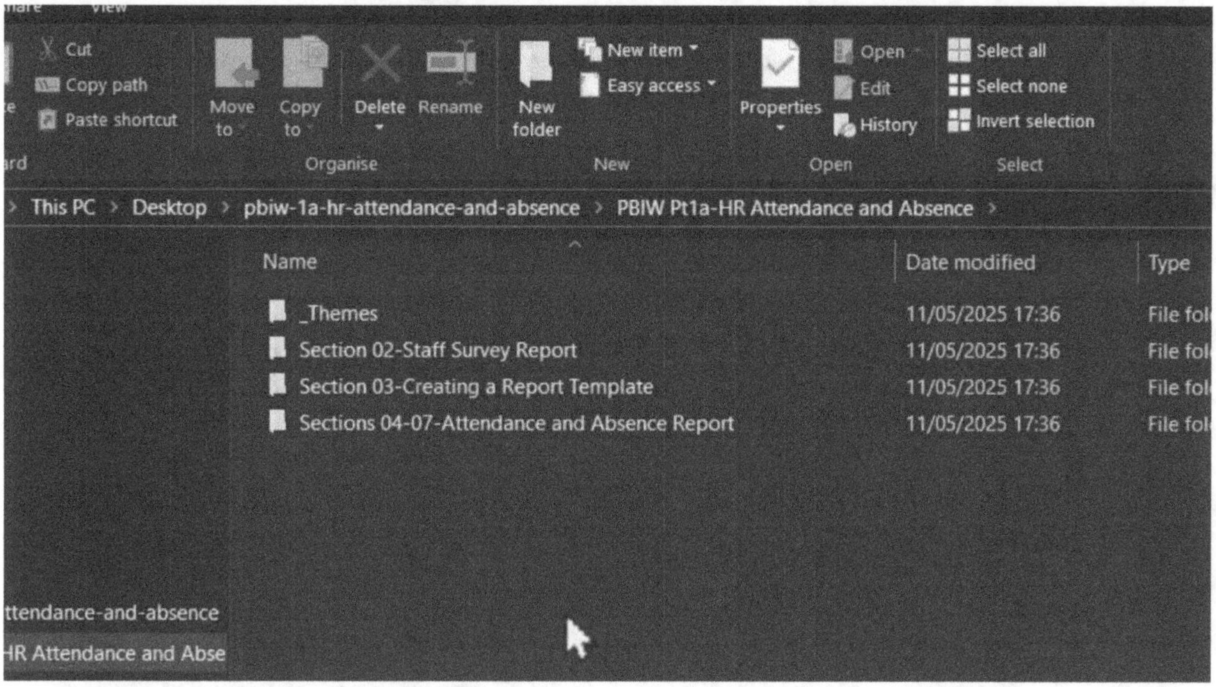

Within each section folder, you'll find two types of files:

- A blank starter file, which you can use to build the report step by step as you follow along.
- A completed version, useful if you're short on time or would prefer to study a finished report to see how everything fits together.

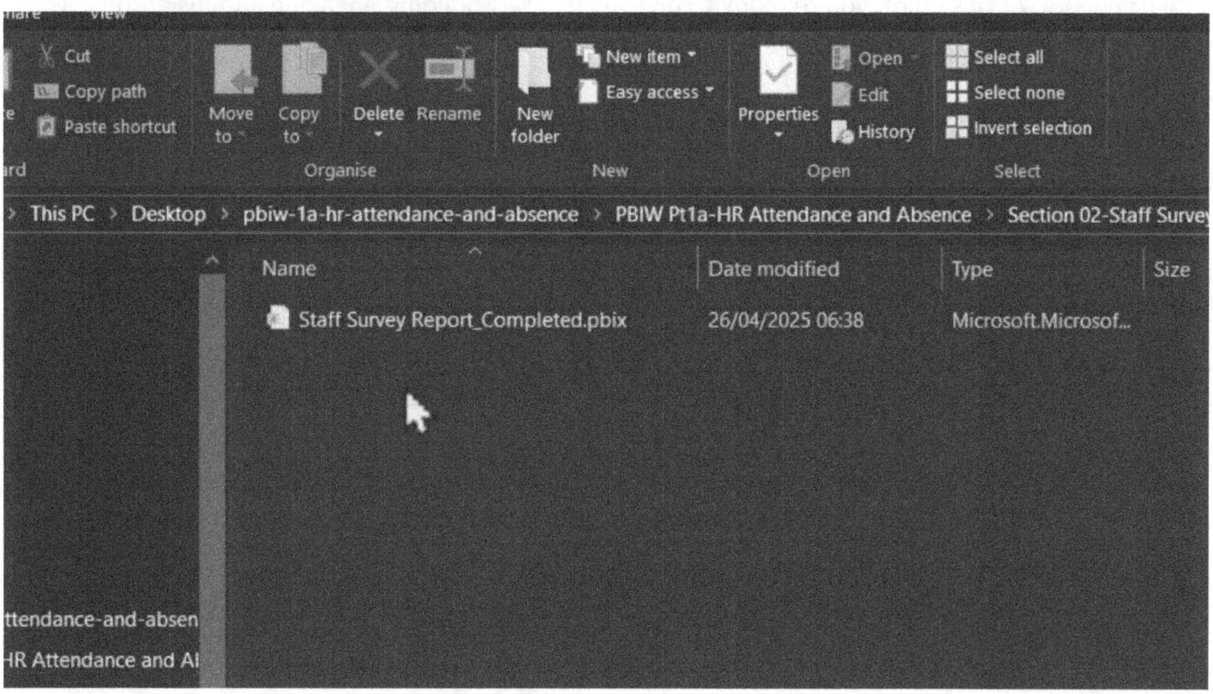

Additionally, there's an assets folder containing essential visuals such as logos, custom Power BI themes, and other elements that help you match the branding used in our examples. These assets include the fictional company branding for KZXP, which is used consistently throughout all the reports.

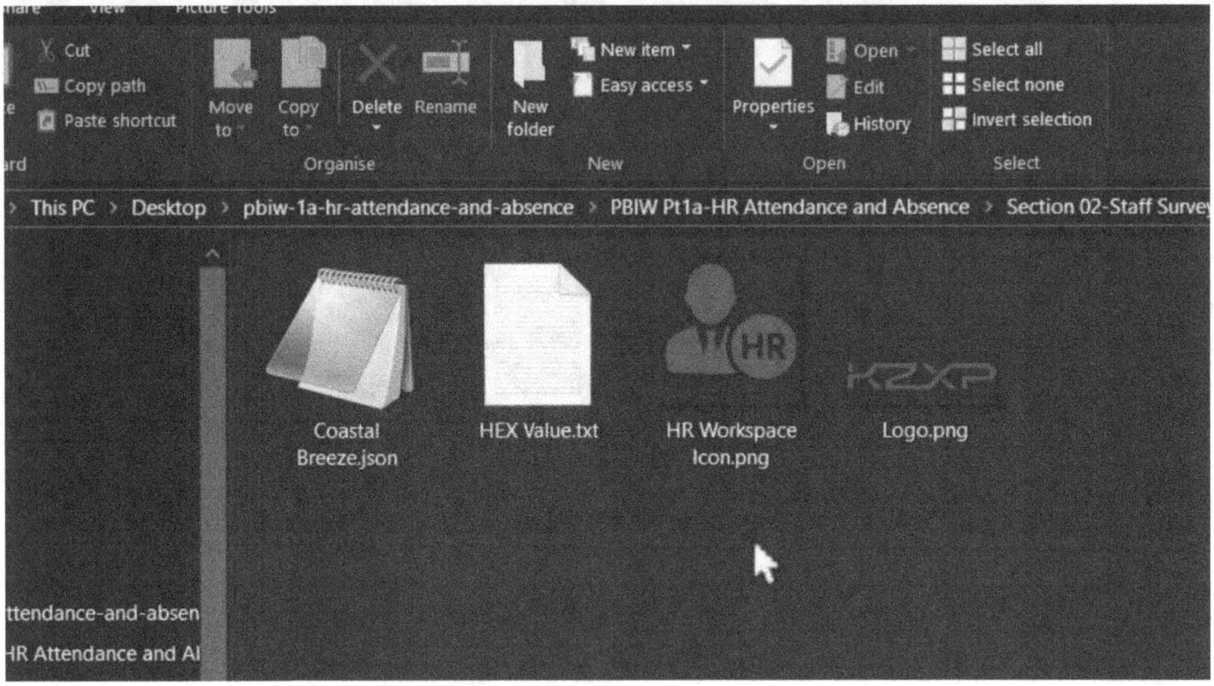

Once you've successfully downloaded and unzipped the folder, you'll have everything you need to begin the practical work. At this point, you're ready to dive in and start building engaging and insightful HR reports using Power BI.

Chapter 2: Staff Survey Report

2.1: Importing and Exploring the Survey CSVs

To begin our report-building process, we start by opening the Power BI file included in the Section 2 folder. This file is named Staff Survey Report.pbix. Alongside it, there is a folder called Data, which contains the two source files we'll be working with throughout this section. These files represent simple flat file datasets: one for survey questions and another for survey results.

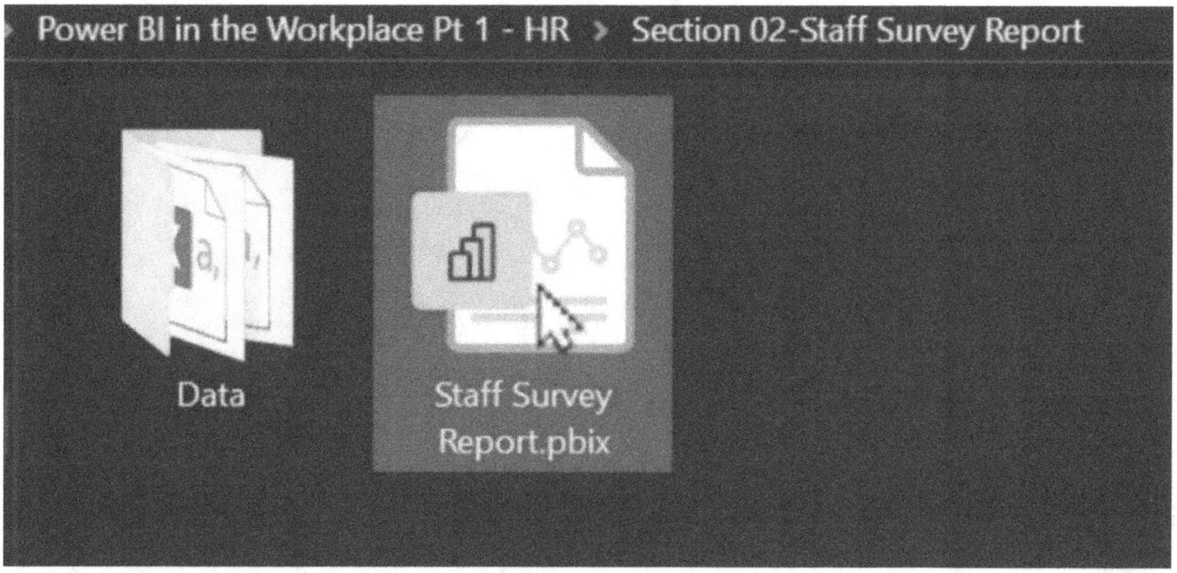

This chapter will take you through the full Power BI report creation cycle. We'll begin with the most straightforward techniques, then progressively introduce more complexity and real-world issues. The goal is not just to import data, but to understand the practical considerations of working with various types of sources, managing transformations, and preparing data for effective reporting.

The first step in any Power BI project is to get some data into your environment. On the Home tab of the ribbon, click the Get Data button. You'll see a list of common data sources in the dropdown menu. Clicking More opens up Power BI's extensive list of compatible sources, which includes files, databases, cloud services, and more.

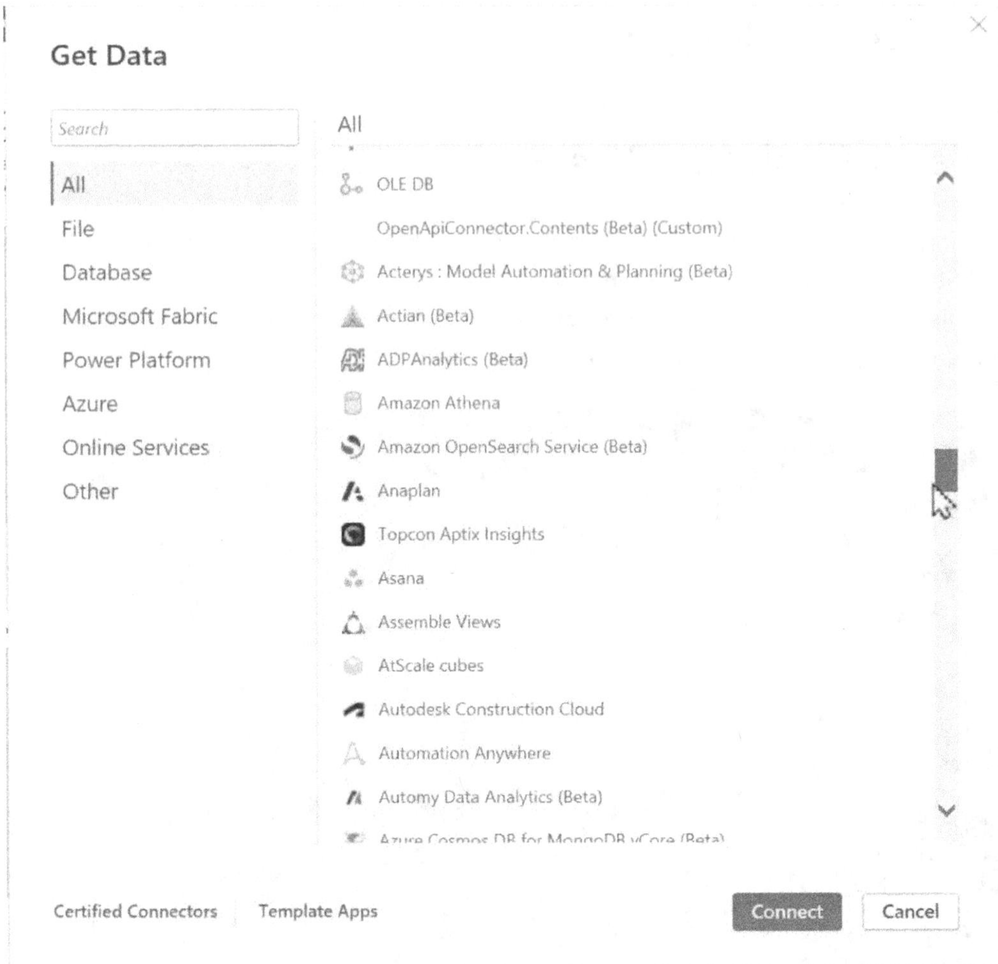

For now, let's cancel this dialog and focus on the simplest type of data source—a flat file. Flat files, such as CSVs, contain just raw data, without the need for credentials, authentication, or complex navigation through database schemas. You connect to them and access the data directly.

So, from the Home tab, choose Get Data, then select Text/CSV.

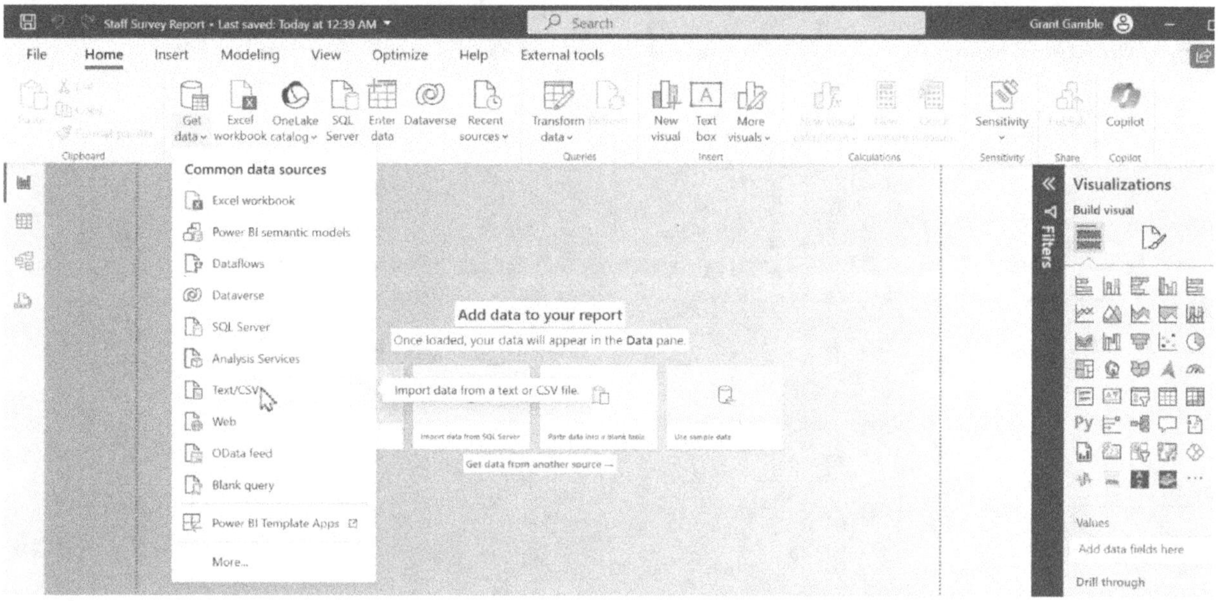

Navigate into the Data folder. You'll see two files: Survey Questions.csv and Survey Results.csv. Since these are stored in separate files, they must be imported one at a time—Power BI does not allow simultaneous loading of multiple files unless you're using folder-based connections or other consolidation methods.

Start by selecting Survey Questions.csv. A preview window will appear, allowing you to inspect the data. Power BI automatically identifies the file's encoding (in this case, Western European), the delimiter (comma), and performs data type detection. For example, it may detect that column one is numeric while column two is text.

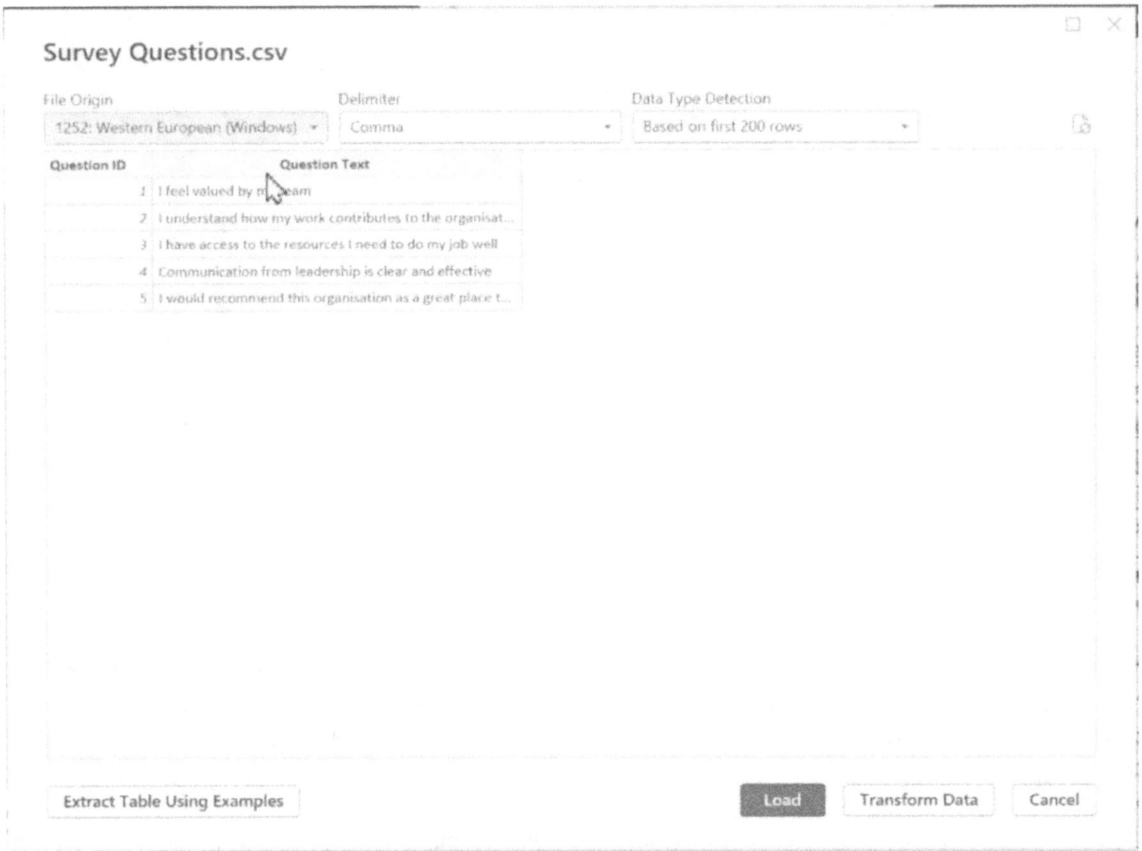

This preview stage is important. It helps confirm that you're accessing the correct file, and that the data appears as expected. The drop-down at the top allows you to determine how Power BI performs type detection: either on the first 200 rows (which is the default and usually works well) or on the entire dataset. You may also turn off detection altogether if you experience delays or want full manual control.

When type detection is turned on, Power BI also checks whether the first row contains headers. For instance, if column one is mostly numeric, but the first row contains text, Power BI assumes the first row is a header row. We'll leave the detection setting at its default: Based on first 200 rows.

At this point, you have two options: Load or Transform Data. Loading is suitable when the data is already clean and requires no shaping. This might be the case if data preparation has already been done upstream—perhaps by an IT or Data Engineering team. But in most cases, even with relatively clean data, Transform Data is the better choice.

By transforming the data before loading, you can reduce the size of your data model, removing unnecessary columns or filtering out rows you don't need. This helps make your report faster and easier to work with. Crucially, this decision is not irreversible. You can always return to Power Query later and make changes, even if you initially chose to Load.

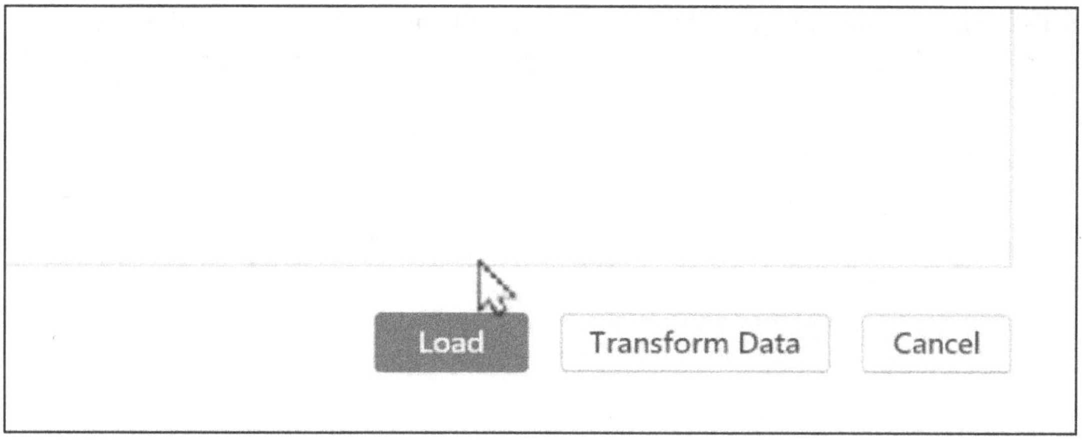

To demonstrate, we'll click Load. You'll now see a new table in the Data pane on the right, created from the Survey Questions file. This table contains the columns found in that file, and represents a straightforward load process.

To perform transformations at any point, simply click the Transform Data button in the ribbon. This launches Power Query, a data shaping environment built into Power BI. You'll notice two application windows in the taskbar: one for Power BI and one for Power Query. This environment is also used in Excel, so the skills you learn here are transferrable.

The process is iterative: enter Power Query, apply transformations, then click Close & Apply to refresh the model with your changes.

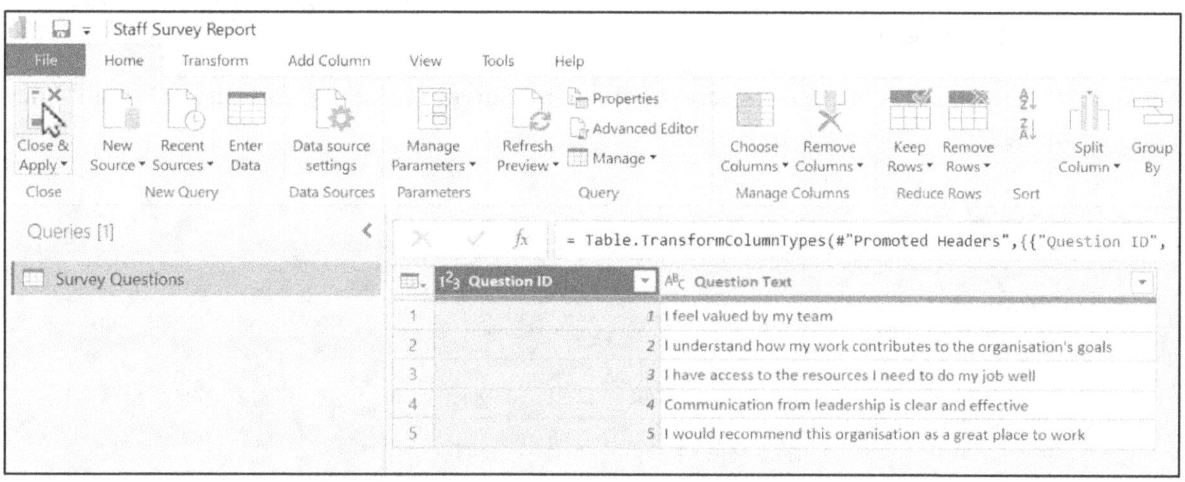

Next, we'll bring in the second file: Survey Results.csv. Once again, use Get Data > Text/CSV, navigate to the file, and a preview will appear. This time, we'll click Transform Data.

Now in Power Query, you'll see both queries—the original one from Survey Questions and the new one from Survey Results. Because we chose Transform Data this time, the second query hasn't yet been loaded into Power BI. If you switch back to Power BI itself, you'll see only the first table for now.

In Power BI, you'll also see a prompt to Apply Changes or Discard Changes, depending on the state of your data. The normal process is to return to Power Query, apply any necessary transformations, and then click Close & Apply.

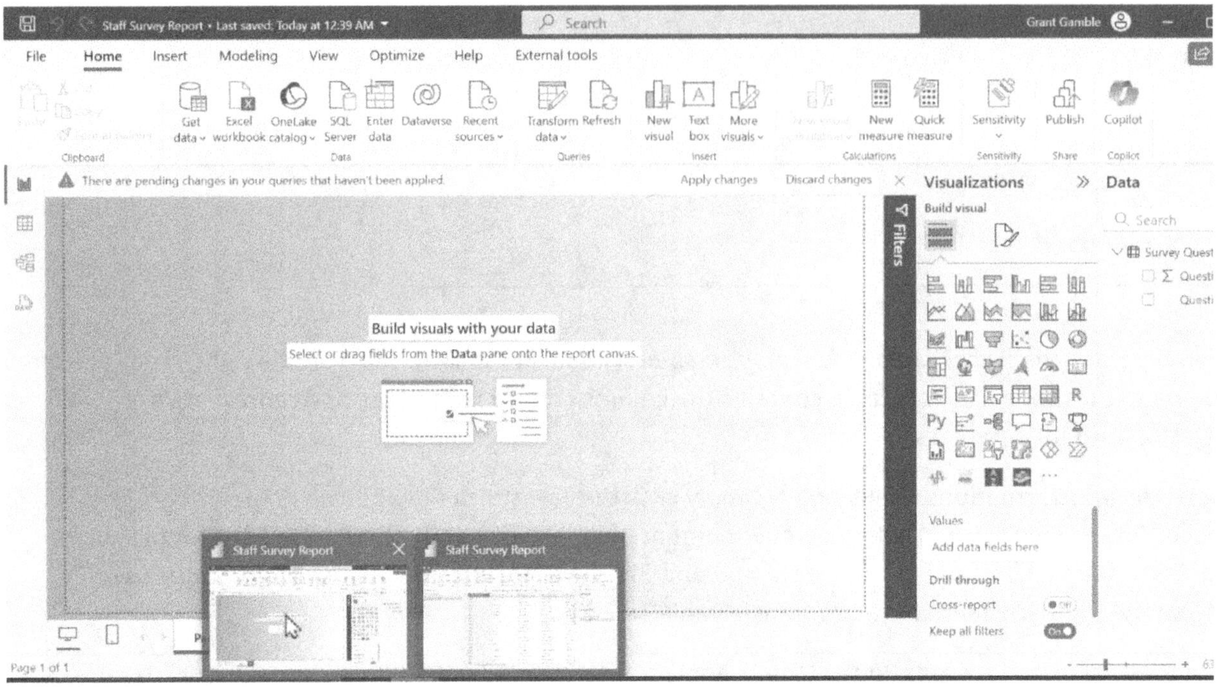

That's exactly what we'll do now. Click Close & Apply in Power Query. The changes will be committed, and the Survey Results data will be loaded into Power BI.

Now, you should see two tables in the Data pane on the right: Survey Questions and Survey Results. You can expand each one to view the individual columns they contain.

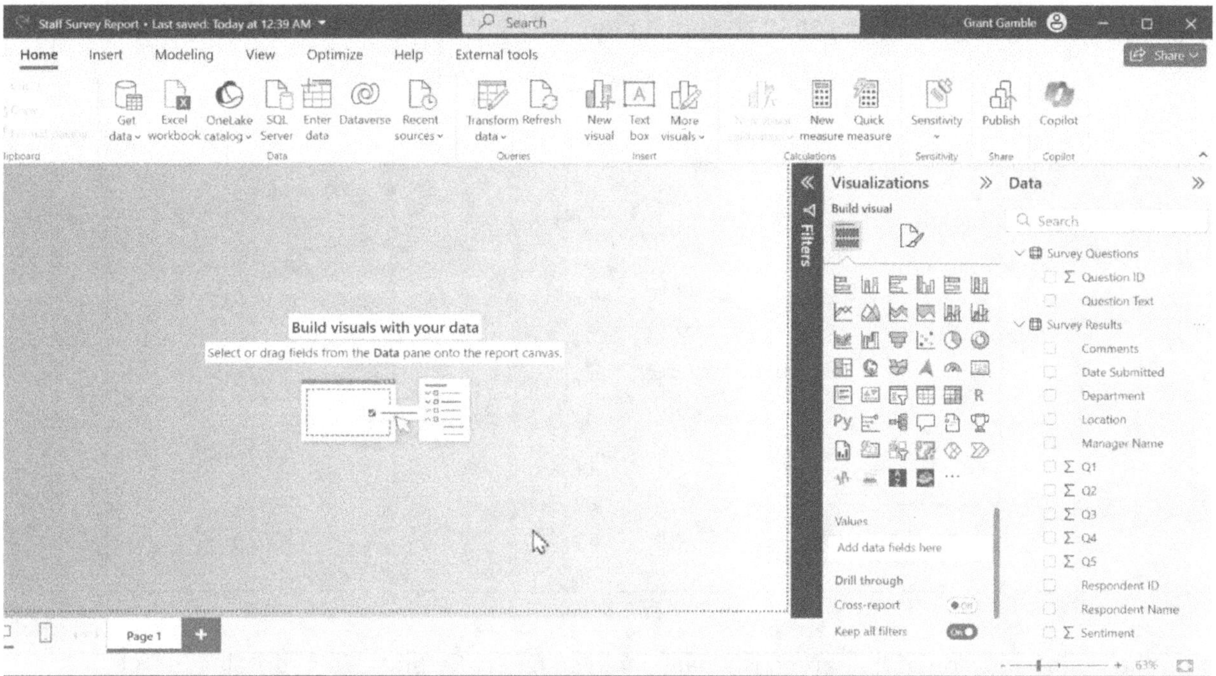

This completes our first look at importing data into Power BI using the most basic data source—flat files. This foundational workflow establishes an essential skill: connecting to data sources, reviewing structure, and choosing the appropriate loading or transformation strategy.

Before moving on, save your Power BI file to preserve your progress.

2.2: Introducing Power Query Transformations

In this section, we take our first proper look at Power Query and how it handles transformations. By now, you should have the Staff Survey Report.pbix file open and be ready to continue working with the data you previously loaded from CSV files.

To launch the Power Query editor, go to the Home tab of the Power BI ribbon and click Transform Data. This will take you into the Power Query environment, where transformations can be visually applied and managed.

On the left-hand side, you'll see the queries that were created when we connected to the two CSV files—one containing survey questions and the other containing survey results. We'll begin by looking at the simpler of the two: the Survey Questions query.

This table contains just two columns. The first column holds the question ID, and the second contains the question text. If you look closely, you'll notice a small icon to the left of each column header. These icons indicate the data type that Power Query has assigned to each column.

In this case, Power Query has made good guesses: the question ID is marked with a [123] icon, meaning it's treated as a whole number, and the question text is marked with [ABC], indicating text. If these types were incorrect, you could click the icon to change them—but here they're accurate, so no action is needed.

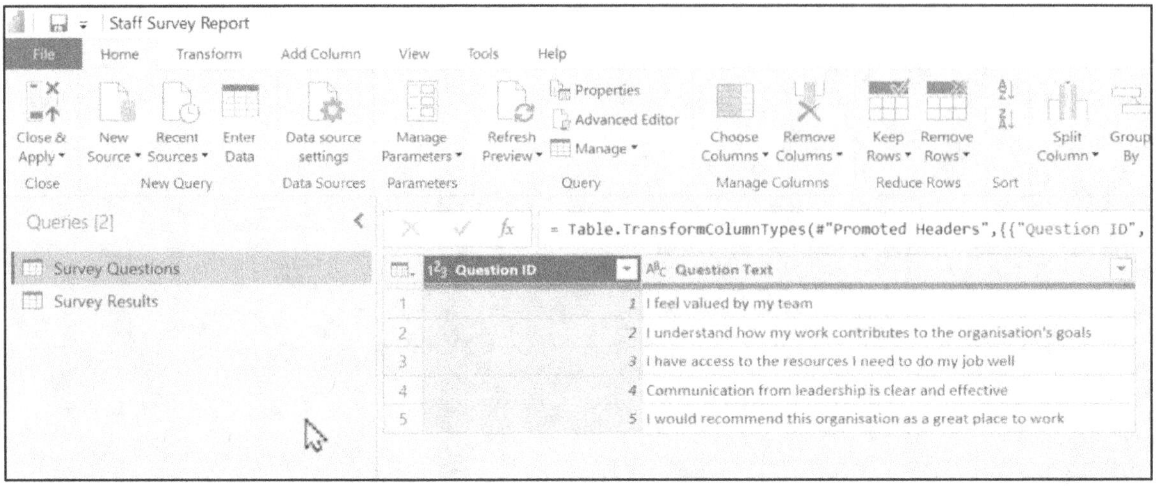

Over on the right-hand side of the screen is a pane labelled Query Settings. This contains useful information about the selected query. At the top, you'll see the name of the query. If you click All Properties, you'll be able to edit its name and add a description, which is a helpful habit when working with complex data models.

Beneath that is the Applied Steps list, one of Power Query's most powerful features. This is how Power Query keeps track of everything you do. There's no "Undo" button in the traditional sense—because you can simply click the "X" next to any step to remove it. This makes it very easy to roll back changes at any point in your transformation process.

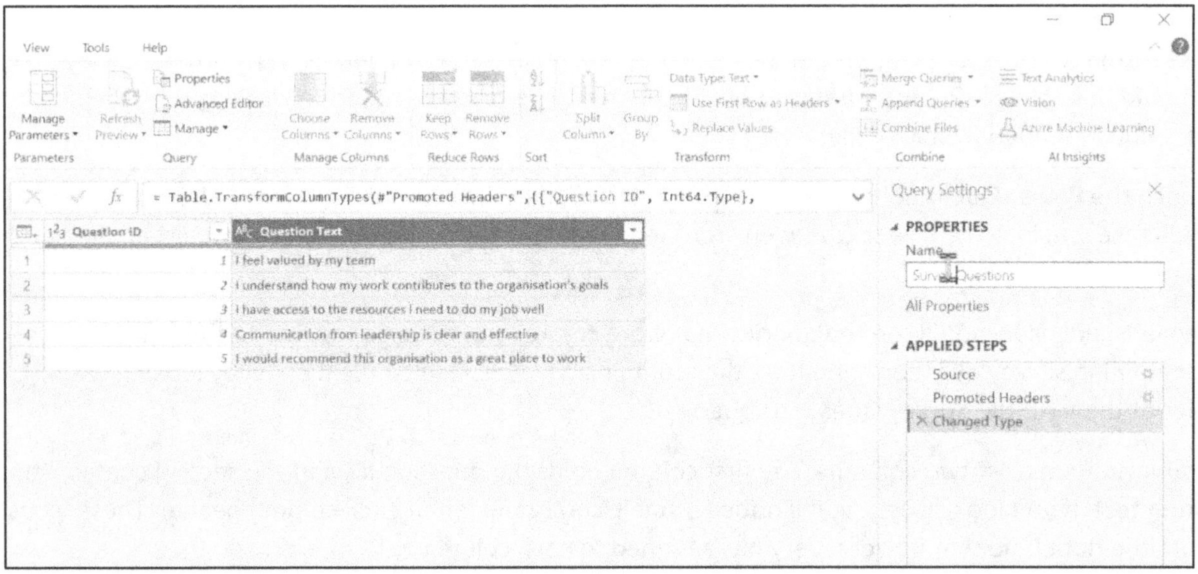

In our example, there's a step called Changed Type, which Power Query applied automatically. If we wanted to remove it, all columns would revert to text. While that might be fine for the second column, it wouldn't be correct for the first, so we would then need to reassign the correct type manually.

Since everything looks good here, we'll leave the Survey Questions query as is and move on to the Survey Results query.

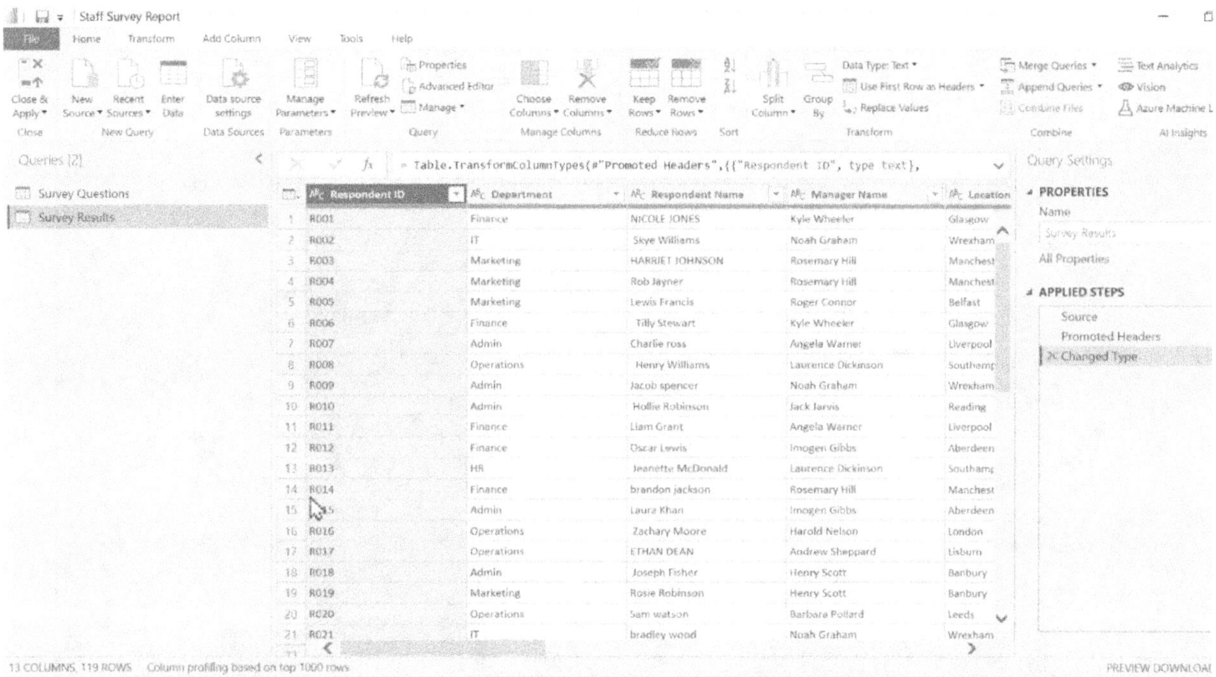

This second table has a different structure. It begins with an alphanumeric identifier starting with the letter "R"—so this should be treated as text. Next, we have the Department column, which tells us where the respondent works—again, text. Then there's the Respondent Name, and here we immediately spot a problem: inconsistencies in capitalisation and occasional leading spaces.

Scrolling across, we see more columns: Manager Name, Location, and then the actual survey questions, labelled Q1 through Q5. Finally, we have Date Submitted, Comments, and Sentiment.

The first step in tidying up is to focus only on the columns we need. Power BI always operates in read-only mode, so you'll never damage your original data source by removing columns within Power Query.

On the Home tab, use the Choose Columns tool. This opens a checklist of available columns, allowing you to tick the ones you want to keep. This is especially helpful when working with large datasets such as CRM systems or databases with hundreds of fields. You can even search within the column list—for example, typing "Q" will narrow it down to the question columns.

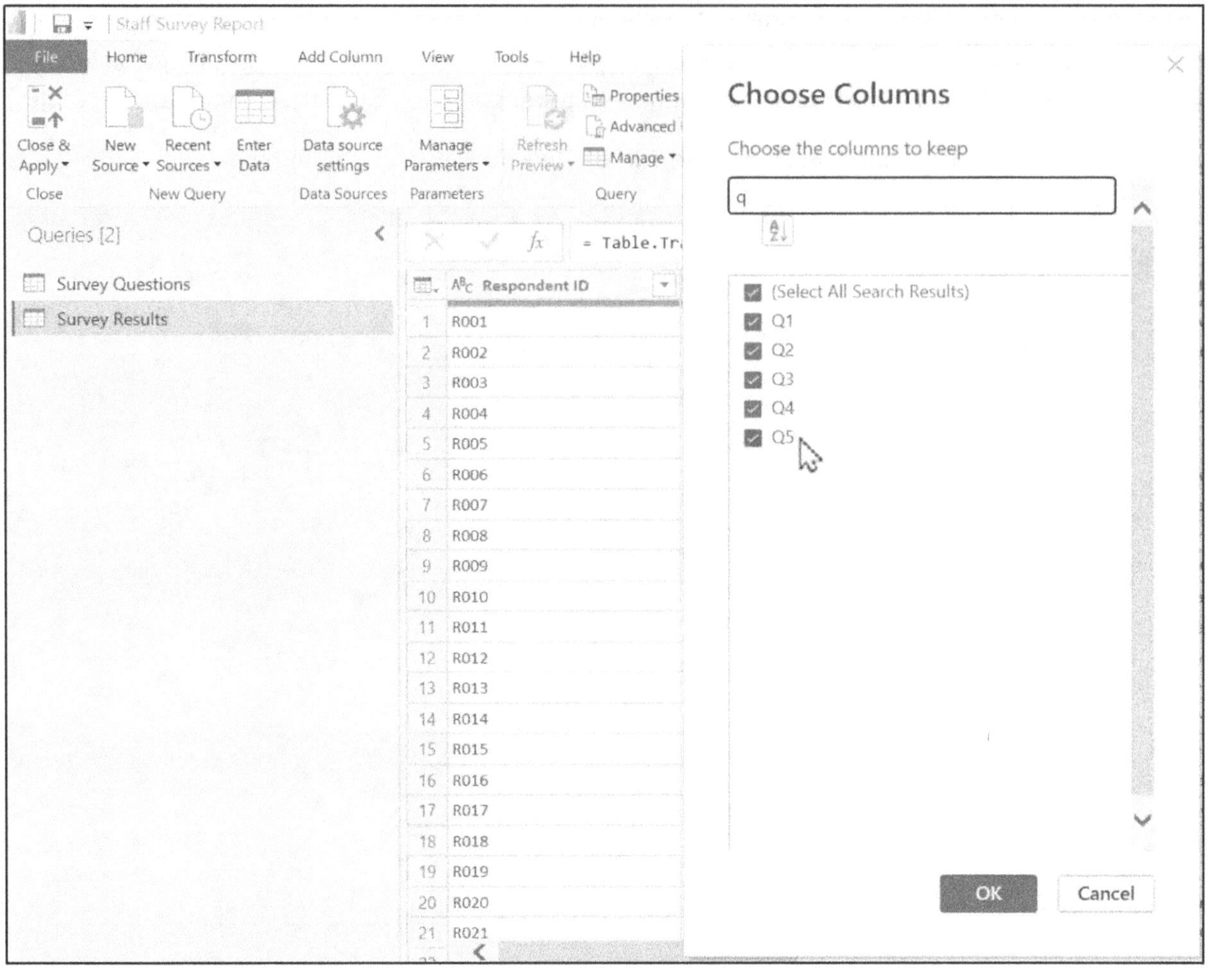

In our case, there are only a few columns, but we'll still use Choose Columns to deselect unnecessary ones. We'll remove Sentiment, Comments, and Respondent ID, since the person's name already uniquely identifies them.

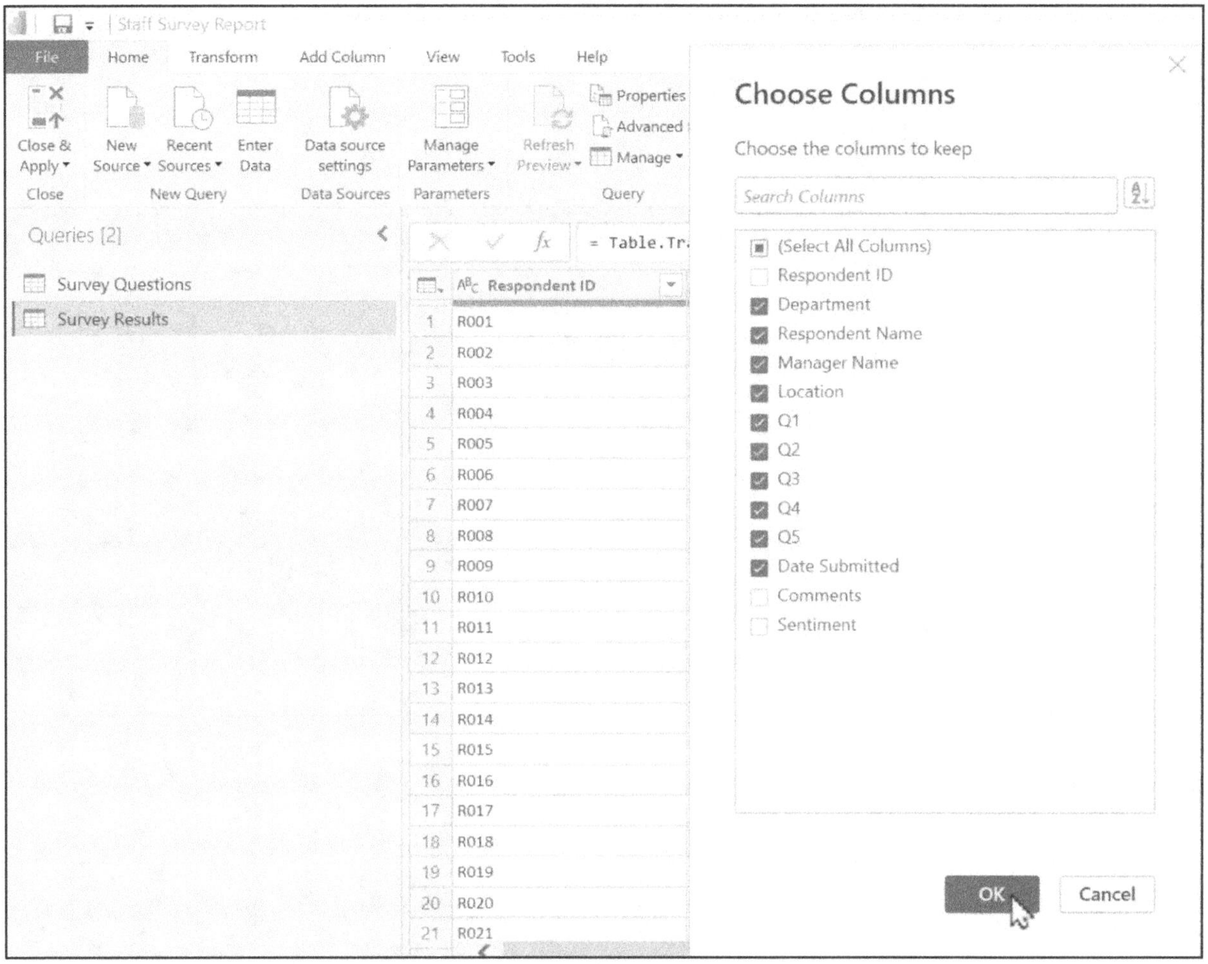

Next, check the data types. Power Query has again made sensible guesses, so we don't need to manually adjust these.

Now we turn our attention back to the Respondent Name column. The inconsistencies here are of two kinds: some names are in all lowercase or uppercase, and others have leading spaces. Ideally, names should follow title case, as seen in row two.

It's also wise to apply these cleanup steps to the Manager Name and Location columns—even if they appear fine—just in case similar inconsistencies are present.

To select a single column, click its heading. To select multiple, hold down Ctrl while clicking each one. For a continuous range, click the first column, then Shift-click the last.

With all three columns selected, go to the Transform tab and look under Format. You'll see options for Lower Case, Upper Case, and Capitalize Each Word. The last is what we want—names should appear in title case.

A quicker way to apply transformations is via the right-click menu, but here's a tip: right-click the column header, not the cell data. Right-clicking a cell will deselect your multiple column selection.

Right-click a selected column header, go to Transform, and choose Capitalize Each Word.

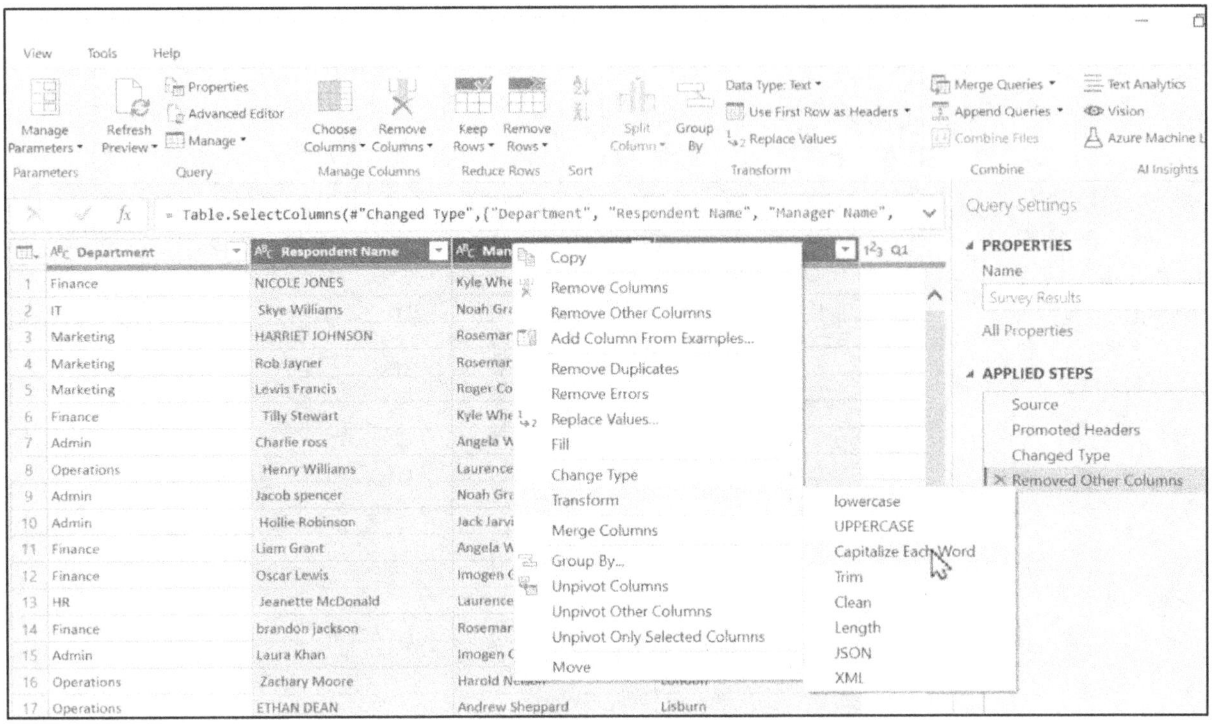

A new applied step will appear in the Query Settings pane.

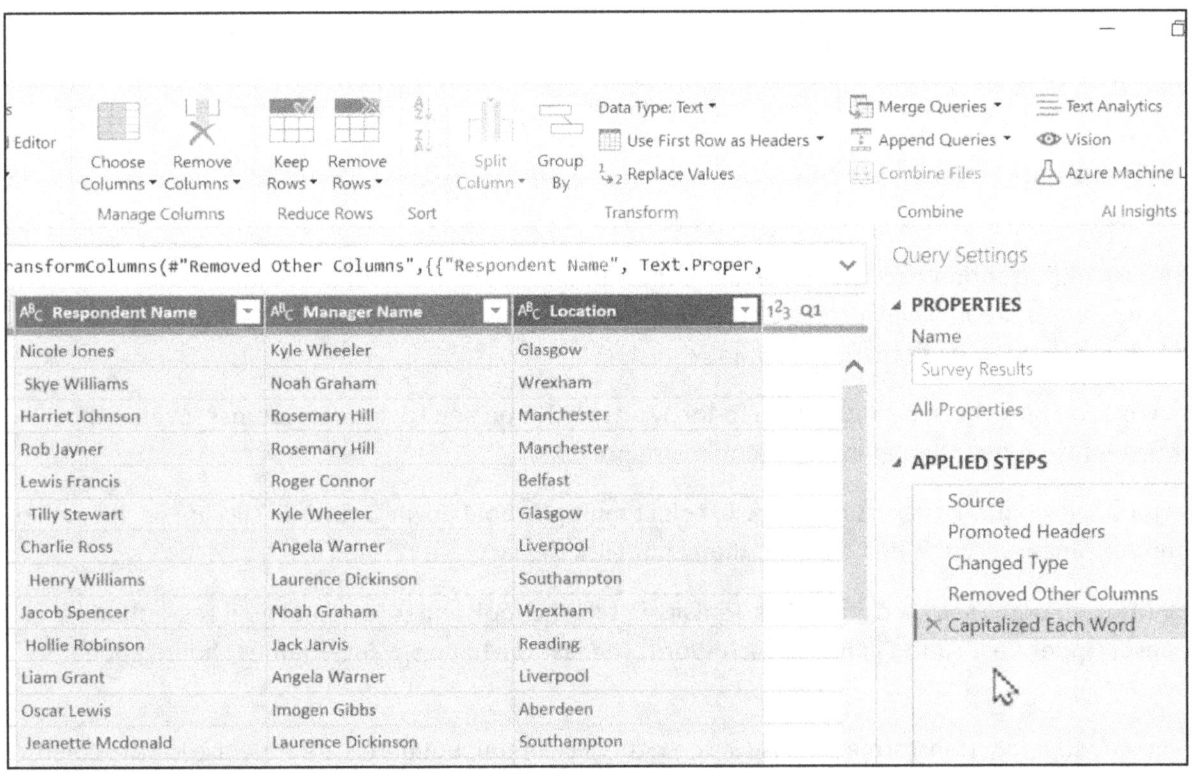

Now we tackle those hidden spaces. Again, select the three columns, then use Transform > Format > Trim. The Trim function removes leading and trailing spaces. (There's also a Clean function, which removes non-printable characters like carriage returns or tabs, but that's not necessary here.)

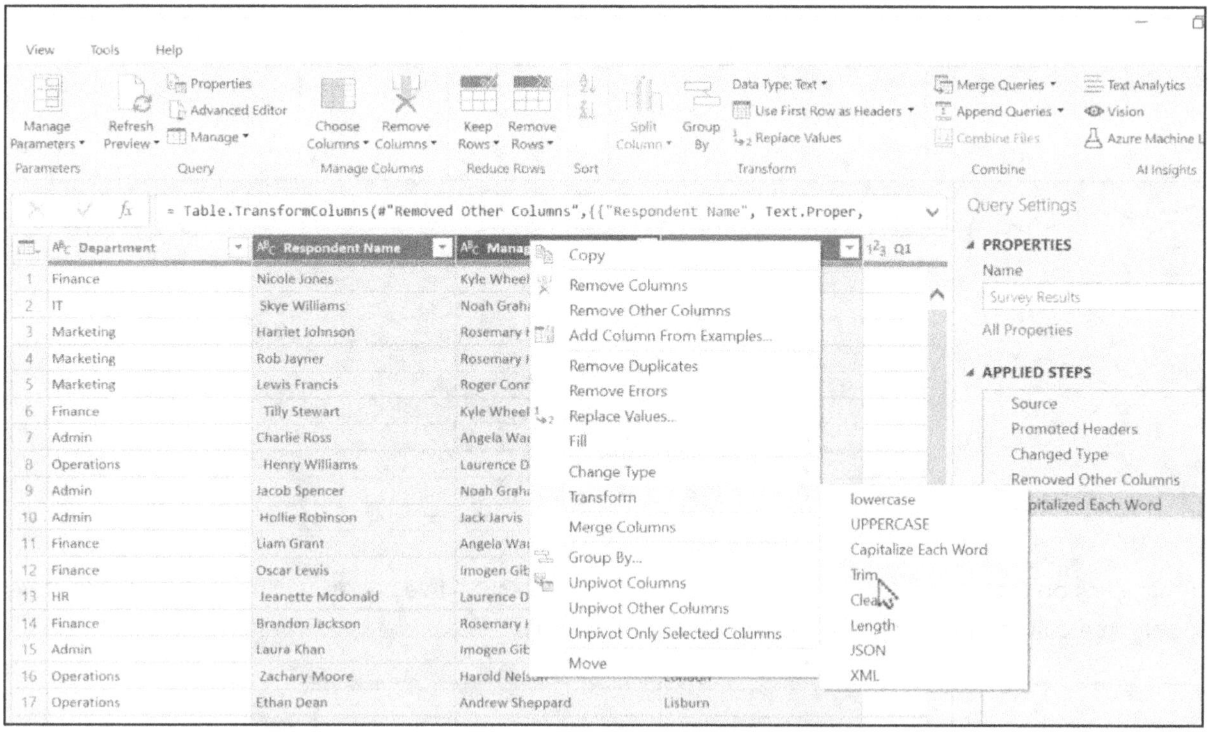

At this point, the basic cleanup is complete. Let's now look at a more advanced transformation: Unpivoting.

If you scroll across, you'll see the five survey question columns: Q1 through Q5. Each one contains a score—essentially the same type of data—but they're split into separate columns. This layout is fine for display, but makes calculations like averaging awkward, since it requires working across multiple fields.

The standard solution is to unpivot the data. This process converts the column-based layout into a row-based one: five columns become two—one for the Question label and one for the Response.

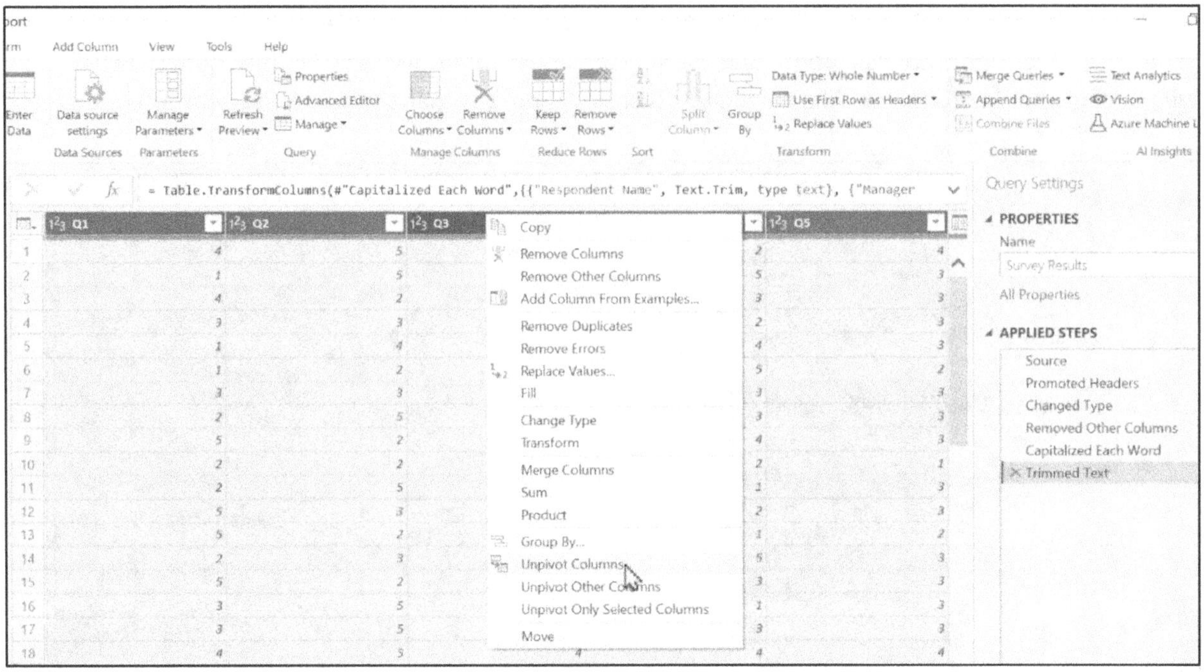

To do this, click on Q1, hold down Shift, and click on Q5 to select all five columns. Then right-click on one of the selected column headers and choose Unpivot Columns.

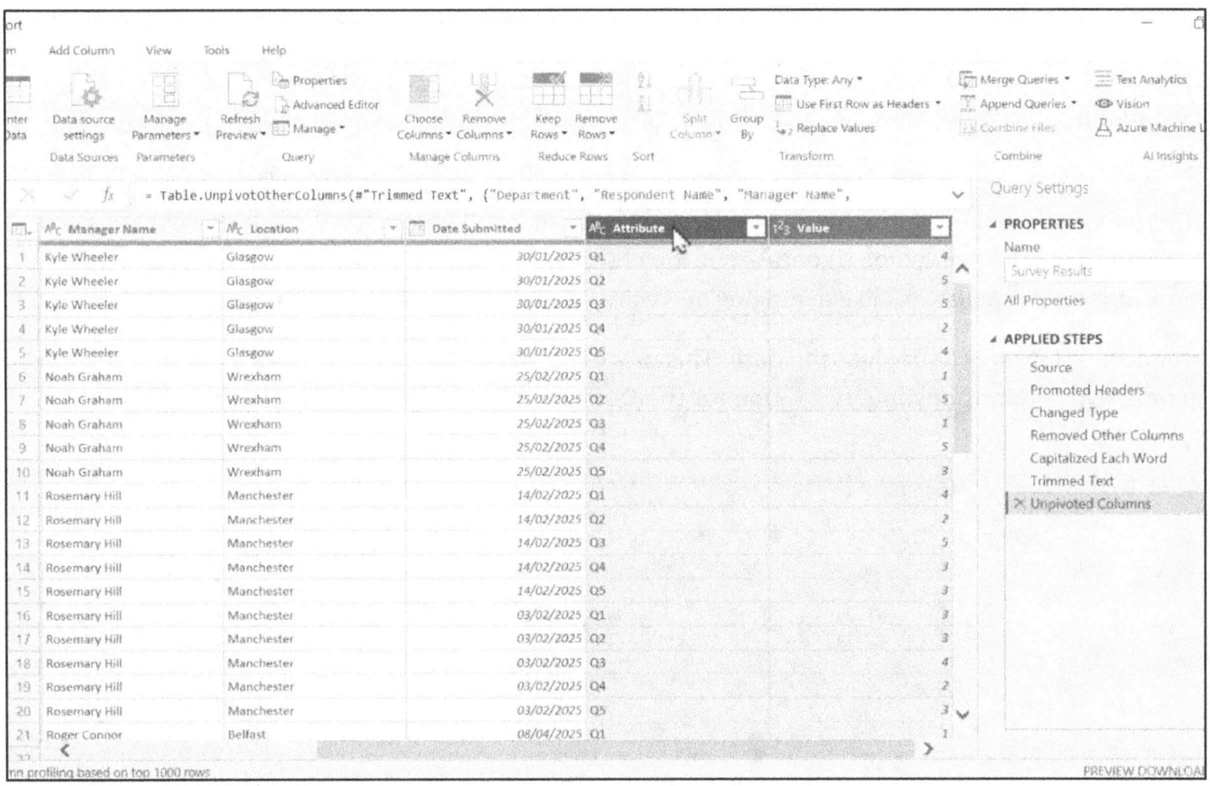

You'll now see two new columns: Attribute and Value. The Attribute column holds the old column names (Q1–Q5), while the Value column holds the scores. Let's rename these to something more meaningful.

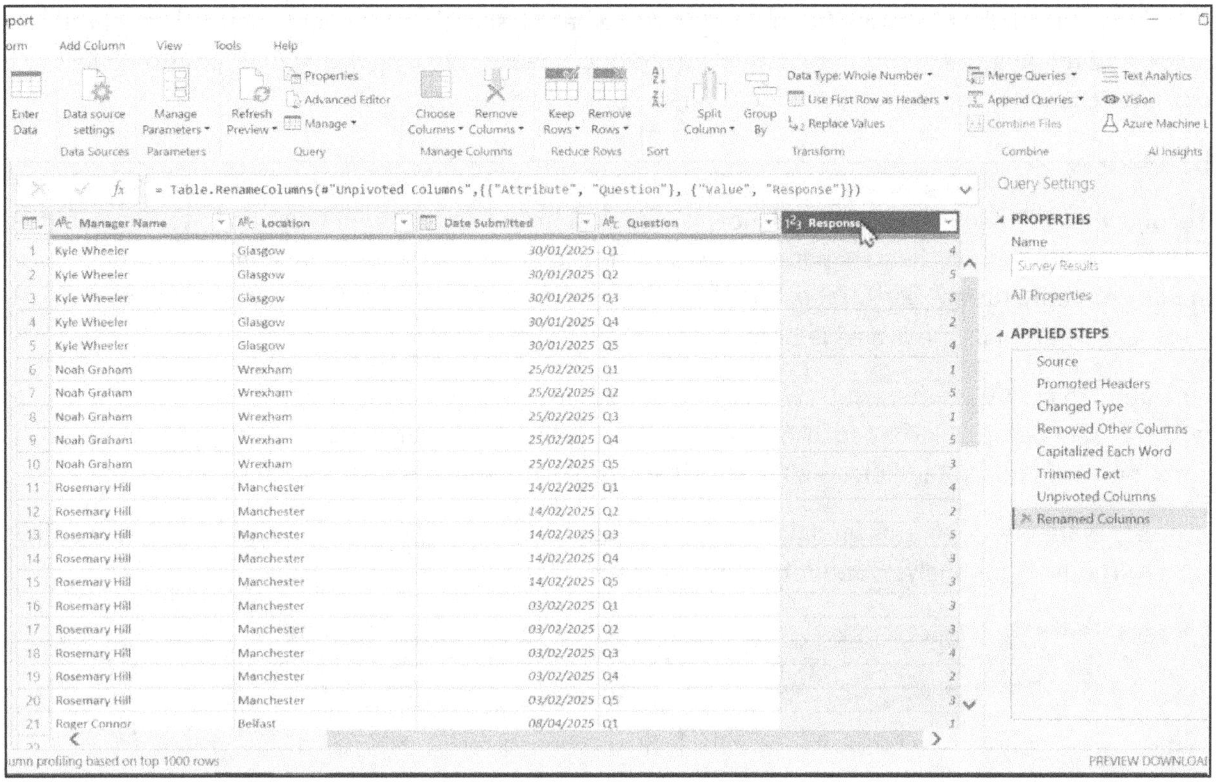

To rename a column, right-click the heading and choose Rename, or simply double-click it. Rename Attribute to Question, and Value to Response.

This completes our introduction to Power Query. As you've seen, it offers a user-friendly visual interface with a clear step-by-step history of every transformation. This makes it easy to trace your work, and just as easy to undo or revise steps.

Just before we finish, remember this: we've made changes to both queries, but only one of them may have been loaded into the data model initially. To ensure everything is updated properly, click Close & Apply in the Power Query window. This applies your changes and returns you to Power BI Desktop.

That concludes our first look at Power Query transformations. In the next section, we'll move into the next phase of report building: Data Modelling.

2.3: Table View, Model View and Data Modelling

In this section, we'll explore the three core views available when working directly in Power BI—Report View, Table View, and Model View. These are distinct from Power Query, which is the environment used for acquiring and transforming data before it reaches Power BI. Understanding how these views fit together is crucial to working effectively in Power BI.

Report View

Report View is where you'll spend most of your time. This is the canvas for building your final output—the report that your audience will interact with. Your goal is to present data in a meaningful and engaging way, so you'll be iterating frequently: creating pages, sharing with your stakeholders, getting feedback, and refining the report until it meets everyone's needs. We'll be diving deeper into Report View in later chapters, so for now, we'll focus on the other two views.

Table View

The second view is Table View. On first glance, it may appear similar to Power Query due to the layout—tables listed to the right in the data pane and a tabular display when you click on a table—but the resemblance is only surface level. Table View is not a data transformation environment; none of the Power Query commands are available here.

Power Query, to clarify, is where you connect to your data source and define transformations that reshape the data before it is loaded into Power BI. You might filter out unnecessary records, reshape columns, or create calculated fields—all of which are applied during data acquisition.

By contrast, Table View operates on data that has already been loaded into the model. It's a behind-the-scenes environment for analysts and report designers, not for end users. Its purpose is exploratory.

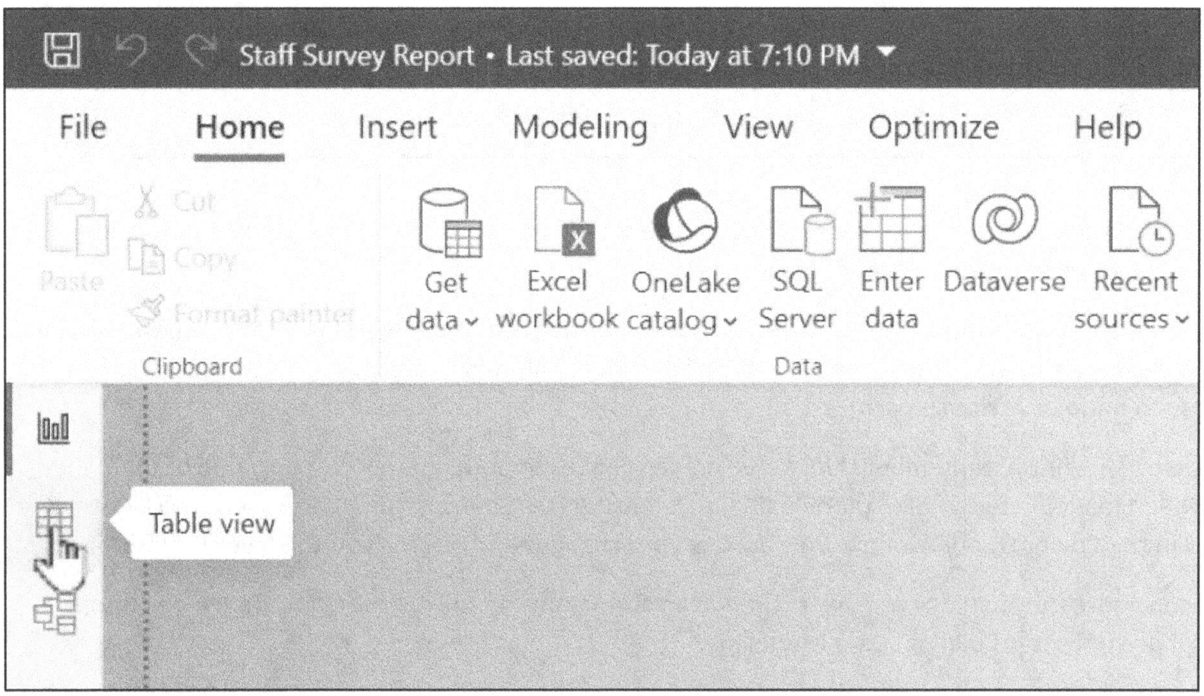

For example, if you're interested in identifying the latest entry in a table, you can click the "Date Submitted" column and apply a descending sort. Instantly, you'll see the most recent date, say 21st April. When finished, simply clear the sort to return to the original order.

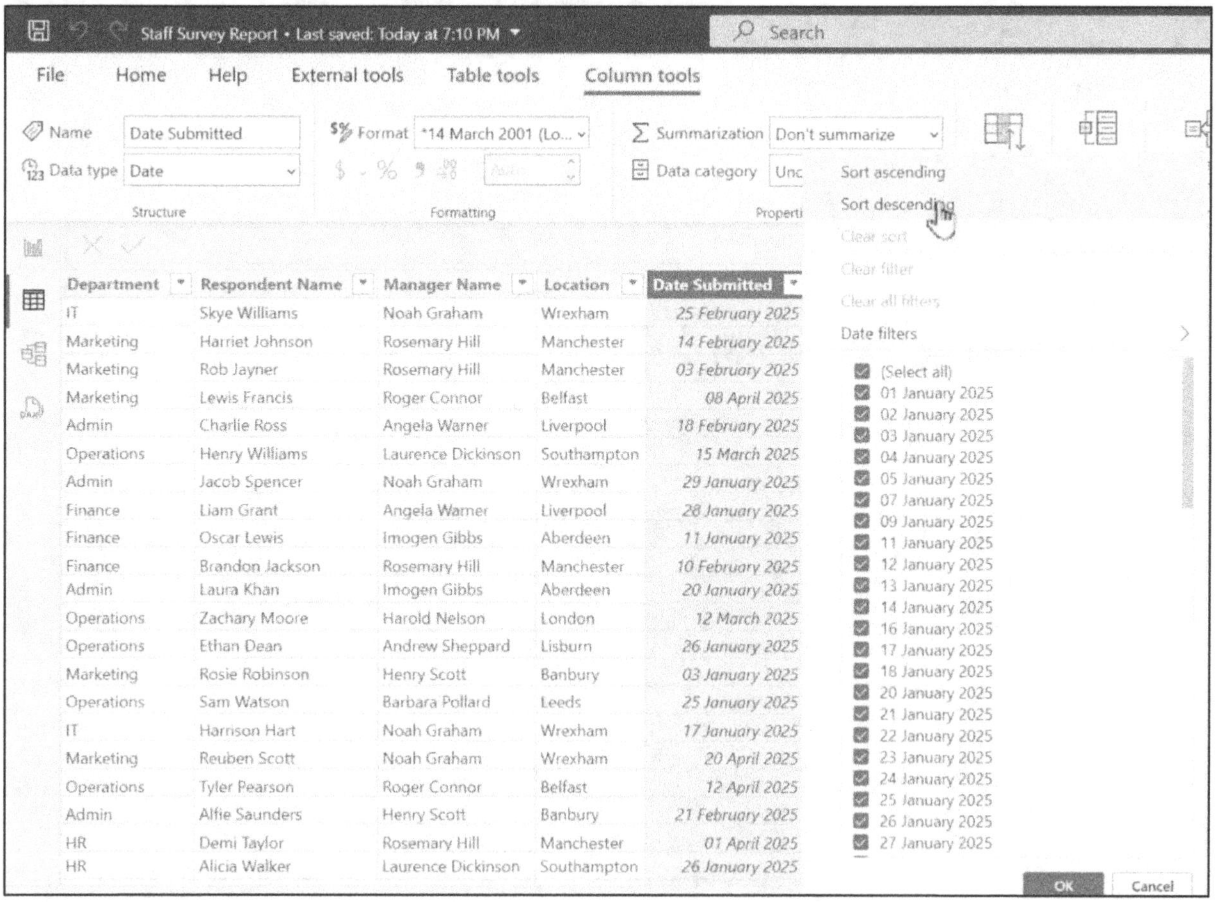

Similarly, suppose you want to look at entries submitted by a particular manager—Harold Nelson, for instance. You can click the filter icon on the "Manager Name" column, deselect all, select only Harold Nelson, and view just his data. When done, clear the filter.

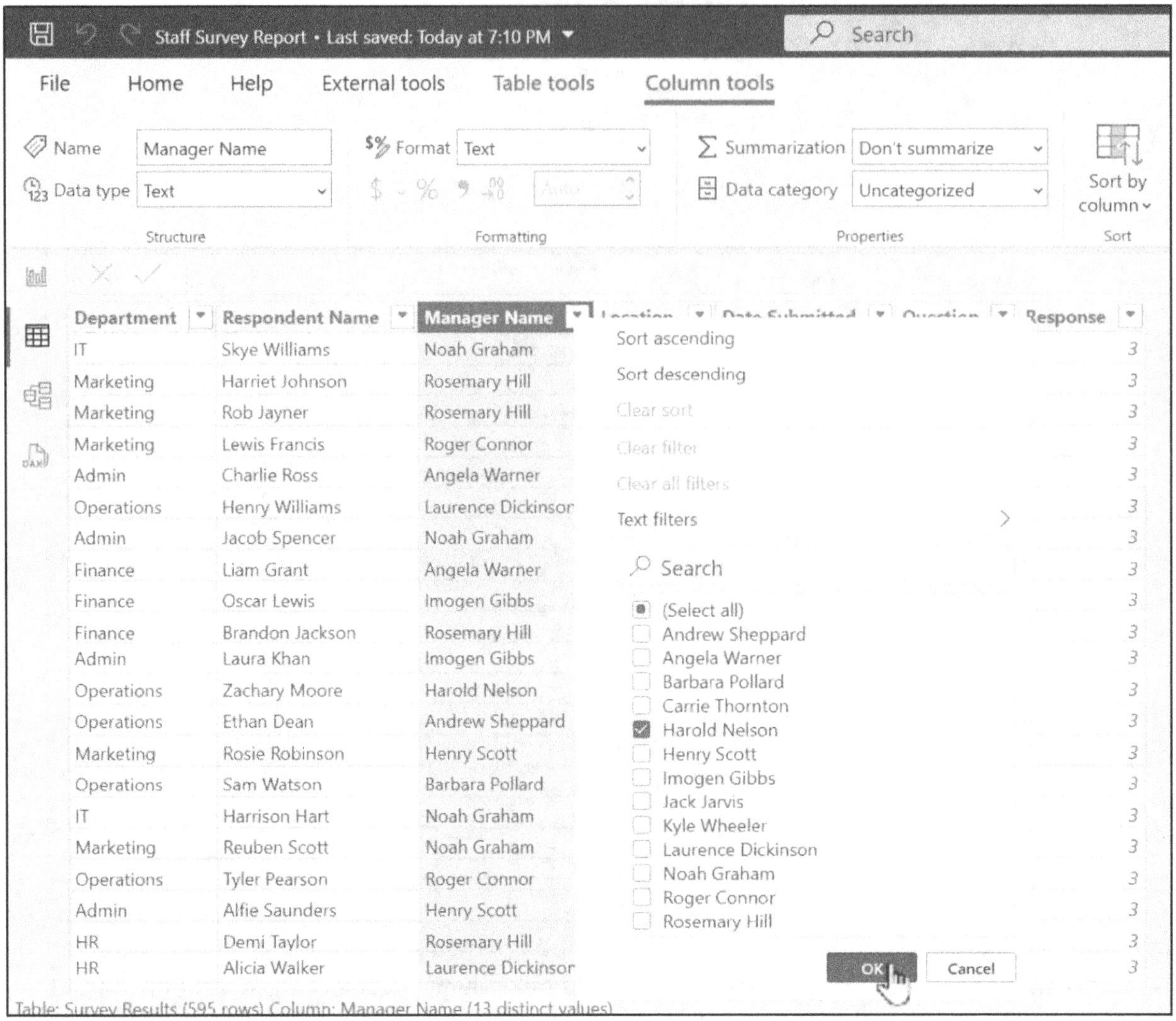

As you perform these tasks, useful summary statistics appear along the bottom of the view, updating automatically. But again, this is only for exploration—no data is being modified.

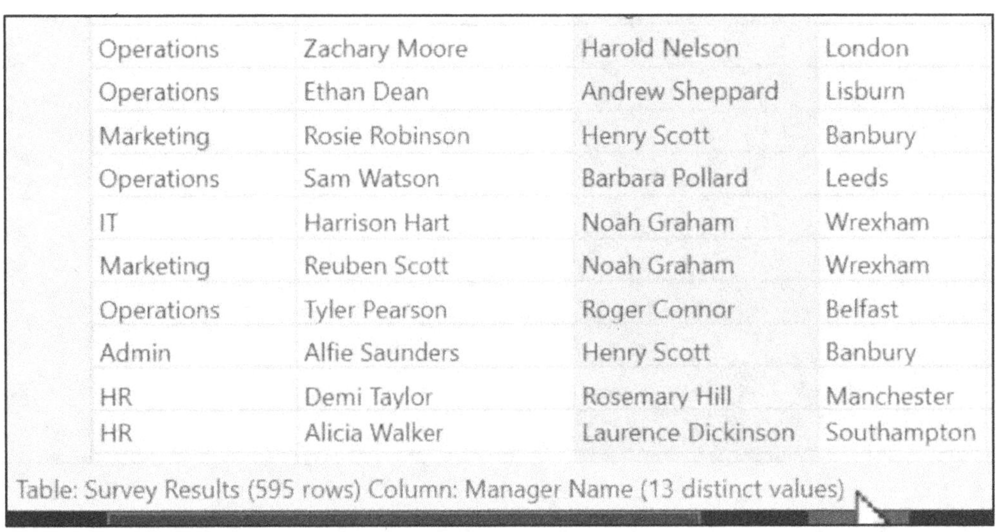

Model View

The third and final view is Model View. This is where data modelling happens—combining and organising the data you've imported via Power Query to ensure it functions as a cohesive whole.

At this stage, your tables exist in Power BI, but they aren't necessarily connected. For example, you might have a "Survey Results" table and a "Survey Questions" table, but unless these are linked, Power BI won't know how they relate to each other.

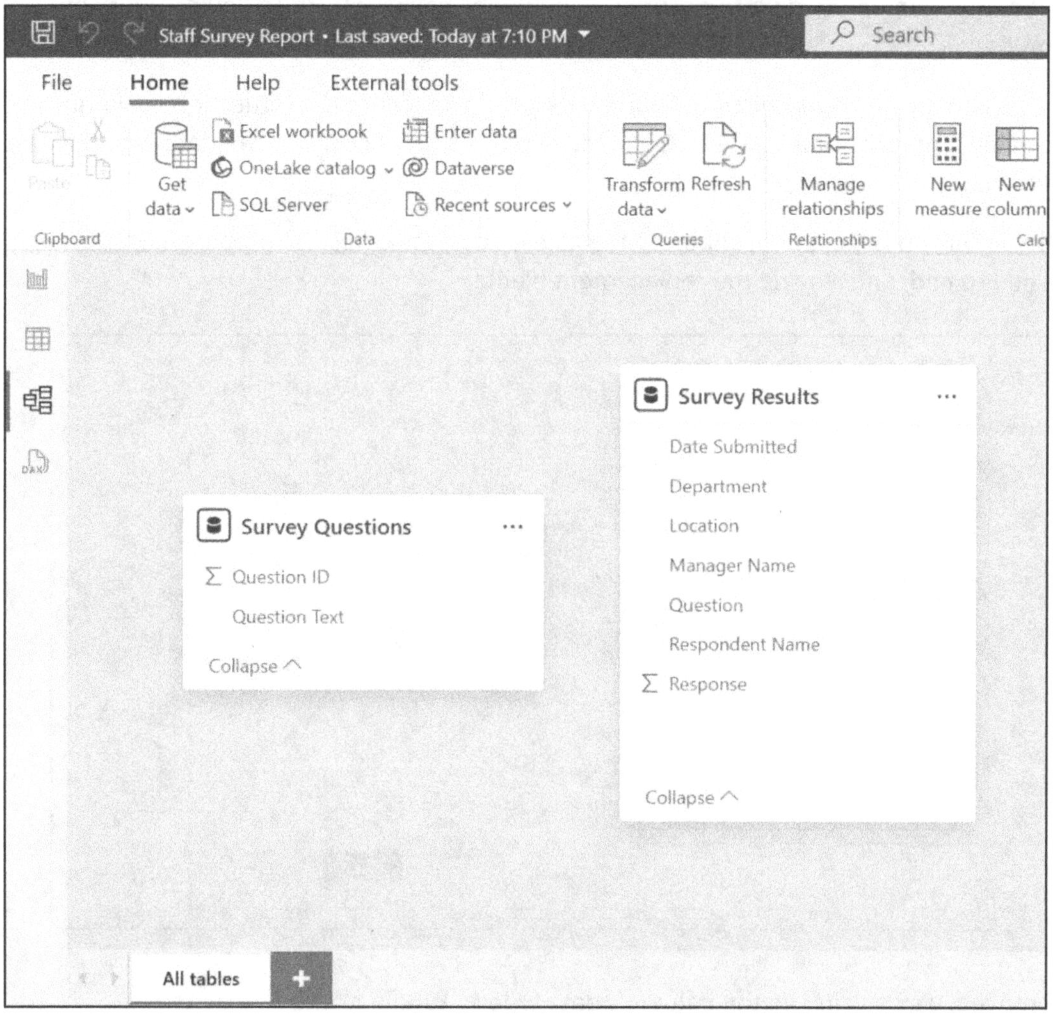

One key objective in Model View is to define relationships between tables. These are the links that allow separate datasets to work together as a unified model.

Let's explore how to build such a relationship. First, return to Table View and identify the column that connects the two tables. In our case, the "Survey Questions" table includes the full question text, while the "Survey Results" table includes only a reference like "Q1" or "Q2".

This means we're looking to connect the "Question" column in "Survey Results" to the "Question ID" column in "Survey Questions." But for a relationship to be valid in Power BI, three conditions must be met:

1. Matching Content – The values in the common columns must match. In our example, we have five question references in both tables.
2. Matching Data Types – The columns must have the same data type. Here, the "Question" column in “Survey Results” is stored as text because of the “Q” prefix, while "Question ID" in “Survey Questions” is stored as a whole number.
3. Lookup Integrity – The table providing the descriptions (Survey Questions) must not contain duplicates in the common column. Each question should be listed only once.

At this point, we need to clean up the data to ensure compatibility. So, we return to Power Query by selecting Transform Data.

“Survey Questions” is already fine. We switch to “Survey Results” and locate the “Question” column. Because it contains alphanumeric values (“Q1”, “Q2”, etc.), we can’t simply change the data type. First, we need to remove the “Q”.

We do this by right-clicking on the column, choosing Replace Values, entering “Q” (uppercase, case-sensitive) as the value to find, and leaving the replacement blank.

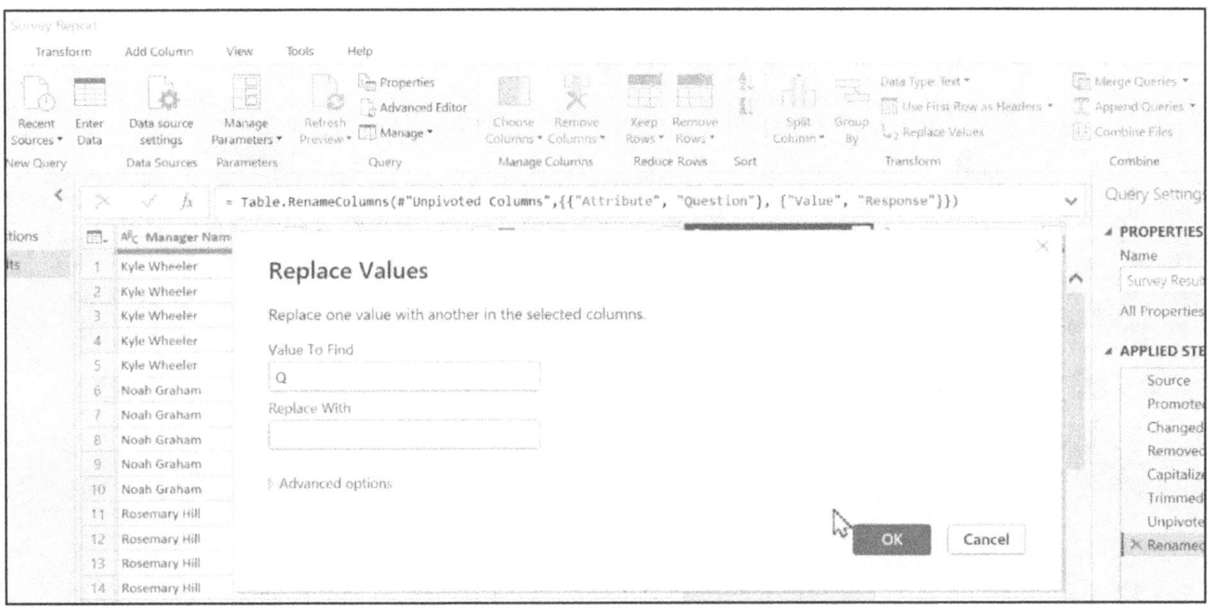

Once the “Q” is removed, we can change the column’s data type to Whole Number.

Now, all three relationship criteria are met:

- Matching content
- Matching data types
- No duplicates in the lookup table (Survey Questions).

We can now click Close & Apply to load the data back into Power BI. Power BI recognises the relationship and creates it automatically.

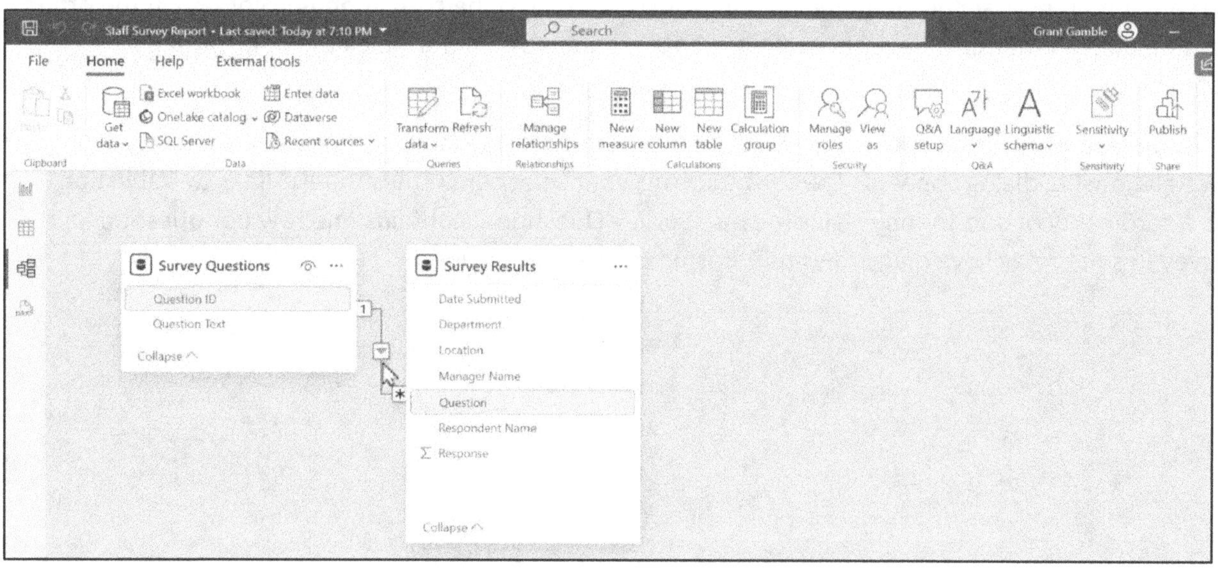

With this relationship established, the two tables behave as one unified table. You can now reference the question text in visualisations and analyses without any additional steps.

If Power BI hadn't detected the relationship automatically, it's easy to create it manually. To demonstrate, we first delete the relationship by right-clicking the connecting line between the tables in Model View and selecting Delete.

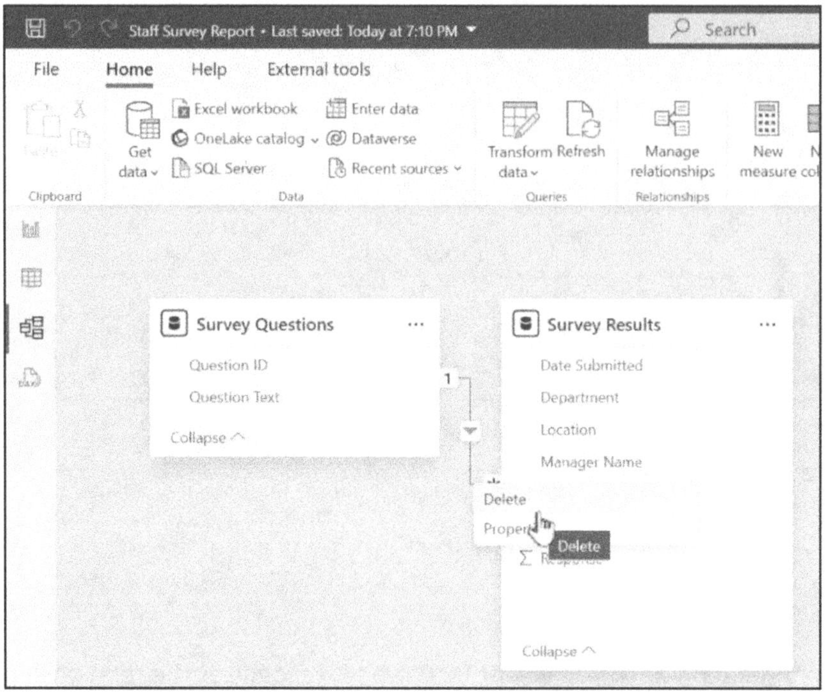

To create it manually, simply drag the column from one table to the corresponding column in the other. Direction doesn't matter—Power BI evaluates both columns and determines the appropriate relationship.

For example, drag "Question ID" from "Survey Questions" to "Question" in "Survey Results". When the New Relationship dialog appears, Power BI confirms your selection: "Question ID" links to "Question", with a cardinality of one-to-many. This means "Survey Questions" contains one row per question, and "Survey Results" may have many rows referencing the same question.

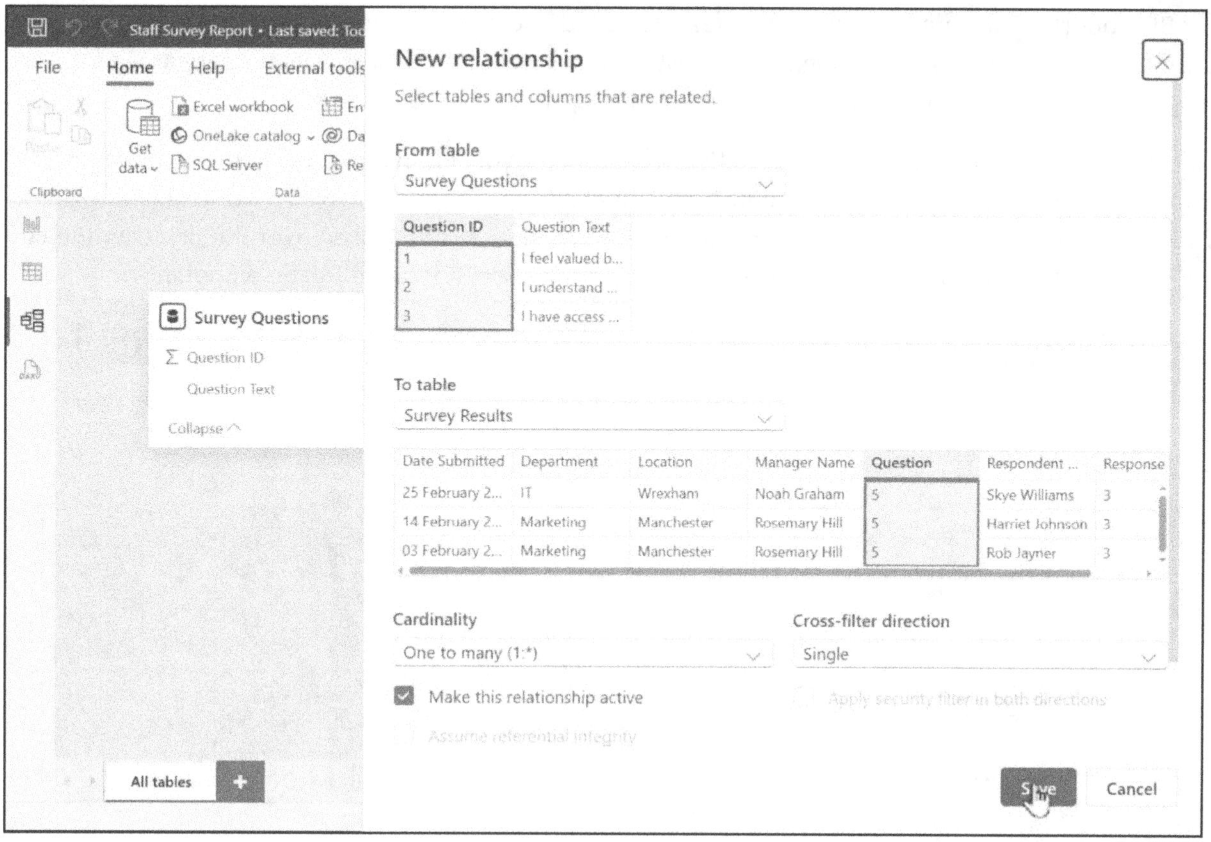

Click Save, and the relationship is established. The tables now work seamlessly together, as if the question text were natively part of the Survey Results table.

This concludes our first look at data modelling. There's a lot more to come, but this gives you a solid foundation for understanding how multiple tables can be brought together to form a coherent and powerful Power BI model.

Save your changes to finish.

2.4: Adding Basic Branding to your Report

In this section, we shift our focus from the data model to the creation of the actual report. This marks the beginning of the design phase, where the visual presentation becomes just as important as the numbers and logic behind it. A critical yet often overlooked step in this process is branding. If your report is to be perceived as polished and professional, it must reflect a consistent visual identity that aligns with your organisation's tone and style.

Branding, in the context of Power BI, refers to the visual cues that give your report a coherent identity—fonts, colours, spacing, layout, and logo use. Many organisations maintain a style guide, and if such a document exists for yours, it's always worth checking. It will often dictate everything from specific colour codes to font usage, preferred logo sizes, and positioning.

Power BI supports visual branding through a feature called Themes. A theme in Power BI is a collection of formatting rules bundled into a single set of instructions. It defines the report's primary and accent colours, fonts, visual defaults, tooltip styles, and even page background colours.

To explore Themes, head to the View tab on the ribbon. Here, you'll find a row of theme thumbnails at the top of the screen. Each represents a different look and feel. In the report we're working with—the staff survey report—there is already a theme applied. If you hover your mouse over the first thumbnail on the left, you'll see it labelled as the current theme. In this case, it's called Rustic Woodland.

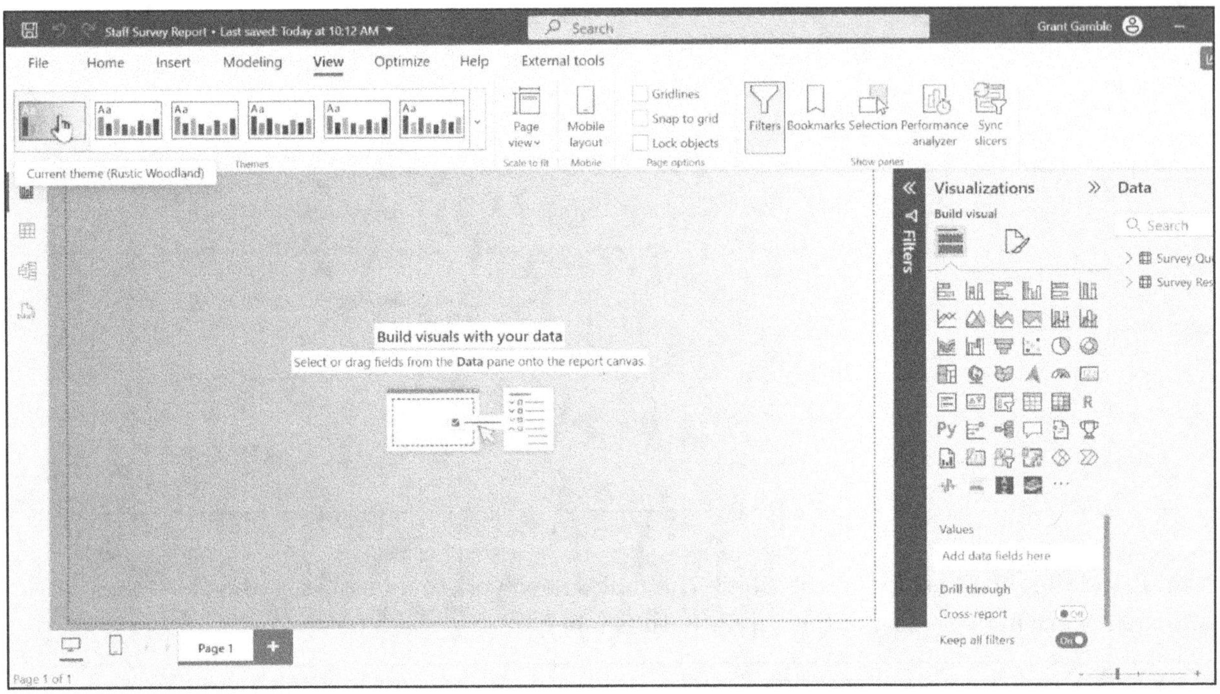

To apply your own theme, a good approach is to begin with a built-in theme that resembles your corporate colours. For this exercise, the fictitious company "KZXP Technologies" uses a blue logo. We'll use this as our starting point and apply the built-in theme called Storm, which features shades of blue.

Click the drop-down arrow next to the themes, and at the bottom of the menu, select Customize current theme. This opens a panel with several categories running down the left-hand side.

Theme Customisation Options

Name and Colors

- This category allows you to define the core colour palette for your report: primary colors, accent tones, sentiment colors (positive, negative, neutral), and more. These are foundational for maintaining a consistent visual identity throughout the report. You can also name your custom theme (e.g. "Storm") for easy reference and reuse.

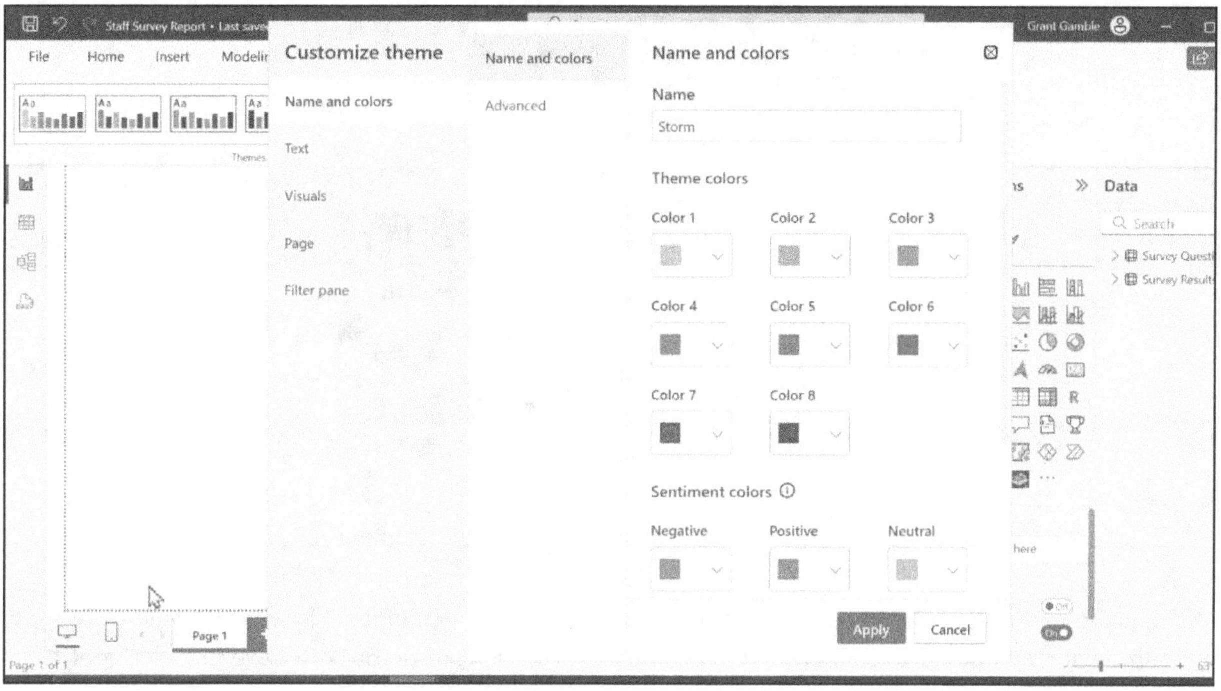

Text

- This section lets you customize the typography across your report. You can define font family, size, and weight for different elements such as titles, headers, labels, and tooltips. Text styling significantly impacts the report's readability and tone—whether it's formal, friendly, technical, or creative.

Visuals

- Here, you can configure the default formatting settings for charts and visuals. This includes options for borders, background colour, shadow effects, and data labels. Setting defaults helps maintain visual consistency and saves time by reducing the need to style individual visuals manually.

Page

- This allows you to customize the appearance of the report page itself, such as page background colour and page size. It affects only the canvas area where visuals are placed (not the surrounding wallpaper).

Filter Pane

- This section enables styling of the filter pane, including its background colour, font colour, and transparency. Customizing the filter pane ensures it aligns visually with the rest of your report and remains accessible and easy to read.

Wallpaper

- While technically part of the "Page" design, the wallpaper refers specifically to the background outside the report canvas (visible when a report is not full-screen). For example, if your company branding includes a deep navy blue, you might apply a light tint of that colour as the wallpaper background. The exact shade can be copied from the branding asset file.

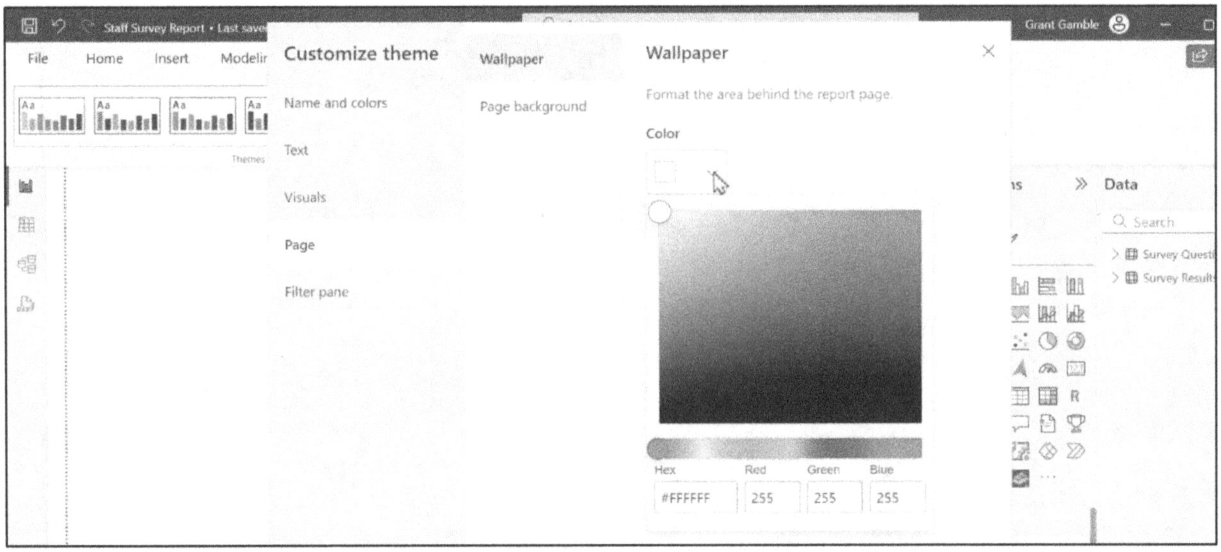

Once the wallpaper colour has been selected, click Apply to see the changes. The report canvas background will now update to reflect the new colour, providing a subtle but effective branded feel.

It's important to note that saving your theme is a separate step. Once you're happy with your changes, go back to the View tab, click the drop-down next to the theme thumbnails, and select Save current theme.

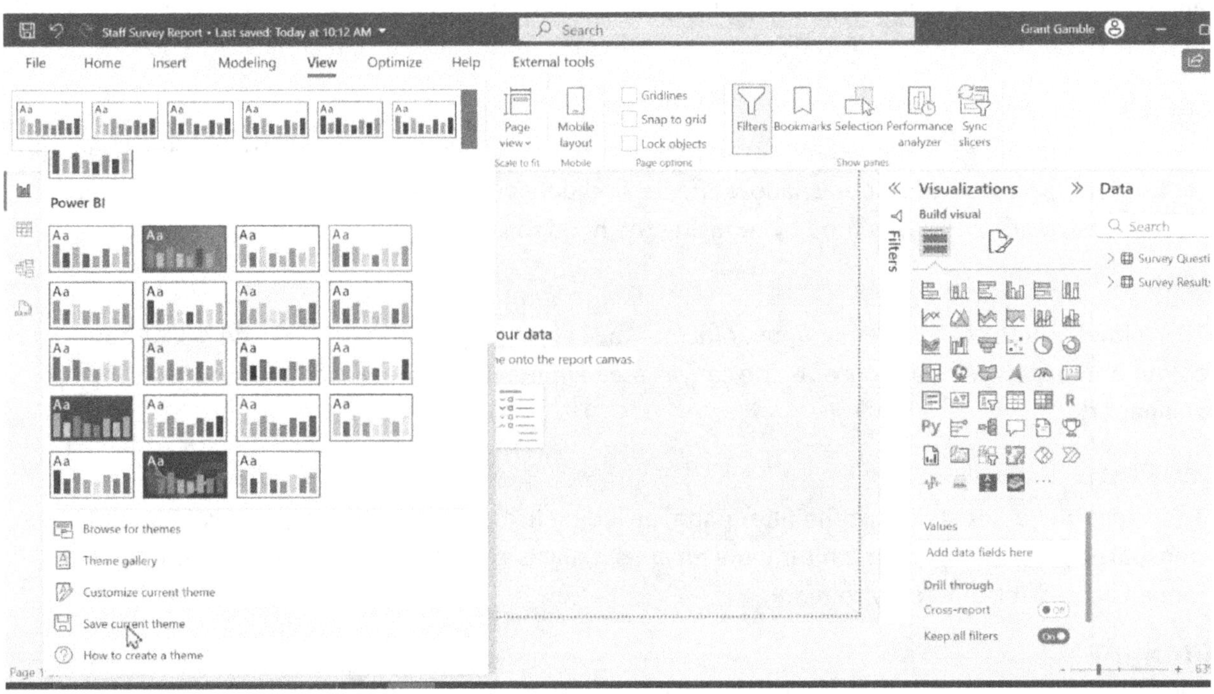

This will prompt you to save the theme as a JSON file, which stores all of your formatting instructions. Once saved, this theme can be reused in other reports. To apply an existing theme later, go to the View tab, open the drop-down next to the themes, and select Browse for themes. You can then locate your saved JSON file.

Inside the section two folder of your project files, you'll find a sample theme file called coastal-breeze.json. This is the official theme for the KZXP Technologies report and can be loaded using the same "Browse for themes" option.

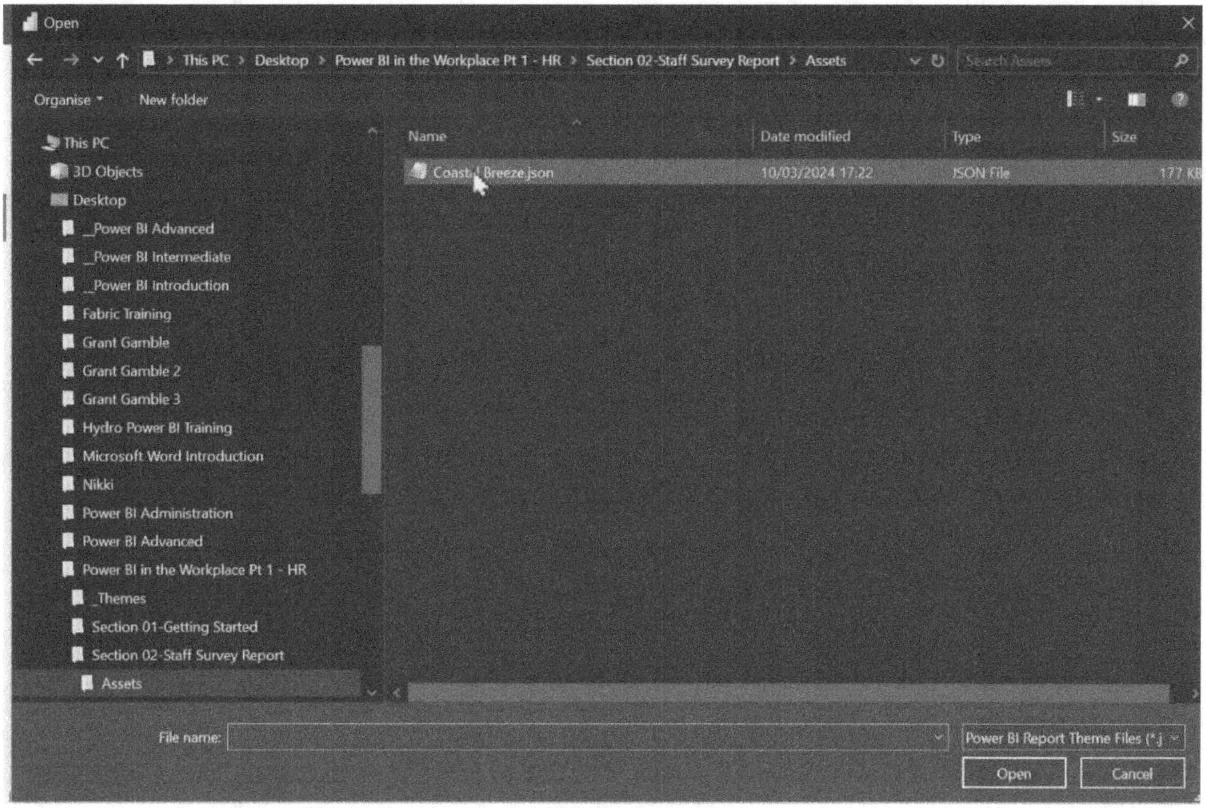

Adding the Company Logo

Once the theme is in place, the next pillar of branding is the company logo. Power BI doesn't treat logos as special components—they're simply images. To insert a logo, go to the Insert tab and click Image.

In the assets folder, you'll find a file named logo.png. This is the logo for KZXP Technologies. Insert it into the report canvas. By default, it appears inside a square-shaped tile, but since the logo is rectangular, we'll need to adjust the tile's dimensions.

To do this, grab the bottom-centre handle of the image tile and drag it upwards to reduce the height. This preserves the original width, aligning the tile better with the logo's natural shape. You can then scale the logo up or down using the corner handles, which retain the image's proportions.

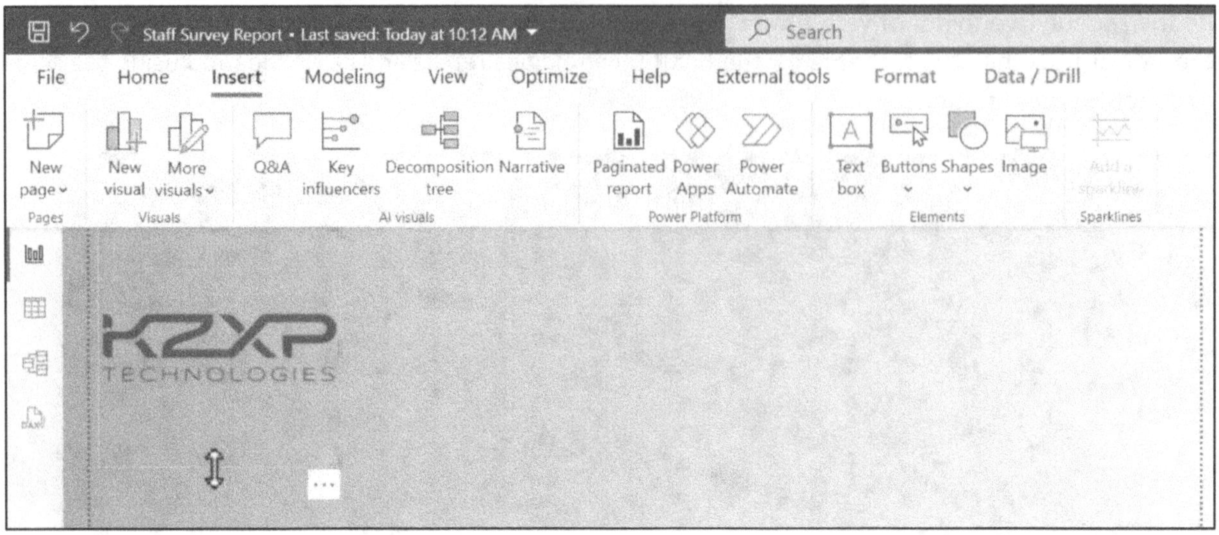

According to the fictional style guide for KZXP Technologies, the logo should appear in the top-left corner of the report. So once the sizing is right, go ahead and drag it into place.

Summary

With these two simple but powerful changes, we've given the report a visual identity:

- Applied a company-branded Power BI theme with a coordinated colour palette
- Inserted and positioned the corporate logo according to guidelines

This kind of visual polish goes a long way in ensuring your report is taken seriously and aligns with the rest of your corporate communications. With the branding now complete, we're ready to begin building the report's content.

2.5: Using the Card Visual

Now that we have our report branding in place, it's time to begin constructing the report itself. The logical starting point is to use the most fundamental visual available in Power BI—the card visual. Despite its simplicity, the card is one of the most commonly used visuals across all Power BI reports.

This is largely due to its ability to clearly and concisely present headline metrics—key performance indicators (KPIs)—in a prominent and digestible format. In short, it delivers the big picture at a glance.

To insert a card, locate the visualizations pane and click on the icon that looks like "123". Once selected, position the card in the top right of your report canvas. This is a common and intuitive position that ensures visibility without distracting from more detailed visuals elsewhere on the page.

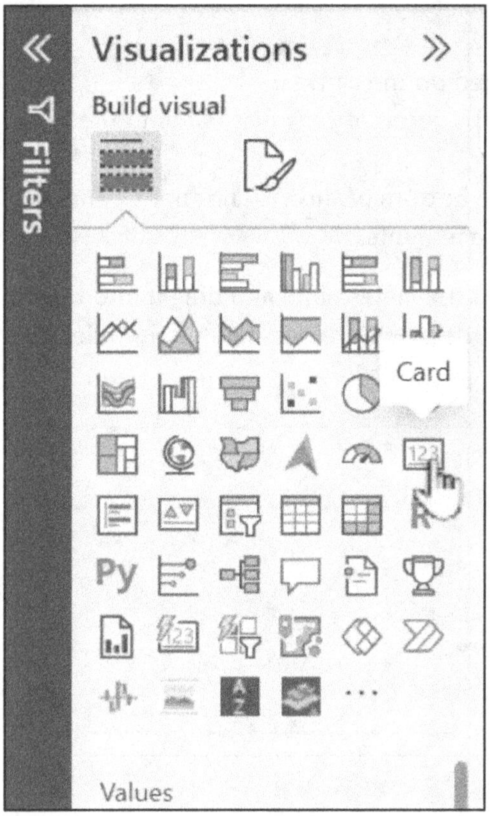

We'll begin by using this card to display one of our most basic but important metrics—the number of responses collected in our survey. In Power BI terms, this can be assessed by counting how many different respondent IDs we have. (When we unpivoted the question columns, we effectively increased the number of rows by a factor of five and each respondent ID now figures on five rows.)

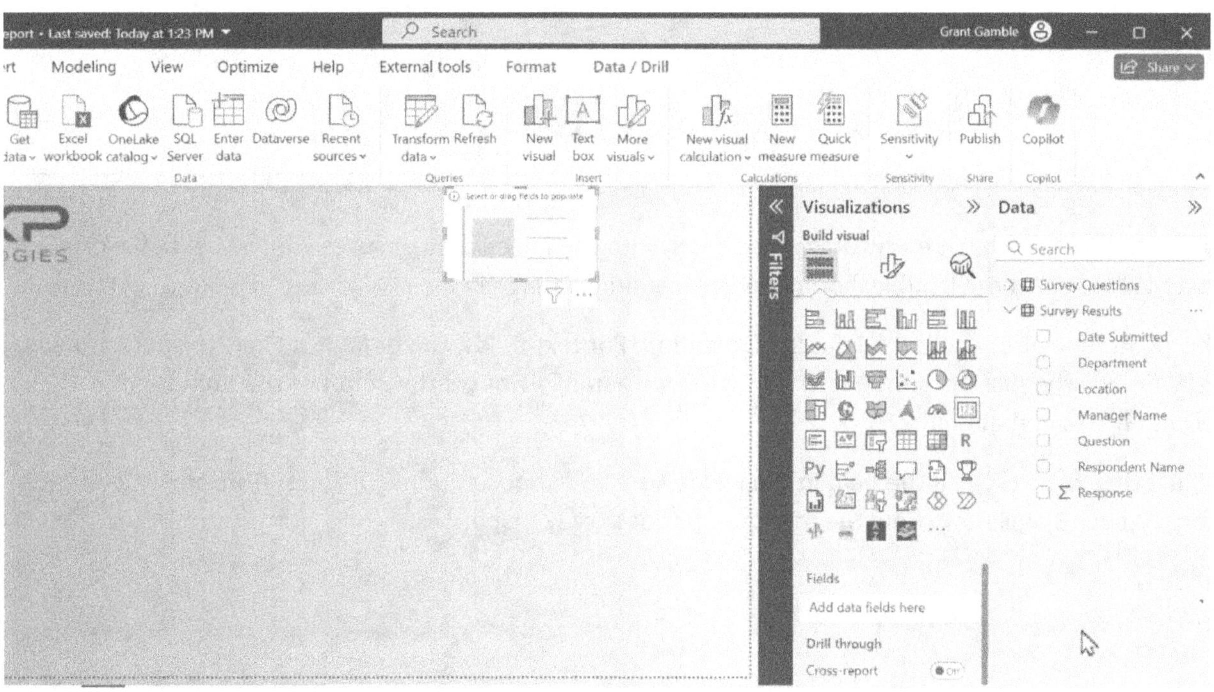

There are three common ways to bring a field into a card visual:

1. Drag the field directly onto the card visual that's already placed on the canvas.
2. Click the checkbox next to the field name in the Data pane; this automatically places it into the selected visual.
3. Best practice: drag the field directly into the Fields well at the bottom of the Visualizations pane, which gives you greater control and helps avoid accidental placements.

Let's focus on the third method. Locate the Respondent ID field in the Fields pane and drag it into the single slot that appears in the Fields area of the card visual. As cards only have one field placeholder, this is straightforward.

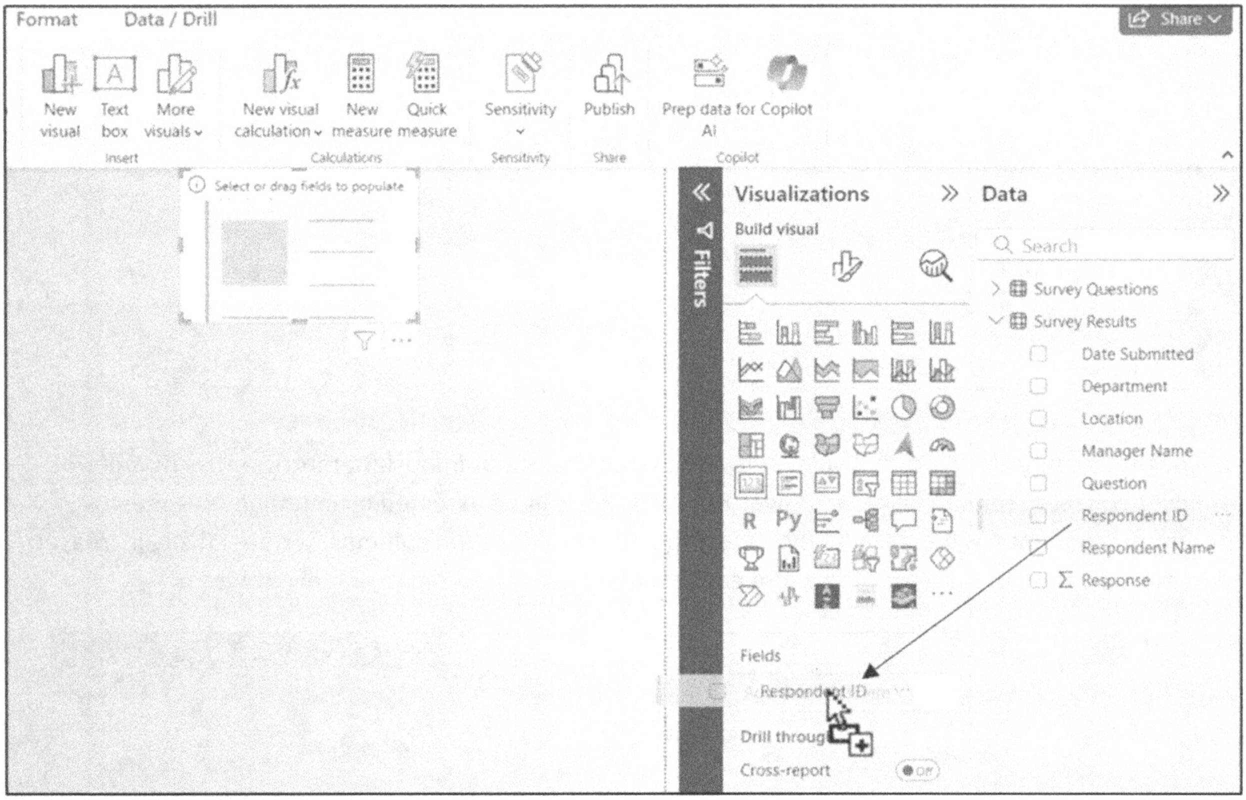

It's good to build this habit early. Dragging directly into the Fields area ensures your visual behaves as expected and saves time troubleshooting misplacements later.

At this point, Power BI applies a default aggregation. For text fields, the default is First, so your card will initially display the first Respondent ID. But what we actually want is the count of the number of different entries in that field.

To adjust this, right-click on the field in the Fields area and choose Count (Distinct) from the aggregation options. Power BI will now show the total number of survey responses.

You may also want to give this card a more descriptive label. Beneath the large number in the card is the category label. To change it, click the dropdown beside the field name in the Fields well and select Rename for this visual.

Type in something clearer like Total Responses.

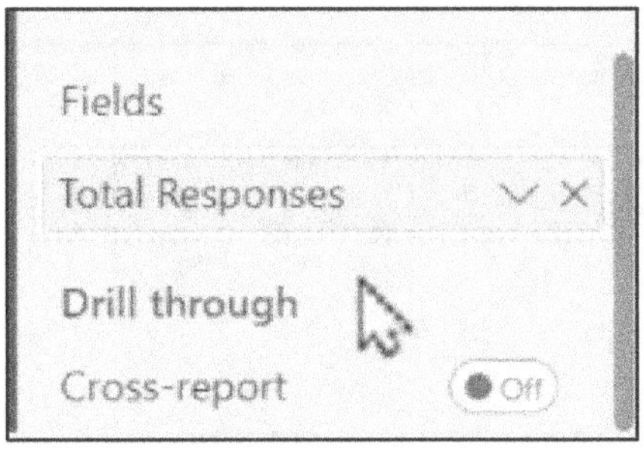

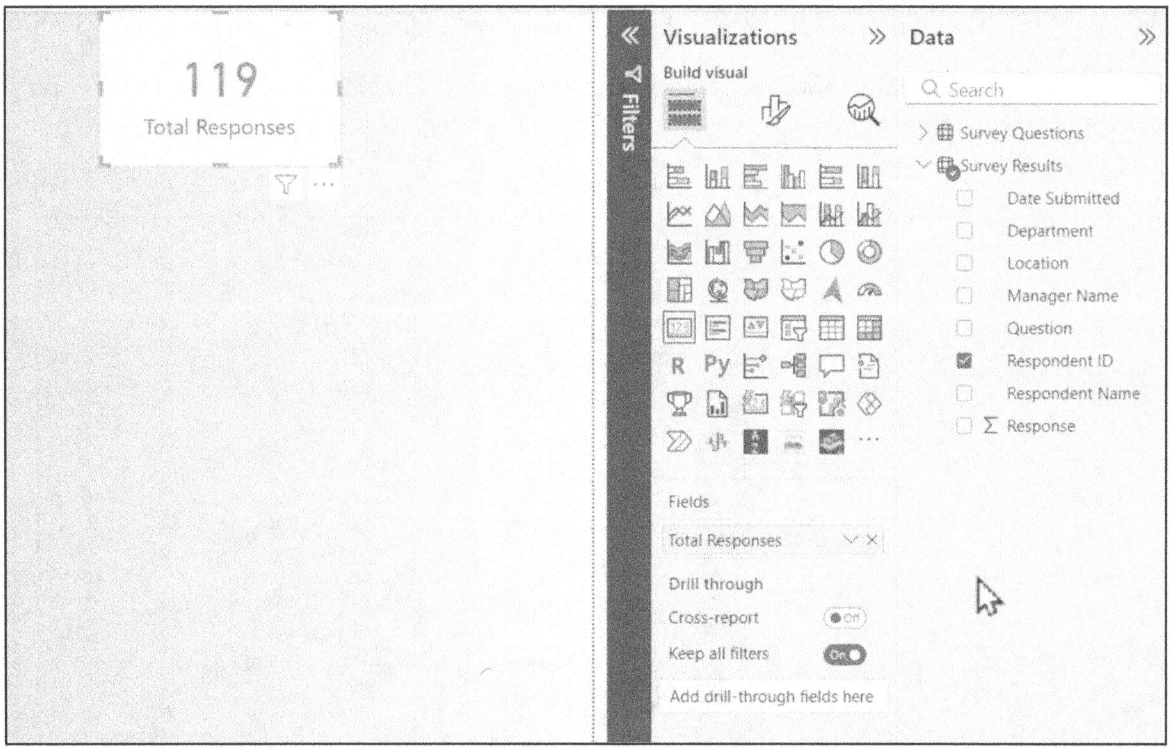

While one card is helpful, most reports benefit from multiple cards to present various key figures side-by-side. In this example, we'll add a second card to display the average response score.

Instead of adding a brand-new visual, it's more efficient to duplicate the existing card. You can do this using Ctrl+C and Ctrl+V, or by clicking the Copy and Paste buttons found in the Power BI ribbon.

Now that you have a duplicate, remove the existing field from the copied card. You can do this by clicking the "X" next to the field in the Fields area, or by unchecking the corresponding checkbox in the Fields pane.

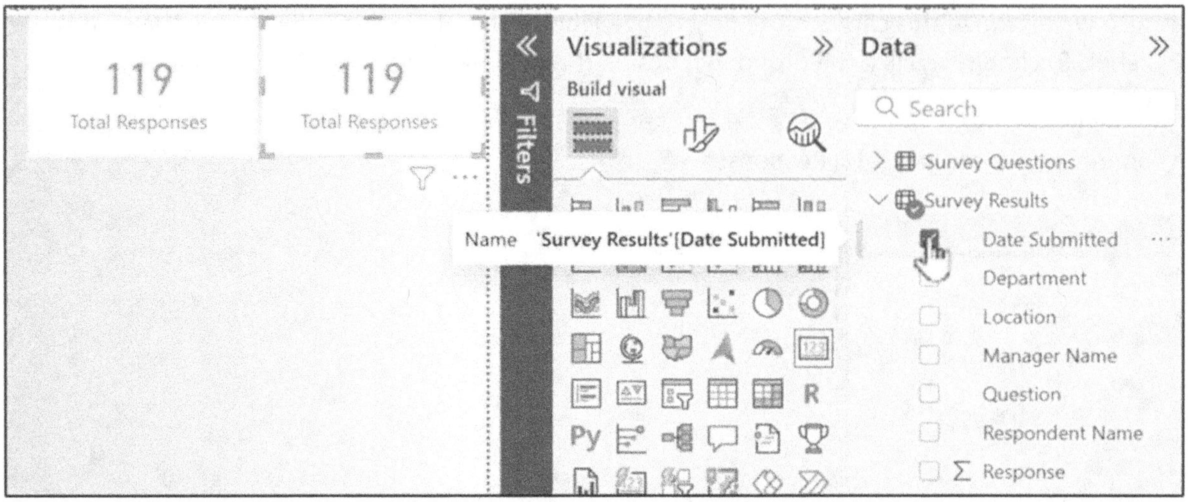

Next, locate the Response field—the column that stores the scores for each question, which range from 1 to Again, use best practice: drag this field into the Fields well of the duplicated card visual.

Since Response is a numeric field, Power BI applies a default aggregation of Sum. That's not quite what we want. To show the average score, right-click on the field and change the aggregation from Sum to Average.

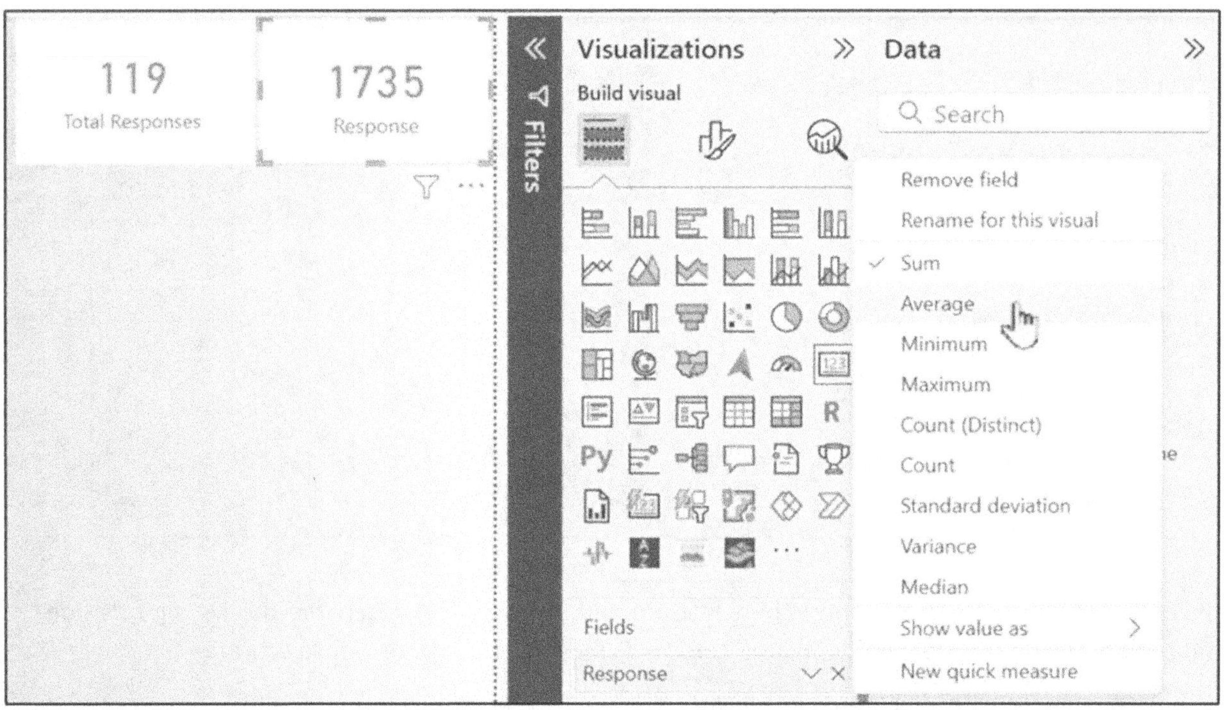

Lastly, let's update the label below the number. Click on the dropdown next to the field name and choose Rename for this visual.

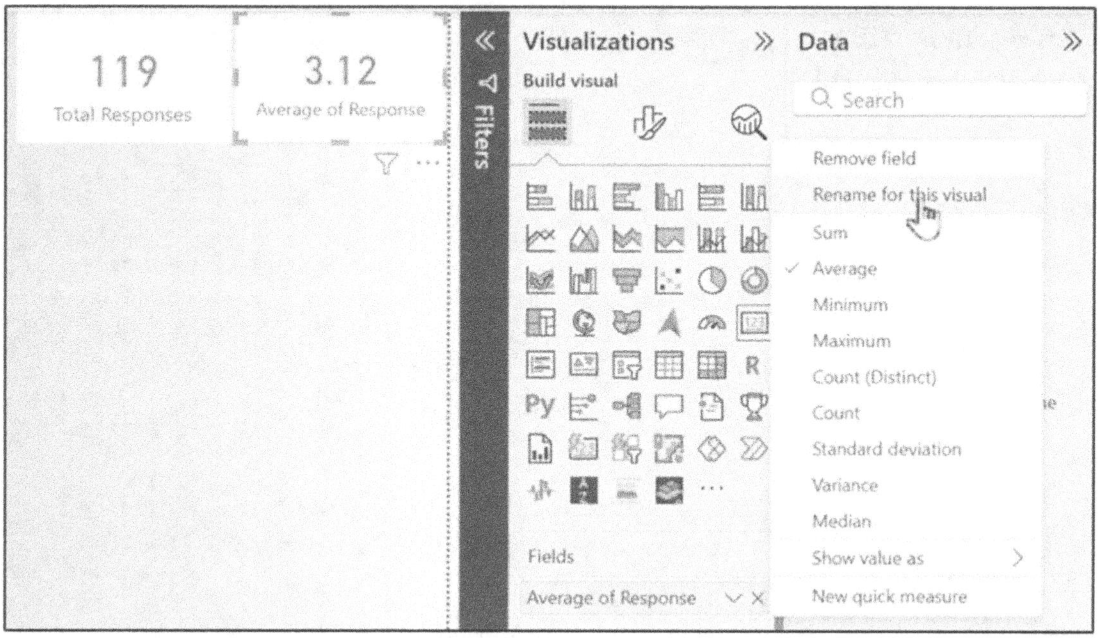

This time, change the label to Average Score.

With those steps complete, you've created two key metrics in your report using card visuals—Total Responses and Average Response. These may seem basic, but they are vital for communicating the overall picture quickly and effectively.

In summary, the card visual is a simple yet powerful way to display headline metrics. It should be part of almost every report you build, offering a clean and focused way to communicate essential figures.

Now that we've covered cards, we're ready to move on to a more advanced visual—the matrix.

2.6: Using the Matrix Visual

The Matrix visual in Power BI is best understood as the report designer's equivalent of Microsoft Excel's Pivot Table. It sits at the more granular end of the spectrum when it comes to visualising data—quite the opposite of the Card visual, which displays only a single, summary figure. With the Matrix, we can view richly detailed, tabular data, making it easier to analyse patterns across multiple dimensions.

To begin, add a Matrix visual to your report canvas. In Power BI, both the Table and the Matrix visuals present data in a structured format. However, for pivot-style analysis with rows and columns forming a grid of values, the Matrix is the correct choice.

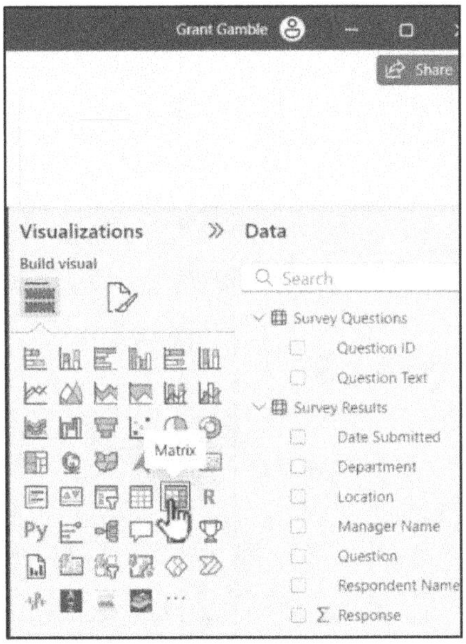

When positioning the Matrix on the page, place it in the bottom-right corner. This provides ample space for multiple columns to be displayed, while leaving room above for a slicer or other complementary visual elements that you might add later.

A good habit when working with visuals is to drag your desired fields and measures directly into the field wells in the Visualizations pane, rather than into the canvas. This gives you better control and ensures each item is placed in the correct section—Rows, Columns, or Values.

To begin constructing our matrix:

1. Drag the Location field into the Rows well. This sets up our vertical axis.
2. Drag the Score measure—this is our numerical response field—into the Values well.

By default, Power BI applies the Sum aggregation to numerical fields. However, in our case, it's more appropriate to see the Average. To change this, right-click on the field inside the Values well and choose Average as the summary function.

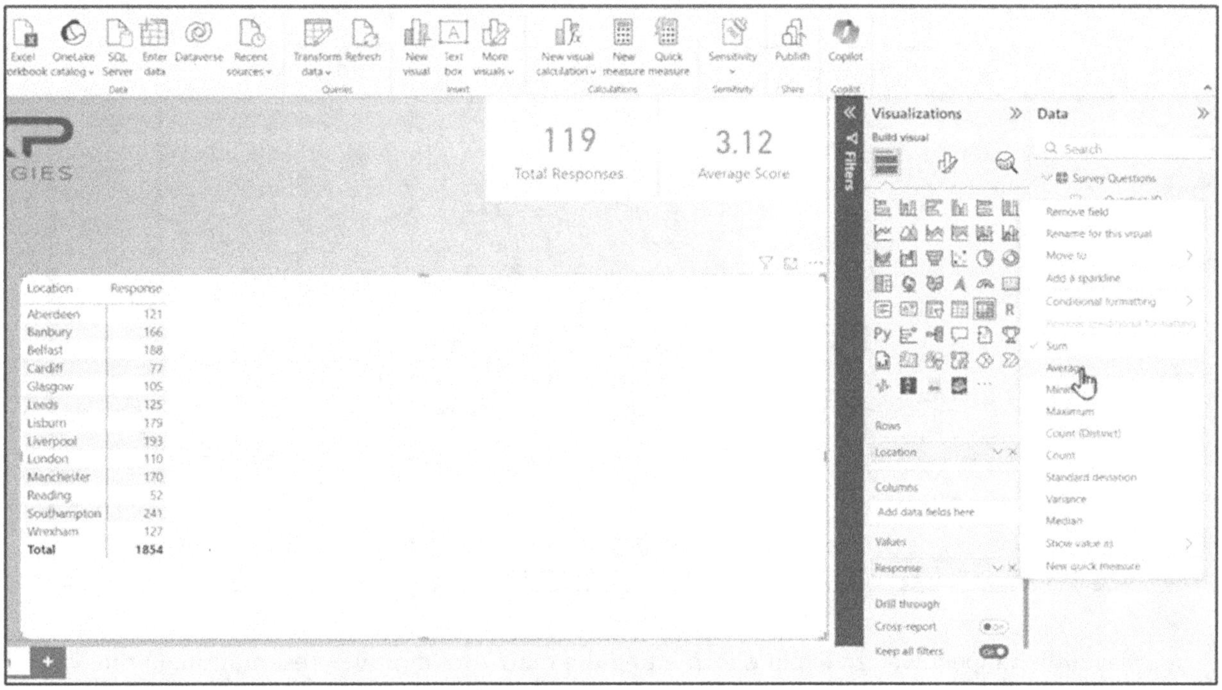

Now we introduce a second dimension, this time across the Columns. From the survey questions table, drag the Question Text field into the Columns well. This turns the matrix into a true pivot-style view, where each question forms a separate column header.

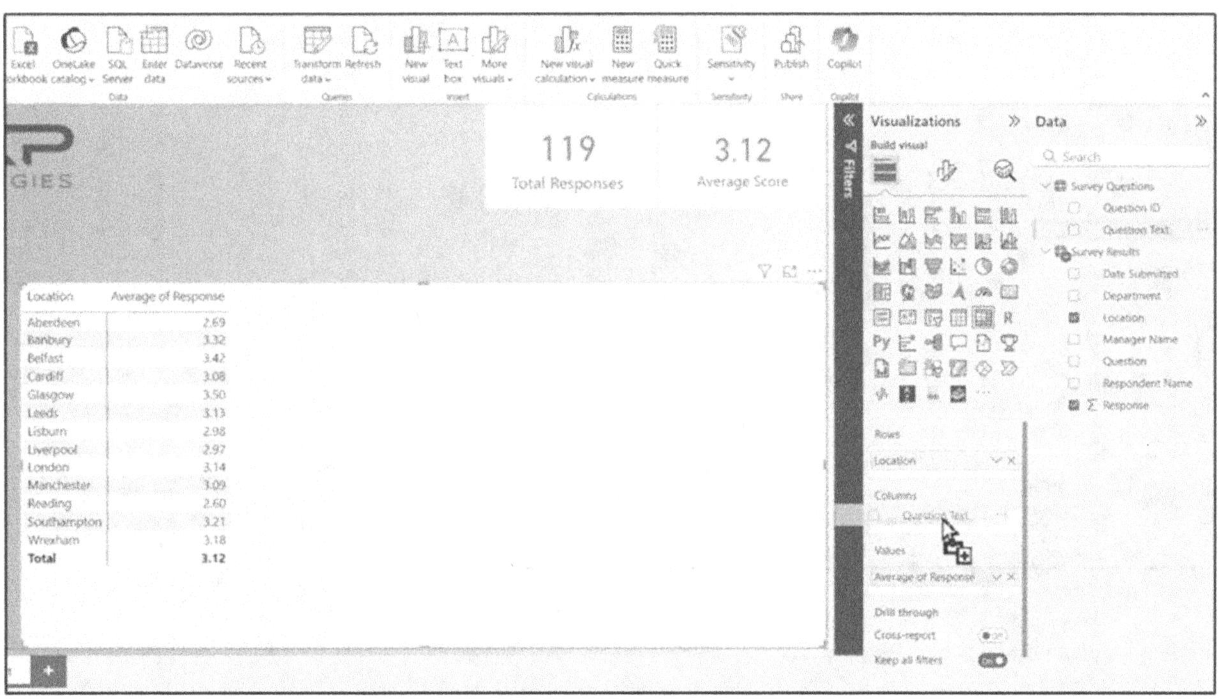

The column headers may contain long text, and you'll likely find that the layout becomes quite wide. Resize columns as necessary to improve readability. If you're familiar with Excel, adjusting column width will feel natural. Column 1 and 2 may already be fine, but for others, aim to reduce them so that the text wraps neatly across about three lines.

Location	Communication from leadership is clear and effective	I feel valued by my team	I have access to the resources I need to do my job well	I understand how my work contributes to the org
Aberdeen	2.11	3.67	2.22	
Banbury	3.30	4.00	3.40	
Belfast	3.64	4.09	3.27	
Cardiff	2.40	3.00	4.00	
Glasgow	3.00	4.17	4.00	
Leeds	2.75	4.50	2.88	
Lisburn	3.00	3.75	2.42	
Liverpool	2.62	4.00	3.23	
London	2.00	4.00	3.57	
Manchester	3.00	3.82	3.36	
Reading	2.50	4.00	1.75	
Southampton	2.93	4.20	2.80	
Wrexham	4.00	3.50	2.88	
Total	**2.92**	**3.93**	**3.04**	

Once your layout is shaped, we can explore formatting the matrix to improve presentation. In the Visualizations pane, click the Format section (indicated by a paintbrush icon).

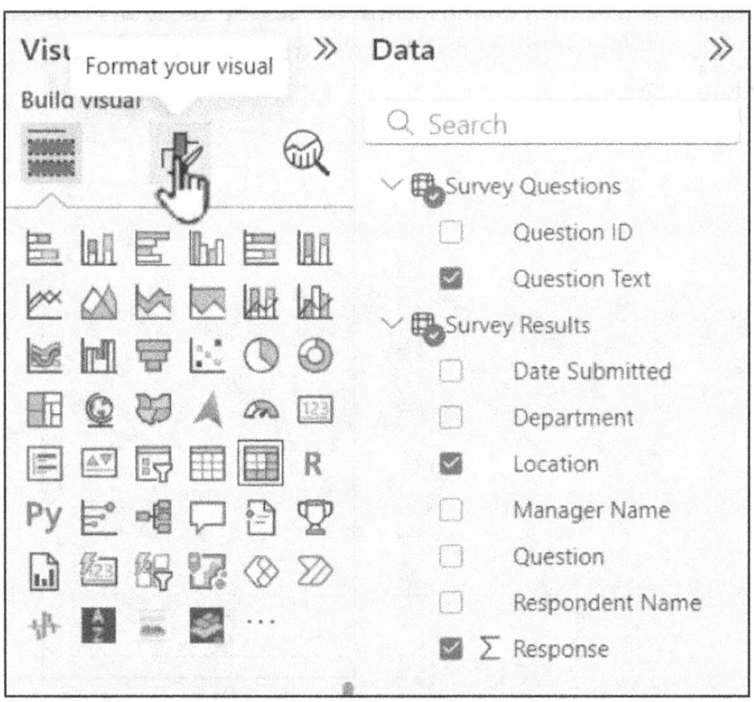

Scroll down and expand the Specific Column section where Apply Settings to Average of Response will be highlighted. Here, you can choose which portion of the Matrix to format: values, totals, headers, and so on.

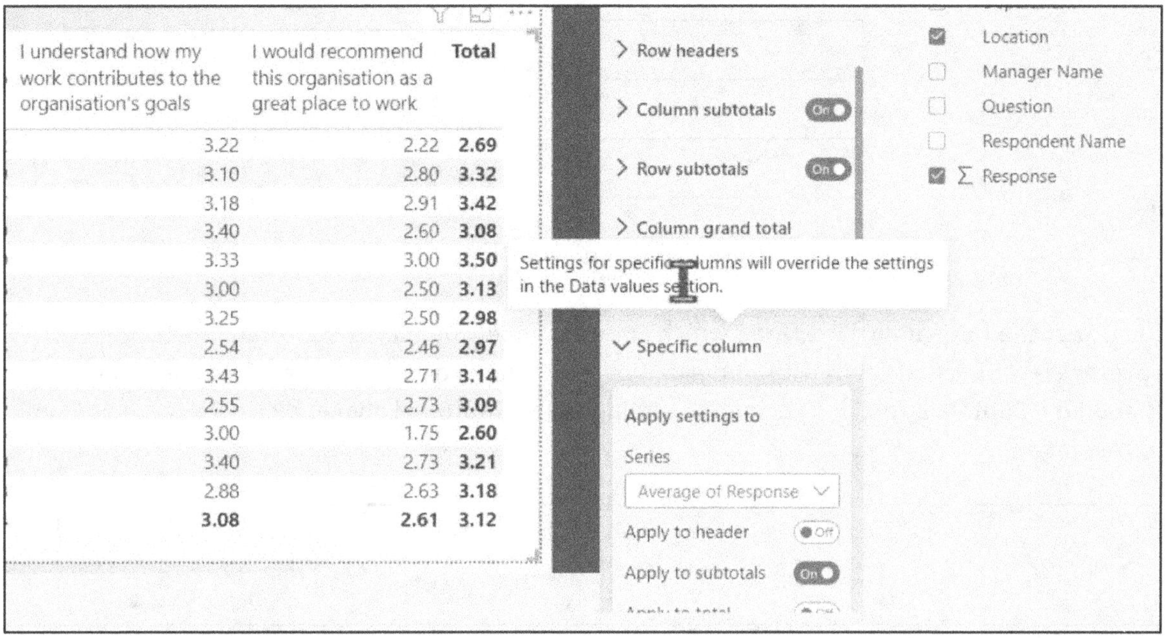

Let's apply two simple but effective adjustments:

- Turn on Apply to total so the formatting also impacts the row and column totals.
- Leave Apply to header switched off. Long headers are more readable when left-aligned, so we'll keep them that way.

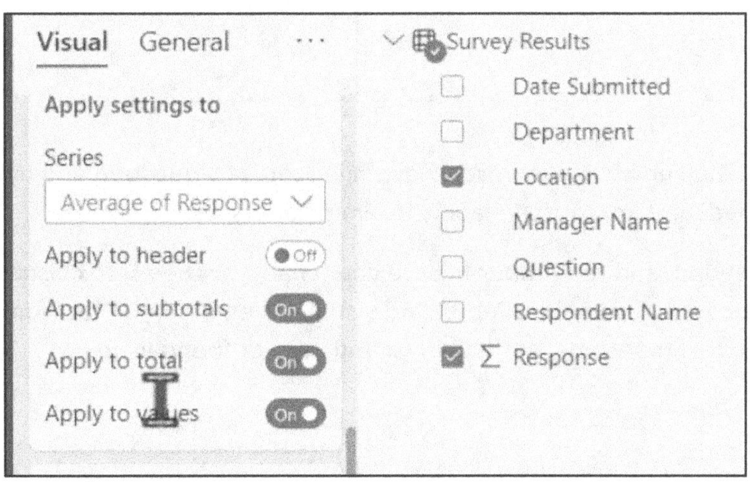

Now, set the alignment for values to Centre. This helps users visually match each score with its corresponding question and location.

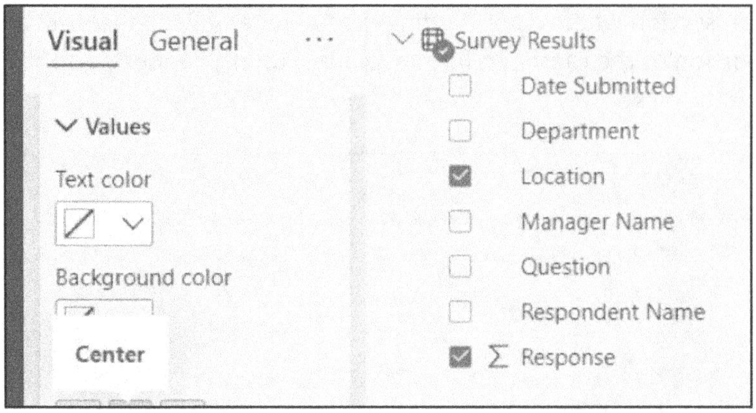

Next, let's correct the misleading label Total which appears under the matrix subtotals. Since we're showing averages—not actual totals—it's important to label them correctly. Under both the Column Subtotals and Row Subtotals sections, locate the setting called Subtotal Label and change the text from "Total" to "Average".

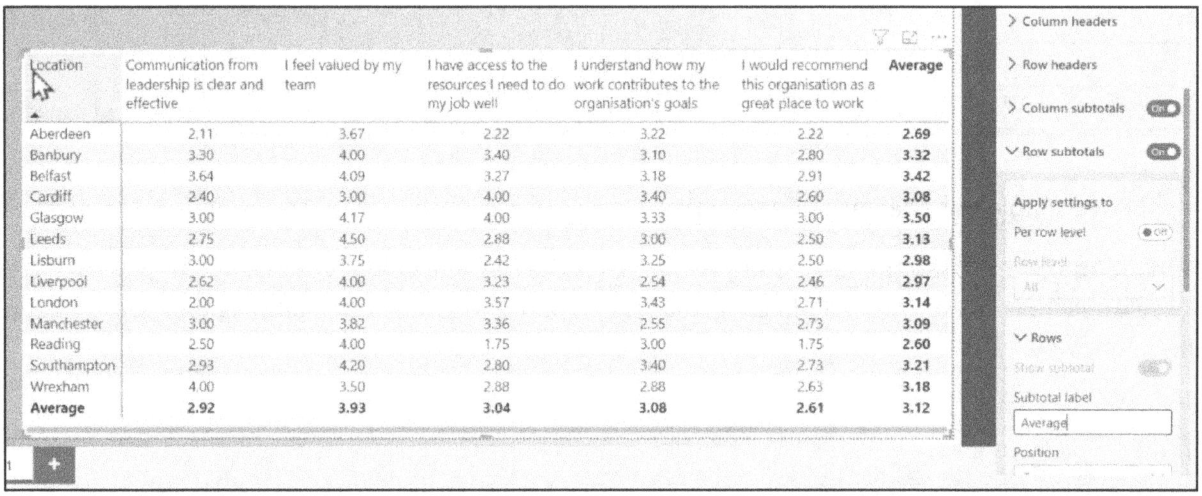

Location	Communication from leadership is clear and effective	I feel valued by my team	I have access to the resources I need to do my job well	I understand how my work contributes to the organisation's goals	I would recommend this organisation as a great place to work	**Average**
Aberdeen	2.11	3.67	2.22	3.22	2.22	**2.69**
Banbury	3.30	4.00	3.40	3.10	2.80	**3.32**
Belfast	3.64	4.09	3.27	3.18	2.91	**3.42**
Cardiff	2.40	3.00	4.00	3.40	2.60	**3.08**
Glasgow	3.00	4.17	4.00	3.33	3.00	**3.50**
Leeds	2.75	4.50	2.88	3.00	2.50	**3.13**
Lisburn	3.00	3.75	2.42	3.25	2.50	**2.98**
Liverpool	2.62	4.00	3.23	2.54	2.46	**2.97**
London	2.00	4.00	3.57	3.43	2.71	**3.14**
Manchester	3.00	3.82	3.36	2.55	2.73	**3.09**
Reading	2.50	4.00	1.75	3.00	1.75	**2.60**
Southampton	2.93	4.20	2.80	3.40	2.73	**3.21**
Wrexham	4.00	3.50	2.88	2.88	2.63	**3.18**
Average	**2.92**	**3.93**	**3.04**	**3.08**	**2.61**	**3.12**

This completes our formatting. The Matrix visual now clearly presents average scores by question and by location, with headers and data neatly aligned, and appropriate labels to avoid confusion.

To conclude, return to the Data section if needed, and remember to save your changes. The Matrix visual represents a big step up in analytical power compared to the simple Card visual. It's an essential tool for anyone looking to explore data across multiple dimensions, particularly if you've ever found value in Pivot Tables in Excel.

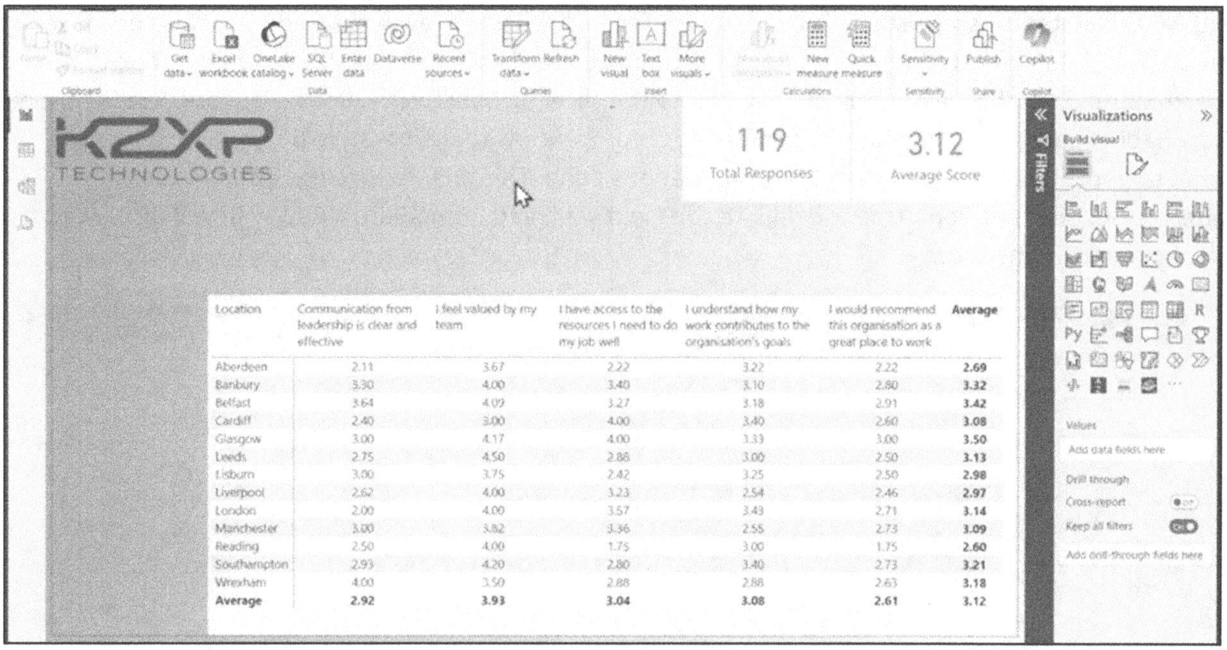

2.7: Adding Slicers to the Page

In this section, we complete our basic staff survey report by exploring and configuring one of Power BI's most interactive and user-friendly tools: the slicer visual. Slicers play a key role in report design by enabling users to filter other visuals on the page. Their primary purpose is to allow the reader to narrow down the view based on a selected value from a field, making analysis more intuitive and personalised.

To begin, we need to add a slicer visual to the report. Navigate to the Visualizations pane, and on row five, locate the slicer icon—it looks like a small funnel. Clicking on it adds the slicer to your report canvas. Power BI may attempt to position the visual for you. Usually, its guess is close enough, but you can always reposition it to better suit your layout.

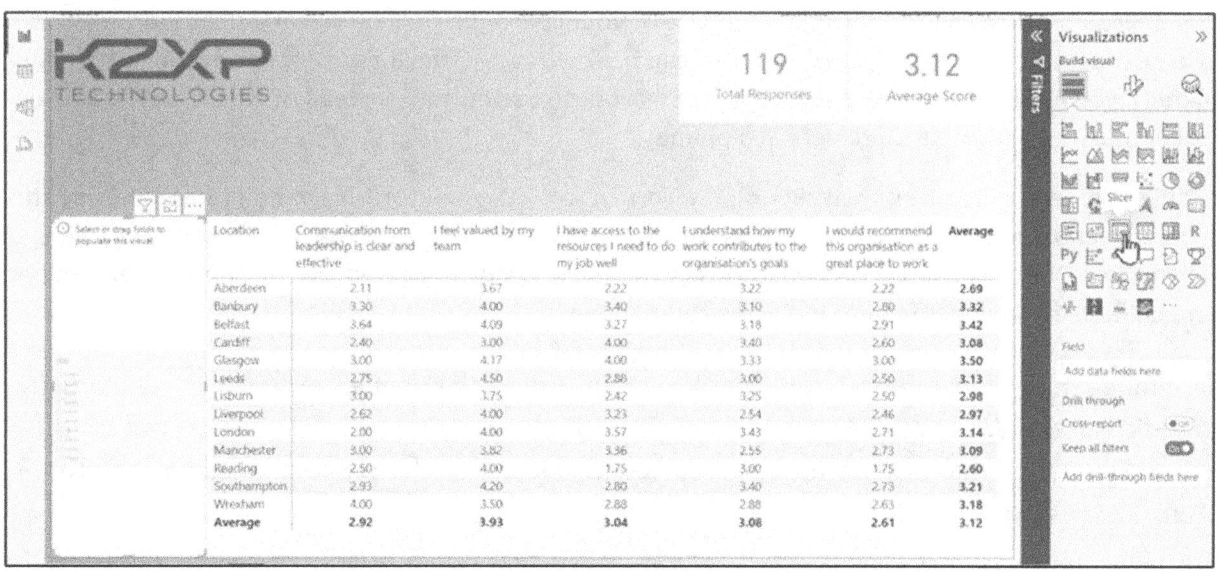

Next, we populate this slicer with the Department field. There are a few ways to do this, but let's take a moment to reinforce best practice. You might be tempted to simply tick the checkbox next to the Department field in the Fields pane or drag it onto the slicer visual directly. Both will work, but the more robust habit—particularly as reports become more complex—is to deliberately drag the field into the correct target zone at the bottom of the Visualizations pane. This ensures accuracy and reduces confusion. So, drag the Department field into the Field well, and immediately Power BI will display a list of departments in the slicer.

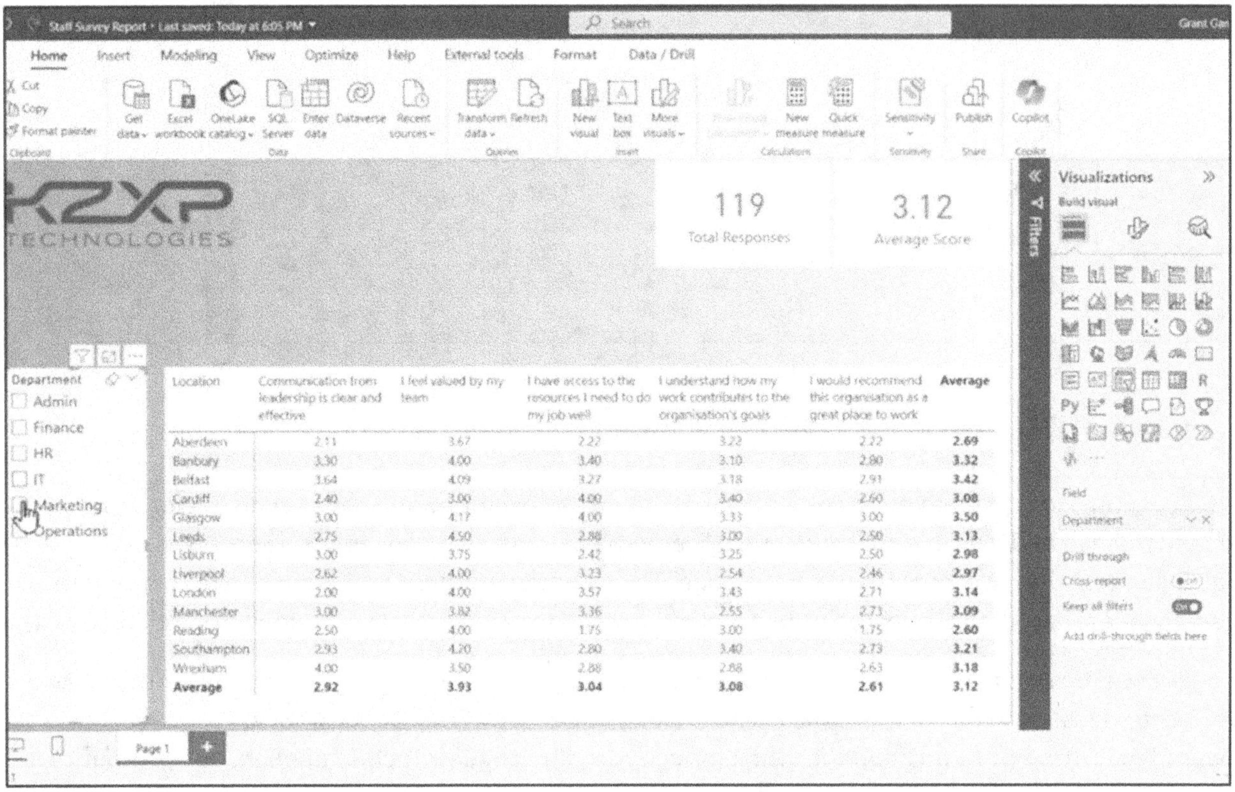

At this stage, it's worth considering your audience. If your colleagues will be viewing the report on mobile devices, these default slicer checkboxes can be frustrating. They're not especially touch-friendly. Thankfully, Power BI allows us to change the slicer layout to use buttons instead of checkboxes—making the slicer much easier to use on tablets and phones.

To enable this, select the slicer, then click on the Format icon (the paintbrush symbol) located beside the data fields section. Expand the Slicer settings category, and within it, locate the Style dropdown. Change the layout from Vertical list to Tile. You'll now see each slicer value displayed as a button—larger, cleaner, and much more suitable for finger tapping on touchscreens.

This change may seem minor, but it significantly improves the user experience, particularly for mobile-first users. While you're in the formatting options, another helpful tweak is to turn off the slicer header. In many cases, it adds unnecessary clutter to the report and can be safely hidden.

So far, we've demonstrated how slicers handle text fields. Now let's briefly explore how they work with dates, which is slightly different.

As before, add a new slicer to the page. This time, Power BI's auto-placement may not be ideal, so simply resize and reposition the slicer to fit neatly—ensuring it doesn't overlap any key elements like logos or headings. Take a moment to balance out the layout so the visuals are evenly spaced and aesthetically pleasing.

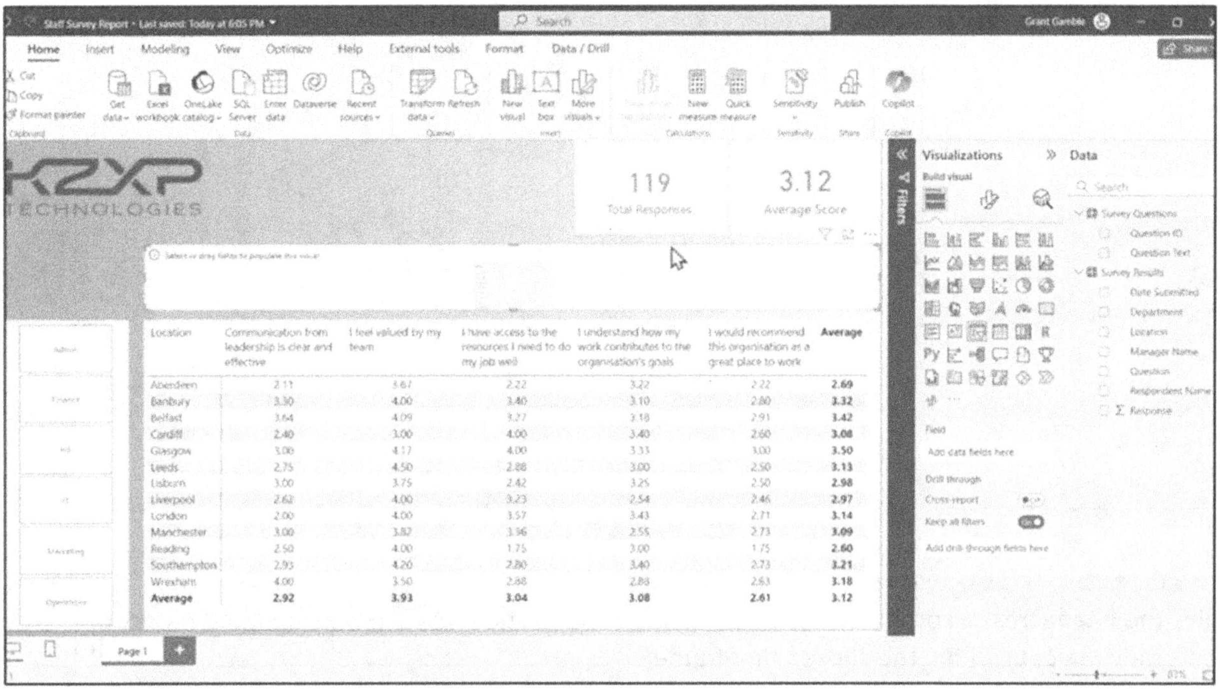

To populate the slicer with a date field, drag the Date Submitted field into the Field section of the Visualizations pane.

Again, let's go into the Format section and turn off the slicer header for a cleaner look.

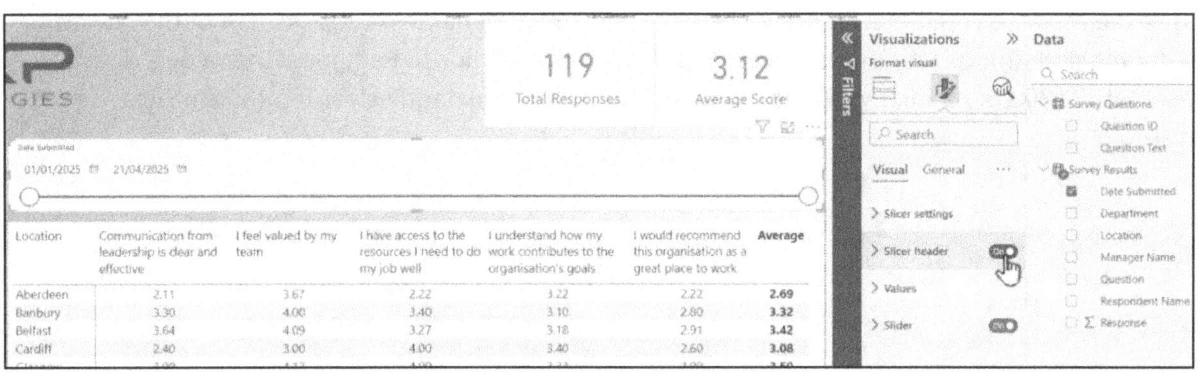

Now observe the default behaviour of the slicer when a date field is used. Power BI automatically uses a "between" style date picker. This provides a pair of slider handles that can be dragged to restrict the date range, or alternatively, users can click the small calendar icons on either side to select a specific start and end date manually.

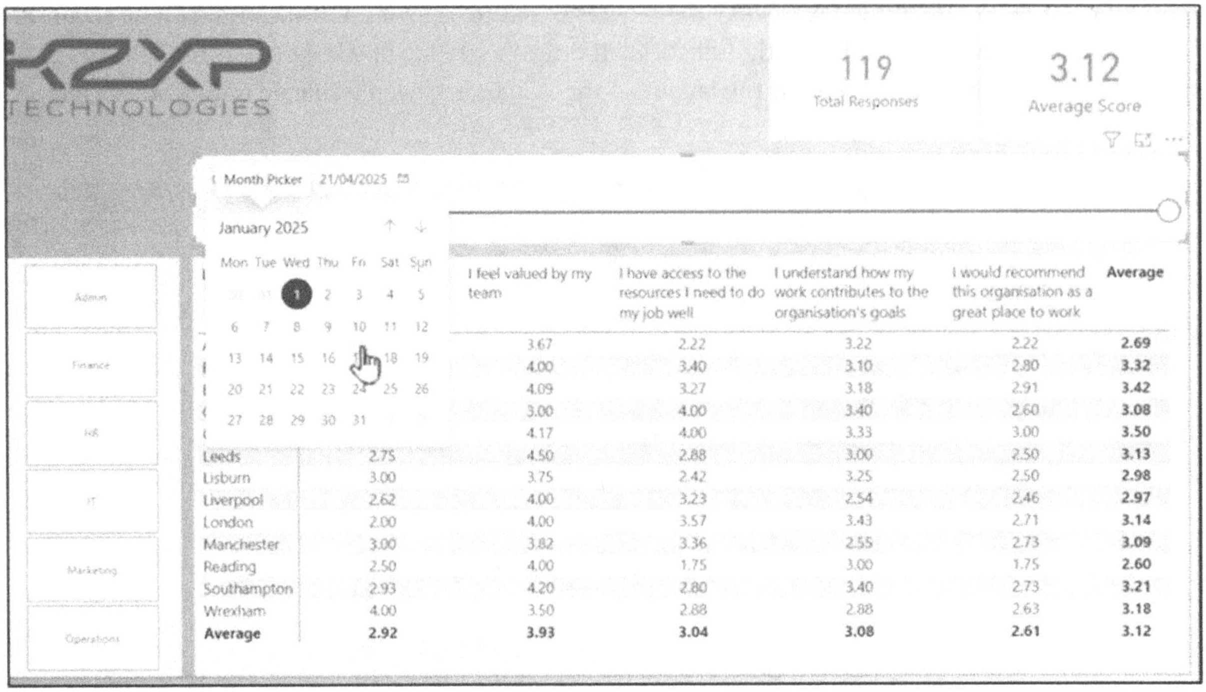

Once a date range is selected—either by dragging or picking dates from the calendar—Power BI instantly applies the filter across all other visuals on the page. The result is a dynamically updated report that reflects only the data within the chosen timeframe.

This interactivity lies at the heart of effective report design. Slicers are not just filters—they are tools for discovery, helping users uncover patterns, trends, and insights relevant to their needs.

Before finishing, let's reset the slicers to a neutral state. Deselect any department and ensure the full date range is selected so the report displays all data once again.

Now that the report is complete, let's give the page a meaningful name. At the bottom of the screen, either double-click the current page tab name or right-click and choose Rename. Enter a descriptive title—something like Staff Survey Report—so that its purpose is instantly clear to others navigating the report.

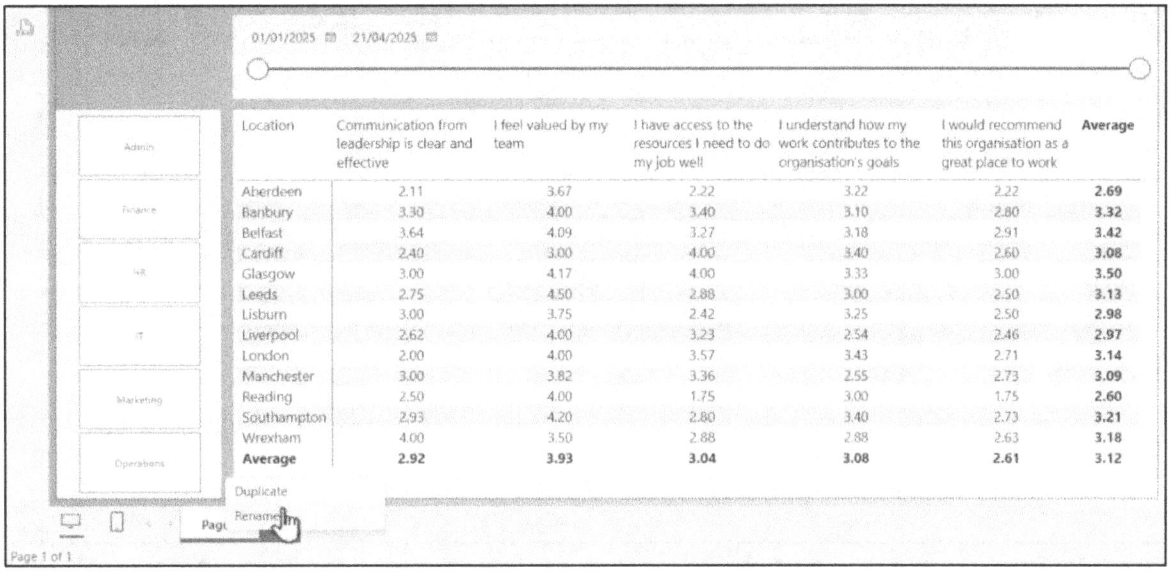

Location	Communication from leadership is clear and effective	I feel valued by my team	I have access to the resources I need to do my job well	I understand how my work contributes to the organisation's goals	I would recommend this organisation as a great place to work	**Average**
Aberdeen	2.11	3.67	2.22	3.22	2.22	**2.69**
Banbury	3.30	4.00	3.40	3.10	2.80	**3.32**
Belfast	3.64	4.09	3.27	3.18	2.91	**3.42**
Cardiff	2.40	3.00	4.00	3.40	2.60	**3.08**
Glasgow	3.00	4.17	4.00	3.33	3.00	**3.50**
Leeds	2.75	4.50	2.88	3.00	2.50	**3.13**
Lisburn	3.00	3.75	2.42	3.25	2.50	**2.98**
Liverpool	2.62	4.00	3.23	2.54	2.46	**2.97**
London	2.00	4.00	3.57	3.43	2.71	**3.14**
Manchester	3.00	3.82	3.36	2.55	2.73	**3.09**
Reading	2.50	4.00	1.75	3.00	1.75	**2.60**
Southampton	2.93	4.20	2.80	3.40	2.73	**3.21**
Wrexham	4.00	3.50	2.88	2.88	2.63	**3.18**
Average	**2.92**	**3.93**	**3.04**	**3.08**	**2.61**	3.12

And with that, congratulations are in order. If you've been building this alongside the tutorial, then you've now completed your first HR report in Power BI. While it may be simple, it marks a significant milestone. It's the culmination of core skills—importing data, creating visuals, adding interactivity—and lays a solid foundation for the more advanced and polished reporting techniques to come.

Let's wrap up by saving your work. This is an essential step, especially as we prepare to move beyond the desktop application. In the next section, we'll learn how to publish the report to the Power BI Service so that it can be shared with your wider organisation.

2.8: Publishing Your First HR Report

When working in Power BI Desktop, you're in what's known as design mode. This is the environment in which you build, test, and preview your reports. However, this is not the final version that your colleagues will interact with. The final version—your published, interactive product—lives in the Power BI Service. This is where consumption happens, and it's where reports become part of the wider organisational workflow.

The Power BI Service acts as the delivery platform for your work. Once your report is ready in Desktop, the next step is to publish it so that others can access it. To do that, we first need to understand where the report is going: a container called a workspace.

A workspace is a logical container within your Power BI tenant that stores related items, including reports, dashboards, datasets, and more. Every Power BI user has at least one workspace available to them, called My Workspace. This is your personal area and anything you publish here is visible only to you. Importantly, if you are using a free Power BI license, My Workspace is the only destination you can publish to.

Publishing to My Workspace is perfectly acceptable when you're learning Power BI or testing out a report. You'll still experience how a report behaves in the cloud and how it appears to users in a live setting.

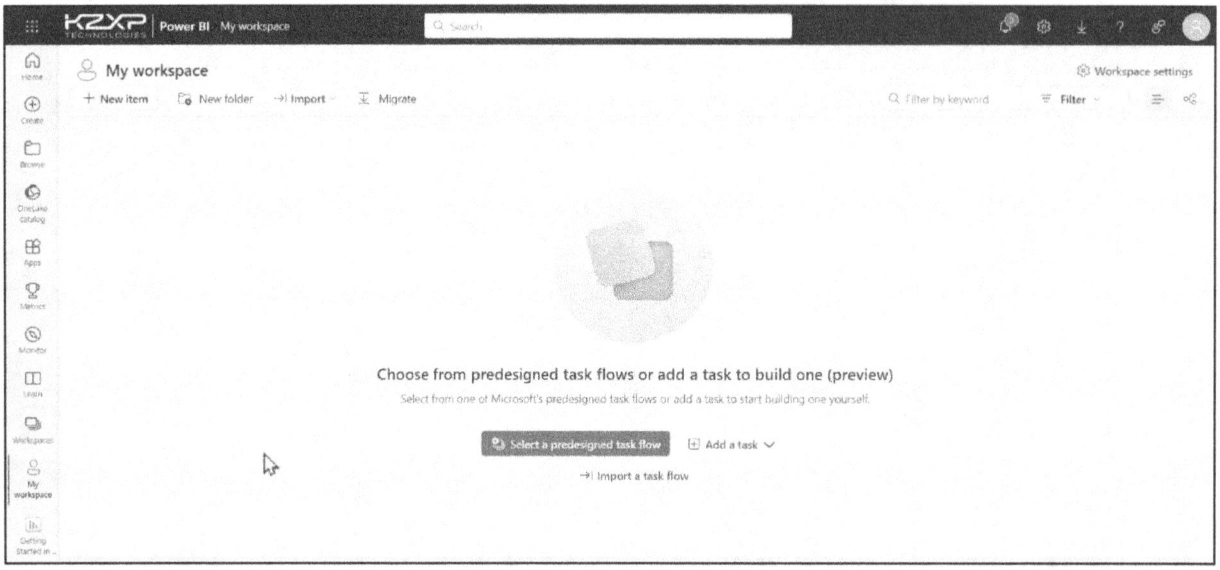

If, however, you have a Power BI Pro license (or Premium Per User), you can publish into shared workspaces—collaborative spaces that allow you to work with others and share reports. This is the key benefit of Pro licensing. You move from personal testing to real collaboration.

Creating a Workspace

To publish into a shared workspace, you may either use one that's been assigned to you by your IT team, or—if permissions allow—you may create one yourself. Many organisations restrict workspace creation for governance reasons, so if you don't see this option, speak to your Power BI administrator.

If you can create workspaces, here's how you do it. On the left-hand navigation bar in the Power BI Service, click on Workspaces. Scroll to the bottom and choose New Workspace.

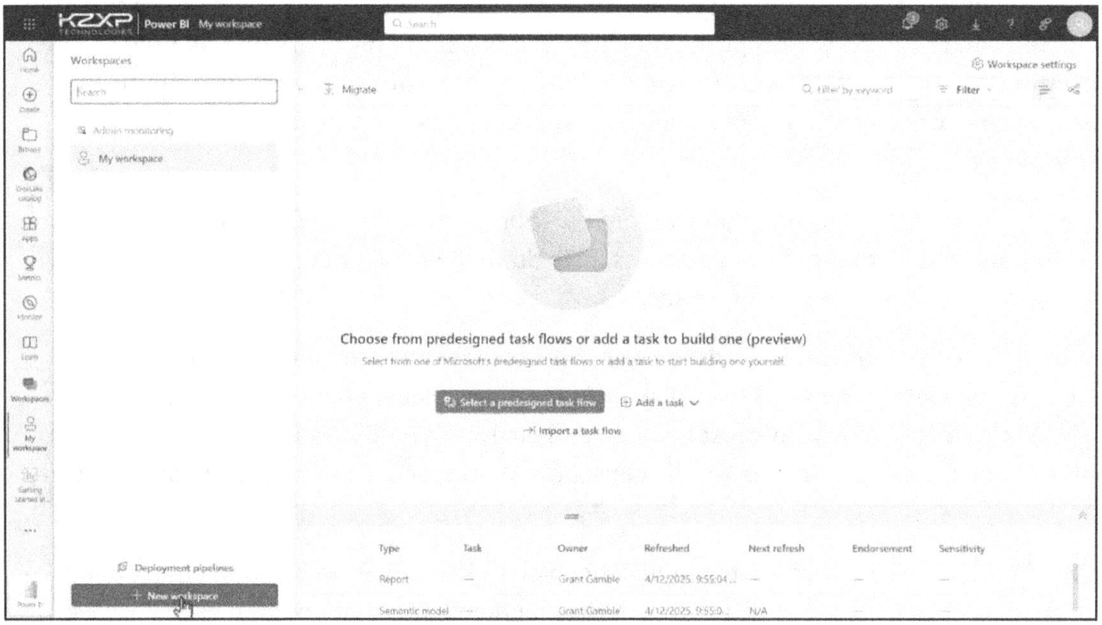

You'll be prompted to give your workspace a name. Choose something clear and descriptive that hasn't already been used within your organisation's tenant. In this case, we'll name it Human Resources.

Next, enter a description to help others understand the workspace's purpose. A suitable example would be: A central hub for all Human Resources reports and dashboards.

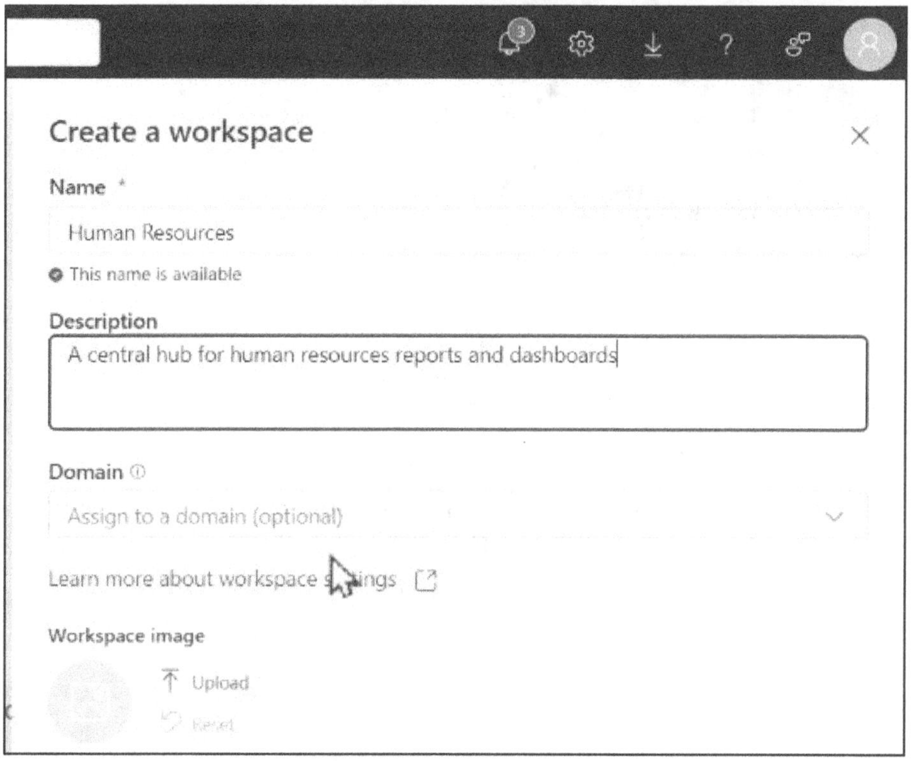

If your organisation uses Power BI domains, you may also assign the workspace to a domain, though we'll return to this feature in a later chapter.

It's also possible to upload an icon for the workspace. This can be very useful when you're part of multiple workspaces, helping you quickly identify the one you need. If you've prepared custom icons for departmental workspaces, simply click Upload, locate the file, and apply the icon. You'll find a suitable file in the Assets folder of the Section 2 folder.

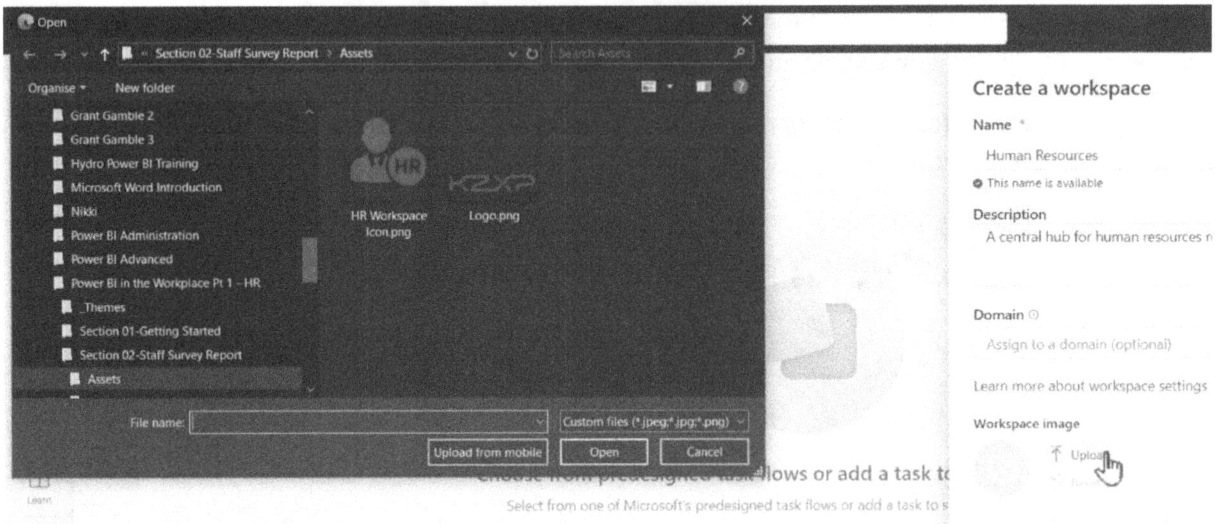

Publishing the Report

With the workspace now created, we'll switch back to Power BI Desktop to begin the publishing process.

On the Home tab in Power BI Desktop, locate the Publish button. This is situated on the far right of the ribbon. Clicking this will initiate the upload process—but before that, Power BI will prompt you to save your file. This is because publishing works from disk, not memory. So go ahead and click Save.

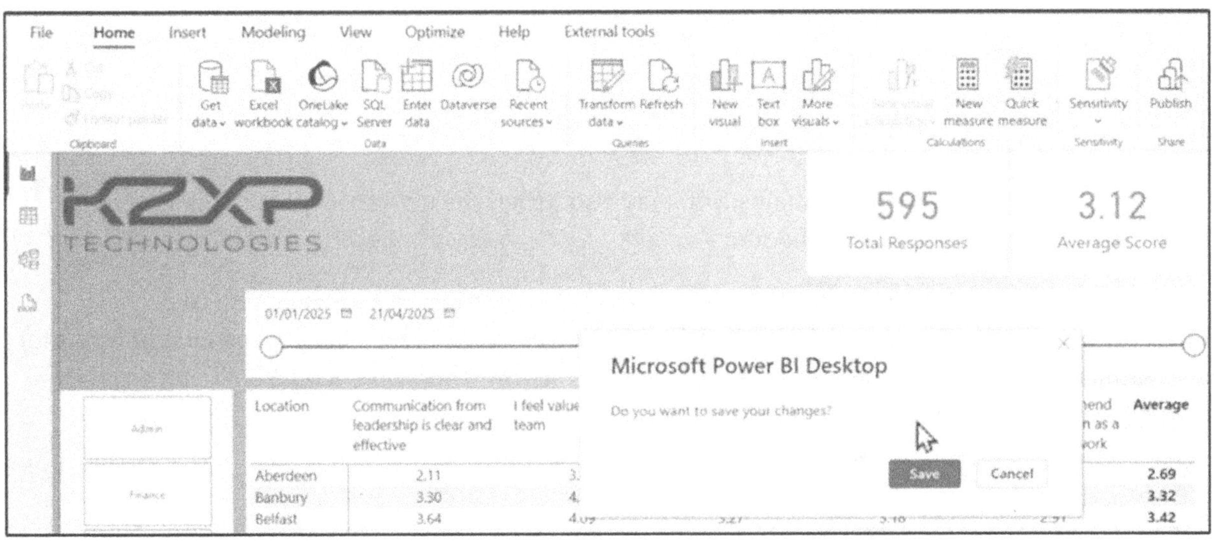

Now, Power BI will list all the workspaces available to you. In our case, you'll see both My Workspace and the new Human Resources workspace that we just created.

Select Human Resources and click Select to continue. Power BI will now upload the report file from your machine into the cloud-based Power BI Service.

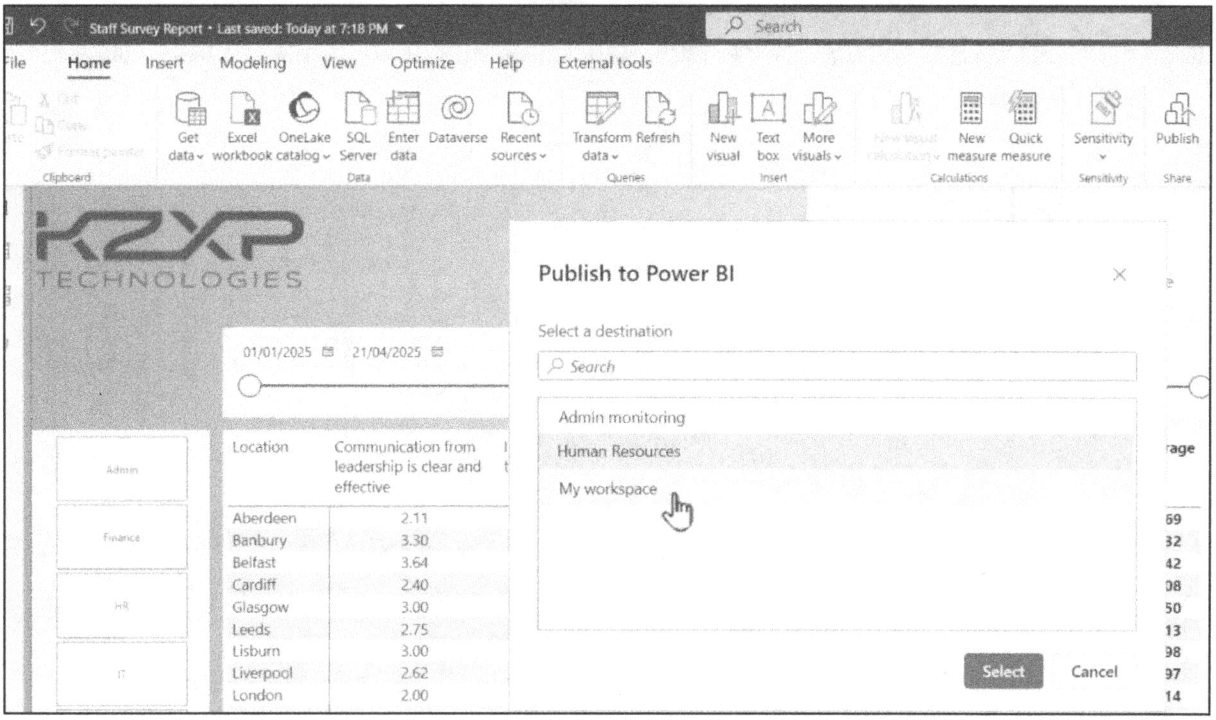

Once the process is complete, switch back to your browser and open the Power BI Service. In your Human Resources workspace, you'll now see two items:

- The report itself—this is the visual and interactive experience you built.
- The semantic model—previously known as the dataset, this is the underlying data and logic that powers your report.

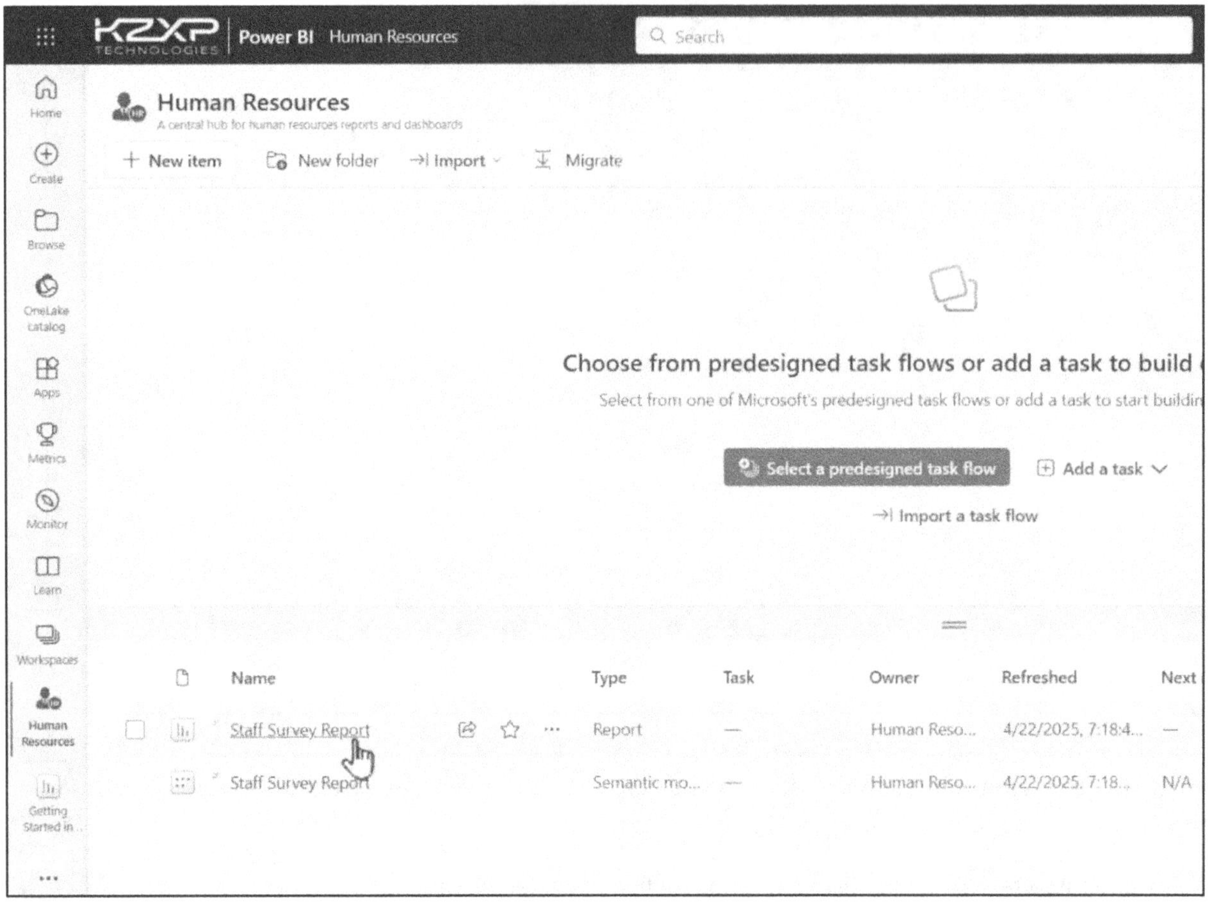

Clicking on the report opens it in reading view. This is what your colleagues will see when they interact with it online.

The Report Experience for Your Colleagues

When users view your report in the Power BI Service, they'll experience the interactivity of slicers, filters, and visuals. However, they won't be able to change or move anything. They are in read-only mode. This is a key concept: you, as the report developer, maintain control of the layout, structure, and logic. Your colleagues are consumers. They explore the report, draw insights, and make decisions—but they don't modify your design.

You can even expand the report to full screen using the button in the top-right corner of the page, making it easier to view in presentations or on shared displays.

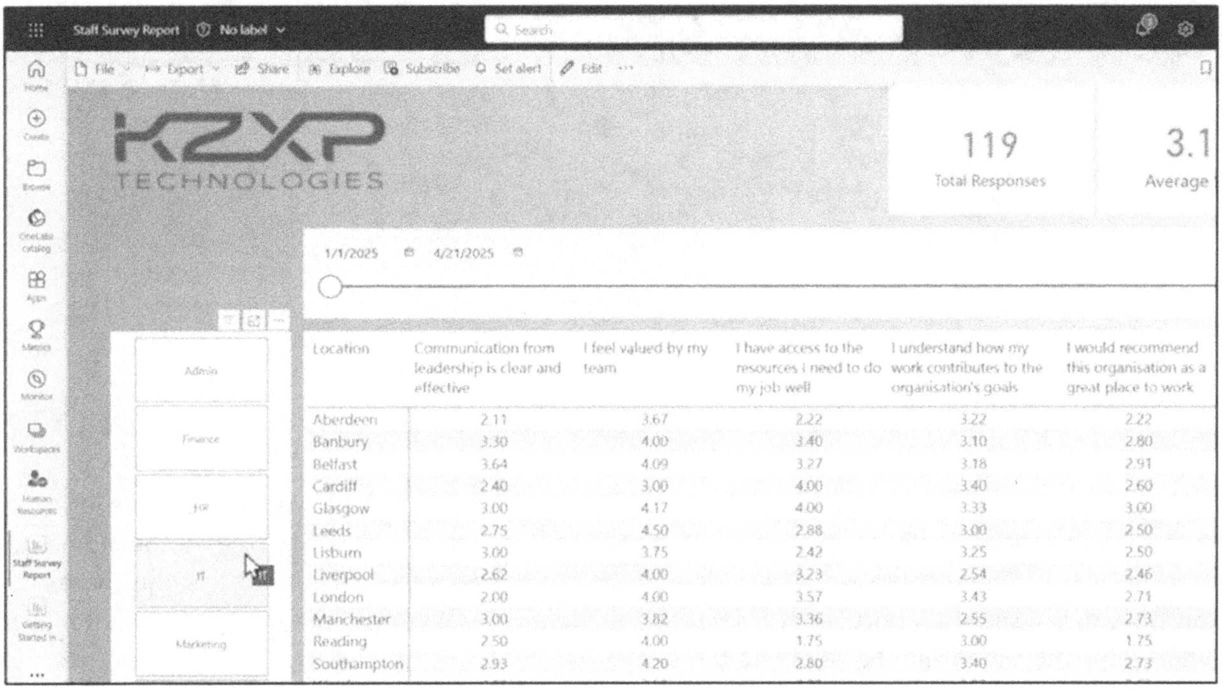

At this point, your report is now live in the Power BI cloud. It's interactive, it's shareable (subject to licensing), and it's part of a structured workspace that supports collaboration and governance.

That completes the core publishing process. You've gone from building in Desktop to delivering in Service—a key milestone in your Power BI journey.

2.9: Sharing your Report with Colleagues

In this section, we'll take our first look at sharing Power BI reports with other users. Sharing is an essential part of the reporting process—after all, creating insights is only valuable if the right people can access and act on them. There are many sophisticated ways to manage access and collaborate across teams, which we'll explore in later sections. But for now, we'll begin with the most basic approach: sharing a single report directly with a colleague.

Let's start by opening the report we created earlier. While viewing the report in the Power BI Service, you'll see a Share button positioned on the menu bar in the top-left of the screen. This button gives you quick access to the sharing options.

Alternatively, you can go back to the workspace level. Click on the name of the workspace in the left-hand navigation pane. This will bring you to the list of all reports within that workspace. At the moment, there might only be one report listed. To the right of the report's name, you'll notice the same Share button. So, you can share a report either from inside the report itself or from the workspace list. It makes no difference—the action and the result are the same.

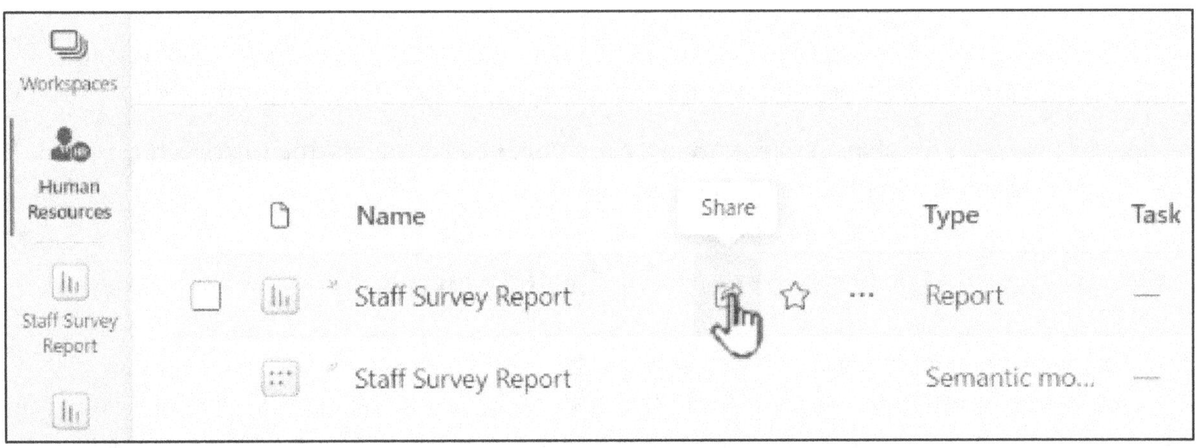

Clicking the Share button opens a dialogue window. Here, you can enter the names or email addresses of the people you'd like to share the report with. Power BI allows you to share reports either with individuals or with groups. For instance, in our environment, there's a group named "IT department", so I could share the report with that group. Or I can share it with a specific person—someone like Peter Parker.

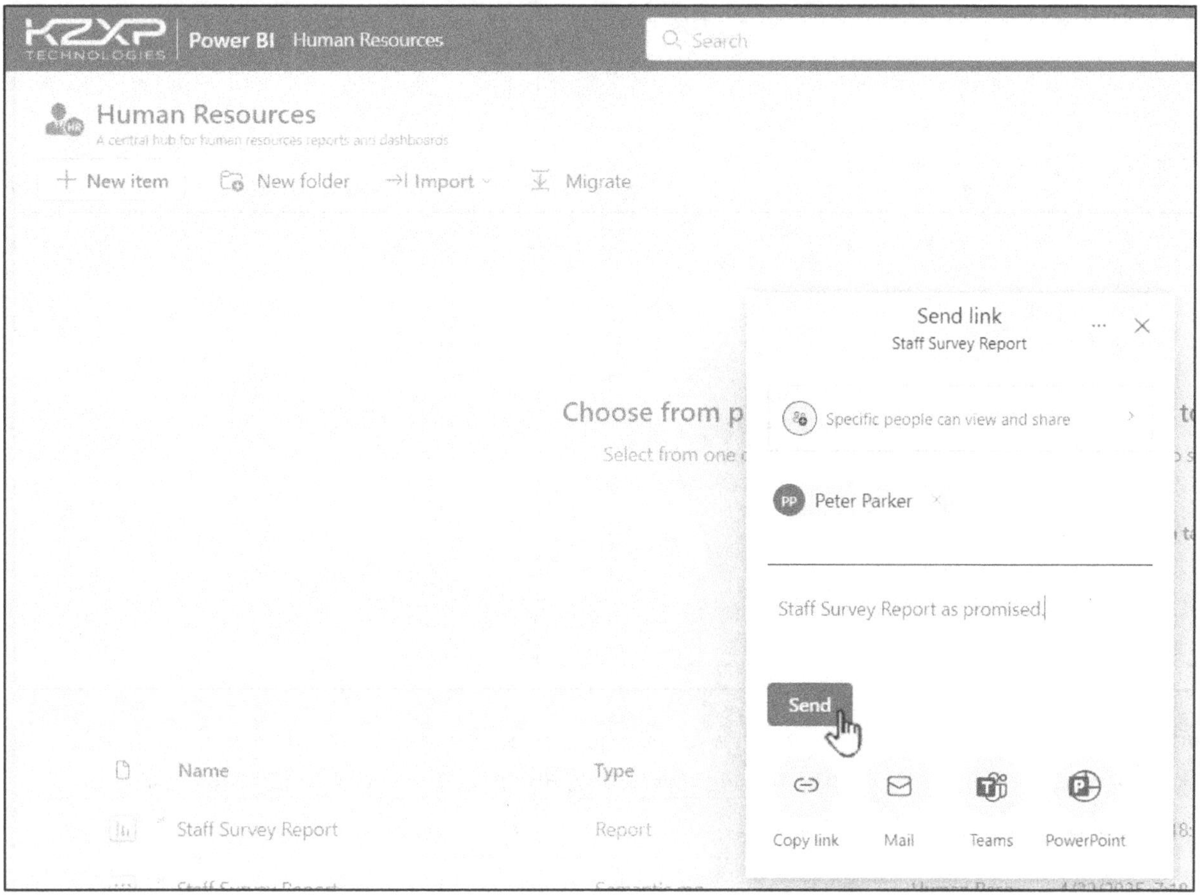

Let's go ahead and share this report with Peter. I type in his name, and then I'm prompted to add an optional message. This message will appear in the notification email Peter receives. It can be a helpful way to provide context or instructions. I'll enter: staff survey report – as promised.

Once I've added the message, I simply click Send. That's it—Peter has now been granted access to view the report.

Now let's look at this from Peter's perspective. I'll log out and sign back in, this time as Peter Parker.

I'll switch over to Outlook so we can see what he receives. Sure enough, there's an email notification from Power BI. The email contains the message we typed, along with a direct link to the report.

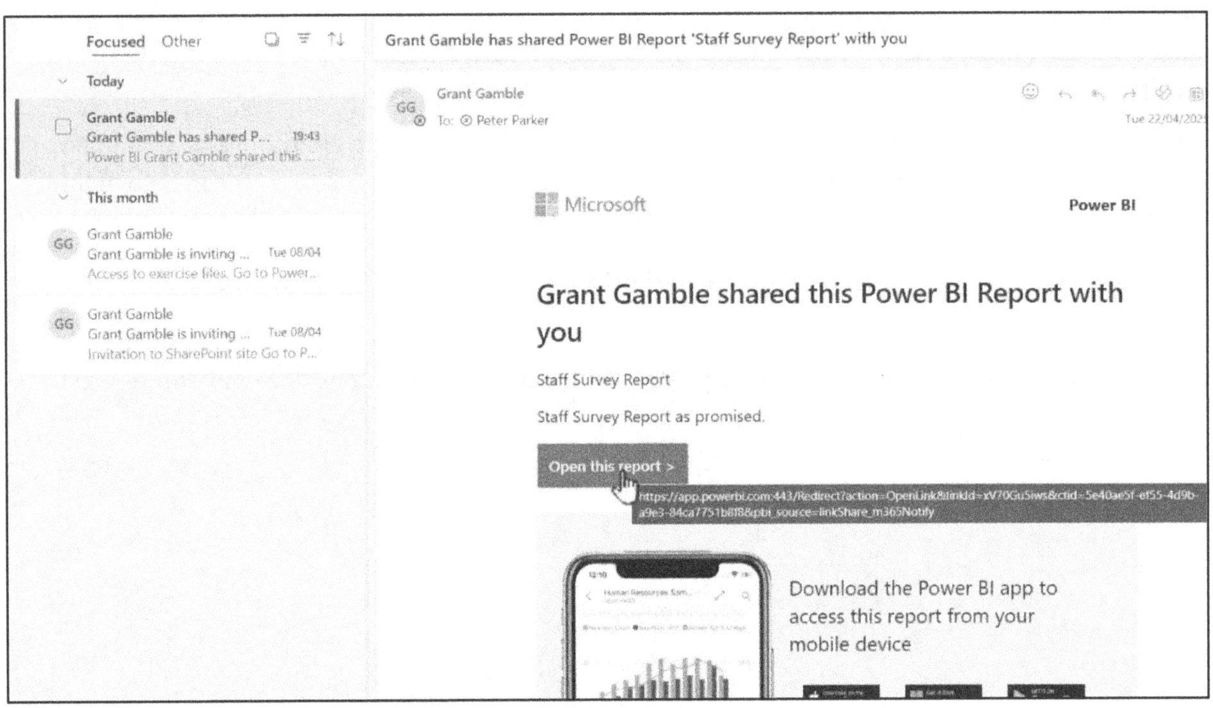

When Peter clicks Open this report, he is taken straight into the Power BI Service where he can view the report in his browser.

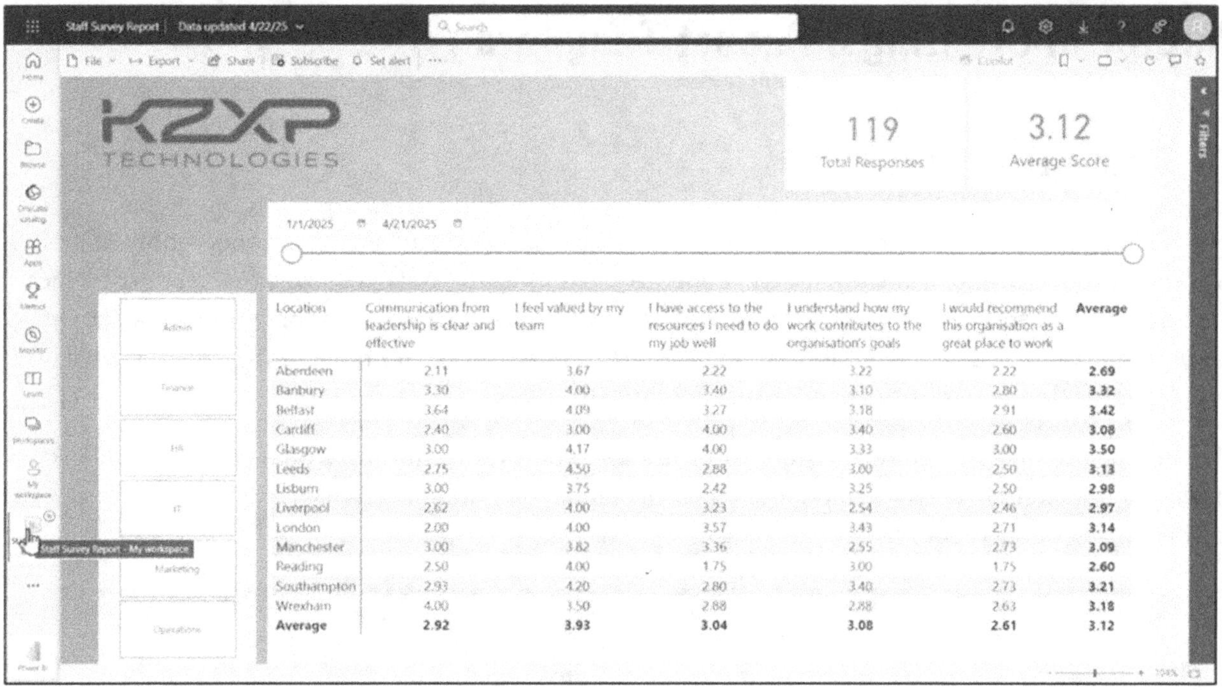

Now, here's a key detail: Peter is accessing the report as an individual user. He doesn't have permission to explore the rest of the HR workspace. I haven't granted him browsing rights or contributor access. All he can see is the specific report that was shared with him.

This kind of sharing is ideal when you want to give someone read-only access to a report without exposing the wider workspace or other reports. It's quick, direct, and works well when you're distributing reports to a small audience or seeking feedback from a colleague.

That's all I wanted to show you in this section. As we progress, we'll explore more advanced sharing options. But for now, if you've built a report and you have a colleague in mind, consider sharing it with them. It's a great way to showcase your progress and demonstrate that you're building functional, professional Power BI reports.

Chapter 3: Creating a Report Template

3.1: Basic Branding

When building reports in Power BI, one of the first considerations should be consistency—both in how your reports function and how they appear. Consistent branding not only improves the user experience but also reinforces trust and professionalism across your reports. A branded report template allows you to apply a unified look and feel without having to start from scratch every time. In this section, we'll walk through setting up the basic branding for such a template.

To begin, open the file named Report Template. You'll see that we're starting with a completely blank canvas. Our goal here is to apply some foundational elements of branding, which will form the basis of a reusable, professional report style.

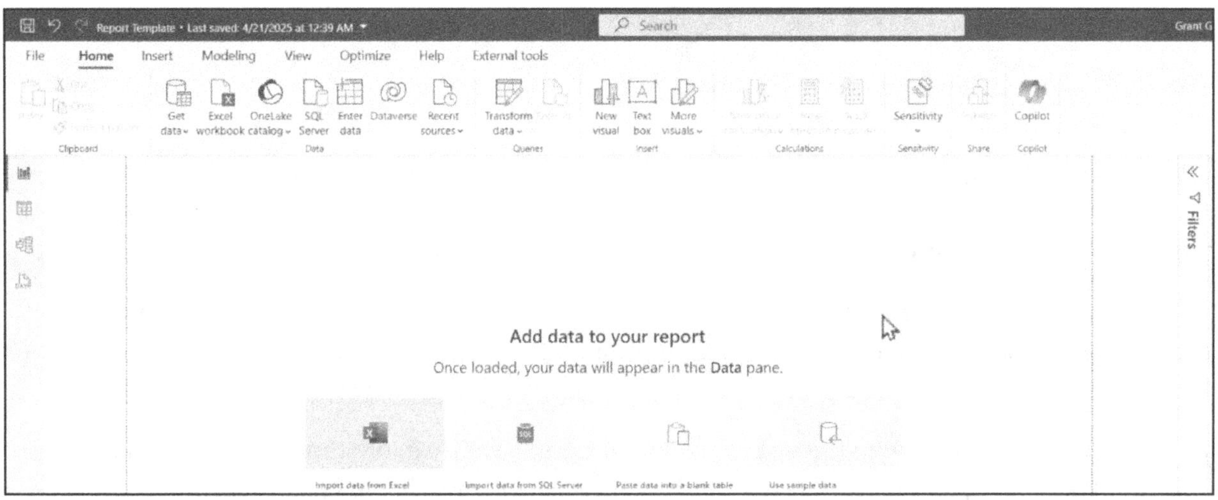

The cornerstone of visual branding in Power BI is the theme. Themes control the colour palette, fonts, and in some cases, background images. To apply a theme:

1. Go to the View tab on the Power BI ribbon.
2. Click on Browse for Themes.
3. Navigate to the Section Three folder, open the Assets subfolder, and select the file named coastal-breeze.json.

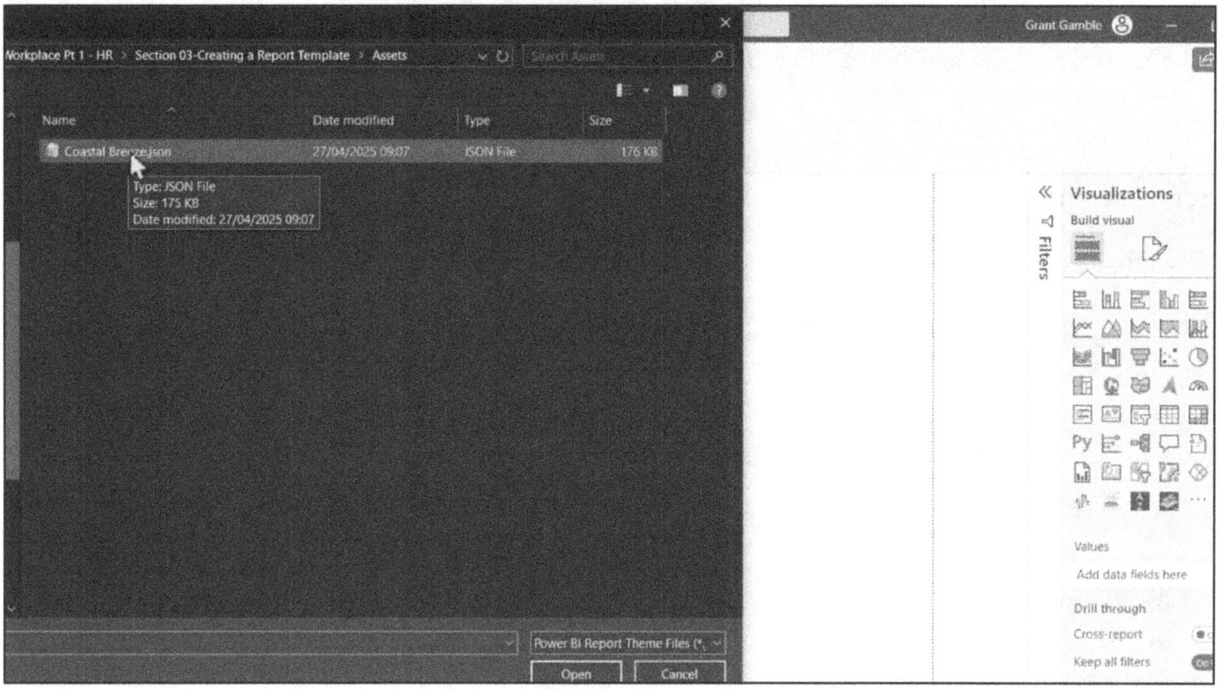

The moment the theme is applied, you'll notice an immediate visual transformation. This particular theme includes a background image, so the page layout itself will subtly change. In addition, interface elements such as the Filters pane will update to use colours defined in the theme.

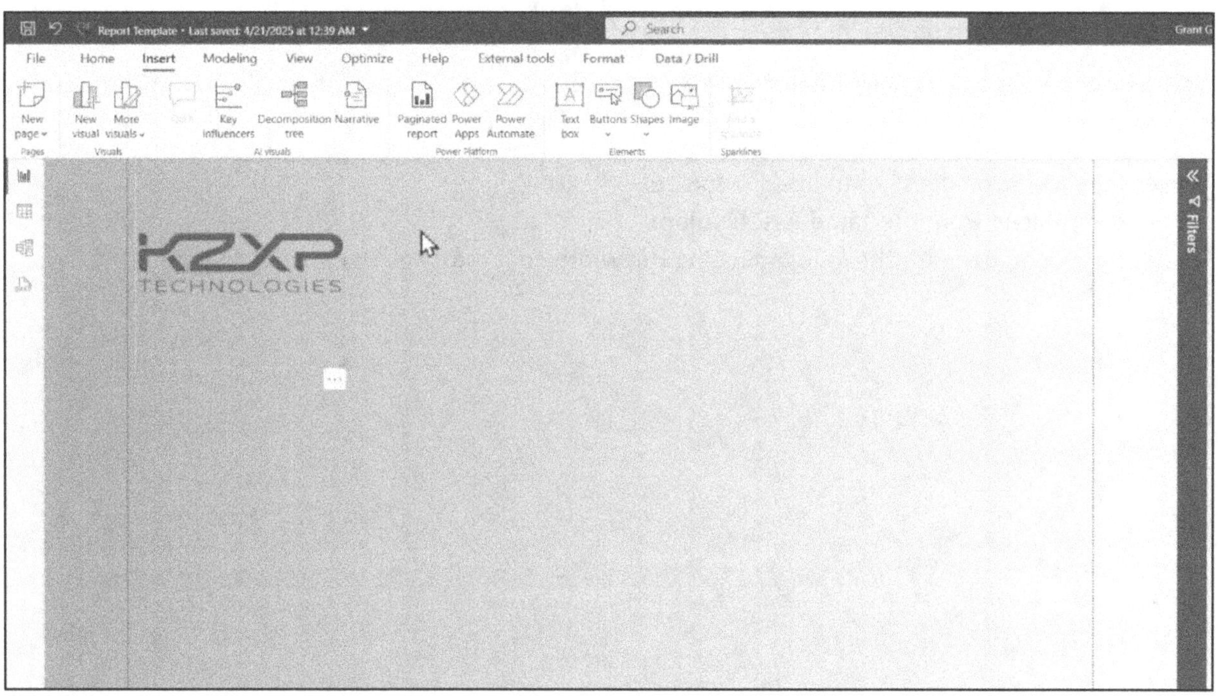

Now that we've set the foundation, the next step is to insert your corporate logo. Logos provide a visual anchor and instantly identify the report as coming from your organisation.

1. Click on the Insert tab in the ribbon.
2. Choose Image, then navigate again to the Assets folder.
3. Select the file named KZXP-logo.

Your style guide may specify logo positioning, and in this example, we're told to always place the logo in the top-left corner of each page. Once the logo is inserted:

- Drag the logo's resize handle (from the bottom centre) to adjust its height without distorting its width.
- Move the logo to the top of the page and nudge it slightly downwards, leaving approximately 10 pixels of breathing space.

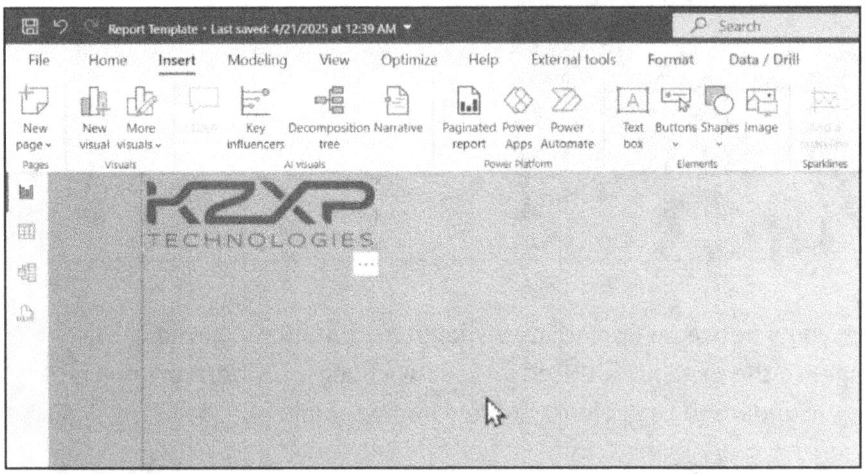

Directly below the logo, we'll insert another image—an HR icon—to indicate that this is an HR-focused report template.

1. Repeat the Insert process: go to Insert > Image.
2. Select the HR icon from the same Assets folder.
3. Position the icon beneath the logo, adjusting the width so it matches the logo precisely.

To refine the layout:

- Reduce the height of the HR icon by dragging its bottom handle.
- Use the arrow keys (specifically the up arrow) to fine-tune its vertical alignment so it sits snugly beneath the logo.

This simple combination—a defined colour theme, a company logo, and a representative icon—lays the groundwork for consistent, branded reporting. It may seem basic, but these are the visual cues that immediately tell a viewer the report is part of a unified suite.

Once you've made these changes, be sure to save your file. Give it a name that reflects its purpose—something like HR Report Template—so it can be reused as a starting point for future reports.

With the branding elements now in place, the next step will be to look at setting up page navigation, which allows report consumers to move between different sections of your report with ease.

3.2: Creating a Navigation Bar

In this section, we'll create a dynamic and visually consistent navigation bar that allows users to move between report pages. This is about more than just functionality—it's about creating a polished and professional user experience that feels coherent every time someone interacts with your HR report.

The navigation bar will sit on the left-hand side of the report and is built using the Page Navigator button in Power BI. The aim is to make navigation intuitive and consistent, regardless of which report a user is viewing.

To begin, go to the Insert tab on the Ribbon, then choose Buttons > Navigator > Page Navigator.

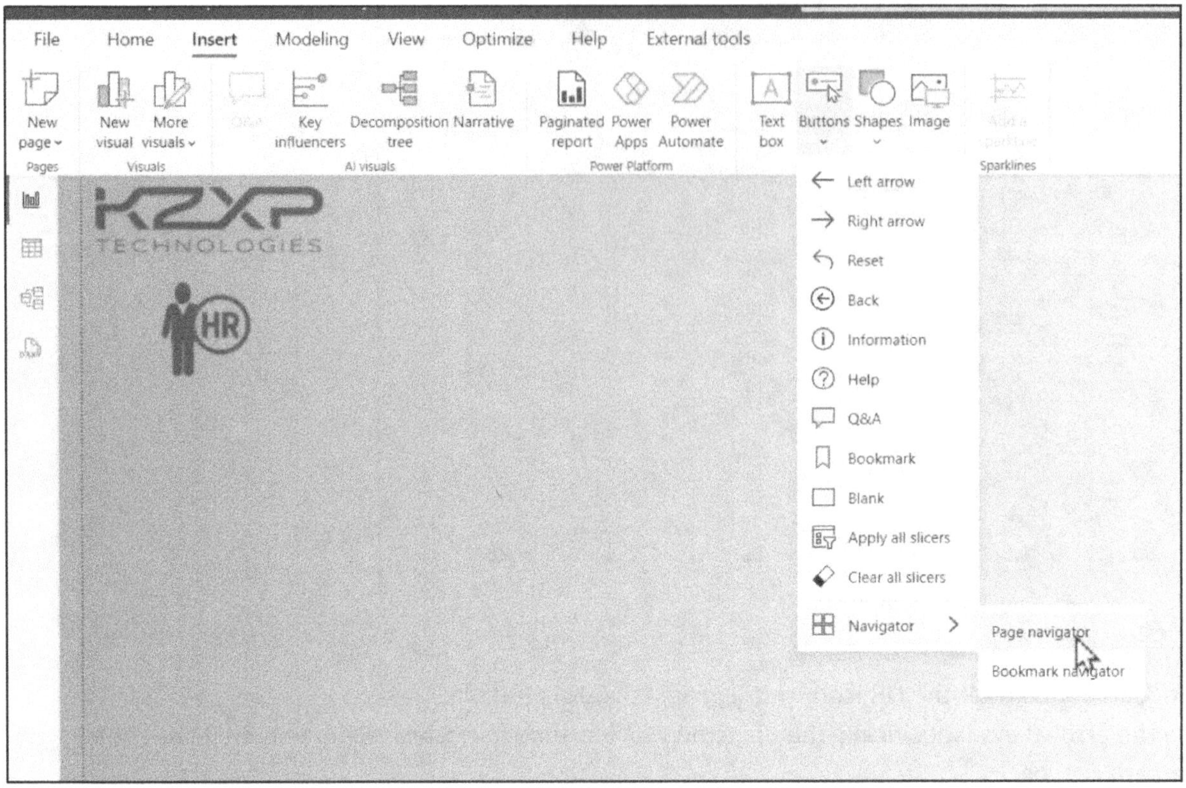

By default, Power BI inserts this element at the top of the canvas.

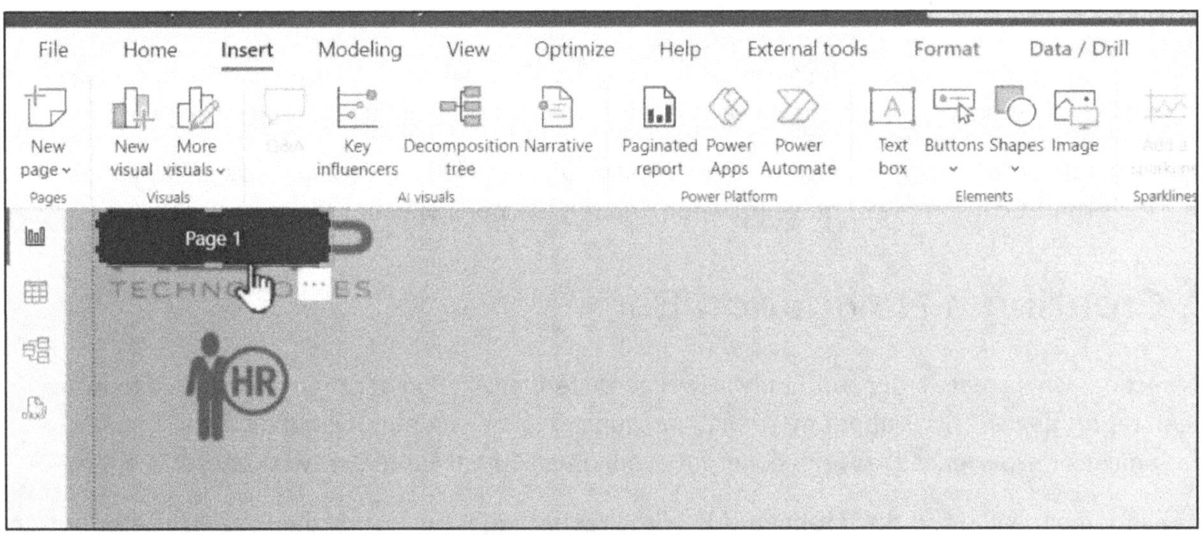

Click and drag the navigator object down to the left-hand side of the page. We'll use a layout that supports five report pages, although this same design works equally well with four, five, or even six.

Next, create the additional report pages. If you only have one page at this point, click the New Page button at the bottom of the screen until you have five in total. Once that's done, return to page one and you'll see the Page Navigator has automatically detected and displayed buttons for all five pages.

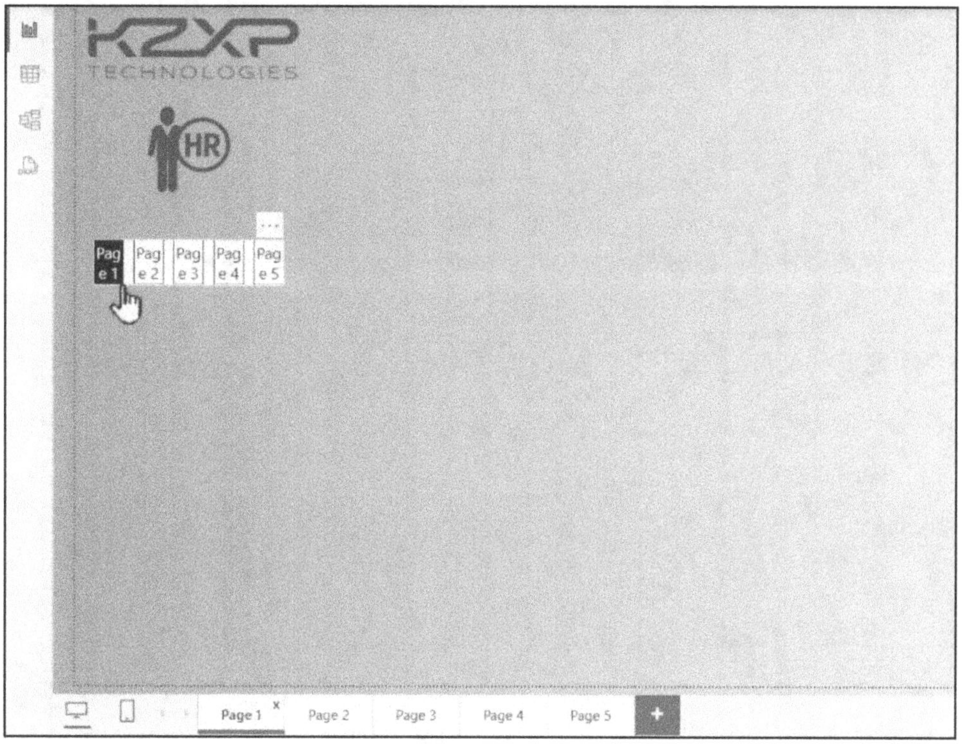

Let's now adjust the layout of the navigation panel. Open the Format pane and expand the Grid layout section. Set the orientation to Vertical so that the buttons run down the side.

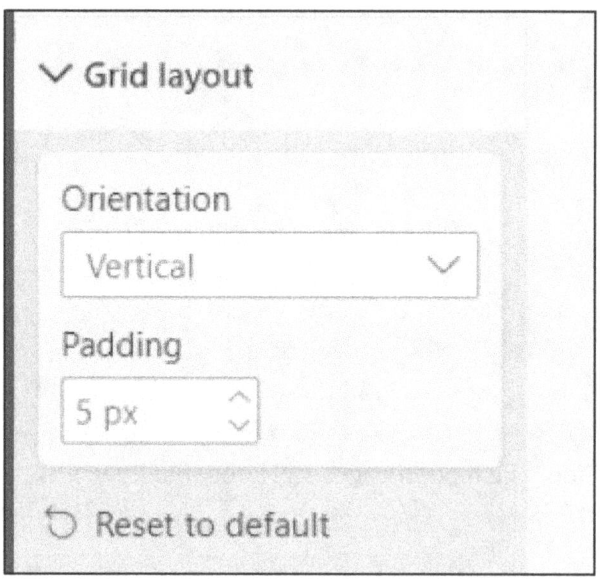

Adjust the height so that all buttons are visible.

Close the Grid layout and open the Shape settings. Change the shape to a Rounded rectangle. Use the corner roundness slider to set the value to 20%. This introduces a softer, more modern design.

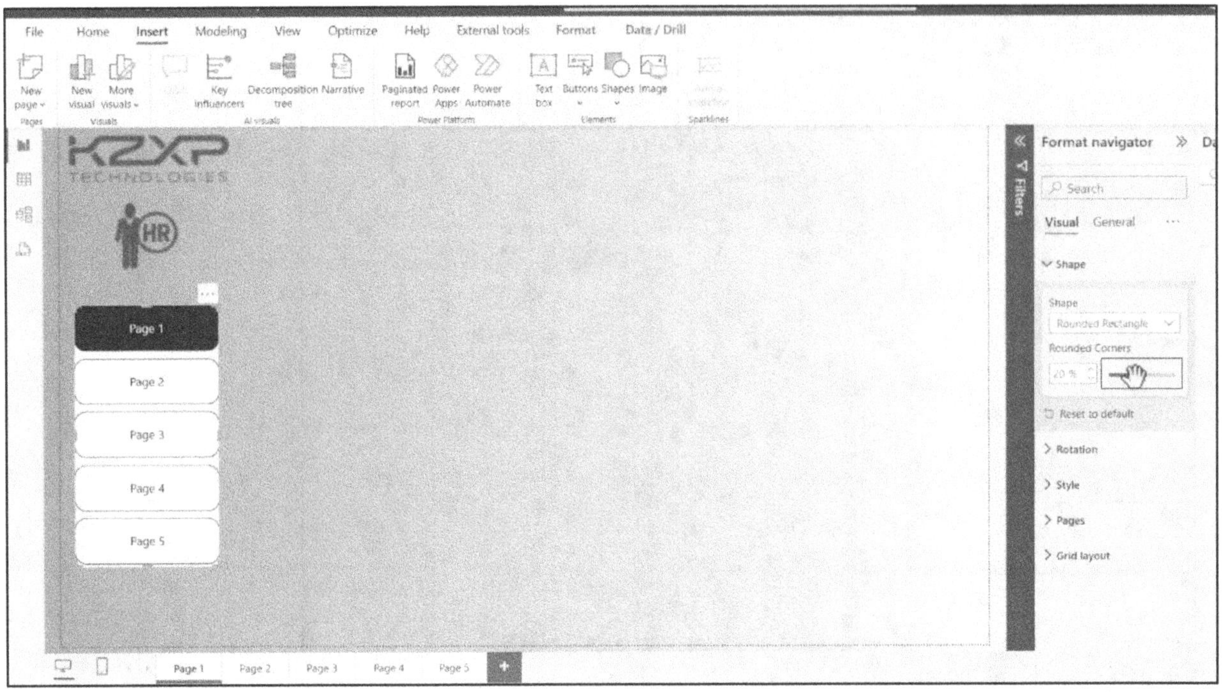

Before continuing, open the Pages section and note that Show Hidden Pages is currently enabled. Best practice is to hide all report pages except one. This ensures that users can only navigate using the custom navigation bar—just like in Excel, where only one sheet must always remain visible.

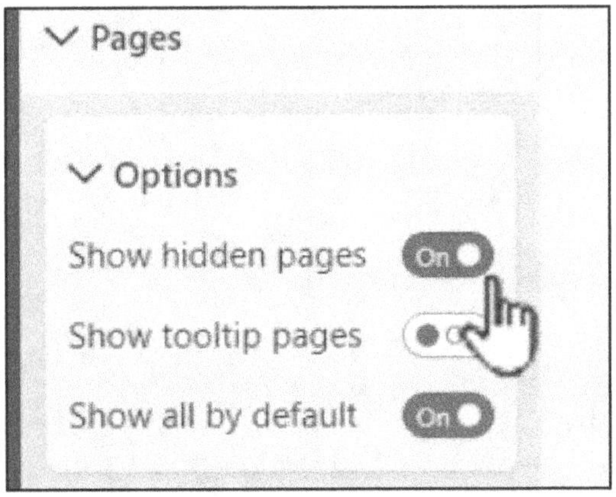

Right-click each page apart from page one and choose Hide. The hidden pages still appear in Power BI Desktop but are invisible to users in the published report.

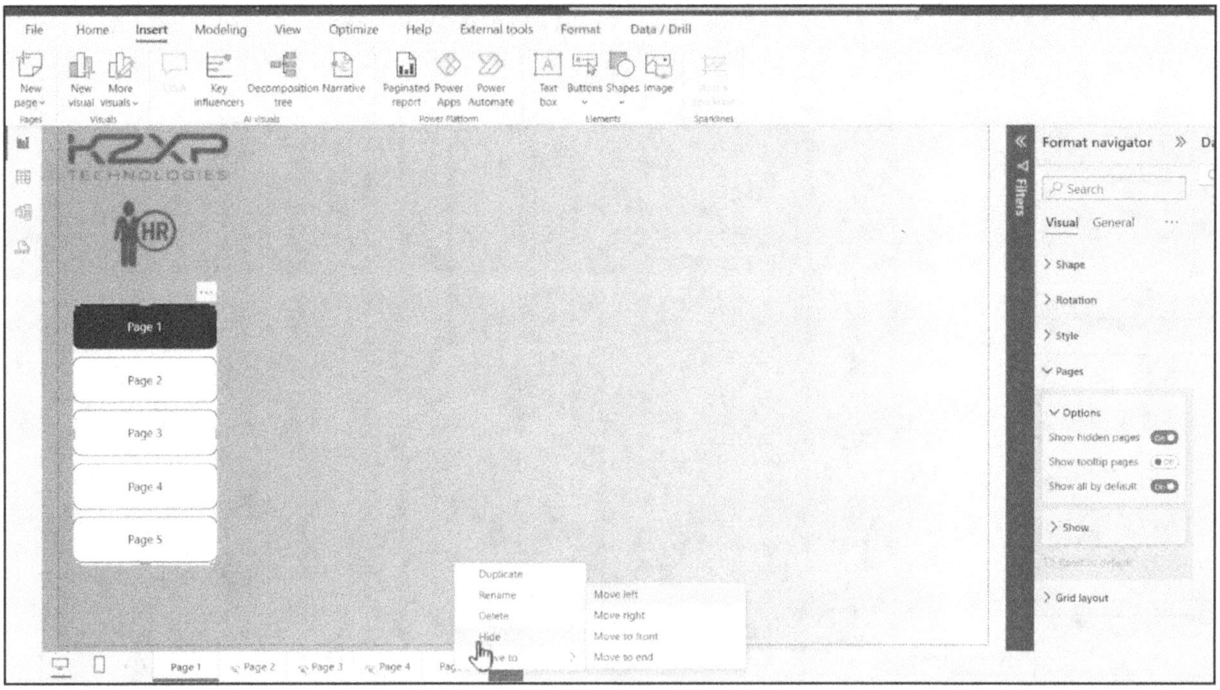

Now let's style the buttons. Power BI offers four visual states: Default, Hover, Press, and Selected. Each state reflects a different moment in the interaction.

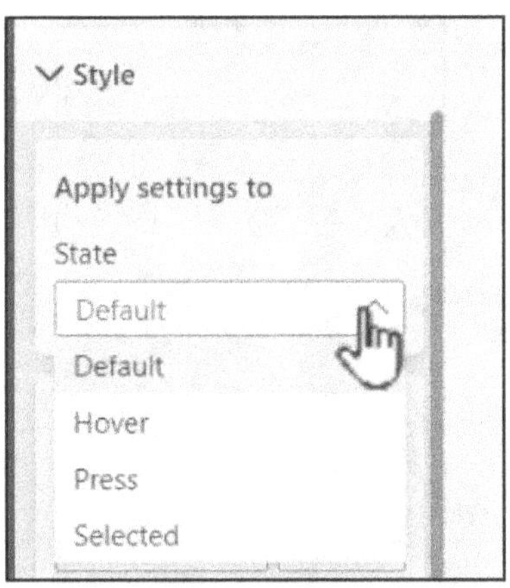

The Default state is the normal appearance of the button. Set the font colour to white and choose the theme's primary blue as the fill—ideally matching your logo or brand palette. Scroll down to enable the Border and optionally add a Shadow for visual depth.

To make the navigation bar feel more integrated, remove the background of the entire navigation object. Switch from the Visual formatting section to the General section. Under Effects > Background, toggle it off. The buttons now rest directly against the report's page background.

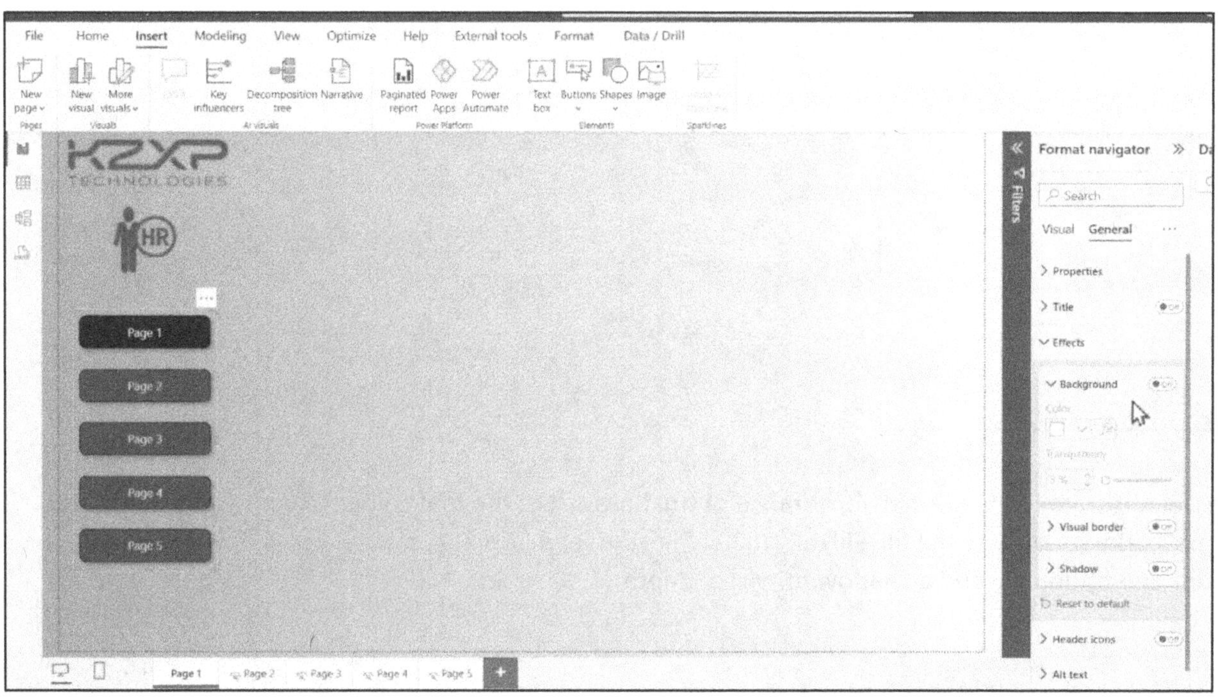

Next, define the Hover state. This activates when the user's mouse pointer moves over the button. Keep the font colour white and set the fill to a peach tone from your theme—a colour that contrasts with the default blue to indicate interactivity.

Now configure the Press state. This is a very short-lived visual state that appears when the button is actively being clicked. Set the font colour to white again and choose a lighter tint of the theme blue as the fill.

For the Selected state—the one that highlights the current page—set the fill colour to a darker version of the theme blue and change the border to white. Increase the border thickness slightly to enhance visibility and help orient the user within the report.

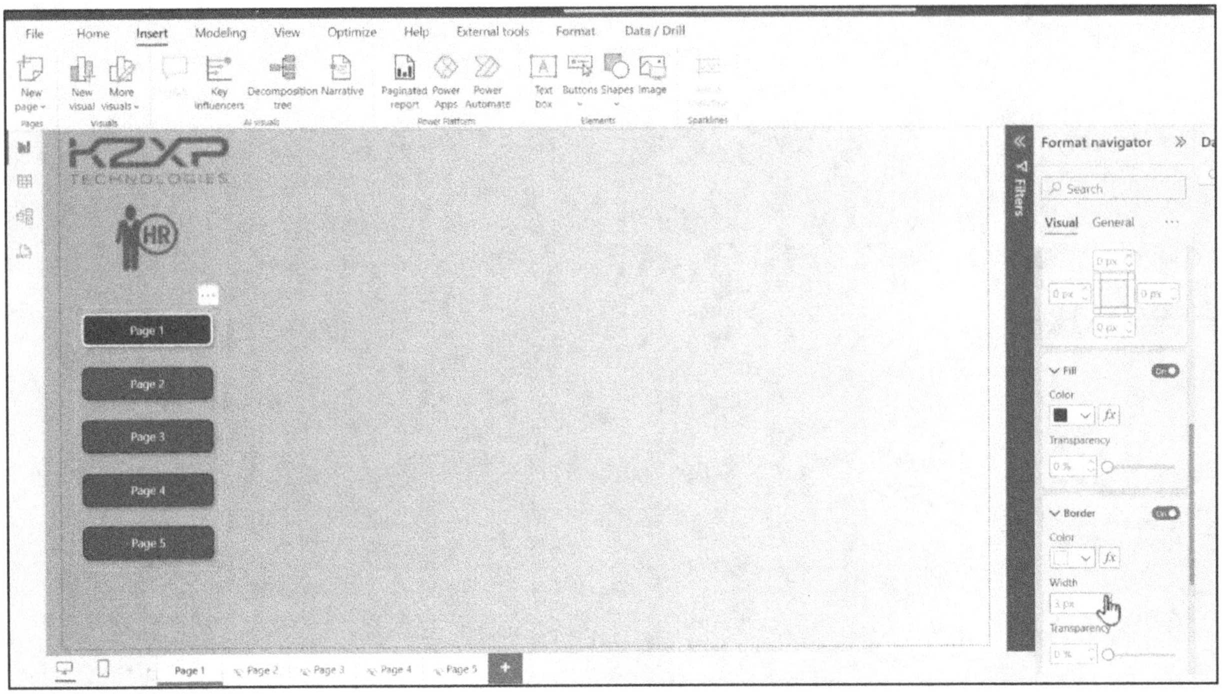

With all four states styled, consider enlarging the buttons slightly. Increase both height and width so that the labels fit neatly and are easy to read, even if they're long.

The page navigator is dynamic. If you rename or reorder pages, the navigation panel updates automatically—no need to manually re-link anything. However, it doesn't automatically appear on every page.

To address this, we'll copy the finished navigation bar across. But first, add a background shape to separate it from the main report area. Go to Insert > Shape > Rectangle and size it to fill the page from top to bottom and completely cover the buttons.

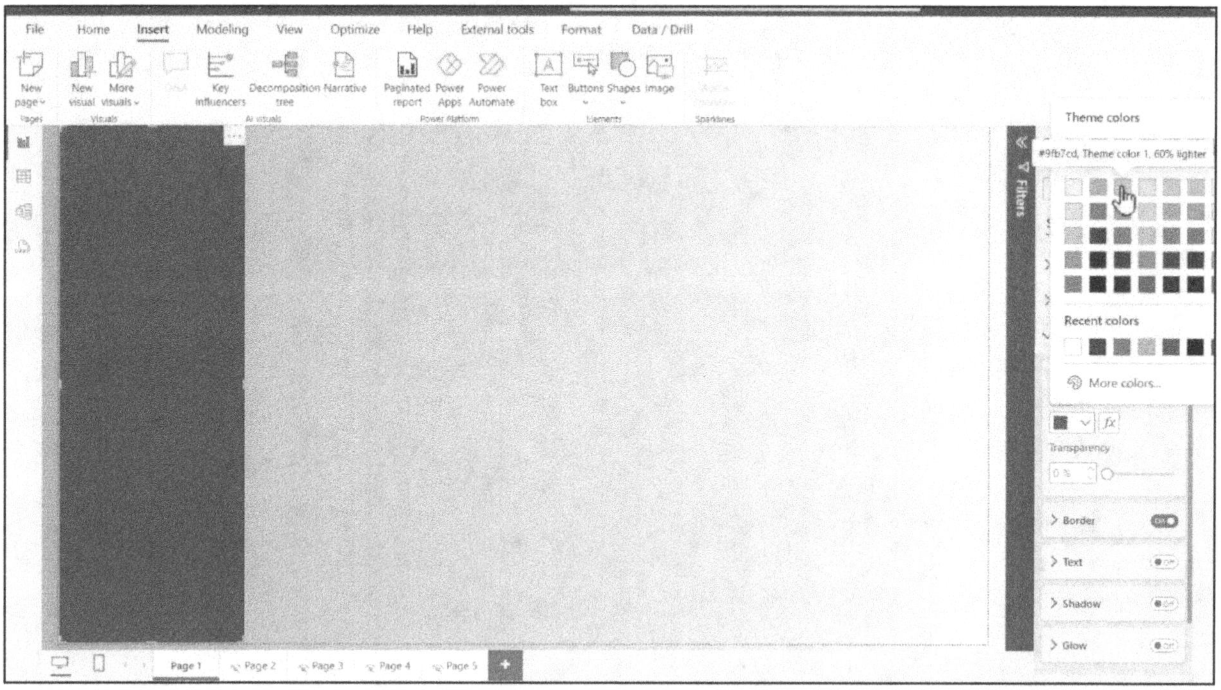

Set the fill of the rectangle to the lightest blue from your theme. Then, with the rectangle selected, go to Format > Send Backward > Send to Back so it sits behind all the navigation elements.

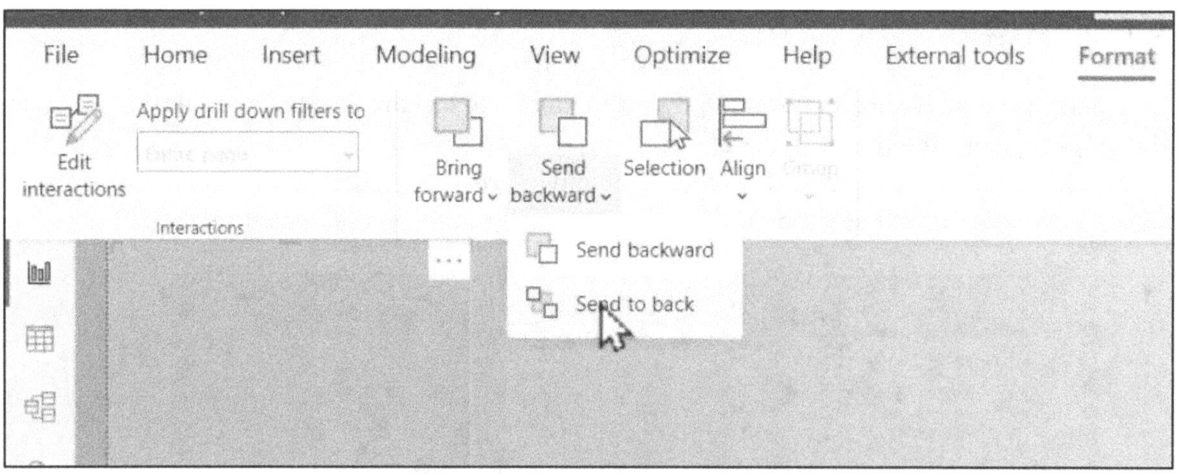

Now select the entire navigation panel—buttons, background rectangle, and any additional graphics. Use Ctrl + A to select all, then on the Home tab, click Copy. Move to each of the remaining pages and Paste. Power BI will preserve the exact positioning of all elements, ensuring consistent alignment across all pages.

To test the buttons in Power BI Desktop, hold down Ctrl while clicking. When published to the Power BI Service, regular clicks will work as expected—no modifier key needed.

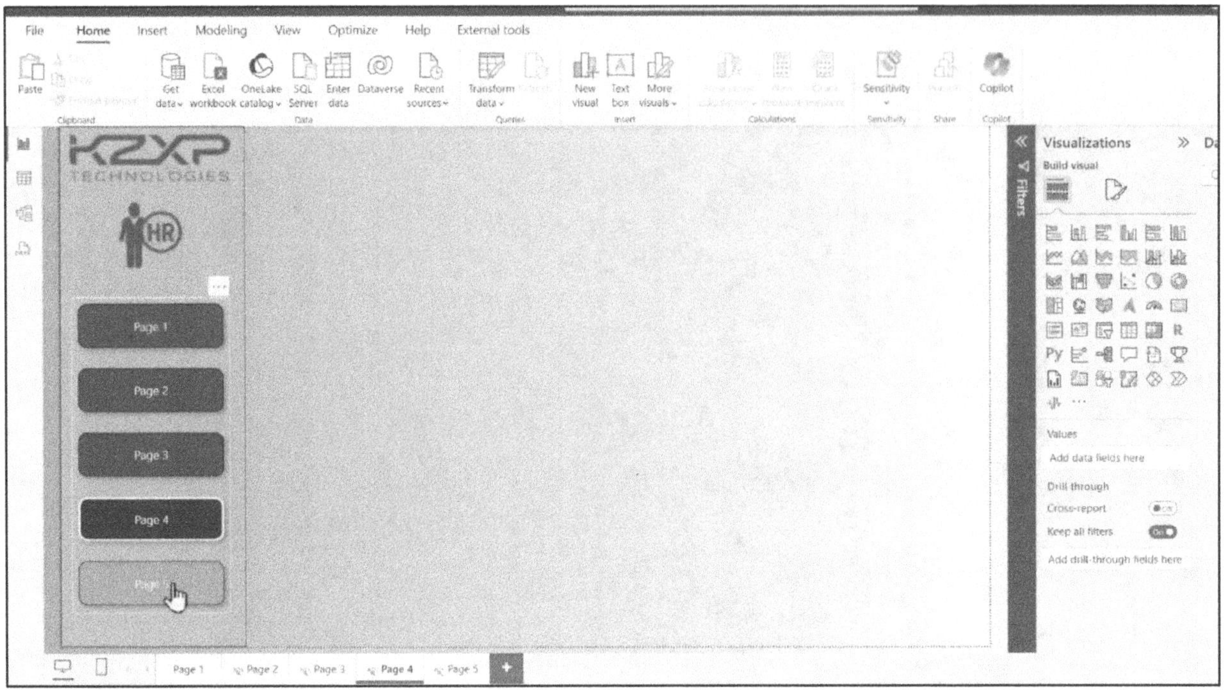

Save your work. The navigation bar is now complete, consistent, and ready to guide users confidently through your report pages.

3.3: Creating a Start Page

When designing corporate reports in Power BI, it's often helpful to include a Start Page—a brief welcome screen that appears when the report is first opened. This page sets the tone, reinforces branding, and communicates essential usage terms such as copyright and internal-only distribution. It is not meant to be interactive beyond a simple navigation button and is typically not revisited once dismissed.

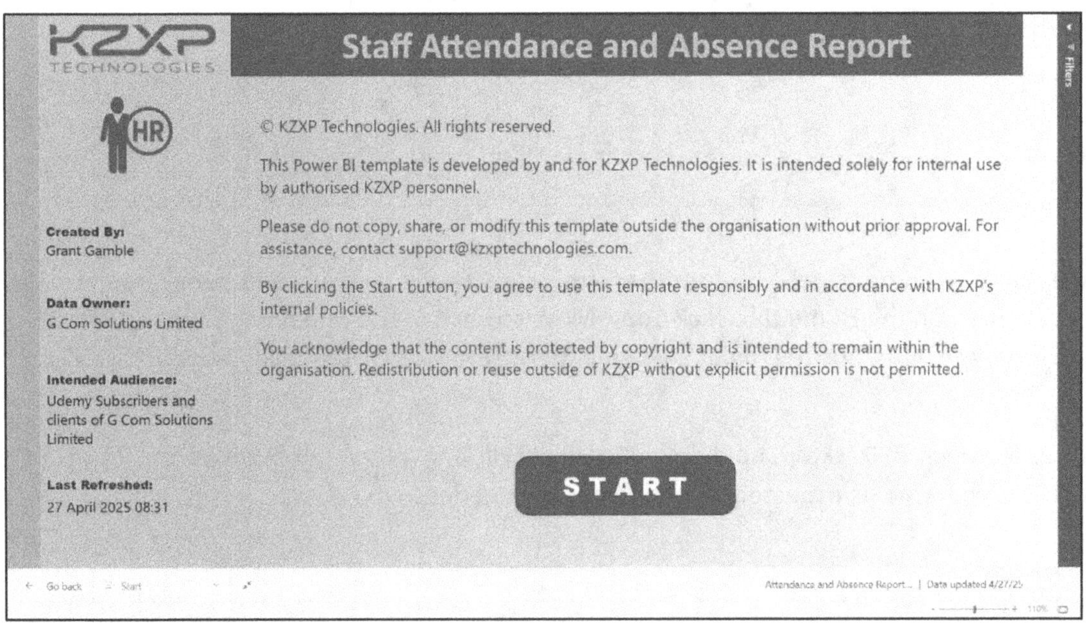

To ensure consistent styling across all report pages, we won't build the Start Page from scratch. Instead, right-click on the existing Page 1 in your report and choose Duplicate. Then, drag the duplicated page to the far left in the page order so that it becomes the first page users see. Rename this page to Start.

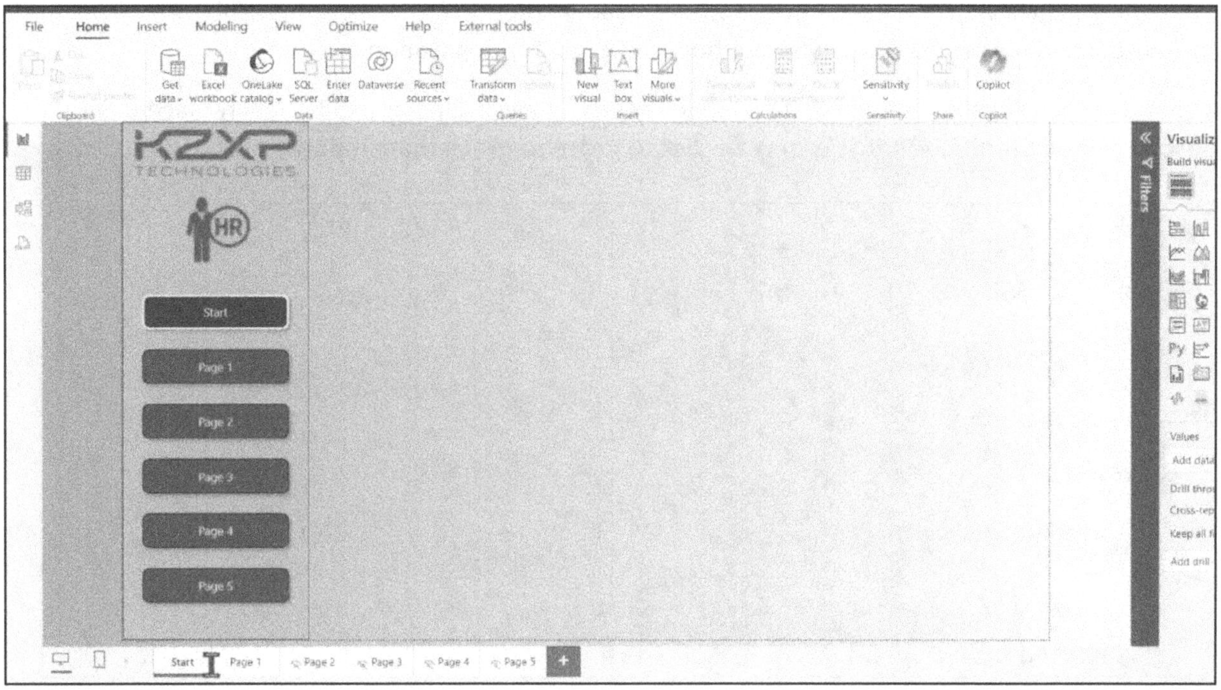

Unlike a traditional home page, the Start Page isn't something users will come back to—it's intended to appear only once, when the report loads. To reinforce this purpose, we'll begin by removing it from the navigation bar.

Click to select the navigation bar visual on the page. Then, in the Format pane, scroll down to the section listing the included pages. You'll find a toggle option labelled Show. Untick the checkbox next to the Start page.

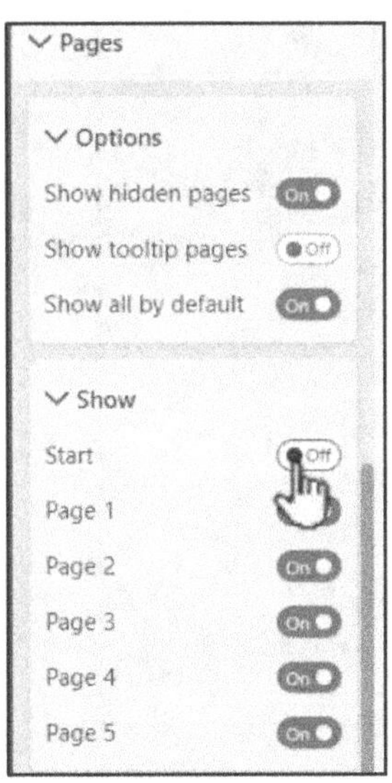

Unfortunately, Power BI currently does not support synchronised navigation bar updates across pages, so you will need to apply this same configuration manually on each remaining report page.

To streamline the process, copy the updated navigation bar from the Start Page and then visit each of the remaining pages. Delete the old navigation bar visual and paste in the new one. This approach ensures visual and functional consistency without unnecessary duplication of effort.

Now that the Start Page is configured, it no longer needs a navigation bar itself. We'll replace it with a single, centralised Start button that users can click to proceed to the main report.

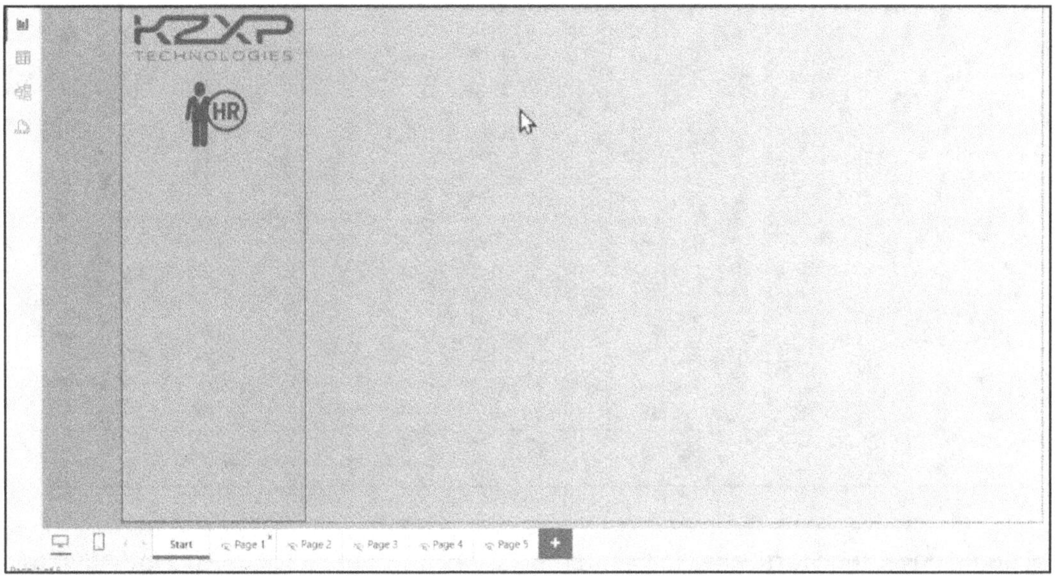

With this setup, Page 1—the actual landing page—can be hidden just like other secondary pages. To do this, right-click Page 1 and select Hide.

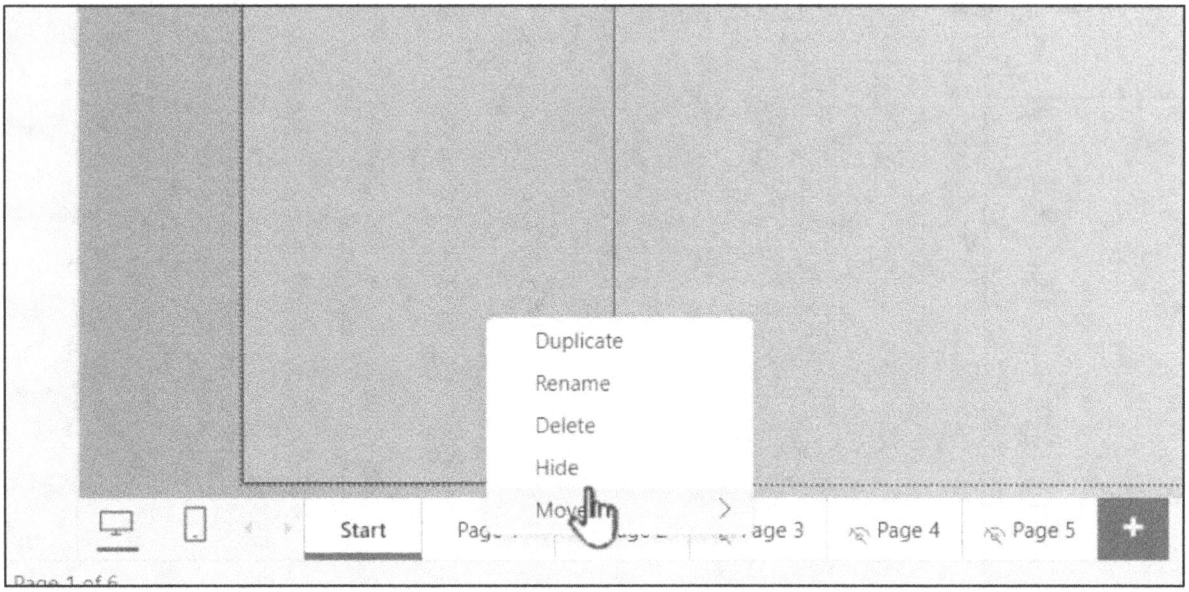

Let's now add the main message to the Start Page. This content is intended to reassure users that the report belongs to your organisation and is intended for internal use only. You can add a message using a Text Box, available either from the Home tab or the Insert menu.

Rather than typing out the text manually, navigate to your Assets folder. Under Section 3, locate the file called Start page text. Open the file, copy the message, and paste it into the text box on your Start Page in Power BI.

By default, the font size may be too small, so increase it for better visibility. Next, change the font colour to your report's theme blue to maintain consistency. To improve the look further, remove the white background behind the text box. You can do this from the Format pane under Effects by toggling the Background setting to Off.

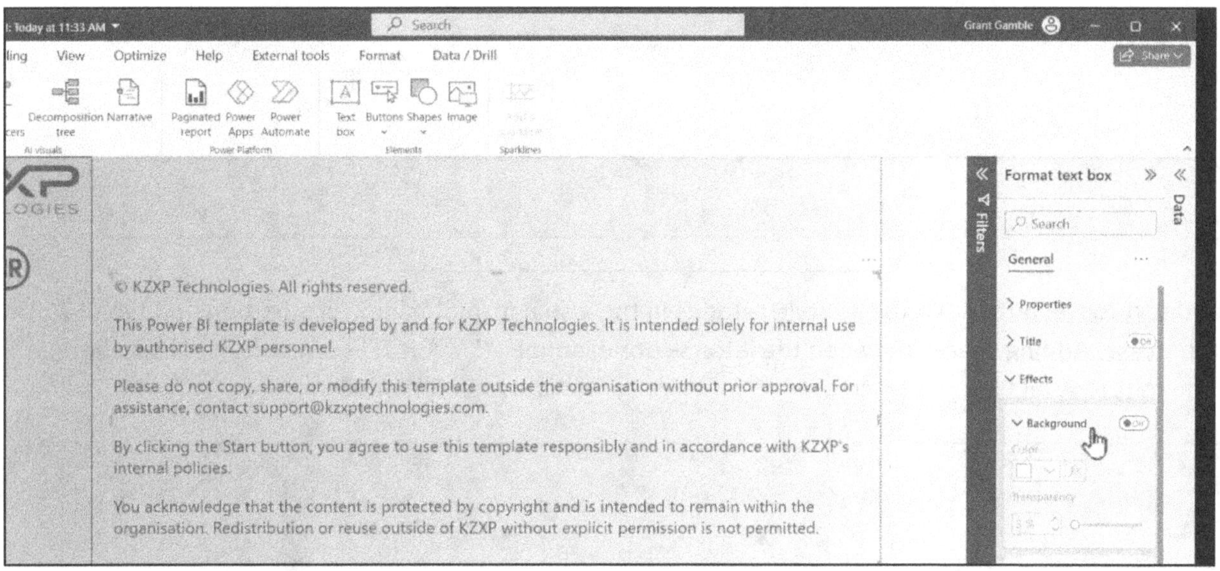

Now let's add the Start button, which will act as the user's entry point into the report. While still in the Insert tab, select Buttons and choose the Blank option. Power BI will usually drop the new button in the top-left corner. Reposition and resize it to your preference, placing it at the bottom centre of the page for clear visibility.

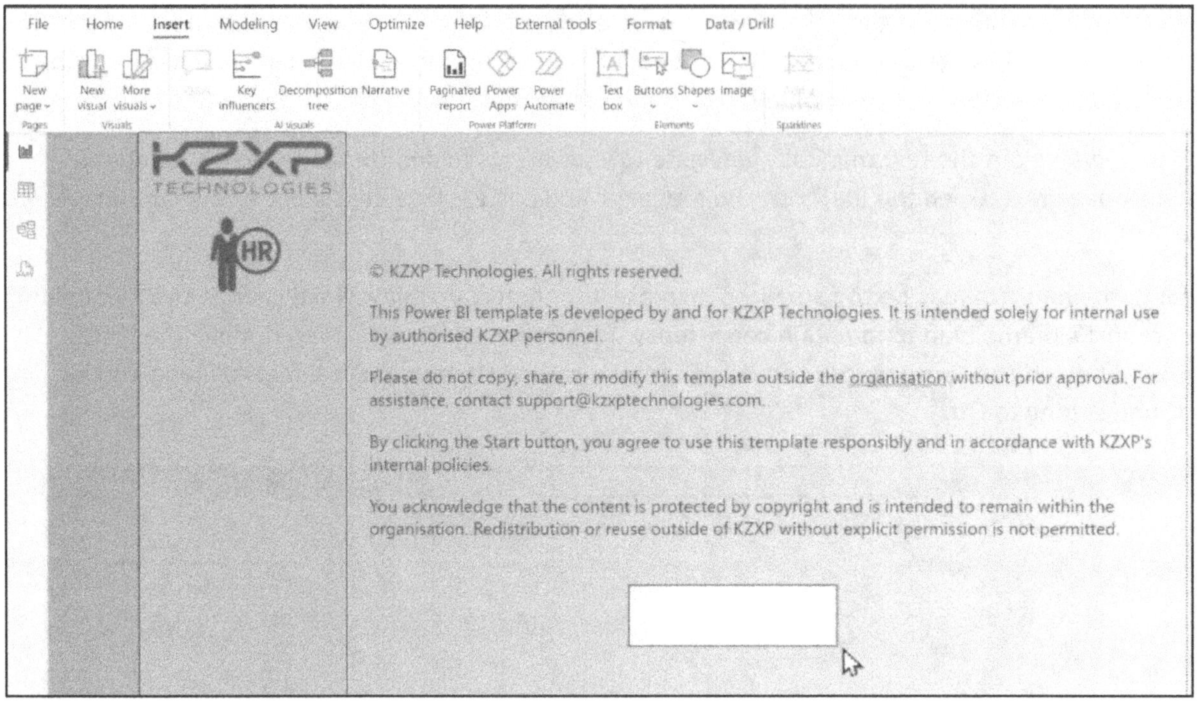

To add text to the button, go to the Style settings in the visual format pane. Turn Text on and type START in uppercase. Adding spaces between the letters—for example, "S T A R T"—can add visual emphasis. Set the font to Arial Black and increase the font size to 24 for maximum impact.

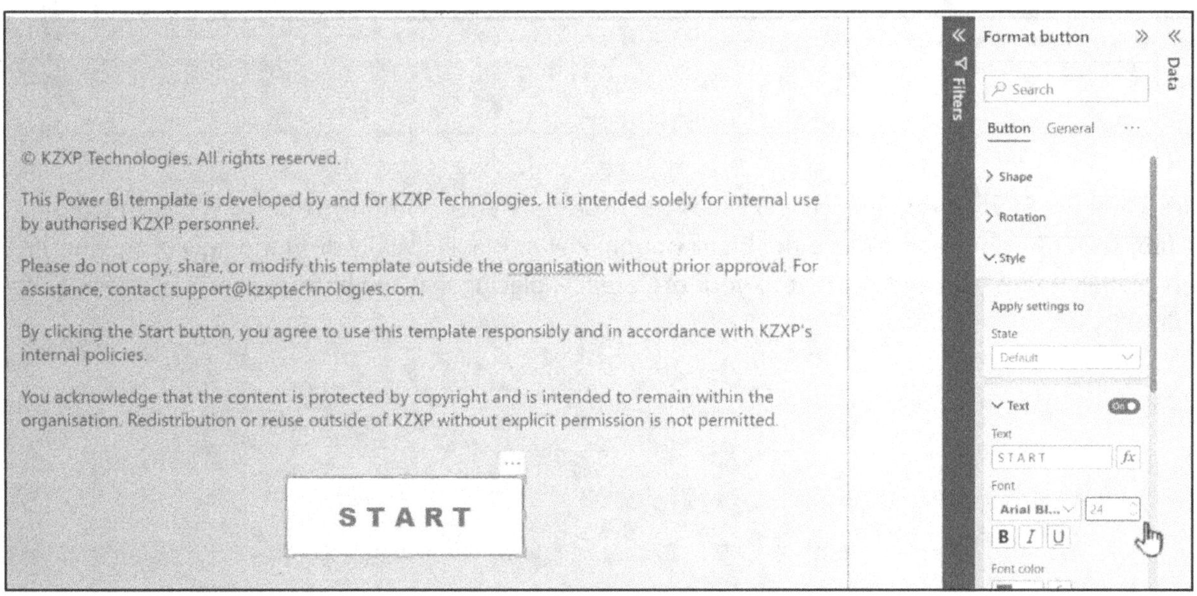

If you've already styled buttons on another page, such as navigation buttons on Page 1, you can try reusing their design.

Highlight the existing navigation bar, click Format Painter from the Home tab.

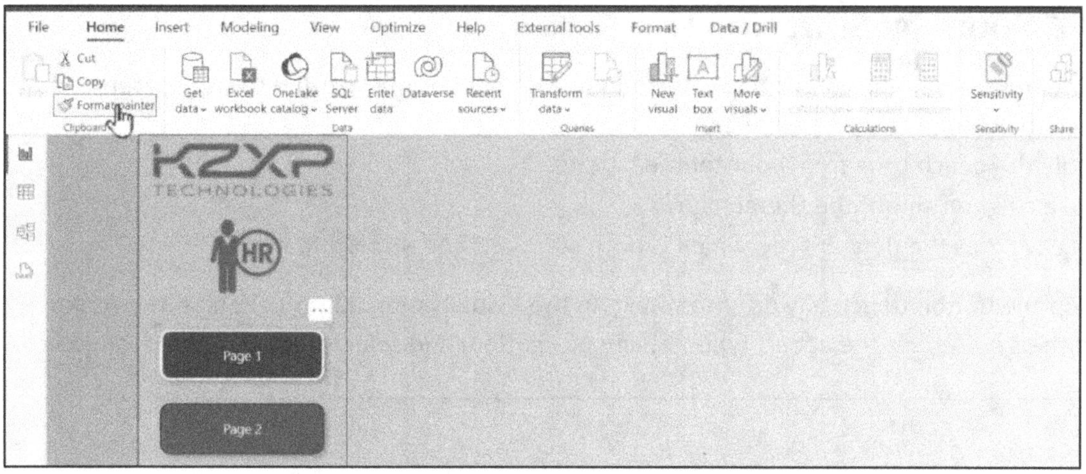

Next, click the new button on your Start Page. (The Format Painter will remain selected when you switch pages.)

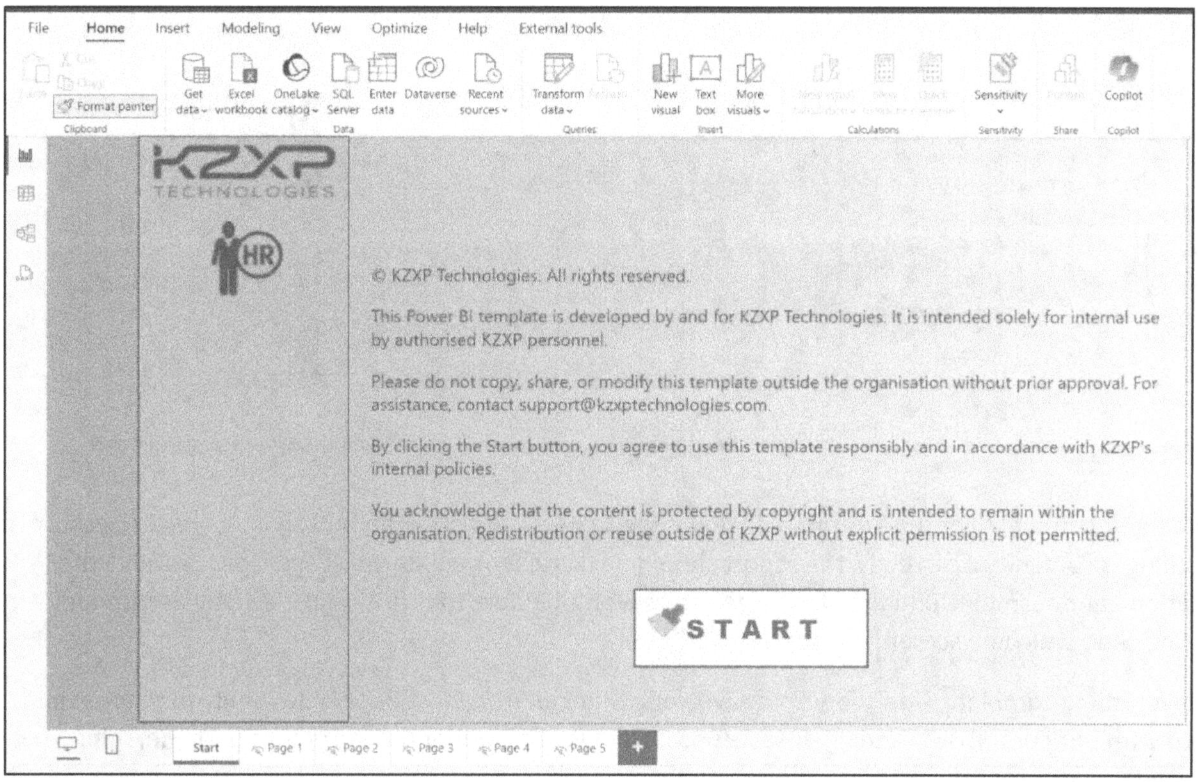

While this process isn't flawless between different types of visuals, it often carries over font and fill styling effectively.

Back in the button's Style settings, you may notice that some formatting was lost during the copy. Reactivate the text option, reapply Arial Black, and ensure size 24 is applied across all button states. The states you'll want to configure are:

Button Fill Colours by State

- Default – Use the theme blue colour. If the button appears faint, it may be due to transparency; set transparency to 0% for a solid appearance.
- Hover – Apply the peach tone from your theme palette.
- Pressed – Use a lighter tint of the theme blue.
- Disabled – Leave it as the default grey, which is both standard and appropriate.

Now let's wire up the button to actually do something. In the Visualisation pane, switch on the Action setting. Expand the section, set the action Type to Page navigation, and select Page 1 as the destination.

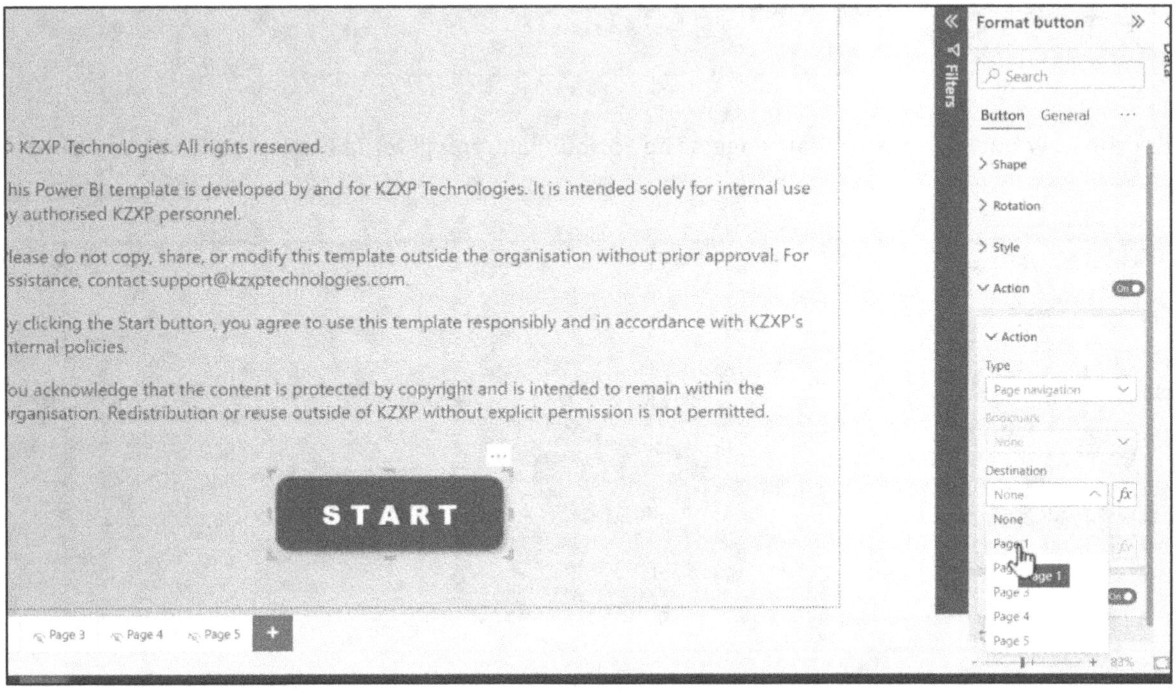

To test the functionality of the button, hold down the Ctrl key and click the button in Power BI Desktop. If everything is configured correctly, the report should navigate immediately to Page One. Because the navigation bar doesn't include the Start Page, users won't be able to return to it—exactly as intended. It's a one-time welcome screen.

With everything complete, don't forget to save your changes. The Start Page is now fully functional and aligned with our corporate branding. It serves as both a gatekeeper and a statement of ownership, ensuring that your report starts on a professional note.

3.4: Creating a DAX Measures Table

In this section, we're going to add a table to our Power BI report template for a very specific and important purpose: storing DAX measures. This is a common best practice when designing professional reports, and it helps ensure that your calculations are organised, consistent, and easy to locate, especially as your report grows in complexity.

DAX, or Data Analysis Expressions, is the formula language used in Power BI. It's designed specifically for data modelling and reporting. With DAX, you can define calculations that aggregate or evaluate data dynamically, based on what's visible in a particular report visual or filter context. Although DAX can be used in calculated columns or tables, its most common and powerful use is in measures.

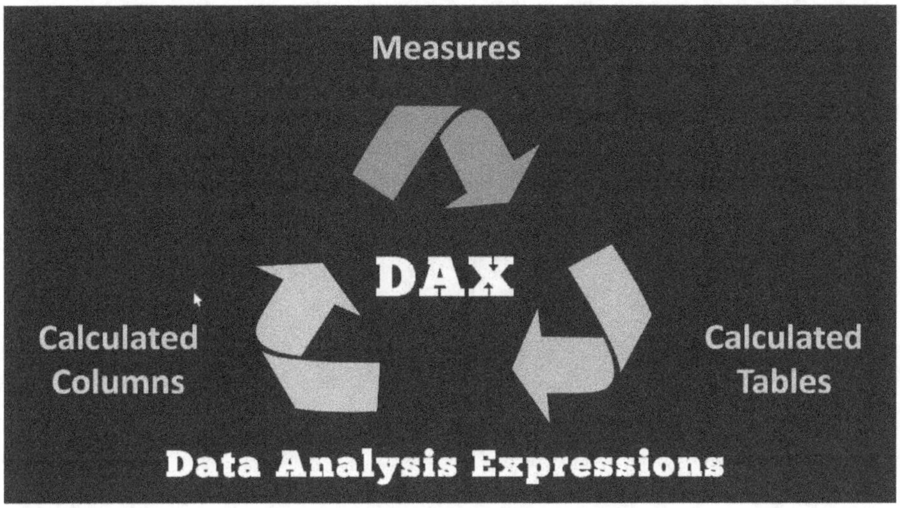

A measure in Power BI is a reusable formula that returns a single value—typically a number—that can be displayed on a visual, such as a card, a table, or a matrix. Measures are always calculated on the fly and respond to filters and slicers, making them ideal for interactive reporting.

Let's take an example. In the upcoming sections of this book, we'll be building an HR report focused on staff attendance and absence. Some of the key metrics we'll want to include are the total number of working days, the number of absence days, and the overall absence rate. All of these will be calculated using DAX measures.

To prepare for this, we're now going to create a dedicated table in our report that will serve as a home for all our measures. Keeping your DAX calculations in one place helps maintain clarity, especially in large reports with many tables and visuals. This table will also be used to store some useful metadata—such as when the report was last refreshed—which will be covered shortly.

Creating the Blank Measures Table

To create a blank table in Power BI Desktop, follow these steps:

1. Go to the Home tab in the ribbon.
2. Click Enter Data. This feature normally allows you to input your own table of values manually.
3. In this case, you don't need to enter any data at all. Just give the table a name.
4. The recommended name is _Measures (with an underscore at the start). This naming convention is widely adopted among Power BI professionals. It helps distinguish the table as a utility table, and the underscore avoids any clash with Power BI's reserved word "Measures."
5. Click Load.

Power BI will now create your new table. It will contain a single column called Column1, which you can ignore entirely. This column only exists because Power BI needs at least one column to create the table, even though we won't use it.

You now have a blank table named _Measures, ready to use. As you begin to build your report, you'll store all your DAX measures here. This helps to centralise your logic and makes it easier to manage your calculations.

Why Use a Dedicated Measures Table?

You might wonder: why not just place each measure in the table where the data originates? Power BI does allow this, and in some small models it might feel natural. However, separating your measures into a dedicated table comes with several advantages:

- Improved organisation – All your calculations are in one place.
- Easier navigation – Especially when you have dozens of measures across multiple data tables.
- Cleaner model design – The data tables remain focused on data, and the logic is abstracted into the _Measures table.
- Template readiness – In reusable templates, the _Measures table provides a clear place for users to look when understanding or editing logic.

This is not something Power BI enforces—you are not required to create a separate measures table. But it's a convention that adds discipline to your development process, particularly in collaborative environments or when building scalable templates.

What Comes Next?

Now that the _Measures table is in place, you're ready to begin adding actual DAX formulas into it. These will power your key report metrics. In the next section, we'll take this a step further by creating metadata measures including one to display the report's last refresh date. These are simple but powerful techniques to give your users confidence that the data they're viewing is up to date.

Here's a small preview of what our first measure will look like:

Last Refresh Date =
MAX('Date Table'[Date])
Later, we'll also learn how to format this result and display it in a card visual to make the report feel complete and professional.

So, with your blank measures table created and saved, you're now well positioned to begin writing your DAX logic.

3.5: Creating a Dynamic Title Measure

In this section, we're going to use the measures table to add dynamic content to the report—starting with a report title that updates automatically based on a measure. This approach is particularly helpful when designing reusable templates, where you want flexibility without needing to manually update text on every page.

We'll focus on building a dynamic report title that appears consistently at the top of every report page. While a standard text box might seem like the obvious choice, it only supports static content. For a dynamic title that can be updated globally via a measure, we'll need a different approach.

Let's begin by inserting a shape rather than using a text box, since text displayed in shapes can be rendered dynamically whereas text is primarily static. From the ribbon, go to the Insert tab and choose Shapes. For this example, we'll select a simple rectangle.

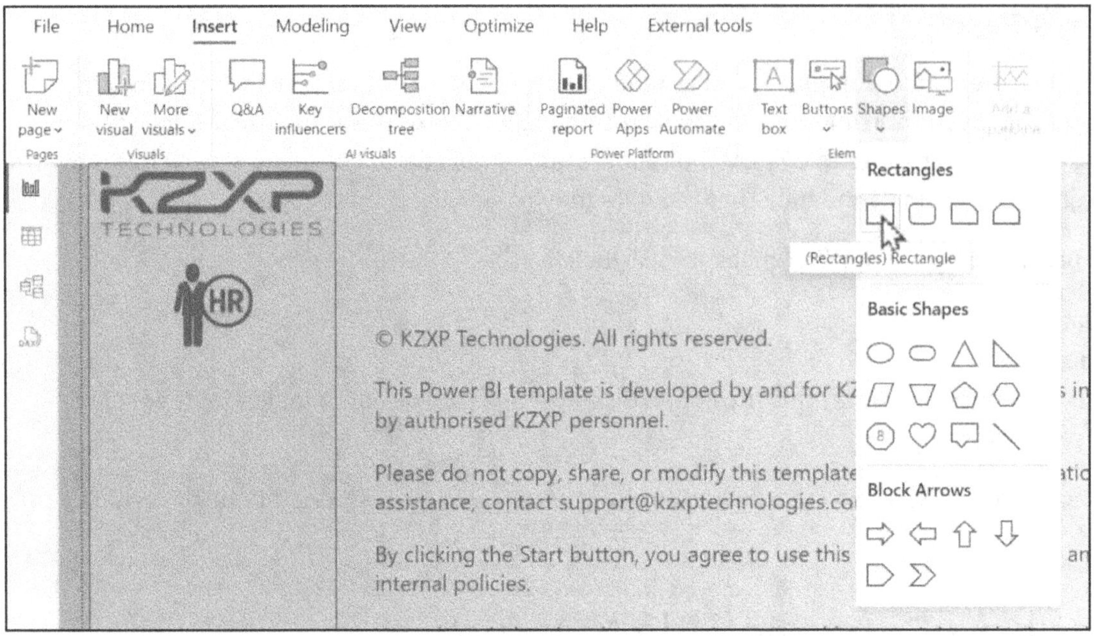

Power BI automatically applies a default theme colour to the shape. If necessary, change the fill colour to theme dark blue.

To enable text within the shape, scroll down in the formatting pane under Style and toggle Text to "On". Type a placeholder message—for instance, "Report Title"—and adjust the font to your preference. In this example, set the font colour to white, the font itself to Arial Black, and the size to 36 points for visibility.

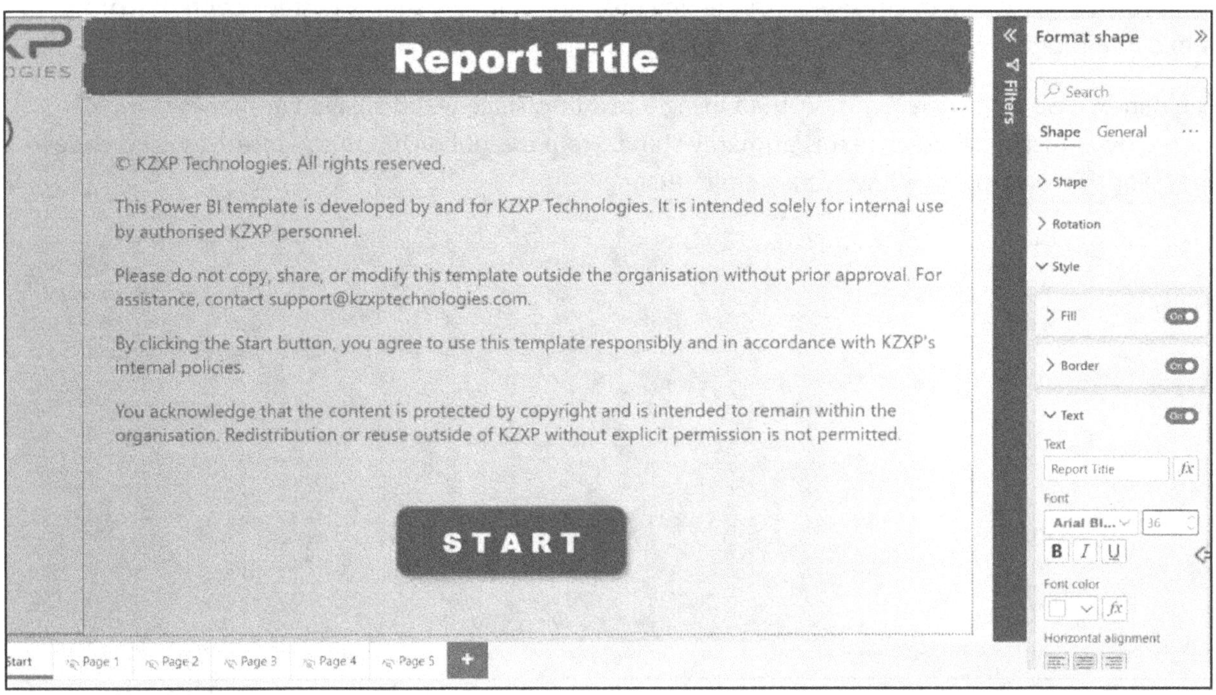

Now comes the key part: making the title dynamic. For that, we need a DAX measure that outputs text. Best practice is to store all measures in a dedicated table, which we've already created earlier.

Right-click on the Measures table and choose New measure.

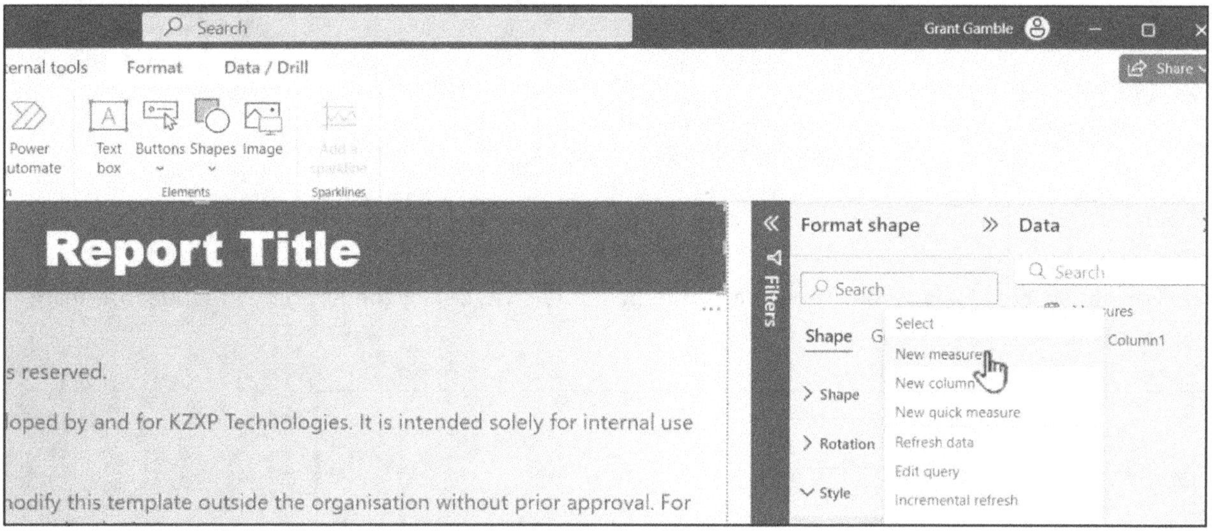

This ensures that the measure will go into the _Measures table and opens the formula bar at the top of the screen. You can press Ctrl and + a few times to increase the font size in the formula bar if needed on the device you are using.

Let's create a basic text-based DAX measure for the title. Call it Report Title. Unlike typical measures that return numbers or aggregations, this one simply returns a string.

Report Title = "Modify ""Report Title"" Measure"

As with Excel, you must enclose string output in double quotes. Since we want quotation marks to appear in the actual text, you'll need to double them, just as you would in Excel—""Report Title"".

Once the measure is complete, click the green checkmark or press Enter to confirm.

You can also hide the formula bar at any time by clicking the small 'X' next to the checkmark.

Now it's time to bind this measure to the shape. With the rectangle still selected, return to the Style section under the formatting pane. Instead of manually deleting the placeholder text, click the fx (function) button beside the Text field. This will open the Conditional formatting dialog.

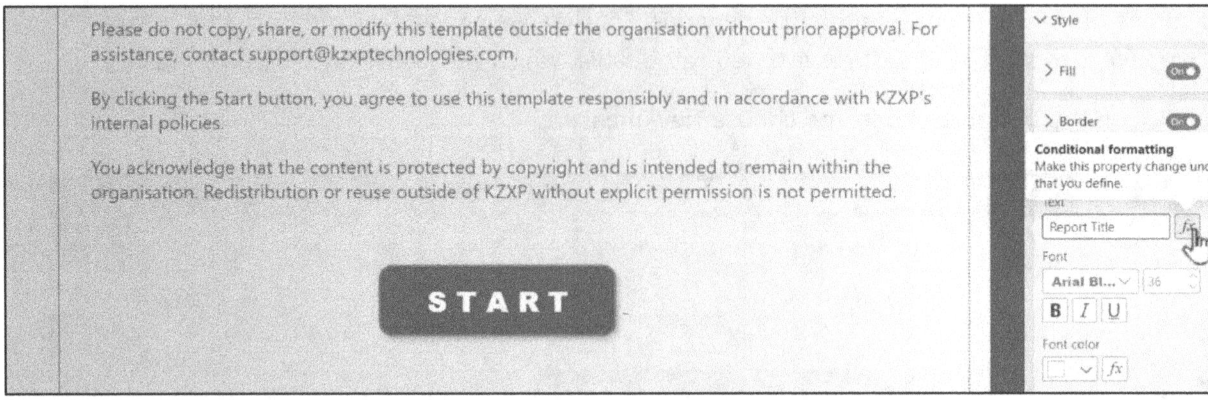

Set the Format style to Field value. Then, from the dropdown list, select the Report Title measure from the Measures table.

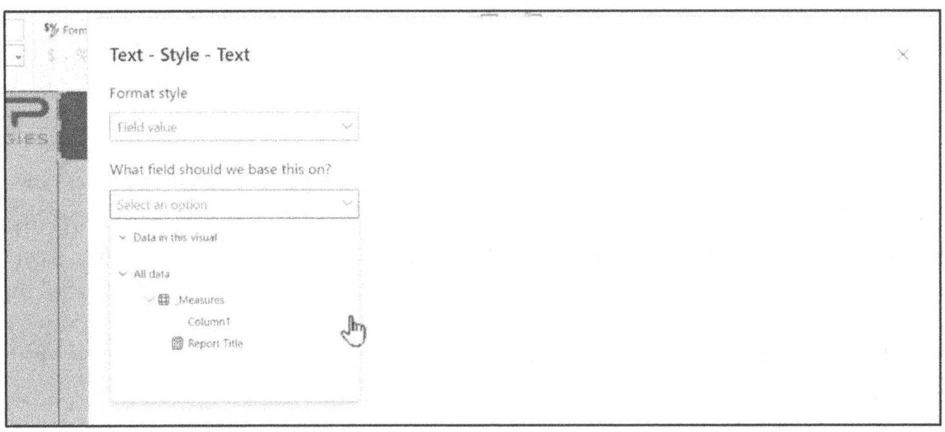

Click OK, and the shape now dynamically displays the content from the DAX measure.

If someone else is using your Power BI template, all they need to do is update the DAX measure—modifying the string between the quotes—and the new title will automatically appear on every page where the shape is placed.

To ensure consistent appearance throughout the report, copy the shape and paste it onto each report page. Go to the Home tab, click Copy, and then paste it onto the desired pages.

Let's test the setup. Open the Report Title measure and update the text to something specific, such as:

Report Title = "Recruitment Pipeline Report"

Once you confirm the change, every report page will display the updated title immediately. This ensures that your report remains consistent and professional, with no need to manually edit page headings.

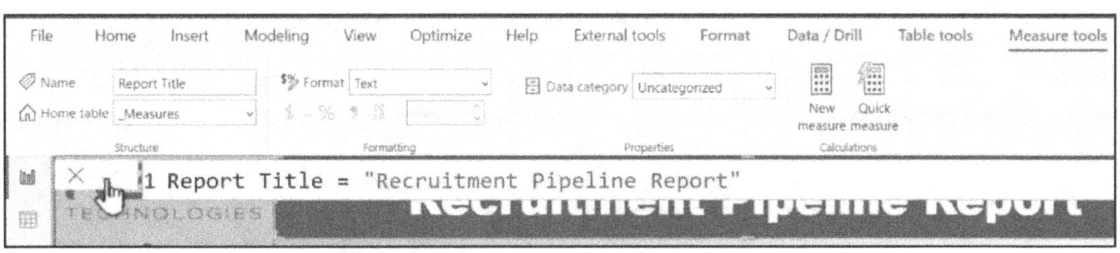

Now, revert the measure back to its default prompt so that users of the template know where to make changes.

Before wrapping up, there's one final housekeeping step. When we created the Measures table using Enter Data, Power BI automatically added a placeholder column named Column. Since we now have at least one proper measure in the table, we're free to delete this default column.

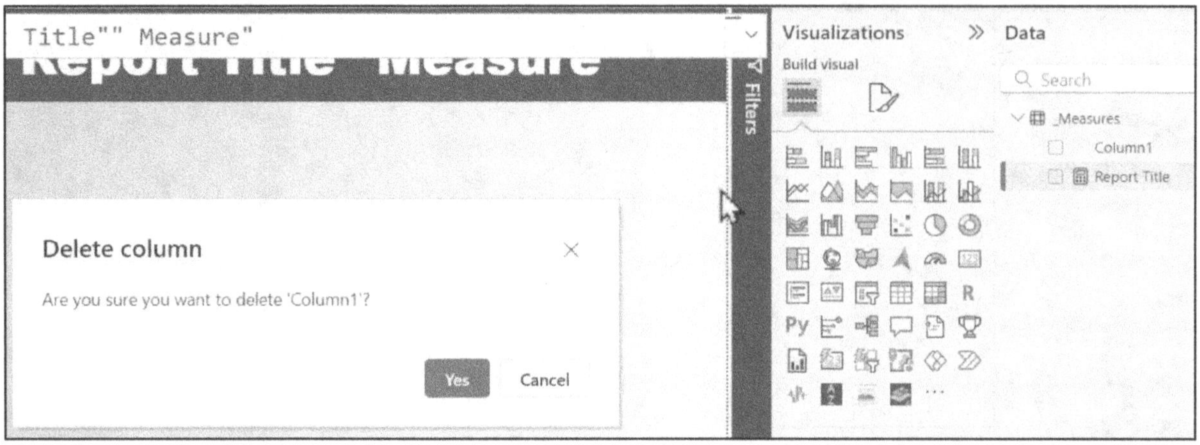

Right-click on Column1 and choose Delete from model. This action changes the icon for the table, signifying that it now contains only measures—just what we want when structuring a clean, reusable model.

With the title measure in place and the placeholder column removed, your measures table is now tidy, and your report is beginning to take shape as a dynamic, user-friendly template.

Let's save the file at this point. In the following section, we'll continue building out our template by adding additional metadata measures.

3.6: Creating Dynamic Metadata

In this section, we'll enhance our report template with dynamic metadata—information that automatically updates within the report. This metadata will be part of the template itself, meaning every report created from this template will already include it. The benefit is clear: consistency and time-saving for future report authors.

For this demonstration, we'll include three pieces of metadata:

- Created by
- Data owner
- Intended audience

In a real-world template, you may wish to expand on this by including metadata like approval status, department, contact email, or version history—whatever is appropriate for your organization's reporting environment.

Adding the First Label – "Created by"

We begin by creating a static label for our first piece of metadata. Static text is easily handled by a standard text box.

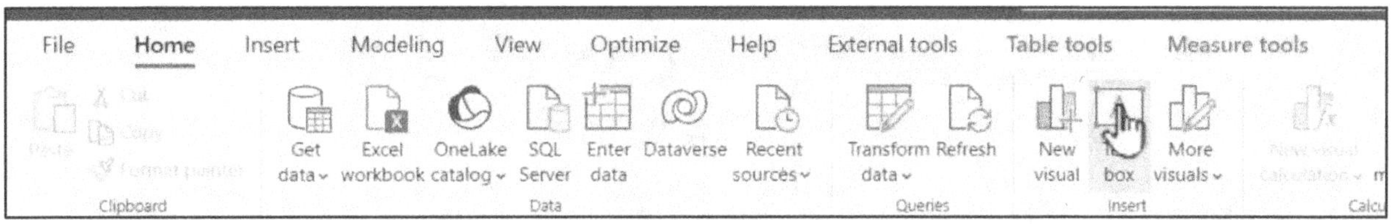

From the ribbon, select Insert > Text Box, and type created by.

To format the label:

- Set the font to Arial Black for a clear, bold appearance.
- Resize the text box slightly so it sits neatly within the layout.
- Position the text box underneath the branding section in the navigation area.
- Go to Format > Effects and switch the Background off—this removes the box behind the text, giving it a cleaner look.

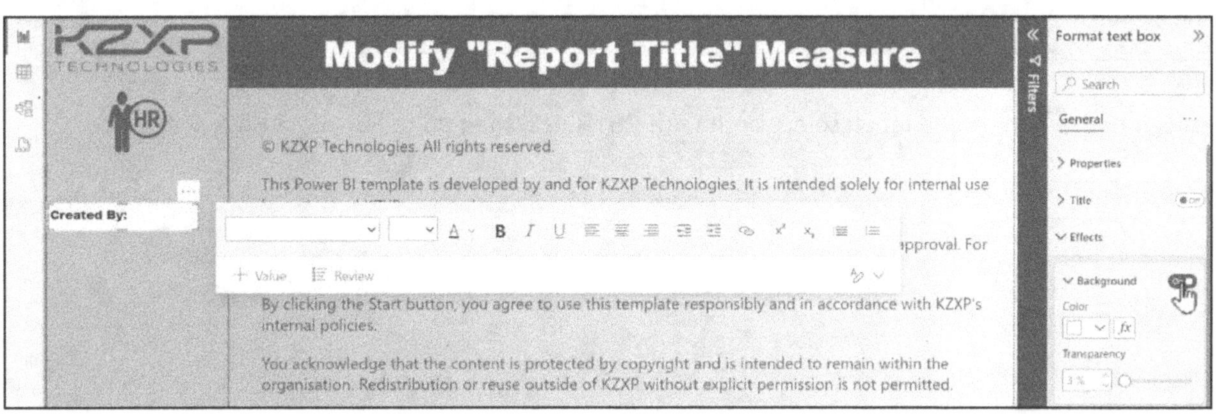

Adding a Dynamic Value for "Created by"

Text boxes don't support dynamic content, so to hold our dynamic value, we need to use a shape.

Insert a rectangle via Insert > Shapes > Rectangle.

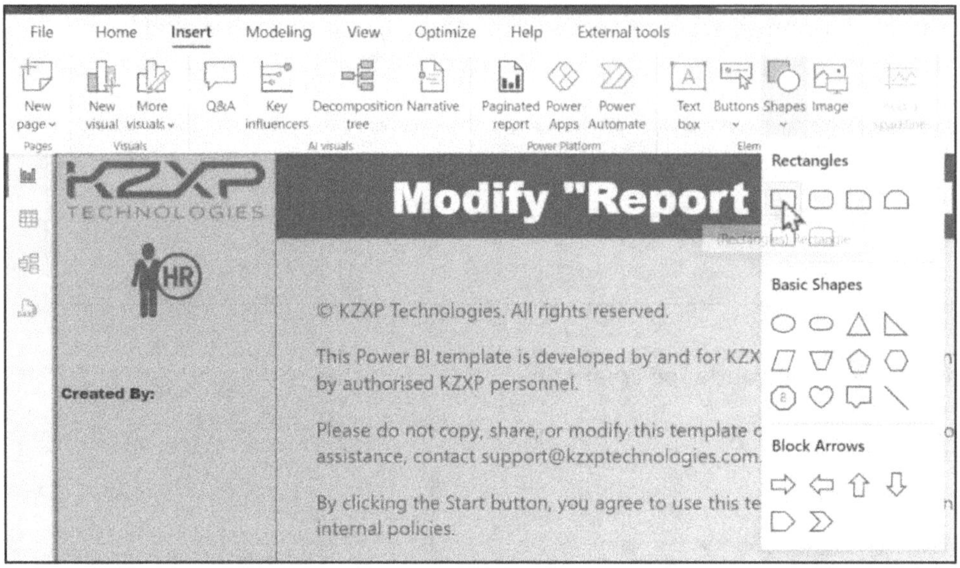

Place it just beneath the "created by" label. Line it up carefully.

Note: The default padding inside the text box can make alignment tricky. To correct this:

- Click the text box.
- In the Format > Properties, set the Left Padding to zero.

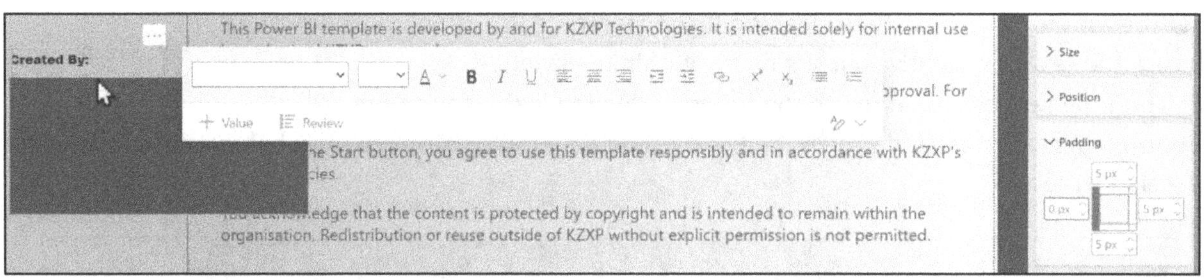

Now align the rectangle and label: select both with Ctrl+Click, then go to Format > Align > Align Left.

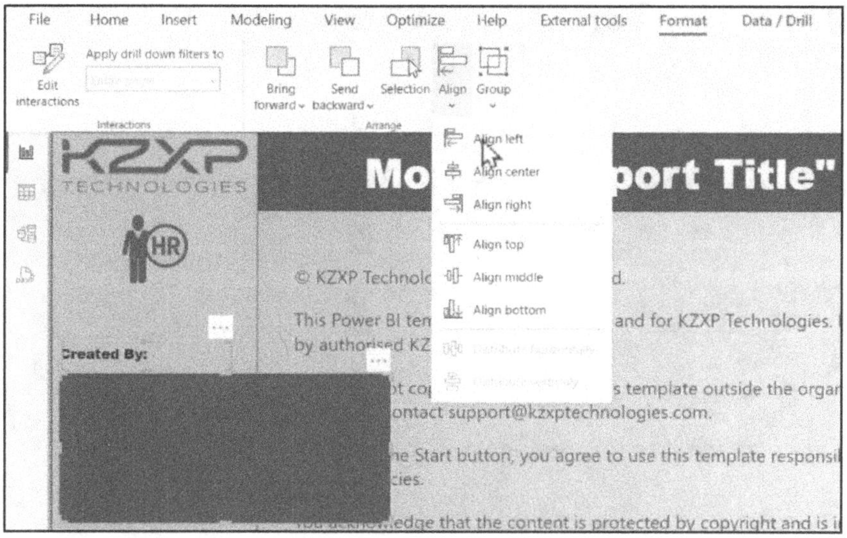

Stretch the rectangle so it fits within the navigation bar. Then, since all we want visible is the dynamic text (not the rectangle itself), remove all visible styling:

- Switch off the background (under Effects).
- Set the shape fill to None (under Shape Style).

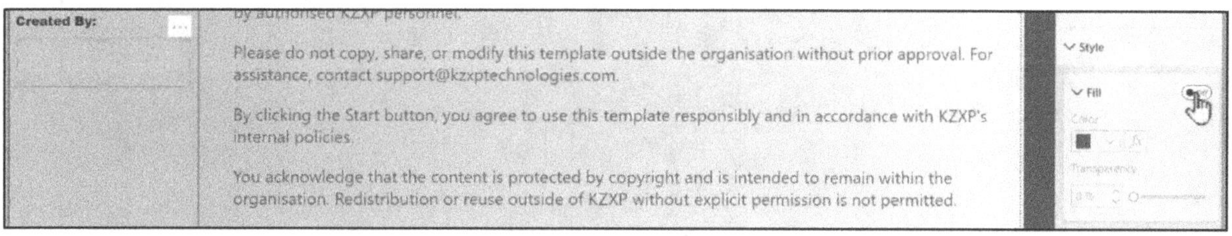

Now that the shape is ready, we need a DAX measure to generate the dynamic text.

To create this measure:

Created By = "Modify ""Created By"" Measure"

You can either type this out or duplicate the measure used in the previous section and then simply modify it.

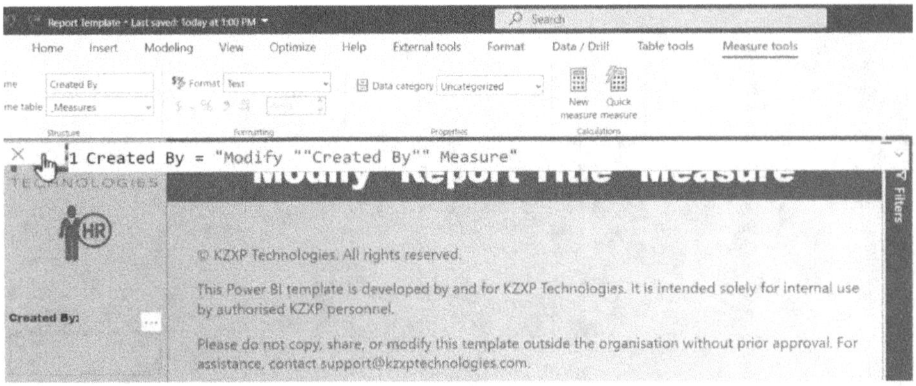

Once the measure is created, we need to attach it to our rectangle. To do this:

- Click on the rectangle.
- In the Format > Style > Text section, click the fx button.
- Change the formatting style to Field value and select the Created By measure.

Set the font size to 14 pt, align the text left and top, and set the font colour to black.

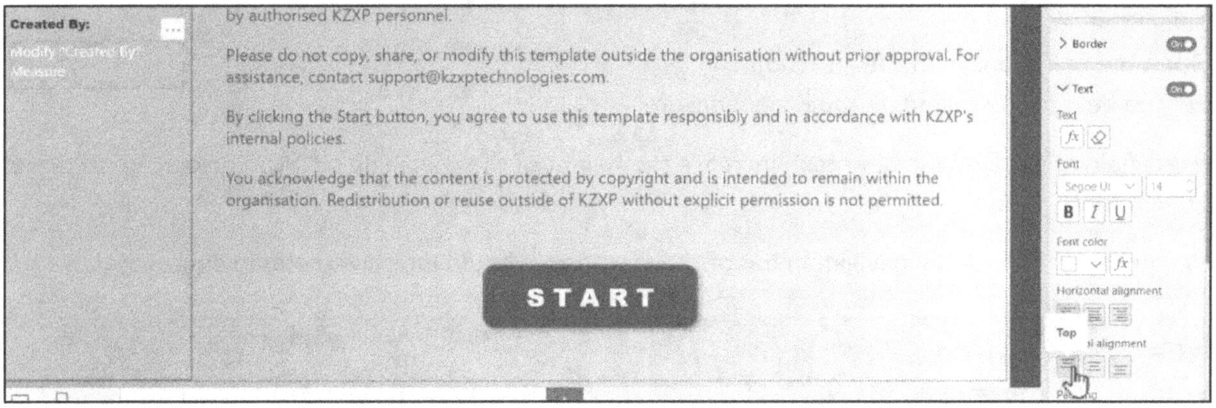

Repeating the Process for "Data Owner"

With the first set done, we can reuse the elements we've created to add more metadata. Ctrl+Click the text box and rectangle together. Copy and paste them. Drag the new pair slightly lower.

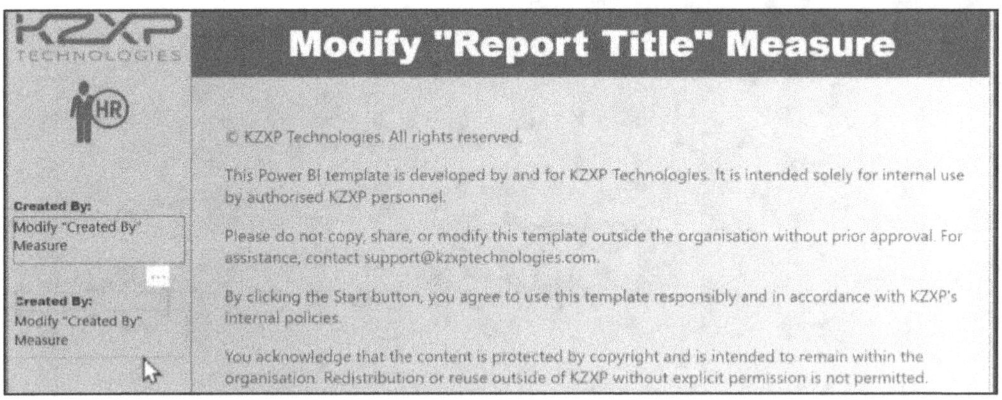

Update the static label to read Data Owner.

Now, create a new DAX measure:

Created By Title = "Modify ""Data Owner"" Measure"

Return to the new rectangle, go to the fx settings, and swap the field from Created By to Data Owner.

Adding the Final Field – "Intended Audience"

Repeat the same steps for the last piece of metadata.

Copy and paste the last pair (label and rectangle), move them below the second set, and update the label to intended audience.

Create a final DAX measure:

Intended Audience Title = "Modify "" Intended Audience "" Measure"

Hook it up just like before:

- Select the rectangle.
- Open the fx options in the Text section.
- Set the field to the Intended Audience measure.

Since this field might contain more text, increase the height of the rectangle so it can display up to three lines of content.

When you have finished, the navigation bar of the start page should look like the following.

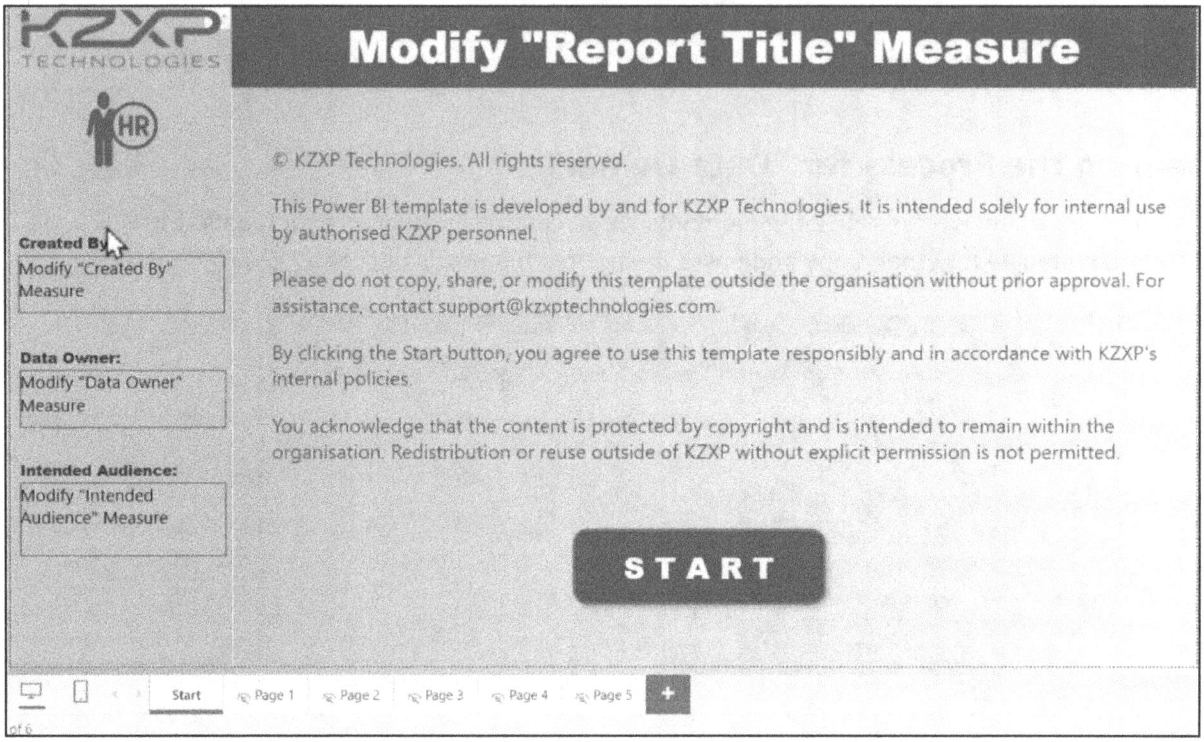

Final Touches and Clean-Up

Before finishing up, check the rectangles. By default, they still have a border applied.

To remove these:

- Click on each rectangle in turn.
- Go to Format > Style and turn the Border option off.

Now the metadata appears cleanly and unobtrusively on the navigation panel—just the text, no frames or outlines.

With this done, we've now added three pieces of dynamic metadata to our report template. These will auto-populate in every report created from this template and can be easily updated by adjusting the DAX measures—no manual editing of visuals required.

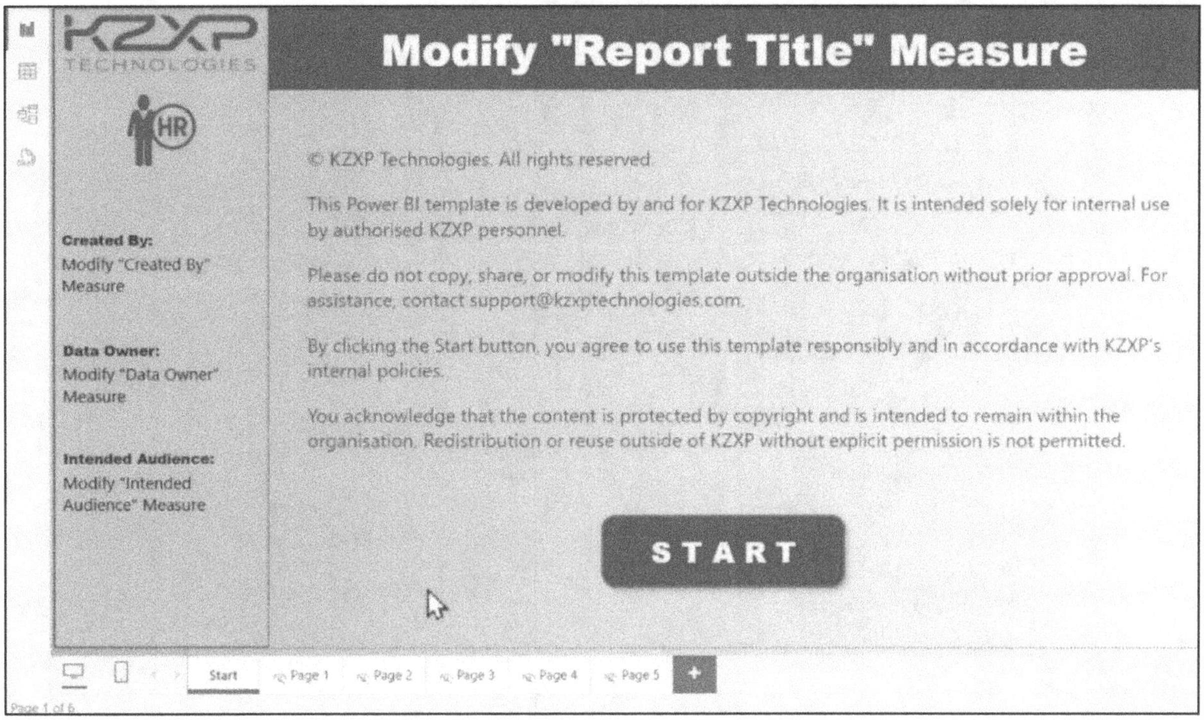

Go ahead and save the file at this point. In the next section, we'll look at how to include a dynamic "last refreshed" message, giving report viewers even more useful context.

3.7: Displaying Last Refresh Date and Time

A key part of creating a professional Power BI report is making sure users know exactly how fresh the data is. Including a "last refreshed" message on your report provides this reassurance. This section walks through how to create a dynamic message that updates automatically to show the date and time the dataset was last refreshed.

When you first connect to a data source in Power BI, the data is imported at the moment you click Close and Apply in Power Query. Later, when the report is published to the Power BI Service, Power BI can be configured to refresh the dataset periodically by reconnecting to the source and replacing the old data.

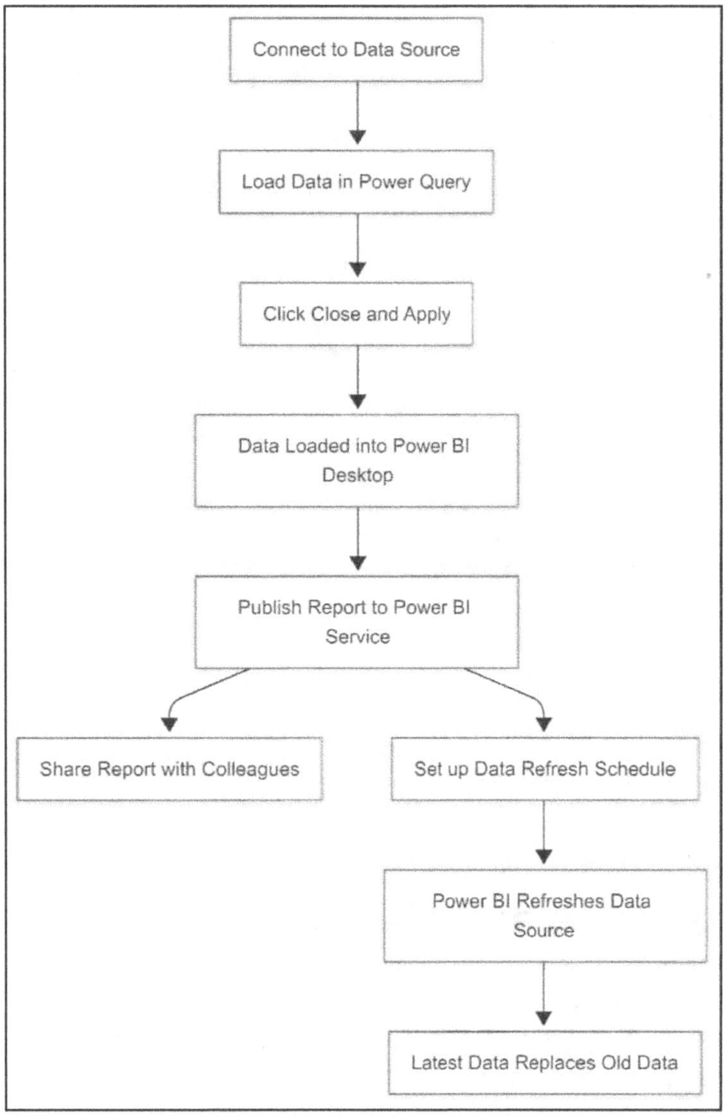

To make that refresh visible to end users, we'll build a dynamic label that displays the most recent refresh time.

Creating a Last Refreshed Query in Power Query

Since dataset refreshes take place via Power Query, we begin this process by creating a new query there. Open Power Query by selecting Transform Data from the Home tab in Power BI Desktop.

The idea is to create a query that returns the current date and time. Every time the dataset is refreshed, this query is also refreshed, updating its value. Importantly, this approach reflects the actual refresh time, not the time the report is simply opened by a user.

To create the query:

1. Go to New Source and choose Blank Query.
2. In the formula bar, or by accessing the Advanced Editor on the Home tab of the ribbon, modify the query to return the current local date and time.

If using the Advanced Editor, you'll see a default variable called Source assigned to a blank value.

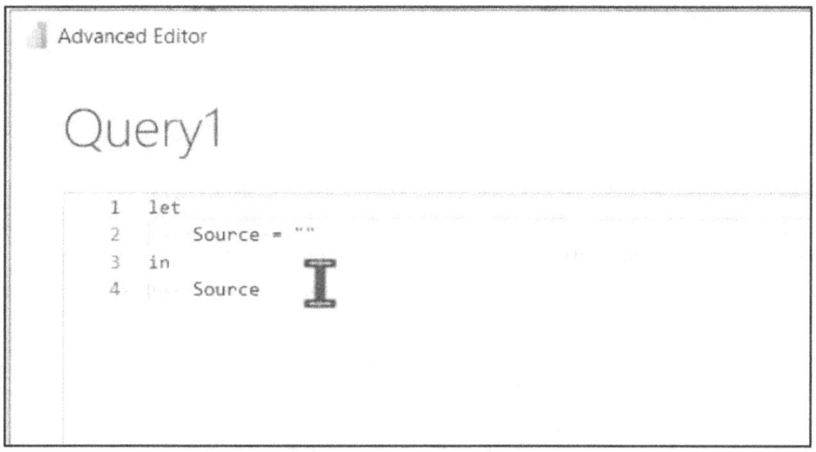

We'll need to change the variable name to something more meaningful, such as lastRefreshed. Be sure to change the name both after the word let and after in, since Power Query evaluates and returns the final variable listed.

```
let
lastRefreshed = DateTime.LocalNow()
in
lastRefreshed
```

The function DateTime.LocalNow() returns the system's local date and time. Note that M is case-sensitive, so you must capitalise exactly as shown, and include the parentheses to execute the function.

After entering the query, click Done. Power Query will recognise the result as a Date/Time type and display a matching icon. Rename the query to Last Refreshed to keep your project tidy and informative.

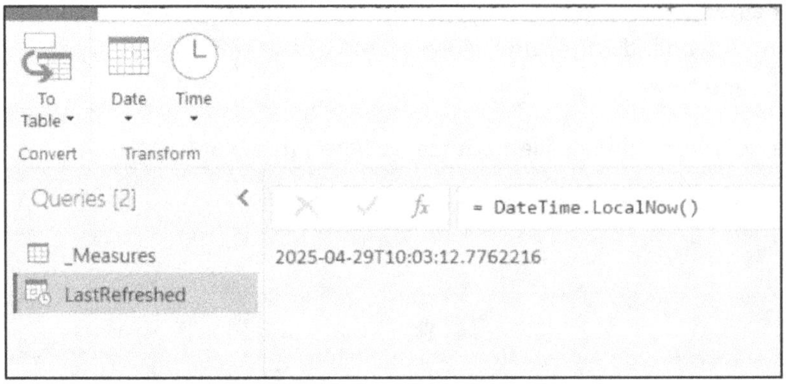

Click Close and Apply to load the query back into Power BI. Once this is done, the query becomes a one-column, one-row table in your data model. In Power BI, all queries become tables when applied, even those that return a single value.

Tidying Up the Model

Since this table serves a metadata purpose and contains no analytical data, let's tidy it away.

1. Switch to Model View.
2. Drag the Last Refreshed table and your Measures table off to one side, separate from your main data model.
3. Hide the Last Refreshed table in Report View by clicking the eye icon next to the table name. This ensures report developers aren't distracted by it.

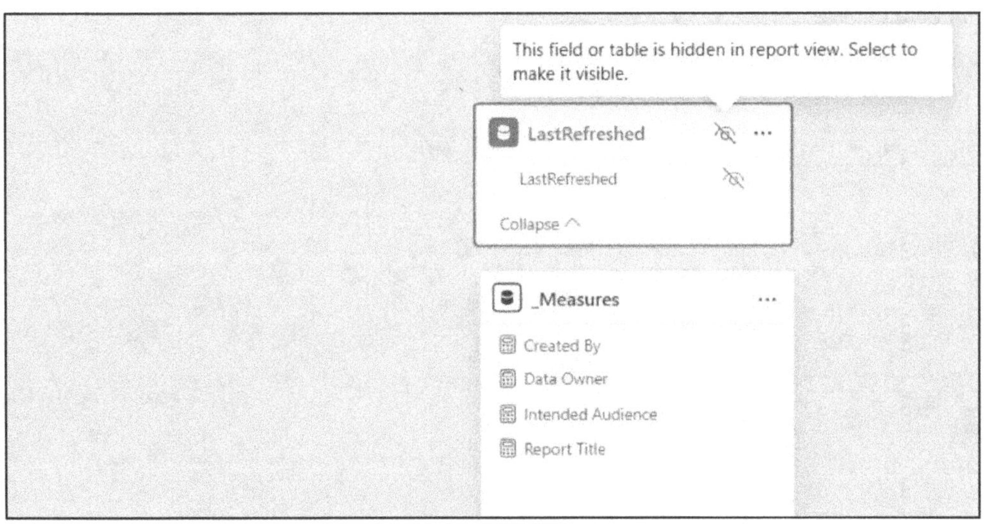

Creating a DAX Measure for the Last Refreshed Value

Next, we'll write a DAX measure to format and display the date and time. Since our goal is to show this information in a text box, we must convert the date/time into a readable text string.

Right-click the _Measures table and choose New Measure. DAX provides a FORMAT function, similar to Excel's TEXT function, which allows us to format values. The syntax is:

Last Refreshed = FORMAT(MAX('Last Refreshed'[Last Refreshed]), "dd mmm yyyy hh:mm")

Even though our table contains only one value, we must use an aggregation function like MAX or MIN to extract it. Since the measure is external to the table, Power BI requires aggregation in measures even if the underlying table only has a single row.

The format string **"dd mmm yyyy hh:mm"** ensures the output looks like **16 May 2025 14:30,** showing the full day, month, year, and time.

Displaying the Measure in a Visual

Now we need to display this value visibly on the report page.

1. Copy one of your existing text box and shape combinations used for other metadata messages.
2. Paste it onto the report canvas and move it to a suitable position near the bottom.
3. Update the label text to "Last Refreshed".
4. Select the shape behind the label, open the Format pane, expand the Style section, and under Text, click the fx button.

5. Choose the new Last Refreshed measure to bind it to the text dynamically.

When you click OK, the shape updates to display the correct last refreshed date and time.

Organising Measures in a Metadata Folder

To keep things tidy, especially in a shared or templated report, it's a good idea to group all metadata-related measures into a dedicated folder.

1. Switch to Model View.
2. Select all the relevant measures by clicking the first and Shift-clicking the last.
3. In the Properties pane, locate the field labelled Display Folder and enter _Metadata.

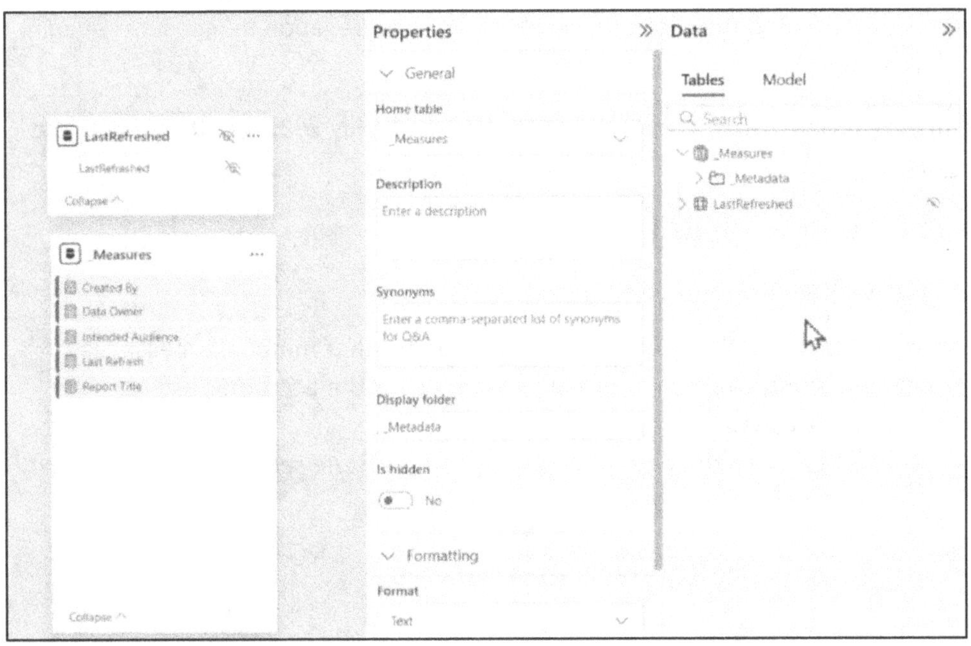

The underscore at the start of the folder name ensures it appears at the top of any alphabetical folder list, making it easy to find.

If you now look at the Data pane on the right, you'll see your measures neatly grouped under a folder called _Metadata.

With this final piece of metadata in place, your Power BI report template is now capable of displaying its most recent refresh date and time, giving users confidence in the freshness of the data they're viewing.

Save your work at this point. In the next section, we'll look at how to export everything we've built into a reusable Power BI template file.

3.8: Exporting the Template File

Now that we've completed the design of our HR report template, the final step is to apply a professional finishing touch and then export the file in a reusable format. This ensures that future reports maintain a consistent style and structure, saving valuable time while promoting visual and functional standards across your reporting suite.

Adding the Footer Copyright Notice

The last design element we need to add is a copyright message to the bottom right corner of each report page—excluding the Start Page, which already features a detailed copyright statement.

Inside the assets folder for section three, you'll find a file labelled footer text. This file contains a short copyright message, including the © symbol. This can be particularly useful if you're on a laptop without an easy way to type that symbol yourself.

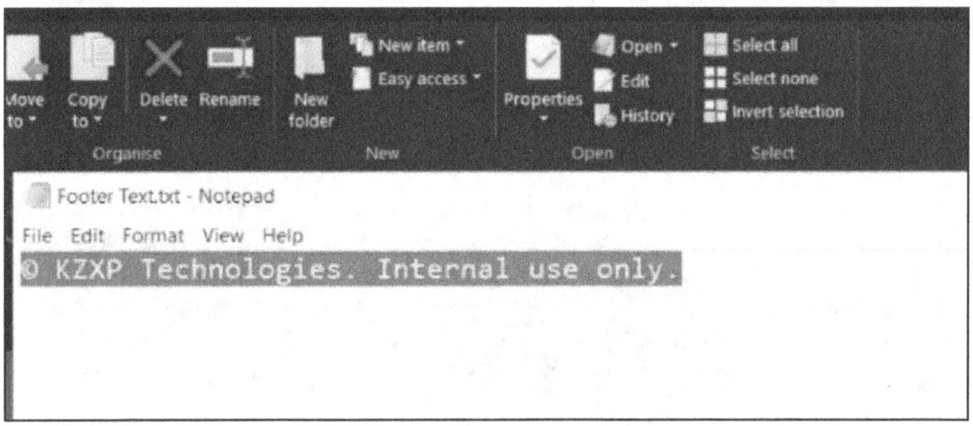

To insert the footer:

1. Go to Page 1 in your report.
2. Insert a new text box near the bottom right corner of the page.
3. Open the footer text file, copy its content, and paste it into the new text box.

We'll now format the text for consistency with our theme. First, click inside the text box and press Ctrl + A to select all of the text. Then apply the following formatting:

- Set the font colour to your theme's blue shade.
- Make the text bold.
- Change the font size to 11 points.

If a scroll bar appears in the text box, this simply means the box isn't tall enough to display all the content. Gently drag the top of the text box up to remove the scroll bar and display the full message.

To ensure a clean visual finish, head to the Format panel, select Effects, and turn off the background. This will remove the visible box around the text and help it sit naturally against the report canvas.

Once you're happy with the footer styling, copy it and paste it onto each report page where you want it to appear—again, skipping the Start Page.

Saving the Master File

With the report template now complete, it's time to save the working version—what you might refer to as your master file. This is the version you'll return to whenever updates to the template are needed.

To save this file:

1. Go to File > Save As.
2. Name the file something like Report Template Master.

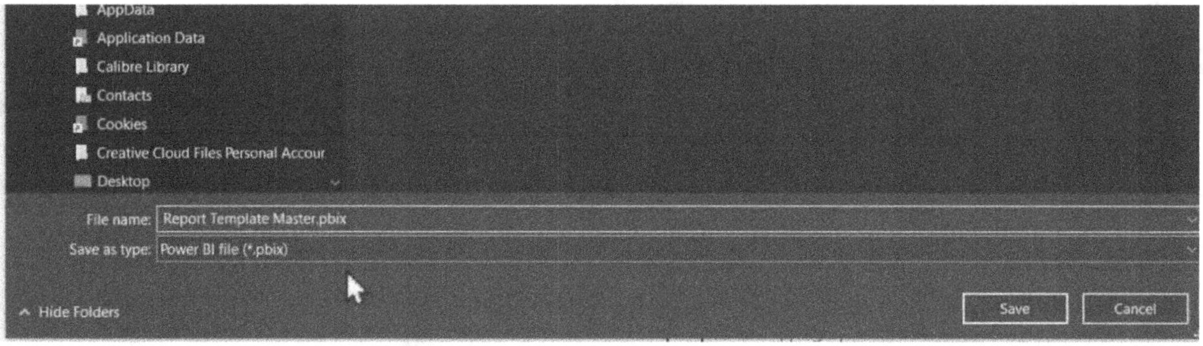

3. Save it in your preferred location.

From this point forward, avoid editing the exported template file directly. All structural changes should be made in this master version, ensuring a clean, controlled process for future template revisions.

Exporting the Power BI Template

We're now ready to export the file as a proper Power BI template file.

To do this:

1. Go to File > Export > Power BI Template.

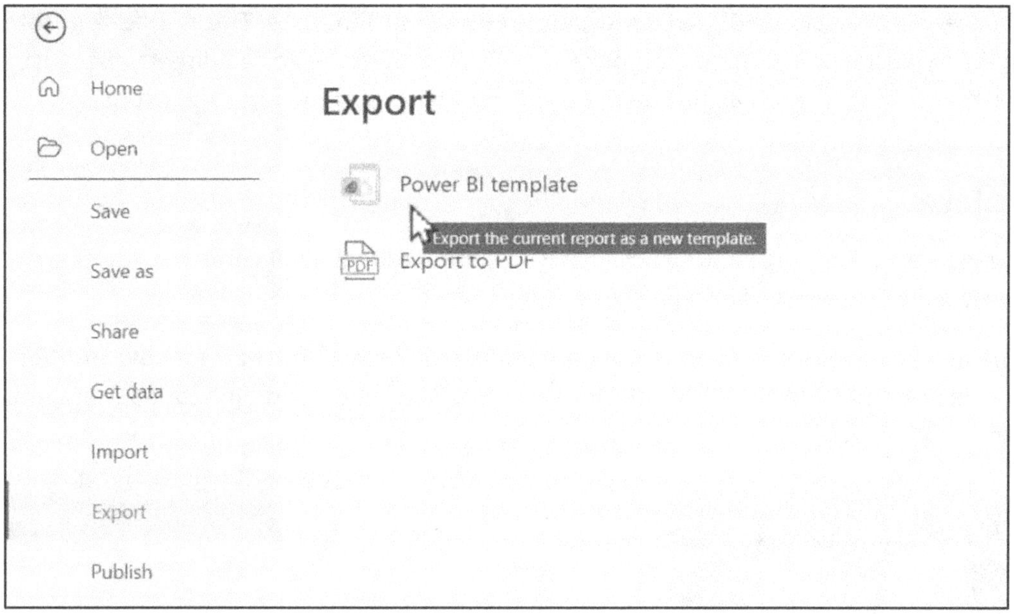

2. When prompted for a description, enter something clear and recognisable, such as KZXP HR Report Template.

3. For the filename, enter the same or similar title.

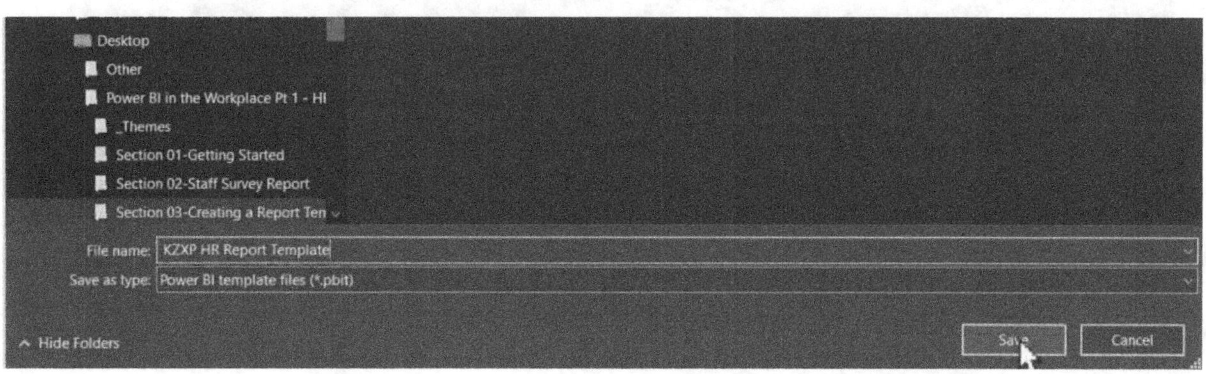

The exported file will have the extension .PBIT, which stands for Power BI Template. This is different from the standard working file extension .PBIX, as the template is not designed to be edited directly. Because we're exporting rather than saving, we remain inside the original PBIX master file after the export is complete.

Using the Template

From now on, whenever a new HR report needs to be created at our fictional KZXP company, the team simply opens the template file by double-clicking it.

When you open a .PBIT file, Power BI doesn't open the template itself. Instead, it creates a new, untitled report file based on it. This new file inherits all visuals, layout settings, themes, and embedded metadata logic from the template.

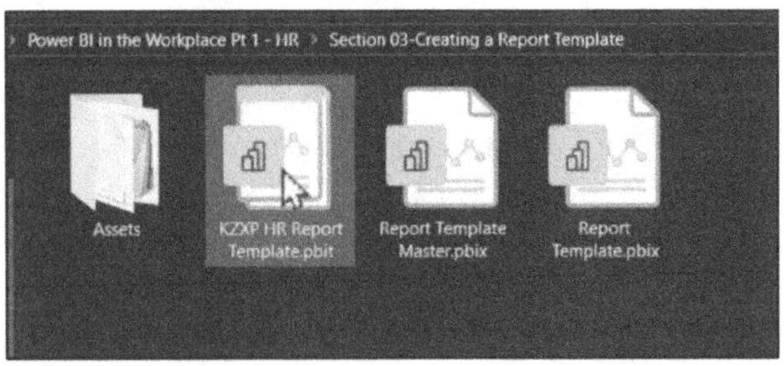

For instance, dynamic features such as the last refresh date will already be functional in the new file.

The first step after launching the new report is to save it:

1. Go to File > Save As.
2. Give the new report an appropriate name, such as Report from Template.

You can now begin personalising the metadata to suit the new report's purpose. A common first task is updating the report title.

To do this:

1. Find the measure used to generate the dynamic report title.
2. Edit the text inside the double quotes.

3. For this example, simply change the title to HR Report.

Once updated, the title will automatically refresh across all pages that reference it, keeping your report consistent and instantly recognisable.

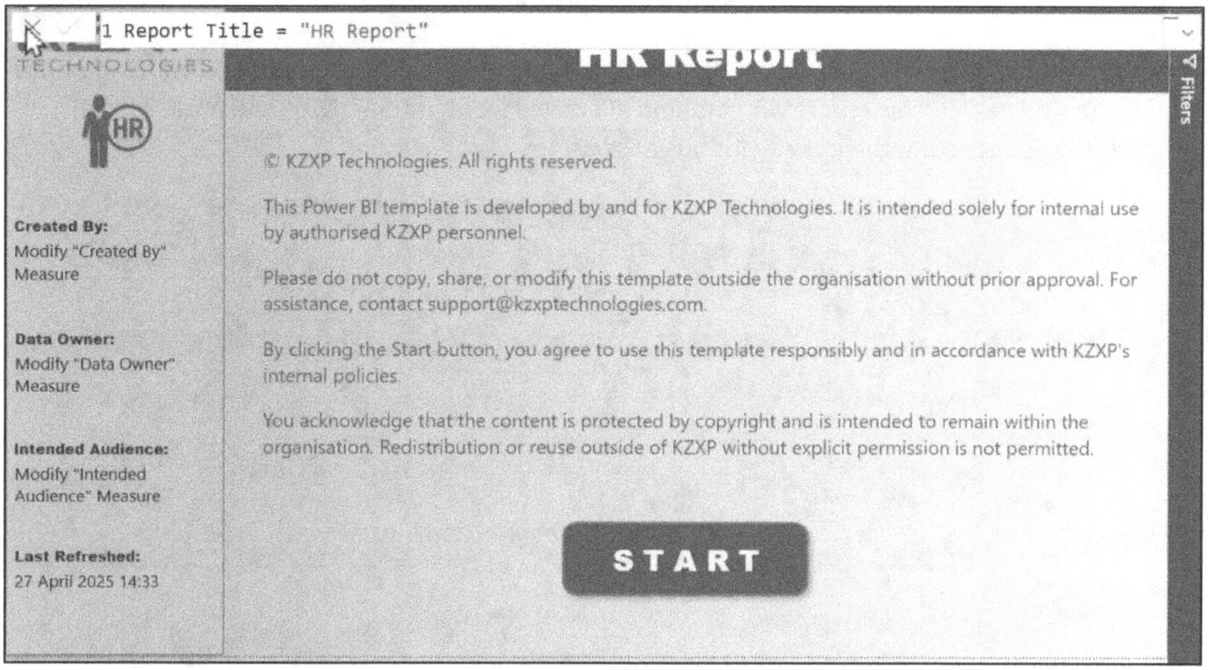

From here, you can click the Start button on the report, connect to your actual data sources, and begin building out the report's contents.

Why Templates Matter

As you can now see, investing time upfront to create a well-structured and branded Power BI template is a wise move. It ensures:

- A consistent, professional appearance across all reports.
- Significant time savings when producing new reports.
- Fewer errors and less rework due to pre-configured logic and layout.

Instead of starting from scratch for every HR report, you begin with a ready-made structure—enabling you to focus on insight and analysis rather than design.

That concludes the work on our reporting template. In the next section, we'll use this template to begin building a real-world report: an Attendance and Absence Report, which will serve as the foundation for all our reporting going forward.

Chapter 4: Attendance and Absence Report - Data Prep

4.1: Welcome to the Absence Report

In this section, we are going to build a full staff attendance and absence report using the branded Power BI template created earlier. This report will combine effective layout, interactivity, and professionally styled visuals to produce something ready for business use.

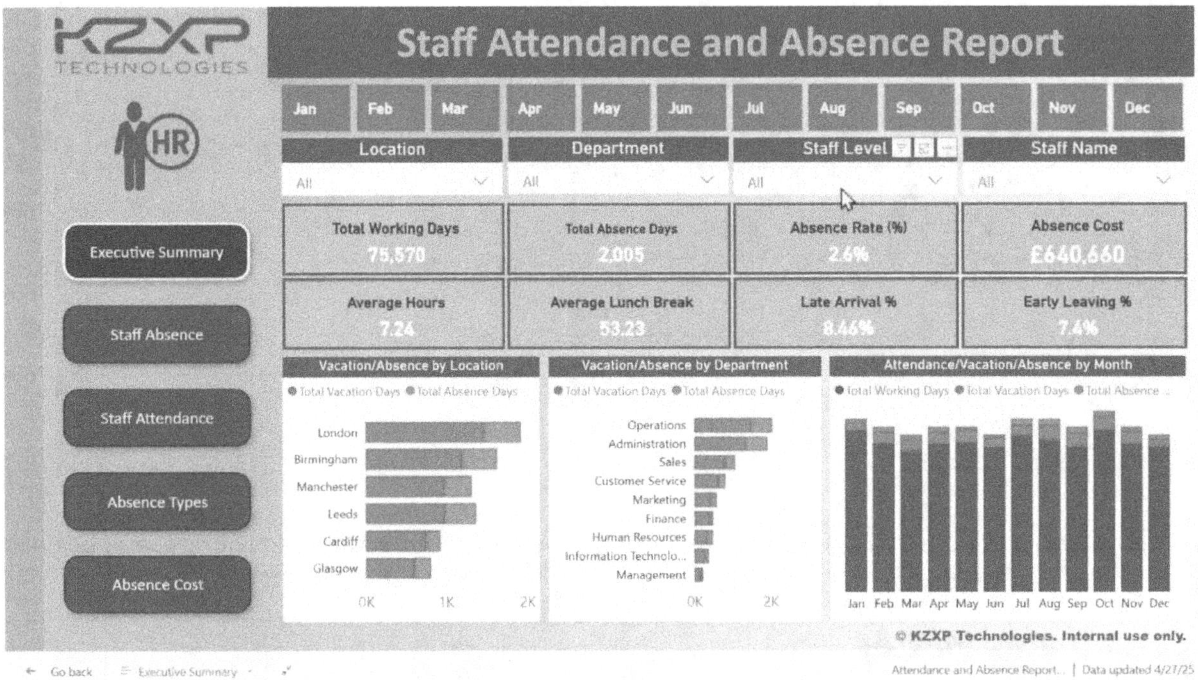

We'll begin by connecting to the data source. This will involve linking to Excel workbooks from multiple locations, including both a local drive and a SharePoint library. You'll also learn how to connect to a hidden workbook—a useful trick when working with source files that contain embedded or background data.

Once connected, we'll use this data to create a complete report with structure and flow. Before we dive into building each page, let's first take a closer look at the data model that will support the entire report.

The Attendance Data Model

At the centre of our model is the Attendance table. This table records key daily timings for staff: arrival times, lunch breaks, and departure times. This table forms the factual backbone of our reporting.

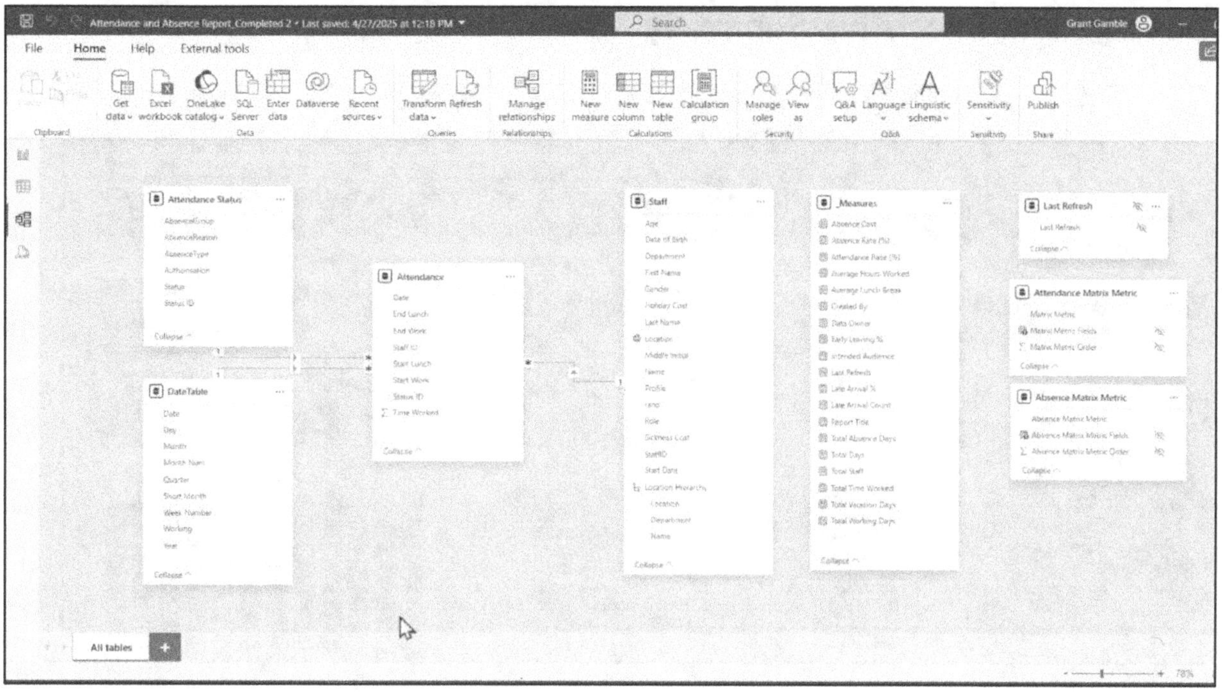

Supporting this are three important lookup tables:

- Staff Table – Contains core information on each staff member, including name, location, department, and staff level.
- Attendance Status – Defines the various attendance categories used, such as 'Present', 'Sick', 'Annual Leave', and 'Late Arrival'.
- Date Table – A standard Power BI date dimension enabling time-based filtering and aggregation.

As we build the report, we'll create a set of calculated DAX measures to drive interactivity and insights.

These measures will be stored neatly in a dedicated Measures table and will drive all the calculations and visuals used throughout the report.

Start Page and Executive Summary

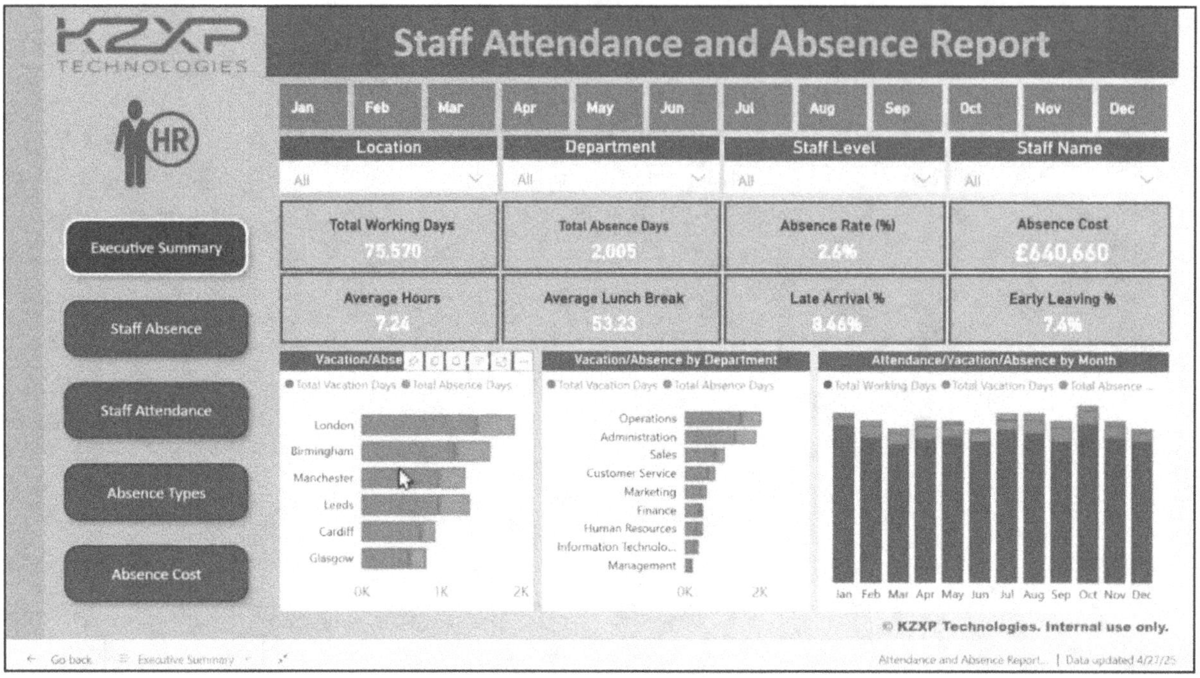

The first page of the report is the Start Page, inherited from our branded template. It contains key metadata including report title, author, creation date, and usage notes. A copyright notice and an internal-use-only disclaimer are prominently displayed. Users access the rest of the report by clicking a clearly labelled Start button.

That brings us to the Executive Summary. This page provides a high-level snapshot of attendance performance using a clean and balanced layout.

At the top are five slicers, arranged to optimise usability:

- A grid-style slicer for choosing a Month.
- Four drop-down slicers for Location, Department, Staff Level, and Staff Name.

These slicers are synchronised across all pages in the report, so any selection made here carries through seamlessly to the rest of the report.

The centre section contains a grid of KPI Cards, each showing key metrics such as total working days, absence days, absence rate, average hours worked, and average lunch break time. These are aligned for clarity and scalability.

Finally, at the bottom, there are three stacked column charts showing:

- Absence and vacation by Location.
- Absence and vacation by Department.
- Absence and vacation by Month, revealing seasonal patterns.

Staff Absence Page

The next page focuses on Staff Absence and introduces a more advanced Power BI feature: field parameters.

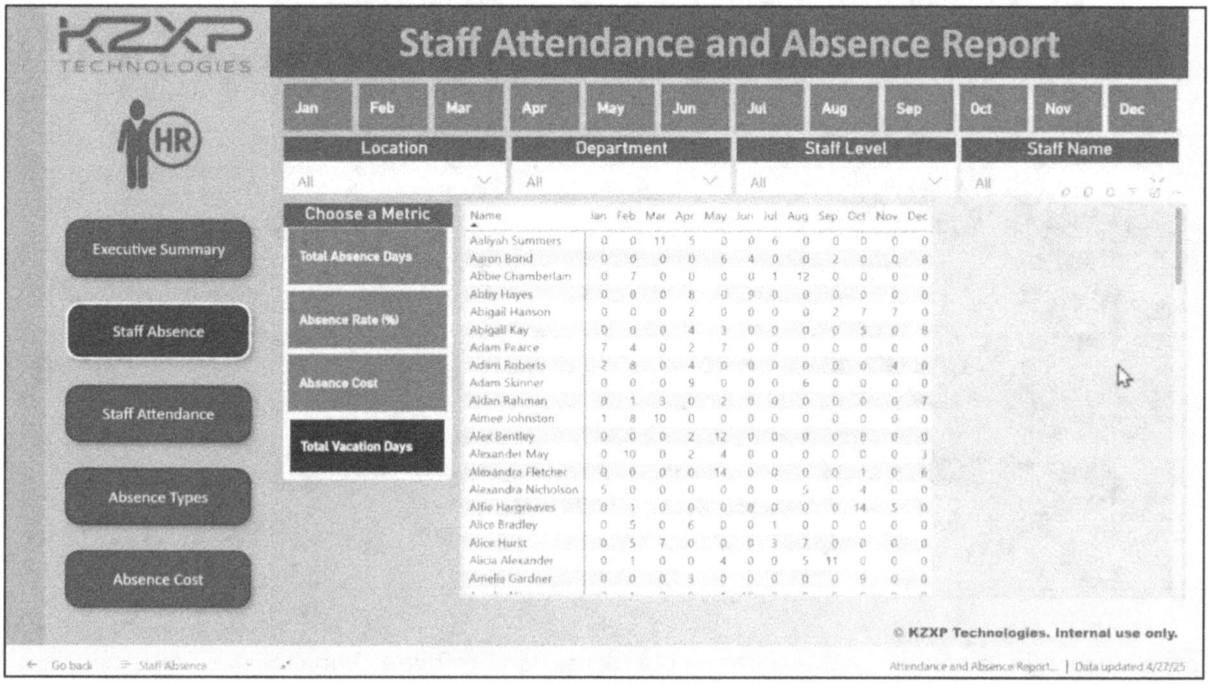

On the left side of the page is a selection panel where users can choose one of several metrics to explore—Absence Days, Absence Rate, Absence Cost, or Vacation Days.

Based on this selection, a matrix visual on the right updates dynamically. The matrix is structured with months as columns and staff names as rows. Thanks to the field parameter setup, we only need one matrix visual that automatically updates depending on the chosen metric. This makes the page both efficient and powerful.

Staff Attendance Page

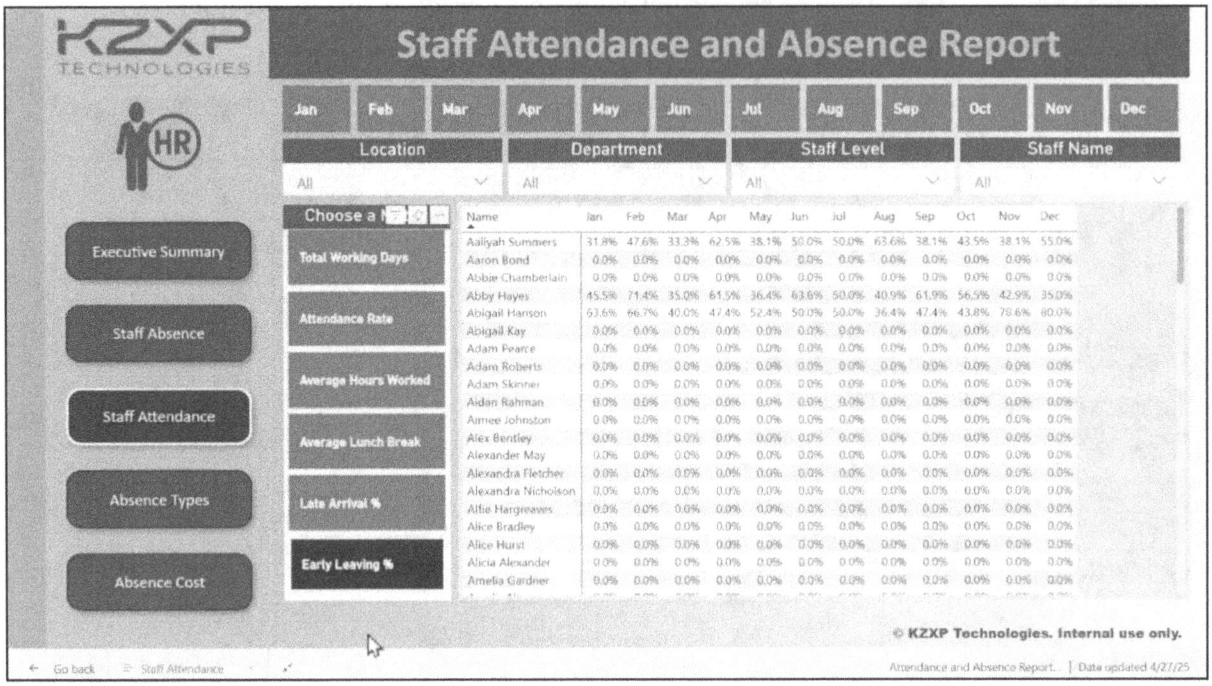

This page mirrors the layout of the previous one but focuses on positive attendance metrics rather than absence. The selectable metrics here include Total Working Days, Average Hours Worked, Late Arrivals, and Early Leavers.

The same field parameter technique is used, with users making a selection on the left and the matrix updating on the right to reflect that choice. Structurally identical to the absence page but offering a different analytical lens.

Absence Types Page

The Absence Types page introduces drill-down hierarchies. This allows the user to explore the composition of absence events in a layered fashion.

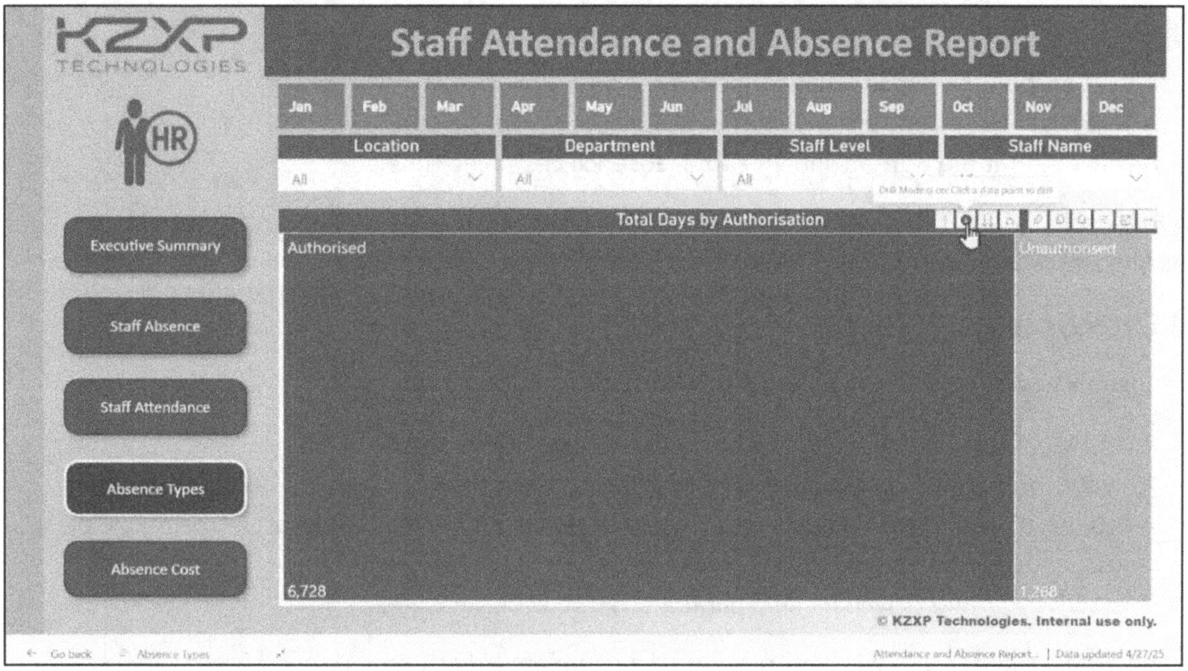

The primary visual is a Tree Map, where each tile represents a top-level absence category. Users can click a tile to drill deeper into subcategories, using the built-in hierarchy capability in Power BI.

This interaction is intuitive, allowing for quick exploration without crowding the visual with too much detail at once.

Absence Cost Page

The final page in the report is the Absence Cost dashboard, focused on financial impact.

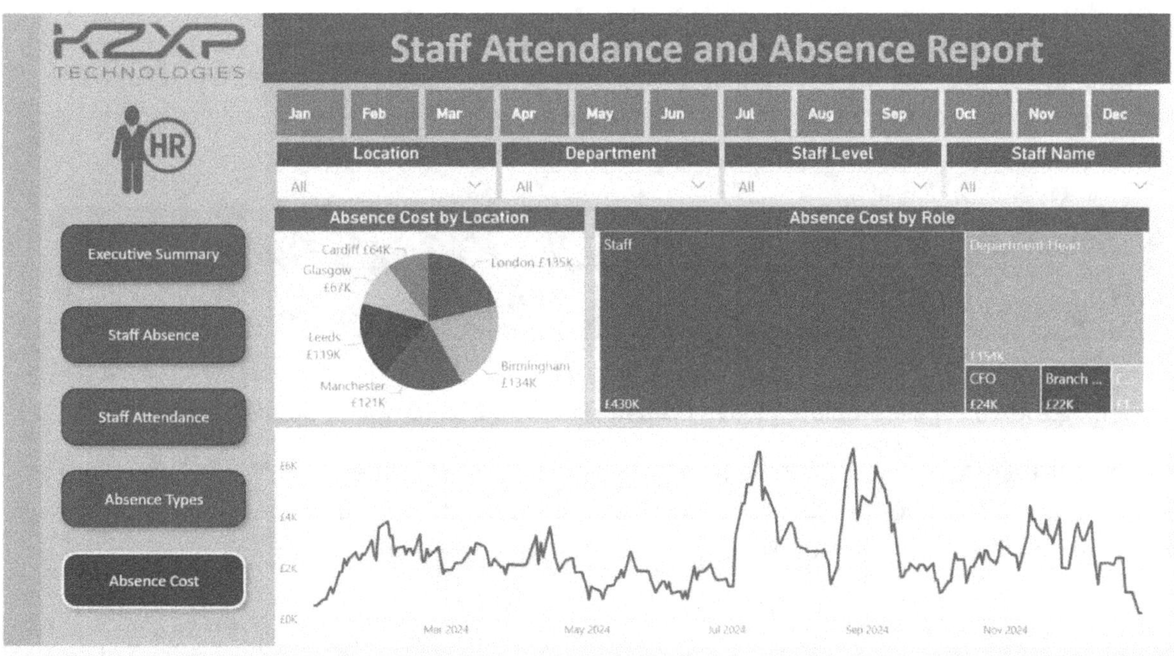

It contains three main visuals:

- A Pie Chart on the left showing total absence cost by Location.
- A Tree Map in the centre showing cost by Role.
- A Line Chart at the bottom showing total absence cost over Time.

This page is designed for finance or HR directors who want quick insights into how absence affects budgets and operational costs.

Final Outcome

Across these six pages, we'll have created a full, professional-grade report with:

- A consistent, branded layout using our custom Power BI template.
- Fully synchronised slicers for a smooth filtering experience.
- A rich mix of visual types including cards, matrices, bar charts, column charts, tree maps, pie charts, and line charts.
- Interactive features driven by field parameters and DAX measures.

By the end of this chapter, you will have developed a complete HR attendance and absence report—ready to deploy, share with colleagues, or adapt for your own organisational needs.

4.2: Connecting to an Excel Workbook

In this section, we begin building the Attendance and Absence Report by connecting Power BI to our first data source—an Excel workbook. This marks the first practical step in bringing together the data that will drive the insights in our report.

foundation for our work, including basic formatting, navigation, and metadata tables, if you followed the setup steps beforehand.

Once the template file is open, it's good practice to save it immediately in the appropriate location so you're working from the correct folder. Navigate to the Section 4 folder and save the file using the name: Attendance and Absence Report.

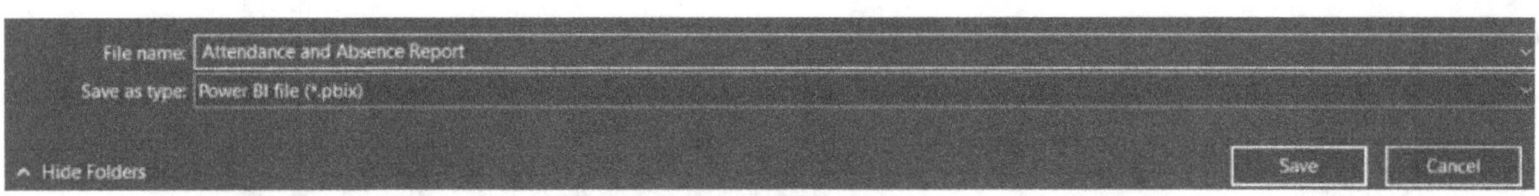

Start by opening the Power BI template file we prepared earlier. This template provides the

To connect to the Excel file, go to the Home tab on the ribbon and select Get Data. While Excel files can be accessed via the standard Get Data menu, Power BI also includes a dedicated Excel workbook button because it's such a commonly used source. Use that button for convenience.

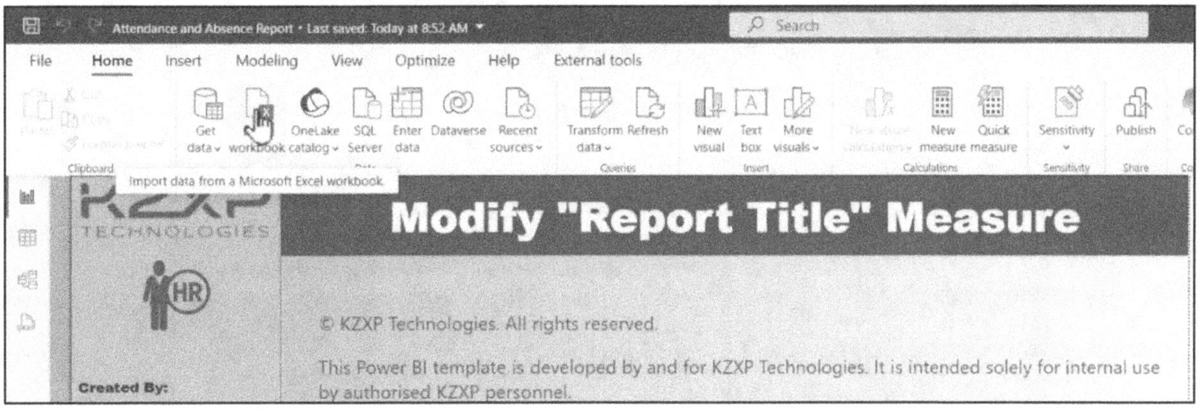

Browse to the Section 4 folder, then open the Data subfolder. Within it, select the file named Attendance and Absence.xlsx. After clicking Open, Power BI will immediately scan the file and present a Navigator pane listing all the data items it has found.

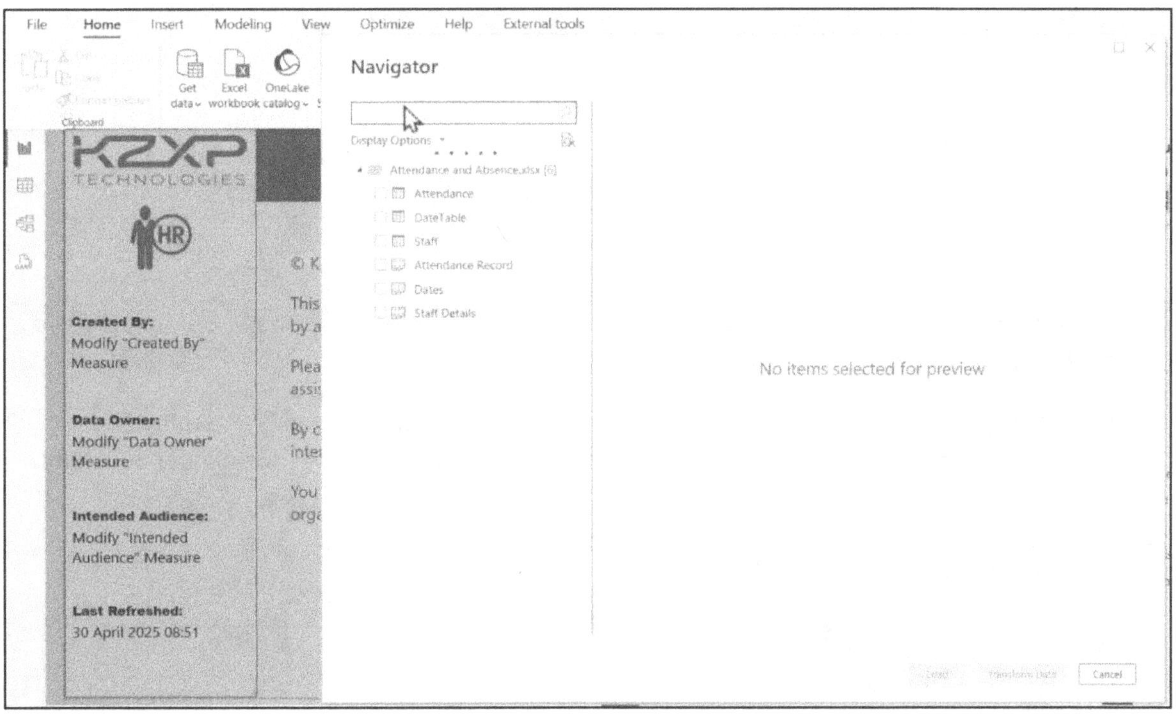

At first glance, you might see six items in the list, but there are in fact only three unique data blocks. Power BI displays both individual worksheets and formal Excel tables separately. This means if a sheet contains a named table, both the sheet and the table will appear in the list.

Whenever possible, try to work with Excel tables—these are created in Excel by selecting a range and using the Format as Table command. Tables provide a cleaner experience in Power BI, allowing for more consistent and predictable data imports. Worksheets do work too, but they often require more tidying up afterward.

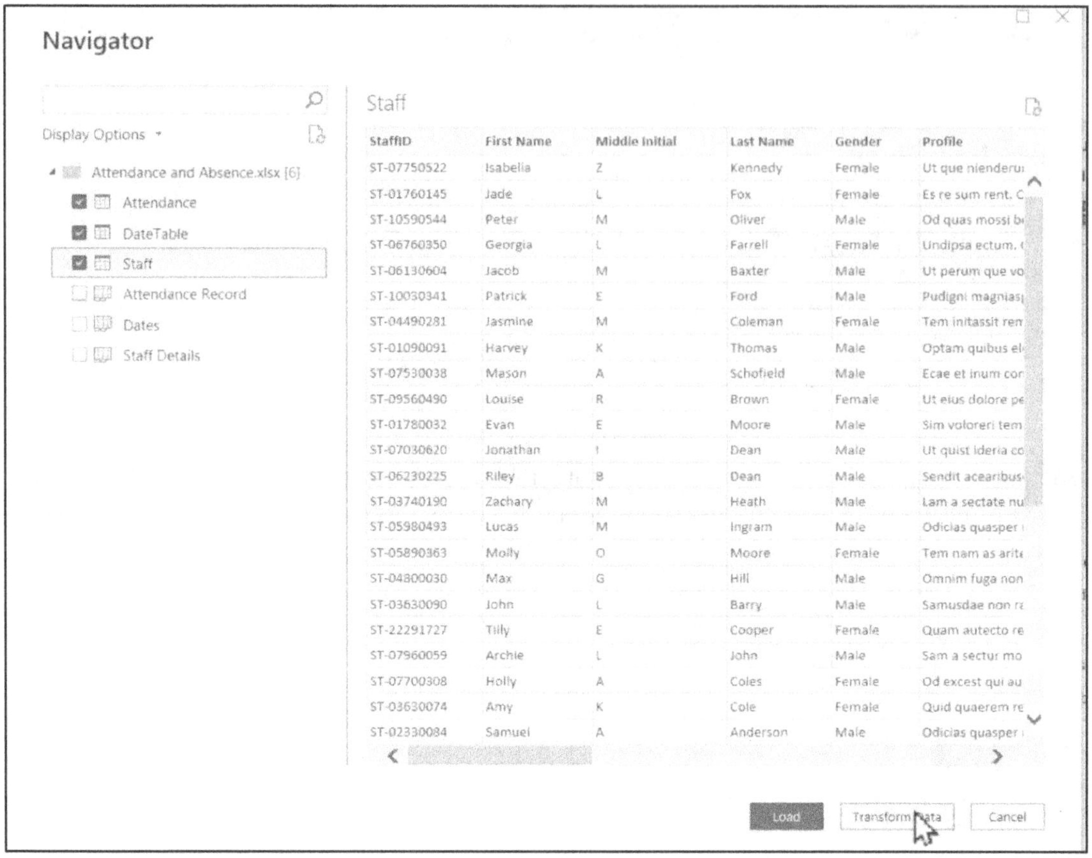

Click Transform Data to proceed into Power Query. This is where we'll clean and shape our data before loading it into the model.

Before we start modifying the tables, let's look at how Power BI connects to Excel files behind the scenes. In Power Query, select any query from the pane on the left. Then, in the formula bar, highlight the Source step. You'll see a line similar to:

Source = Excel.Workbook(File.Contents("..."))

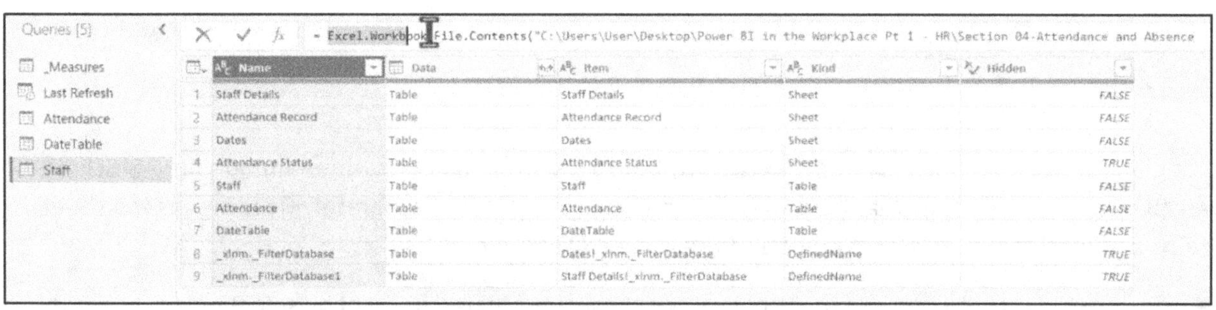

This formula tells us that the file is stored locally or on a network path. The Excel.Workbook function generates a metadata table, listing all accessible objects inside the Excel file.

Power BI recognises three types of objects when connecting to Excel:

- Defined Names – named ranges you've manually created in Excel.
- Sheets – standard worksheets within the file.
- Tables – formal Excel tables formatted via "Format as Table".

You can navigate to any of these objects by clicking into the Data column within the metadata preview. For example, suppose you delete some of the applied steps in the query editor and then click on the Staff table in the metadata. Power BI automatically creates a Navigation step that opens that table directly.

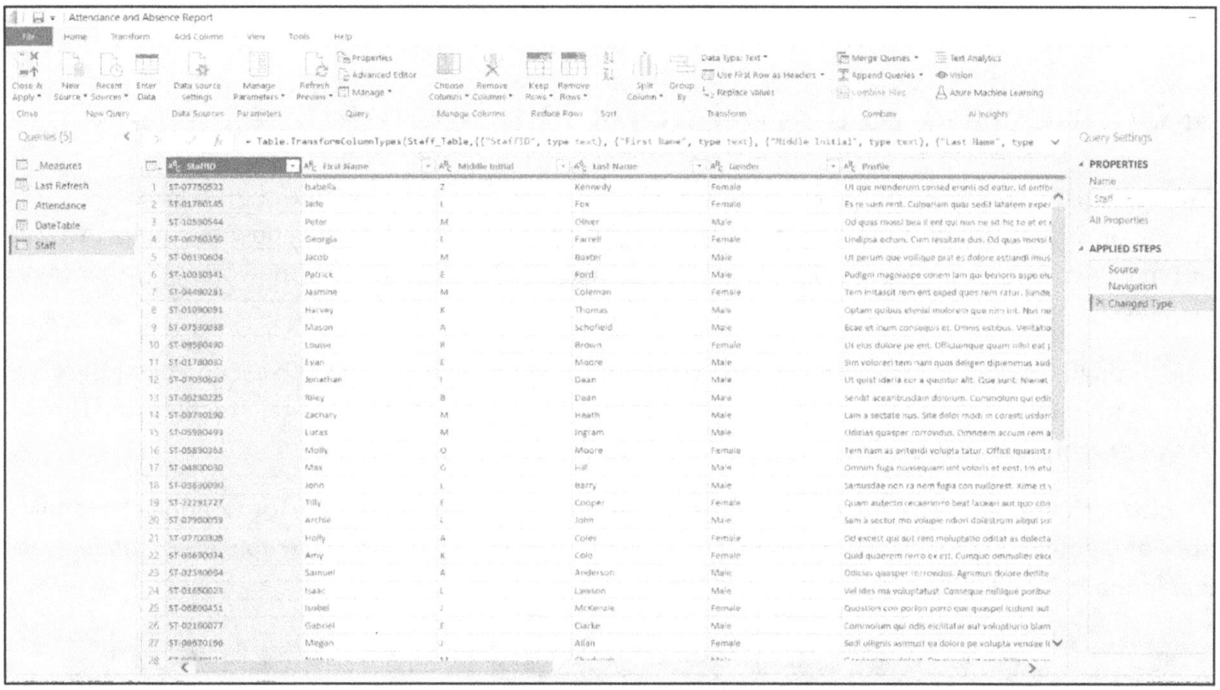

After this navigation step, Power BI often applies automatic changes to the data types of columns. These changes are based on what it assumes the data represents—for example, converting a text column to a date type. If these assumptions aren't correct for your purposes, you can override them at any time. None of the changes are permanent until you load the data.

At this point, we're nearly ready to start cleaning and prepping the tables for the model. But before we dive in, there's one more connection method worth exploring: connecting to Excel workbooks stored in a SharePoint library.

If your organisation stores files in SharePoint or you're collaborating in Microsoft Teams, this method will likely be important to you. However, if you're not using SharePoint or online workspaces, feel free to skip ahead and move directly into the table cleanup phase.

To wrap up this step, go ahead and delete the three queries we've brought in so far. Click Close & Apply to commit any changes and return to the report view. Save your Power BI file again to preserve your progress.

In the next part of this chapter, we'll revisit the same Excel file, but this time we'll connect to it via SharePoint to demonstrate how to integrate online data sources efficiently.

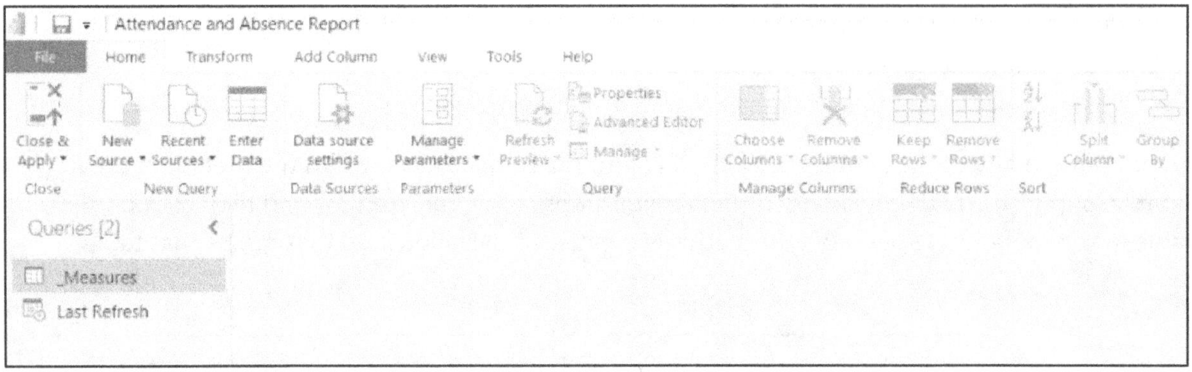

4.3: Connecting to a Workbook in a SharePoint Library

In many modern workplaces using Microsoft 365, it is common for teams to store shared Excel workbooks in SharePoint document libraries rather than on local drives. Knowing how to connect to such files from Power BI is an essential skill—especially because the process differs from working with locally stored files.

To walk through this process, let's imagine we've already created a SharePoint site called Power BI Reports. Within this site's document library, we've created a folder named HR Data. The first step is to upload our Excel file into this folder.

Click Upload, then select Files. Navigate to the relevant folder on your machine—for example, Section 4 > Data—and double-click the Excel workbook Attendance and Absence.xlsx. Once uploaded, the file will appear in the HR Data folder.

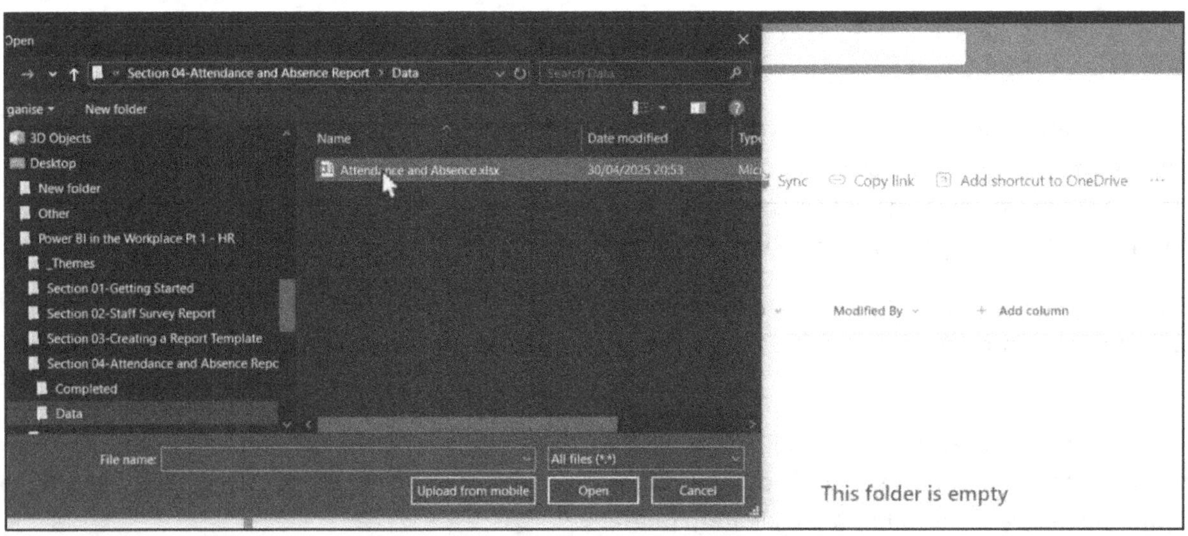

This next step is absolutely critical: to connect this file from Power BI, we need its direct web path—not a sharing link. Locate the file in the library, click the three-dot menu (More Actions), and look carefully at the available options. You might instinctively go for Copy Link but resist the temptation!

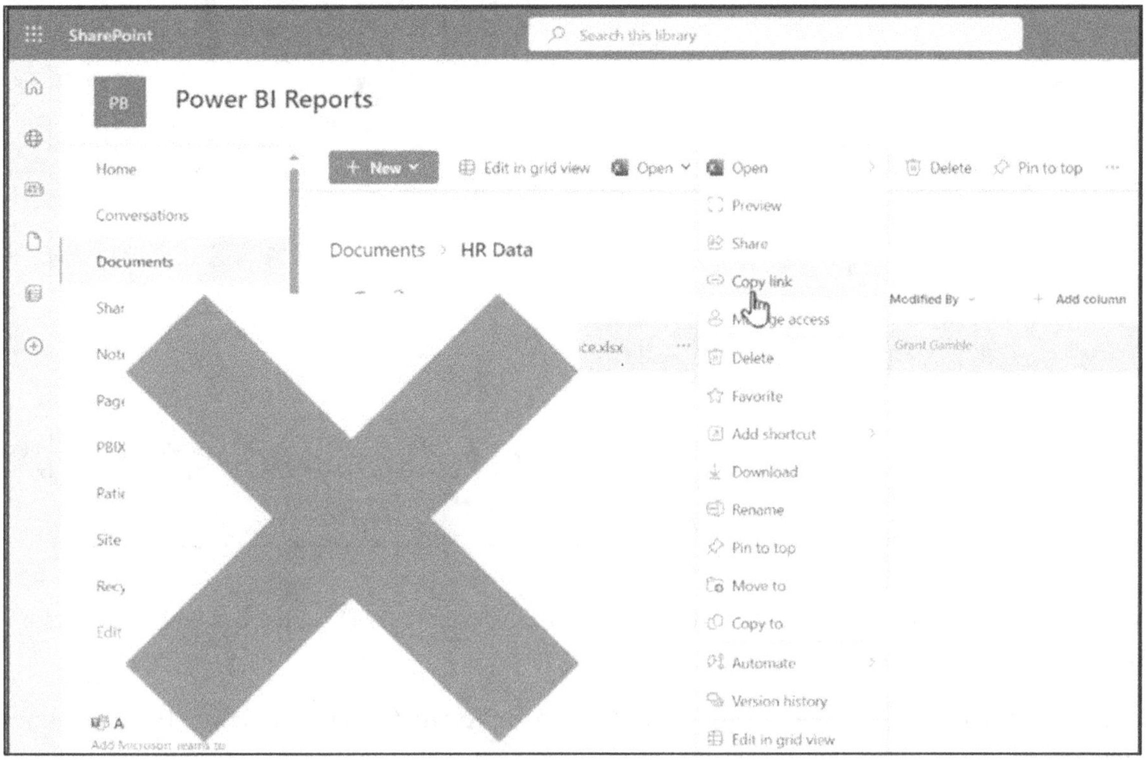

That link is designed for sharing within Teams or SharePoint and won't work for Power BI connections.

Instead, scroll to the bottom of the More Actions menu and choose Details. This opens the file's Properties pane on the right-hand side. Scroll all the way down until you see a field labelled Path. Next to it is a Copy button with a tooltip that reads Copy Direct Link. That's the link you want. Click to copy it to your clipboard.

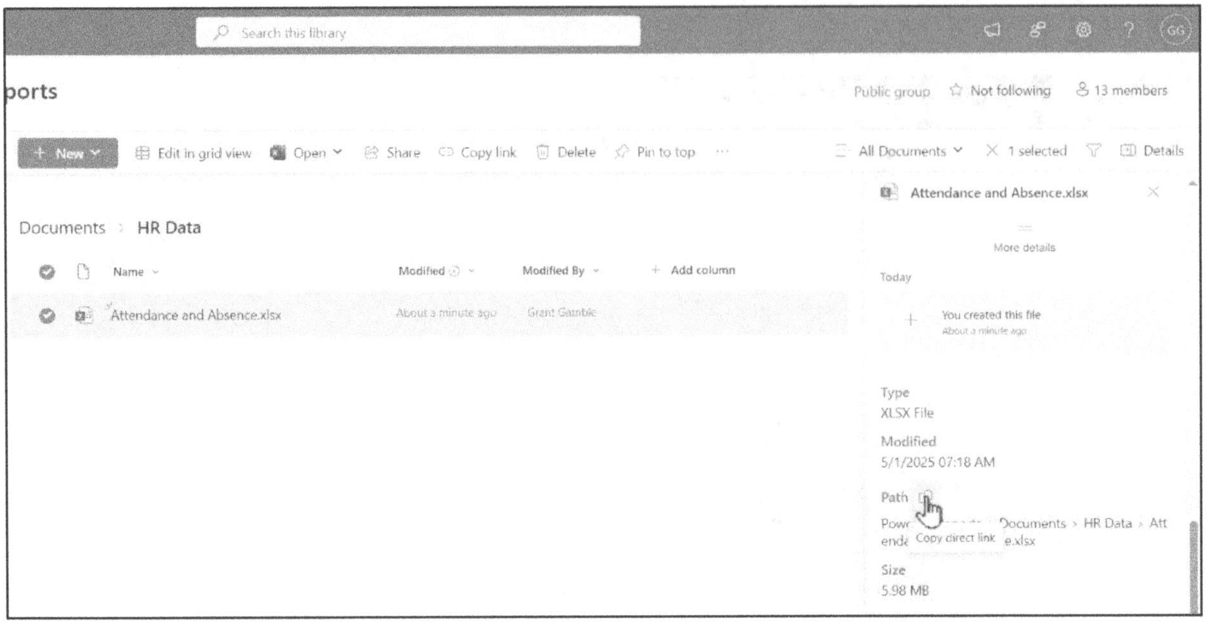

This is the golden rule: Do not use Copy Link. Always use Copy Direct Link. This ensures Power BI gets a direct URL to the file, suitable for data connections.

Now that you have the correct URL, switch to Power BI Desktop to create the connection. Here's where a lot of people make a common mistake.

Although we're connecting to an Excel file, because it's stored online, the Excel Workbook connector is not the right tool. Let's briefly demonstrate why.

Click Get Data > Excel Workbook, paste in the URL you copied, and click Open. Almost immediately, you'll receive an error. This is your signal: you're using the wrong connector.

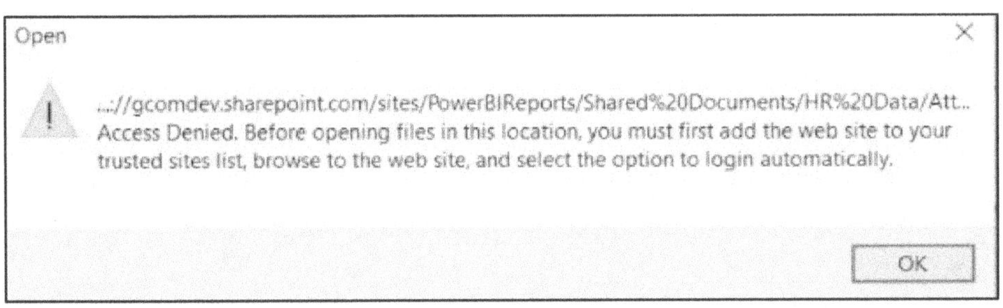

When working with files hosted online—in SharePoint, OneDrive, or any web-based system—you must use the Web connector, regardless of the file type (Excel, CSV, JSON, etc.).

So, close that dialog and instead click Get Data > Web. Paste in the same direct link URL. Power BI now recognises it correctly and begins the connection process.

You will be prompted to authenticate. By default, Power BI selects Anonymous, which will not work for secure SharePoint sites. Change this to Organizational Account, then click Sign In and provide your Microsoft 365 credentials. Once you authenticate successfully, click Connect.

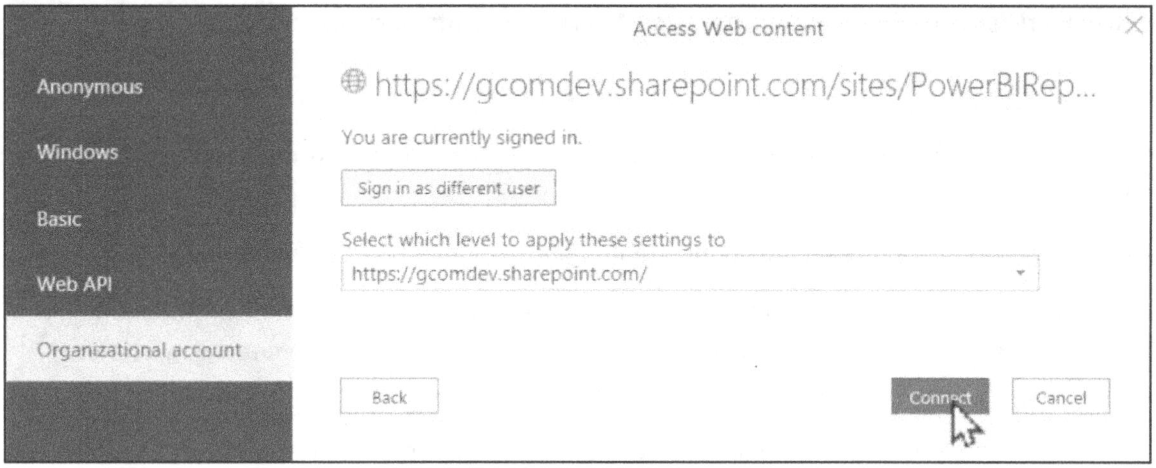

At this point, Power BI presents you with the content of the workbook. You'll see any formal Excel tables defined within the file. Just as with locally stored Excel files, you should select the tables (not the raw sheets) for better reliability and structure. Then click Transform Data to load these into Power Query.

Inside Power Query, it's worth pausing to examine what's happening behind the scenes. In the Applied Steps list, click on Source. This reveals the formula Power BI is using to connect to the file.

Source = Excel.Workbook(Web.Contents("https://yourcompany.sharepoint.com/sites/.../HR Data/filename.xlsx"),null, true)

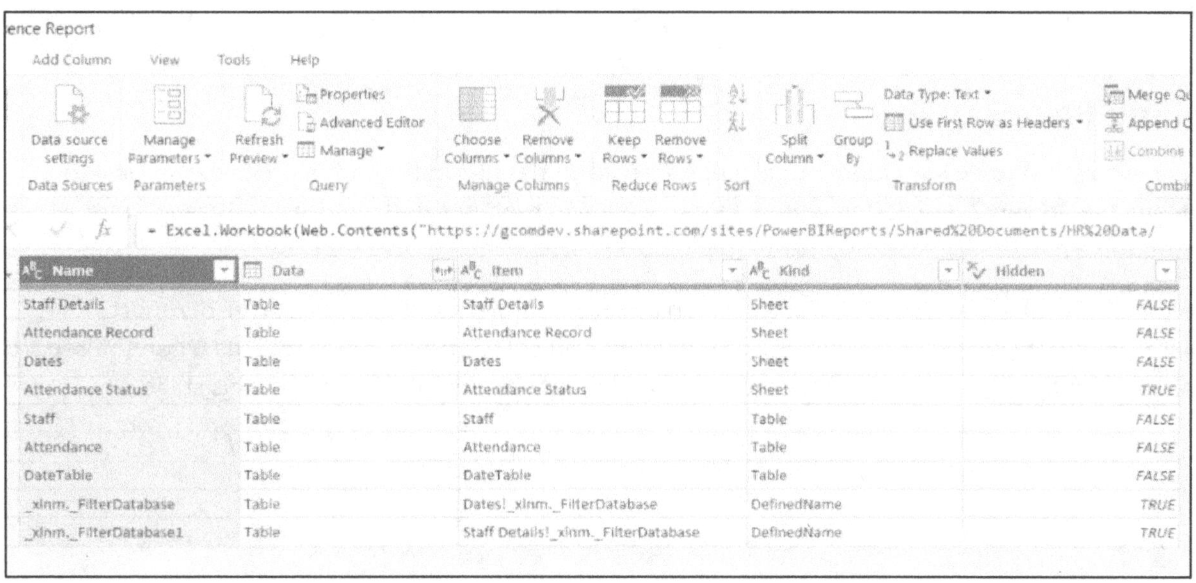

This tells us two important things. First, we are using the Excel.Workbook function, which is normal. But more importantly, we're using Web.Contents, confirming that the connection is genuinely to an online resource—in this case, a SharePoint-hosted file.

Compare that to what we would see when connecting to a file stored locally. In that case, the source step would include File.Contents instead:

Source = Excel.Workbook(File.Contents("C:\Users\YourName\Documents\filename.xlsx"), null, true)

So, here's the key difference:

If you see File.Contents, the file is local—even if someone originally shared it from SharePoint but you manually downloaded it.

If you see Web.Contents, it's a true online connection to SharePoint or another web source.

Understanding this distinction is important. If your report is meant to update from a central online file, but you see File.Contents, it means the report is pointing to a local copy—and updates won't reflect changes in the shared version. Always confirm the connection type by checking this step.

With our connection verified, we're ready to begin transforming and preparing the data. But we'll leave that for the next stage. For now, click Close & Apply to load the data into Power BI, and don't forget to save your changes.

For teams who don't use SharePoint, this process might not apply—but for organisations who do, it's a vital step in building dynamic and connected Power BI reports. Everyone can now move forward with preparing the tables for analysis and modelling.

4.4: Transforming Tables in Power Query

Before building any visuals or writing DAX measures, it's important to ensure that our imported tables are clean and properly structured. In this section, we'll review the data we've brought into Power BI and apply any necessary transformations using Power Query.

Opening Power Query

To begin, we return to Power Query by selecting Transform data from the ribbon in Power BI Desktop. This opens the Power Query Editor, where we can view and modify the structure and types of our imported tables.

At the top of the Queries pane, you'll see two tables that we inherited from our Power BI report template: Measures, which holds our DAX calculations, and Last Refresh, which records when the report was last updated. These tables are pre-configured and don't require any changes at this stage.

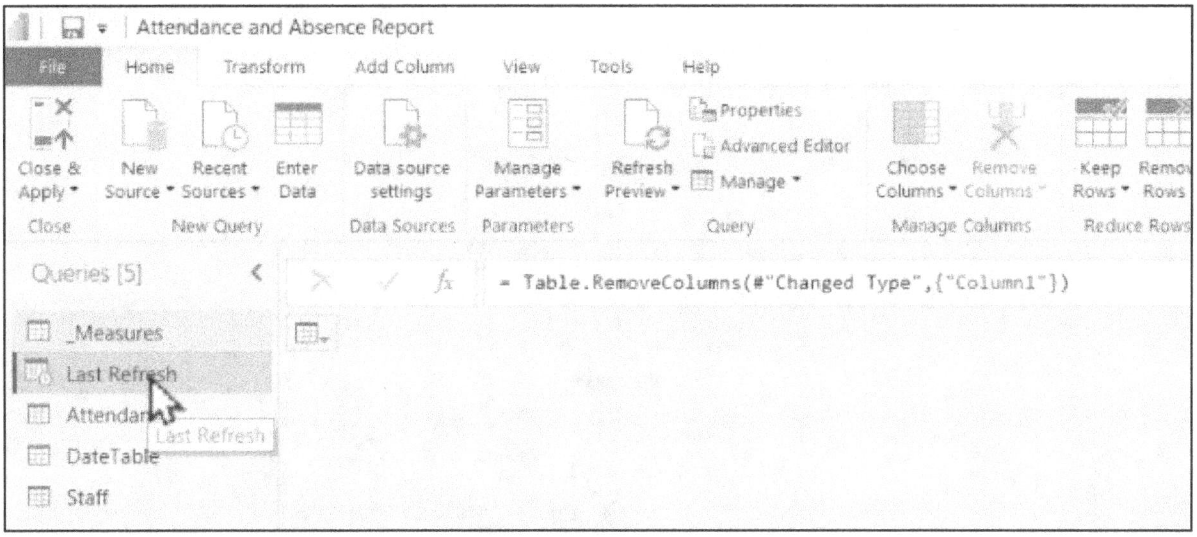

Reviewing the Attendance Table

Let's begin with one of the three main tables we imported: the Attendance table.

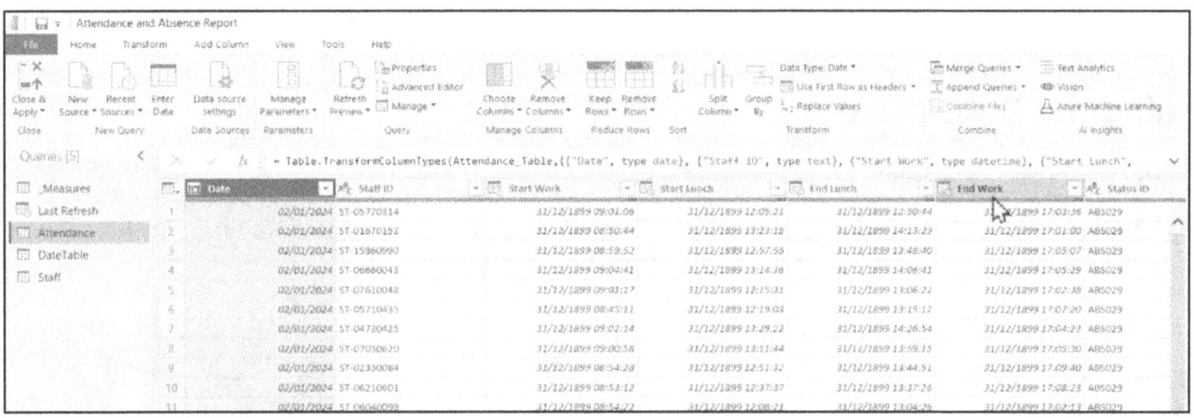

One thing that stands out immediately is the data type assigned to the time-related columns: Start Work, Start Lunch, End Lunch, and End Work. Power Query has defaulted these columns to the Date/Time type, likely as a general precaution.

However, these columns only contain time values, not full dates. To better reflect the actual contents and avoid confusion in later reporting, we should change their data type to Time.

Here's how we can do that:

1. Click on the Start Work column header.
2. Hold down the Shift key and click on End Work to select all four of the time columns.
3. Right-click on any of the selected columns and choose Change Type > Time.
4. Power BI will prompt us to confirm whether we'd like to replace the existing (Change Type) step or insert a new one. In this case, we'll choose Replace Current.

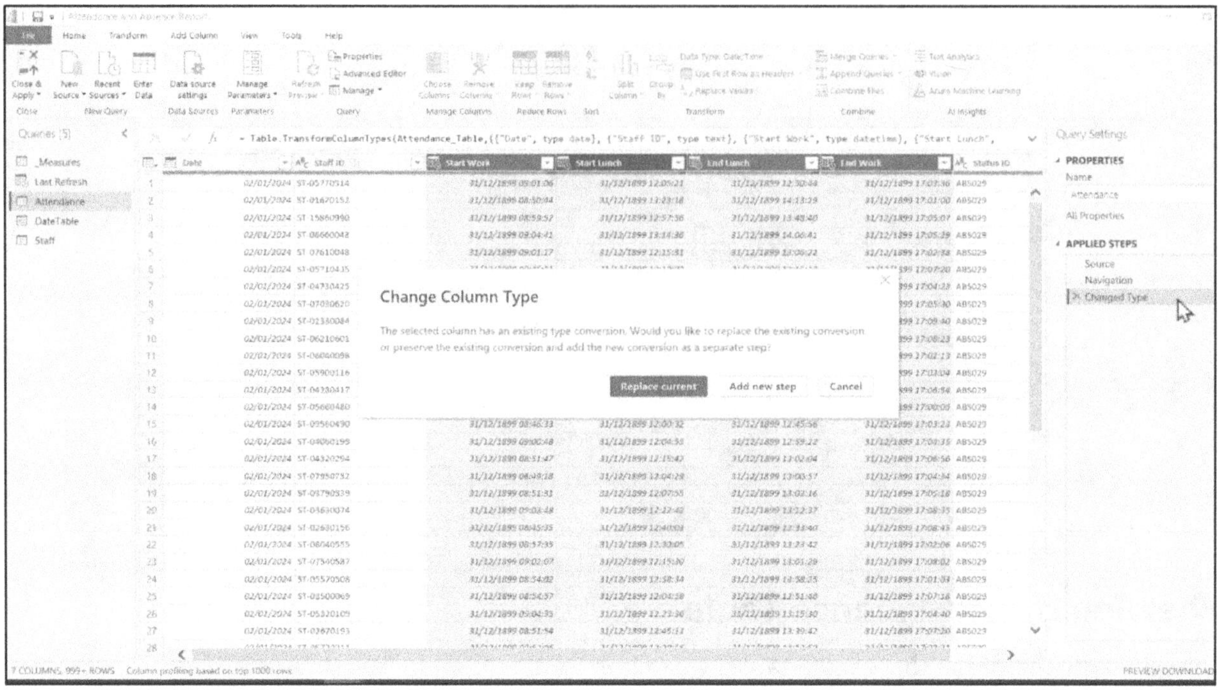

That completes the clean-up for the Attendance table. Everything else in this table looks fine.

Cleaning the Date Table

Next, let's turn to the Date table.

Unlike the Attendance table, Power Query hasn't recognised any of the column data types in this table, so we need to correct that.

1. Click on the first column in the table.
2. Scroll to the last column, hold Shift, and click on the last column's header to select all columns.
3. On the ribbon, go to the Transform tab and click Detect Data Type.

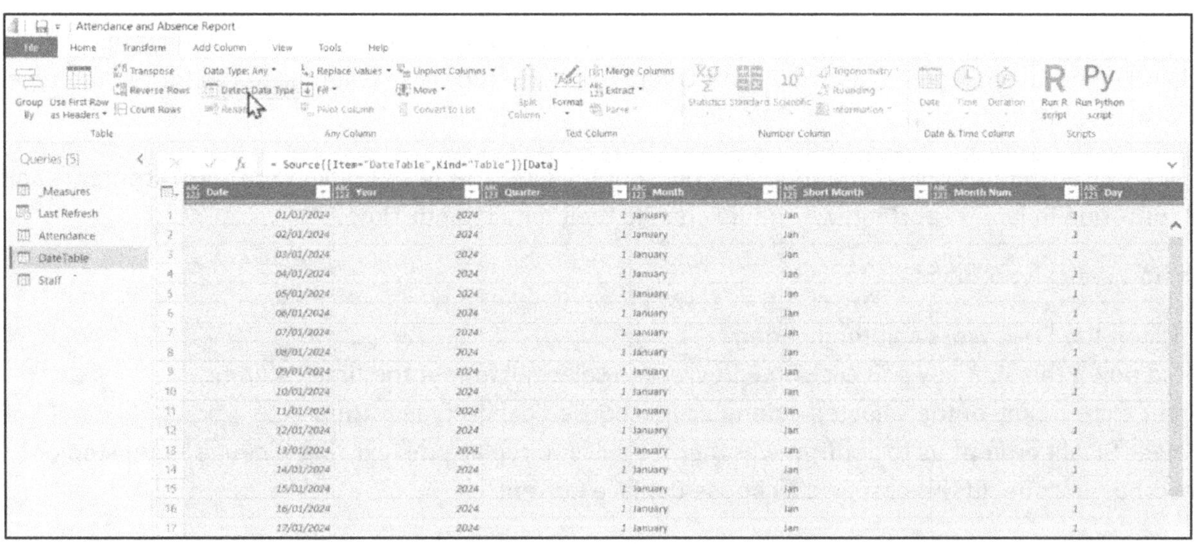

Power Query will attempt to assign the correct data types automatically. Since the columns in this table are straightforward—mostly dates, numbers, and text—it should get everything right. This small step helps ensure downstream calculations and filters behave as expected.

Updating the Staff Table

The final table we'll transform is the Staff table.

As you'd expect, most of the columns here are text fields. Two columns—Date of Birth and Start Date—are date fields. These are typically handled well by Power Query. However, there are two cost-related fields, Holiday Cost and Sickness Cost, that we need to refine.

Even though the values in these cost fields are currently stored as whole numbers, we want to treat them as monetary amounts. The appropriate data type in Power Query is Fixed Decimal Number, which is the best match for currency fields.

1. Select both Holiday Cost and Sickness Cost columns.
2. Right-click and choose Change Type > Fixed Decimal Number.
3. Click Replace when prompted.

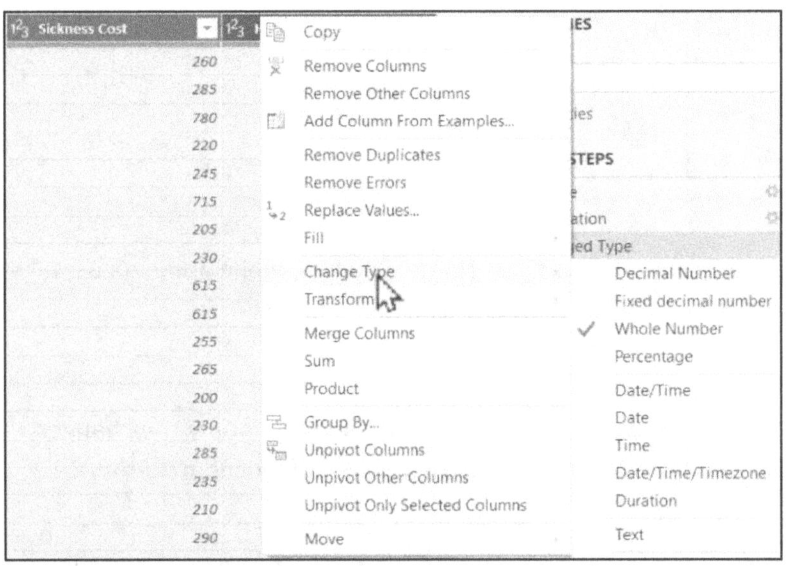

Using the correct data type is essential for accurate calculations later on, especially when aggregating or formatting currency values.

Creating a Full Name Column

To make our reports more user-friendly, we'll create a new column that combines the First Name and Last Name fields. This gives us a neat Full Name column that can be used in slicers, labels, and tooltips.

Here's how to create it:

1. Click on First Name to select it.
2. Hold down Control (Ctrl) and click on Last Name.
3. Go to the Add Column tab and choose Merge Columns.

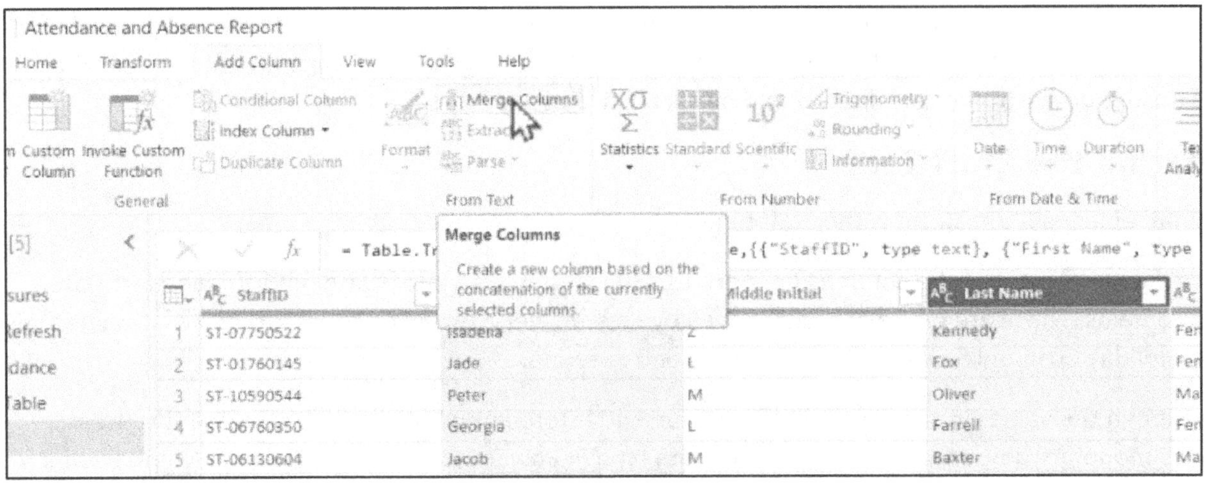

The Merge Columns dialog will appear. Choose Space as the separator so that the full name appears with a space between first and last names. Then, give the new column a name such as Name and click OK.

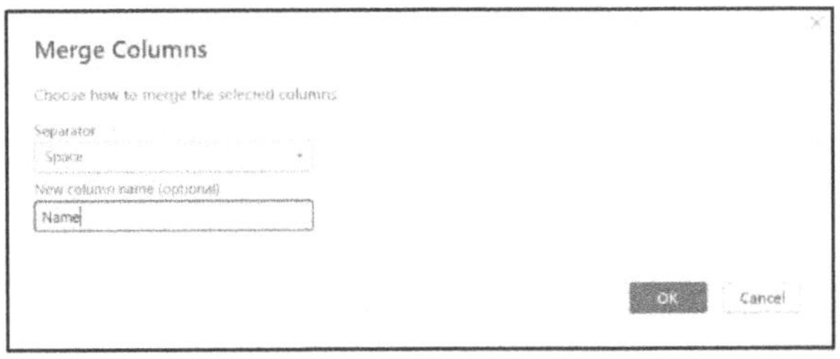

This approach ensures we retain the original First Name and Last Name columns, while adding a useful combined field for reporting.

Finishing Up

At this point, we've finished all necessary transformations for our existing tables. To apply the changes, click Close & Apply in Power Query. This will return us to the Power BI main window and load the updated tables into the data model.

There is one final table we still need to bring in—this one is stored in a hidden worksheet within our original Excel file. In the next section, we'll cover how to import that table and prepare it for analysis.

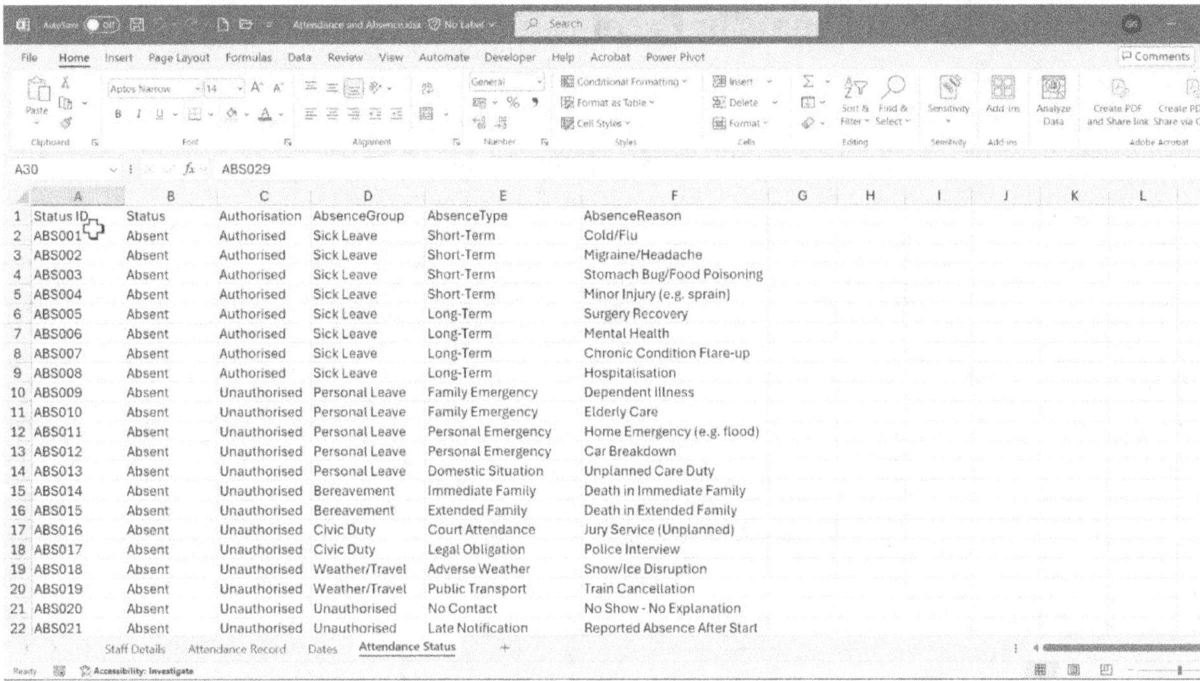

4.5: Connecting to a Hidden Sheet

When working with Excel files in Power BI, it's not uncommon to encounter sheets that have been hidden—either for tidiness, to avoid user interference, or even as a basic layer of security. In this tutorial, we'll walk through how to bring data from a hidden or even a "very hidden" worksheet into Power BI using Power Query.

Understanding Hidden Sheets in Excel

Before we move into Power BI, let's clarify how sheet visibility works within Excel. When you open an Excel workbook, only the visible sheets appear along the bottom tab bar. If a sheet is hidden, you can reveal it by right-clicking on any visible sheet tab and selecting Unhide.

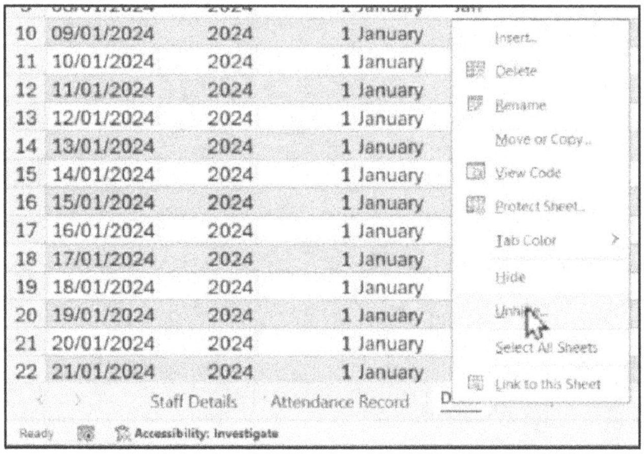

A dialog box will list all hidden sheets, and you can select any of them to bring back into view.

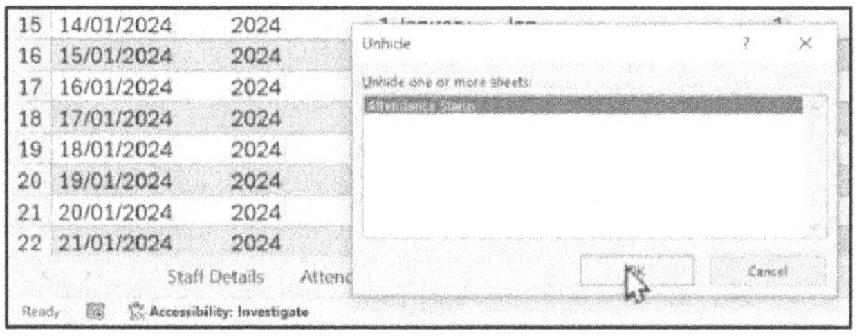

To hide a sheet, simply right-click its tab and choose Hide. This is especially useful for reference tables or data ranges you want to retain in the file but keep out of sight for end users.

There is an additional, lesser-known level of hiding available via the Developer tools. If the Developer tab is enabled, click into Visual Basic to open the VBA editor. In the Properties panel (F4), selecting a worksheet reveals its Visible property. By changing this to xlSheetVeryHidden, the sheet becomes completely hidden.

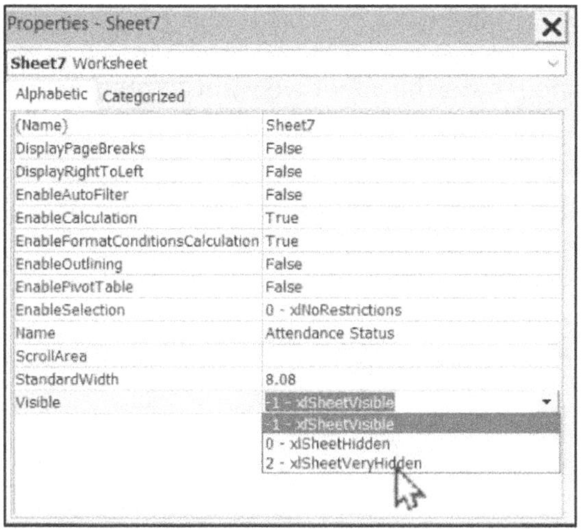

It won't even appear in the Unhide dialog. Unless someone accesses the Developer tools, it's unlikely they'll discover it by accident.

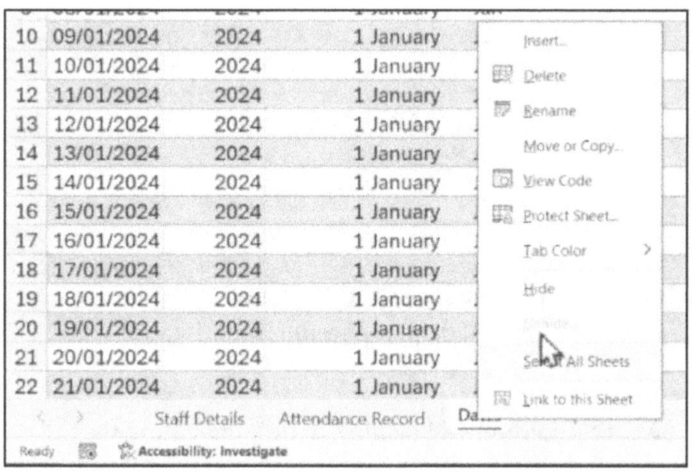

It's important to note that whether a sheet contains a formal Excel table or just a regular range of cells, its visibility status can still be set to hidden or very hidden. The structure of the data does not affect the ability to hide a sheet.

Why Power BI Doesn't Show Hidden Sheets by Default

When connecting to an Excel workbook in Power BI—whether it's stored on your local drive, in SharePoint, or elsewhere—you're only shown visible sheets by default. The connector window omits any sheet that's hidden or very hidden.

The easiest way to access a hidden sheet in an Excel workbook—once you've already connected to the file—is through Power Query. Begin by clicking Transform Data to open the Power Query Editor.

Rather than creating a brand-new connection, the simplest approach is to duplicate one of the existing queries that already connects to the same workbook. Any existing query will do; the goal is just to reuse the connection.

In this example, we'll right-click on the "Staff" query and select Duplicate.

Next, rename the duplicated query to "Attendance Status", since that's the sheet we want to bring in.

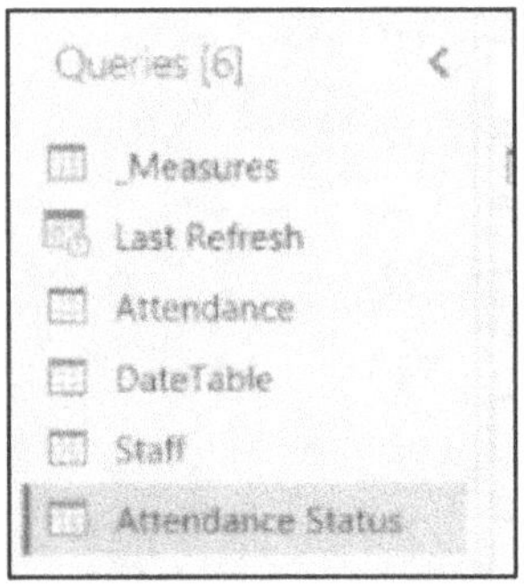

Resetting the Query to the Source

Navigate to the Applied Steps pane and delete all steps except for the Source step.

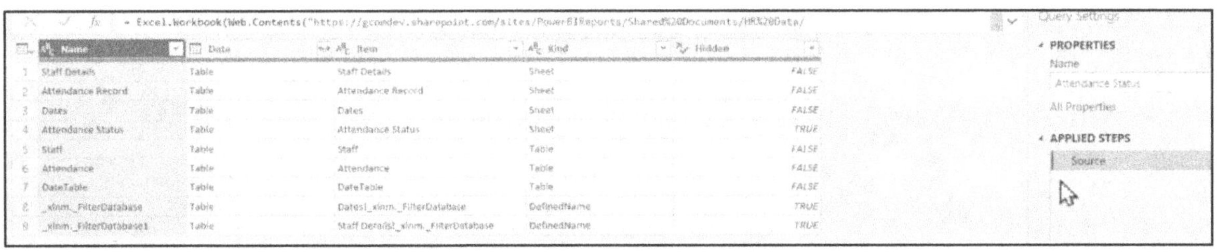

This keeps the query connected to the Excel file, but resets the navigation, allowing us to explore all available sheets—visible or hidden. At this point, Power Query will display the full metadata for the workbook.

Look for a column named "Hidden". For certain rows, this column will display "true", indicating that those sheets are hidden.

If you scroll through the "Name" column, you'll find "Attendance Status" listed. Its Kind is set to "Sheet", confirming it's a worksheet—even though it's hidden.

Navigating to the Hidden Sheet

To access the data, locate the row labelled "Attendance Status" and click the small table link in the Data column. This takes you directly into the hidden worksheet.

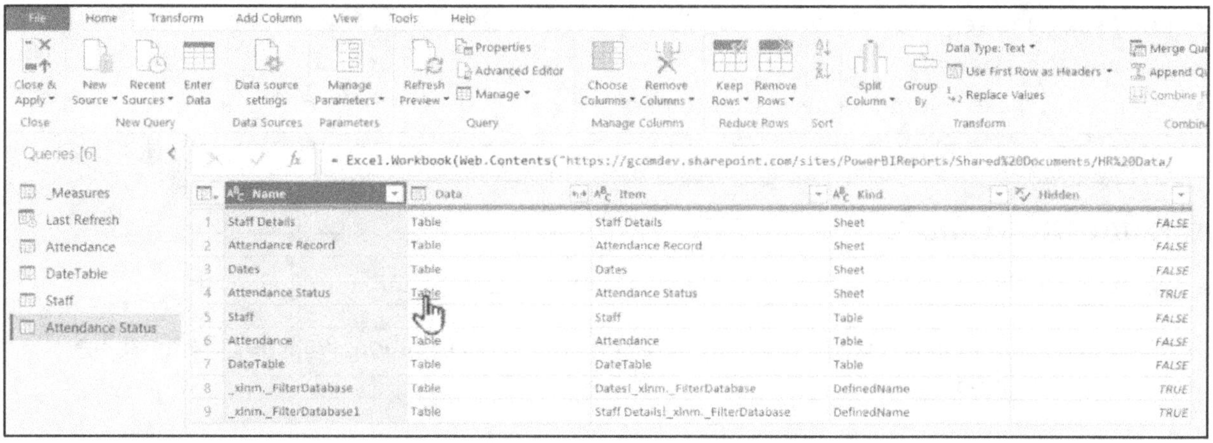

At this stage, you may notice that Power Query hasn't promoted the first row to headers. This often happens when every column is interpreted as text—Power Query assumes there are no headers.

Fixing Column Headers

To correct this, follow two steps:

1. First, delete the "Changed Type" step—it's based on placeholder column names and will be incorrect.
2. Then, apply "Use First Row as Headers".

You can apply the header promotion either from the Home ribbon or by clicking the drop-down menu in the top left corner of the preview table.

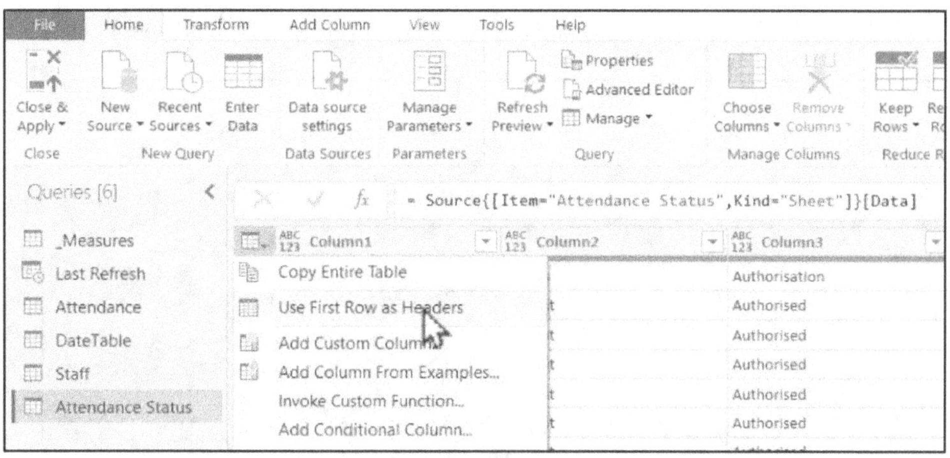

Once you do this, Power Query will automatically reapply a new Changed Type step—this time correctly using the newly promoted column headers.

Tidying Column Names

The final step is to tidy up your column names. Imported Excel sheets often use system-friendly headings like AbsenceGroup or AbsenceReason. It's a good idea to:

- Add spaces to separate words
- Fix any abbreviations
- Generally, make column names easier to read

This will make it much easier to build reports and visuals later on.

Finalising the Import

Once everything looks good, click Close & Apply to load the updated query into Power BI.

Now that all tables are in place, we're ready to move on. In the next section, we'll put the finishing touches on our data model.

4.6: Completing the Data Model

In this chapter, we complete the foundational data model required for our attendance and absence reporting. This model is crucial because it defines how different pieces of data relate to each other, enabling us to build accurate, insightful visuals and metrics.

Switching to Model View

To begin, we switch into Model View in Power BI. This view gives us a visual layout of all our tables and the relationships between them. For a cleaner workspace, it's helpful to close both the Properties and Data panes, giving us more room to arrange our tables.

We then position our tables thoughtfully. All primary data tables—the ones containing actual attendance information—should be grouped on the left side of the screen. Non-data tables, such as those containing only measures or metadata like last refresh details, can be positioned to the right, safely out of the way.

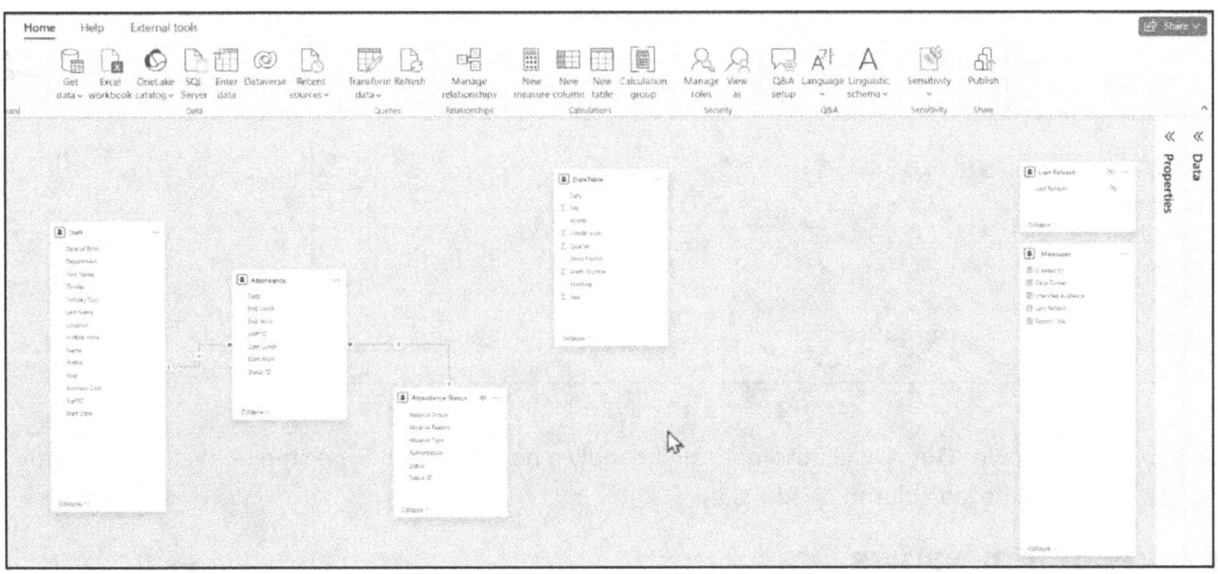

If needed, we can use the zoom controls in the bottom right corner of the screen to focus on the central part of our model.

Identifying the Fact Table

At the heart of our model is the Attendance table. This is our fact table, containing all the transactional records we want to analyse—each row logging an event like someone starting work, going to lunch, or clocking out at the end of the day.

In data modelling, a fact table stores the measurable events or transactions. These records are often numeric or timestamp-based and are connected to dimension tables—which provide context for the facts.

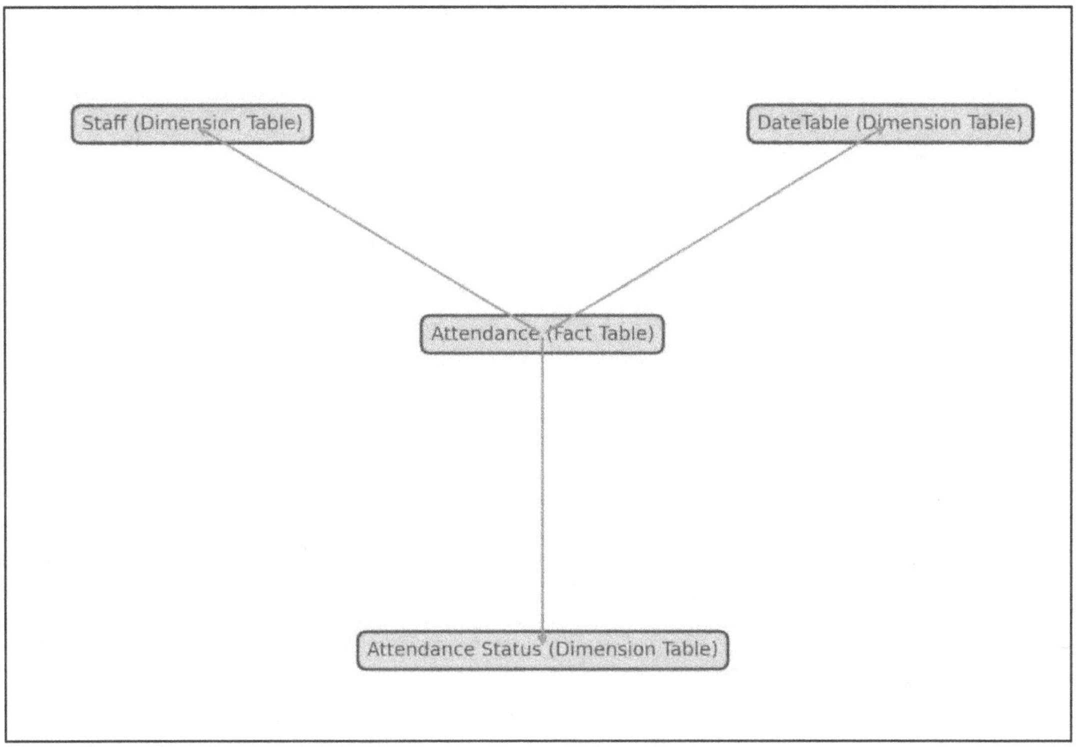

Understanding Dimension Tables

To enhance our analysis, we link the fact table to several dimension tables:

- The Staff table describes who each person is, their department, and other personnel details.
- The Date table provides calendar context—such as month, quarter, and year—enabling time-based analysis.
- The Attendance Status table categorizes each attendance event—such as Sick Leave, Holiday, or Authorised Absence.

This design, with a central fact table surrounded by connected dimension tables, is known as a star schema. It's named for its star-like appearance in the diagram, with one main table in the centre and others radiating outwards.

Auto-Detected Relationships in Power BI

When we initially clicked Close & Apply after loading the data, Power BI automatically tried to detect relationships between tables based on column names and compatible data types.

For instance:

- It correctly recognised that Staff ID appears in both the Staff and Attendance tables and created a relationship.

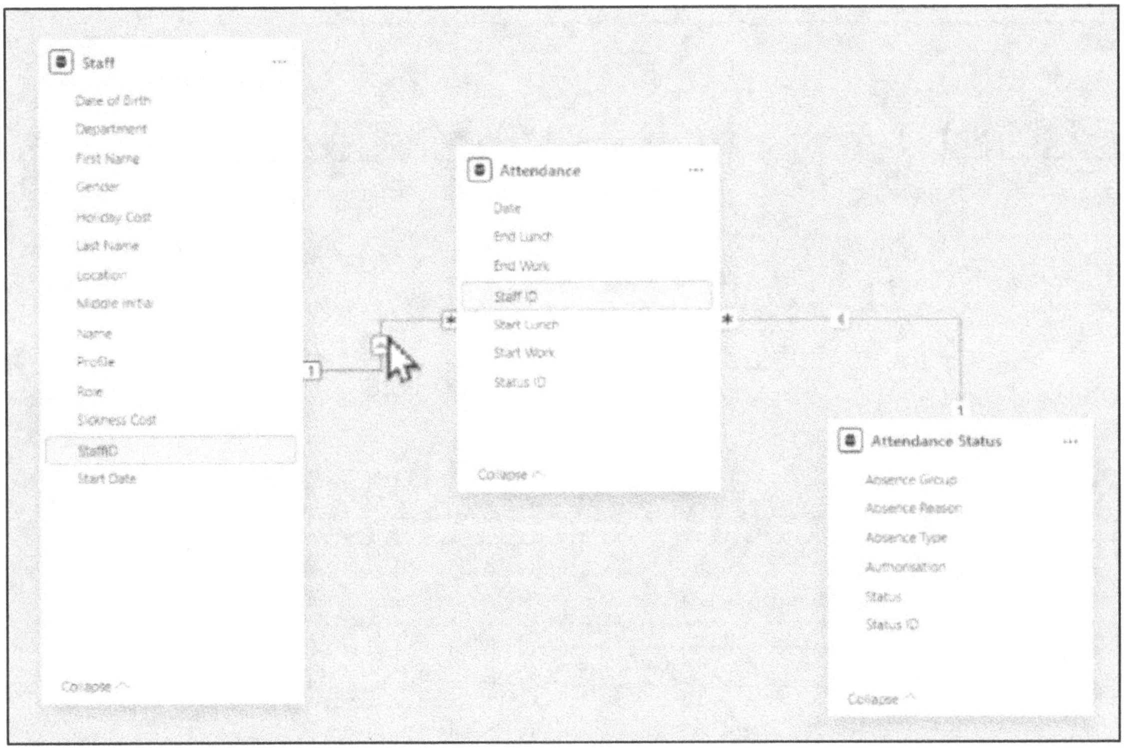

- It also created a link between Status ID in the Attendance Status table and the Attendance table.

This behaviour is known as relationship detection. Power BI checks for similar column names and compatible data formats to infer connections.

However, one limitation is that Power BI usually does not create relationships based on date columns, even when column names match. That's why we still need to connect the Date table to the Attendance table manually.

Examining Relationships in Model View

Once the auto-detected relationships are in place, we review the diagram:

Each connecting line represents a relationship. Hovering over a line highlights the two fields that form the relationship—useful for confirming connections. For example, hovering over the line between Attendance and Staff shows it's based on Staff ID.

At either end of the line, you'll see small symbols:

- A "1" indicates the one side of the relationship.
- An asterisk ("*") indicates the many side.

So, the relationship between Staff and Attendance is one-to-many, meaning each staff member can have multiple attendance records.

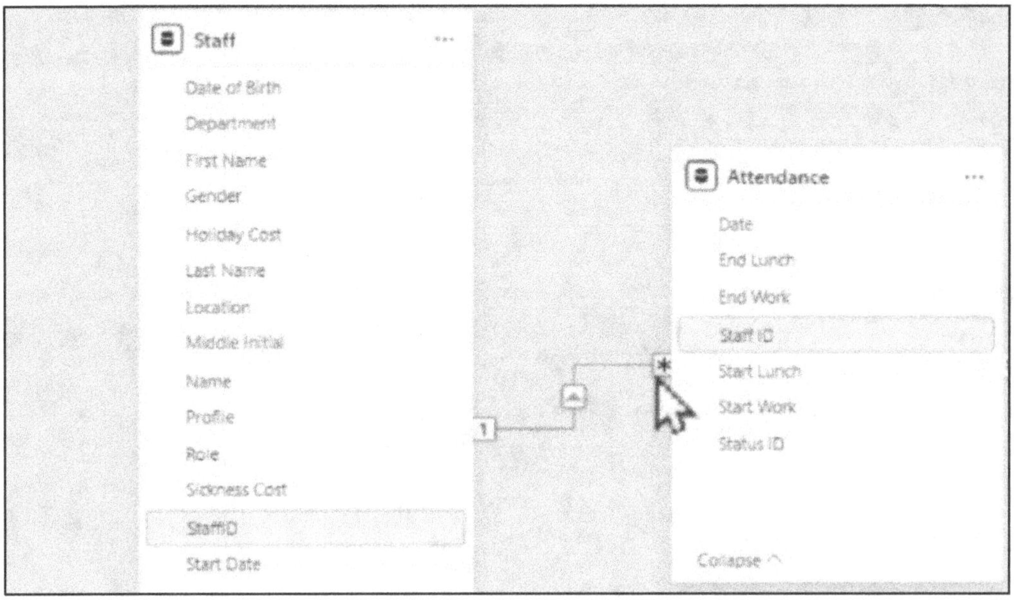

To edit a relationship, right-click on the line and choose Properties. Here, you can:

- Change which columns are used.
- Adjust the cardinality (e.g., one-to-one, one-to-many).
- Activate or deactivate the relationship.

Active and Inactive Relationships

Sometimes Power BI adds a relationship but leaves it inactive. This often happens when Power BI detects multiple potential relationships and is unsure which one should be used in calculations.

For example, the relationship between the Attendance and Attendance Status tables was automatically created using Status ID. It appears as a solid line, meaning it's active.

To demonstrate relationship deactivation:

Right-click the line, choose Properties, and uncheck the box labelled Make this relationship active. Click OK.

You'll see the line change to a dotted line—signalling the relationship is now inactive.

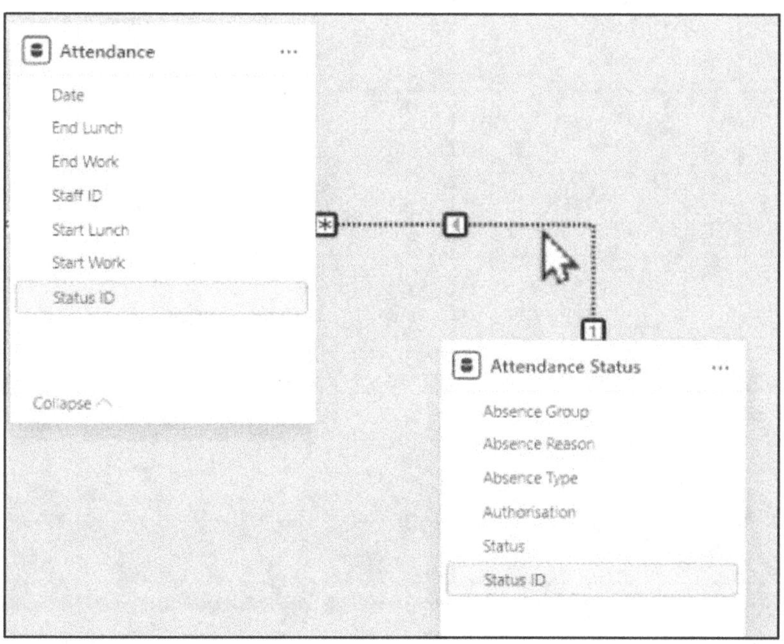

This can be useful in more advanced models, where multiple relationships between the same tables might exist, but only one is used at a time. We'll cover such cases when we explore inactive relationships later in the book.

To reactivate the relationship, repeat the process and check the Make this relationship active box again. The line will return to a solid state, and the connection becomes usable again in visuals and calculations.

Creating the Date Relationship Manually

To finish the data model, we need to manually create a relationship between the Date table and the Attendance table.

Click and drag the Date column from the Date table onto the Date column in the Attendance table. This opens the Create Relationship dialog box.

In the dialog, double-check the following:

- The tables and columns being connected are correct.
- Cardinality is set to one-to-many—one date in the calendar can appear many times in attendance records.
- The relationship is active.

Once confirmed, click Save. The new relationship appears in the model, completing the star schema.

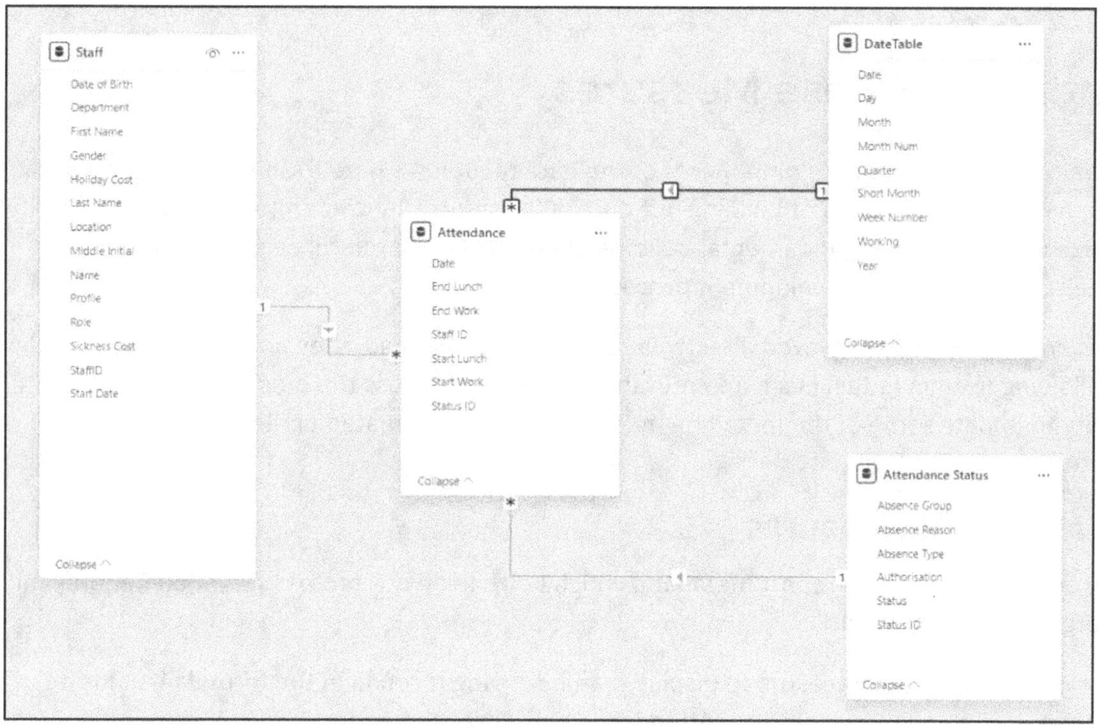

Saving the Model

With our data model complete, we are ready to start building visuals and calculations. The relationships we've defined ensure our analysis will be accurate, structured, and easy to maintain.

Be sure to save your Power BI file at this point, preserving the model setup.

In the next stage, we will begin defining a set of base measures—calculated values that serve as foundational blocks for further analysis, including metrics like total hours worked, number of absences, and average attendance.

Chapter 5: Attendance and Absence Report - DAX

5.1: Creating DAX Base Measures

Now that we've completed the static components of the data model, it's time to shift our focus to DAX. In this chapter, we begin the process of building out our DAX measures by creating a set of base measures. These will serve as the fundamental building blocks that we'll reference and build upon throughout the rest of the report development process.

Base measures are not typically displayed directly in report visuals. Instead, they underpin more complex calculations, allowing us to maintain clean and reusable expressions across the model. We'll also take this opportunity to update some of the metadata measures that were created earlier as part of the report template.

Updating Metadata Measures

We'll begin by editing our dynamic report metadata, which helps keep our reports self-documenting and aligned with organisational standards.

Click into the existing report title measure to display the underlying formula in the formula bar. Inside the double quotes, update the value to: Staff Attendance and Absence Report

For the Created By field, enter your name or the appropriate author.

For Data Owner, type: G Com Solutions Limited

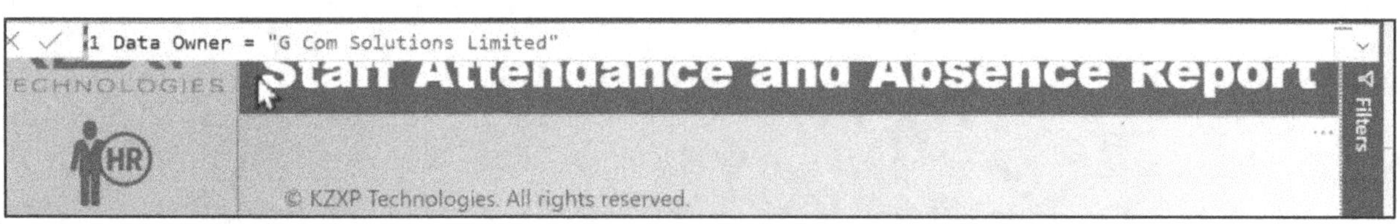

Enter your audience information in the Intended Audience measure.

That concludes the metadata update. With this in place, we can move on to our first base measure.

Total Attendance Days

Our attendance table is the main fact table in this report. Each row represents one attendance record—essentially one person on one day. A common and useful base measure is a simple count of rows in this table, which gives us the total number of attendance days recorded.

To create this measure:

1. Right-click on the Measures table in the Fields pane.
2. Select New Measure.
3. Enter the following formula:

Total Attendance Days =
COUNTROWS(Attendance)

Use Shift + Enter while writing DAX to format your code neatly across multiple lines (Excel's Alt + Enter shortcut also works). This is not only good practice but also improves readability, particularly in complex expressions.

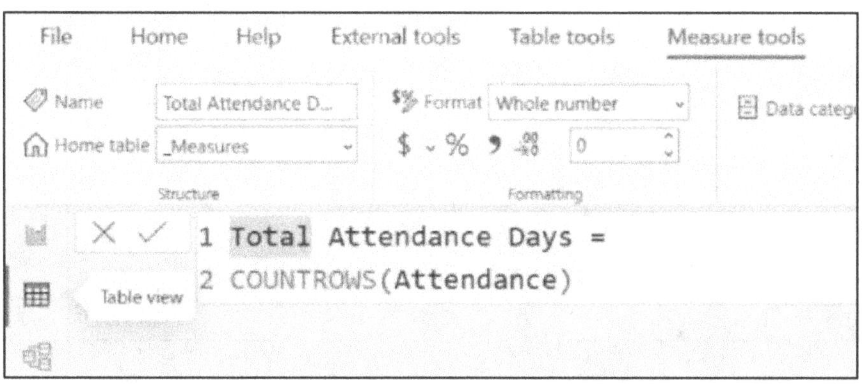

The COUNTROWS function is your go-to for counting rows in a table. It's more straightforward than COUNT and COUNTA which always require careful consideration of the column on which to focus. COUNTROWS is reliable, predictable, and doesn't care what types of values the columns hold—it simply returns the number of rows in the table.

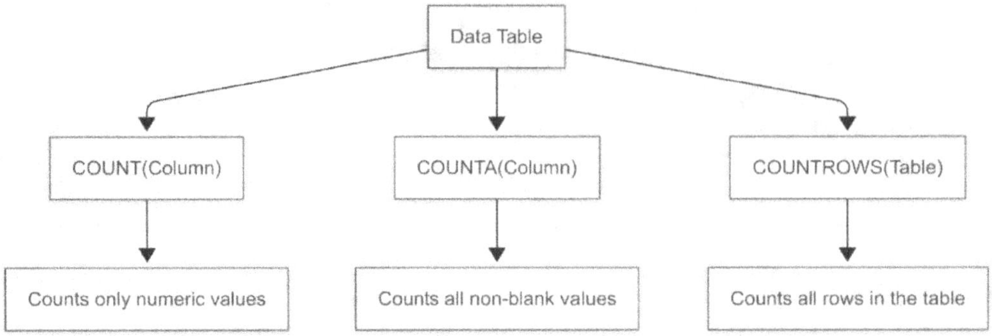

Once the measure is created, let's tidy things up by placing it into a Display Folder.

1. Switch to Model View.
2. Select the Total Attendance Days measure.
3. In the Properties pane, type Base Measures in the Display Folder field.

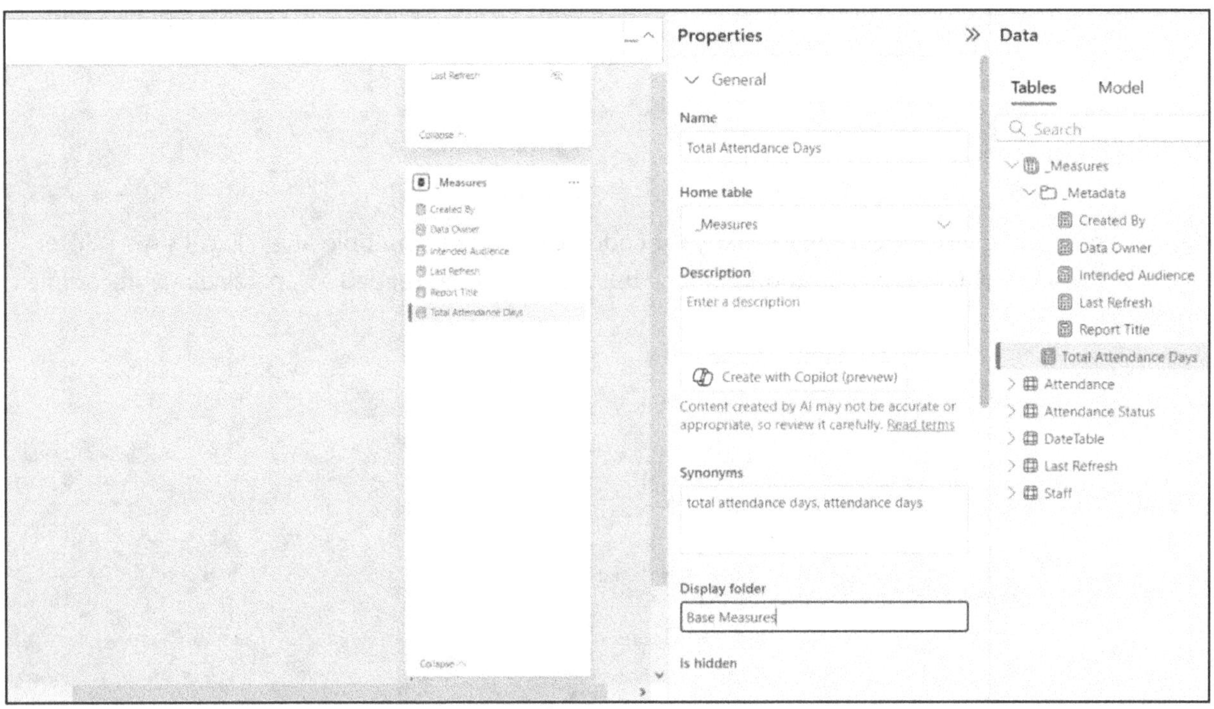

Next, we want to know how many unique staff members have attendance records. For this, we'll use the DISTINCTCOUNT function to count unique values in the staff ID column.

1. Right-click on the Base Measures folder.
2. Choose New Measure.
3. Enter the following formula:

Total Staff =
DISTINCTCOUNT('Attendance'[Staff ID])

The DISTINCTCOUNT function is ideal when you need to know how many different values exist in a column. It eliminates duplicates before counting, giving us an accurate count of individual staff members.

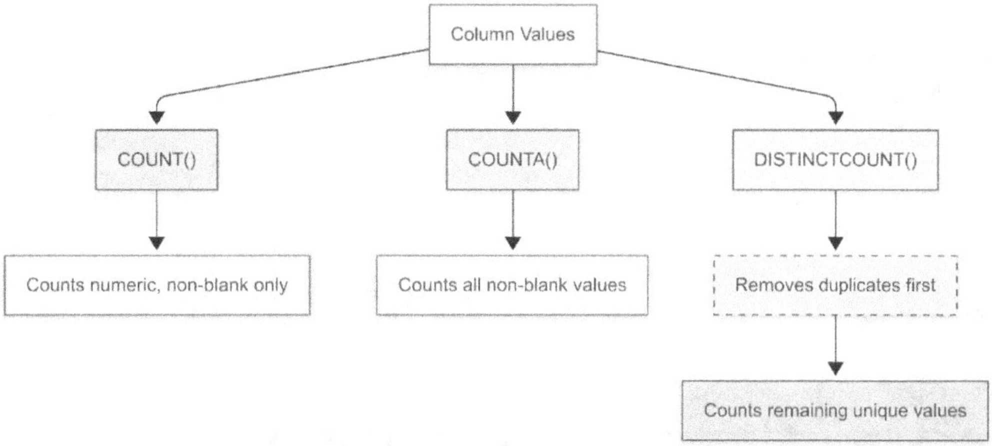

Average Start and End Times

Now let's capture the average start and end times. These are time-based values stored as decimals in Power BI. The number 1 represents a full 24-hour day. For example:

- 0.25 = 6 AM
- 0.50 = 12 PM (midday)
- 0.75 = 6 PM

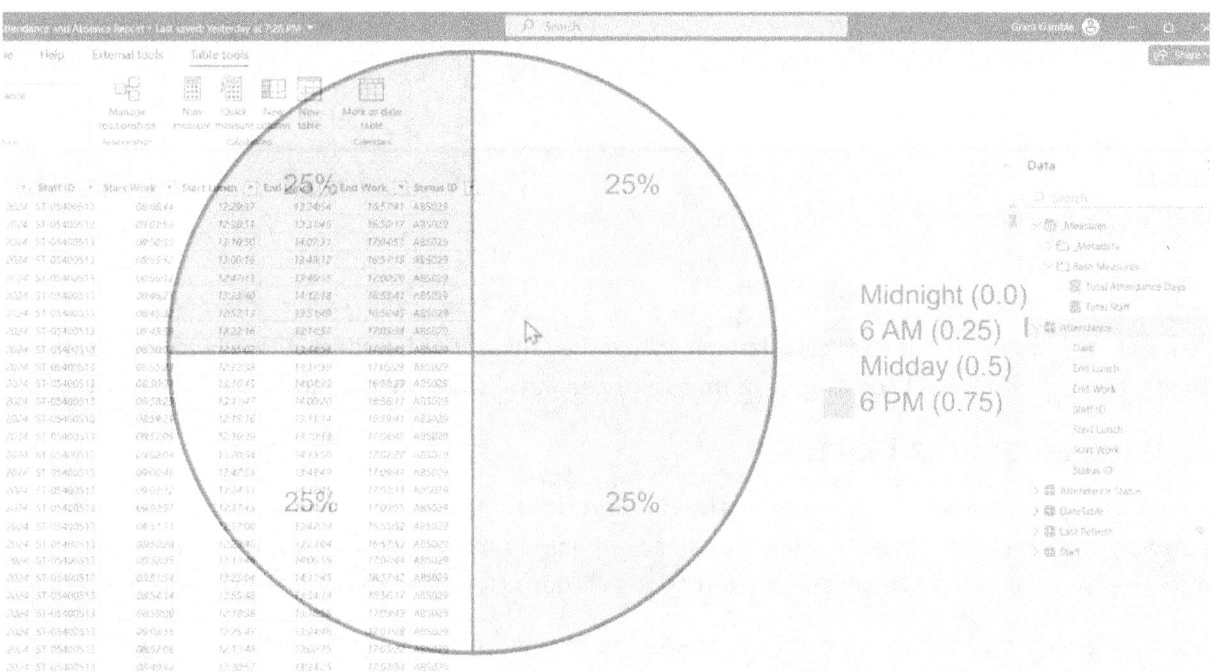

So, when we take averages of these fields, we're averaging decimal values. Later, we'll apply formatting to display these correctly as time values in visuals. For now, we just want the raw average numbers.

Start with the average start time:

1. Right-click on the Base Measures folder.
2. Choose New Measure.
3. Enter:

Average Start Time =

```
AVERAGE(
 'Attendance'[Start Work]
)
```

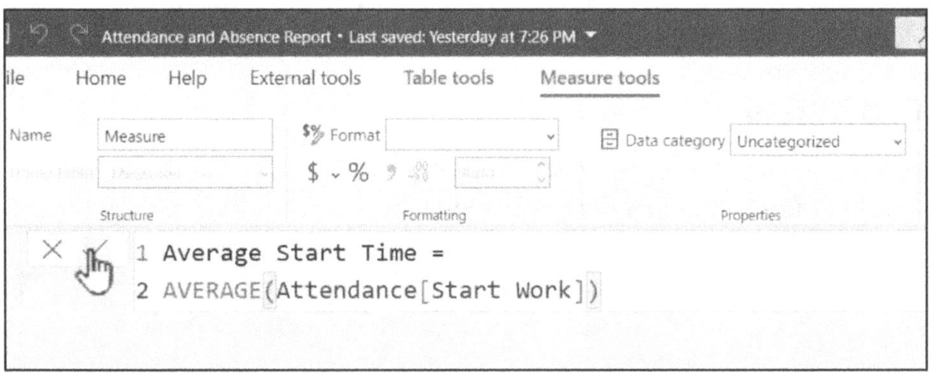

Then repeat for average leaving time:

```
Average Leaving Time =
AVERAGE(
 'Attendance'[End Work]
)
```

These measures round off our base calculations. While they might not be added directly to visuals, they are fundamental to how we'll construct summary and analytical views in later stages.

Why Base Measures Matter

Base measures play an essential role in structured report development. They reduce repetition, enforce consistency, and simplify troubleshooting. By using well-named base measures like the ones we've just created, we can compose more advanced expressions without cluttering them with low-level logic.

That completes our foundation layer of DAX. Make sure to save your changes now.

In the next section, we'll build on this foundation by introducing iterator functions—powerful tools that let us perform row-by-row calculations within a virtual table in memory. These will allow us to construct calculated aggregates that respond to context in dynamic ways.

5.2: Row Context Iteration Functions

In this chapter, we round off our foundational work by introducing two powerful DAX functions—AVERAGEX and SUMX. These are known as iterator functions, and they unlock more advanced logic than the basic aggregation functions we've used so far. While traditional aggregators like SUM or AVERAGE operate on entire columns at once, iterator functions take a row-by-row approach, allowing us to define custom logic for each row before aggregating the results. These functions can easily be identified since most of them end with an "X".

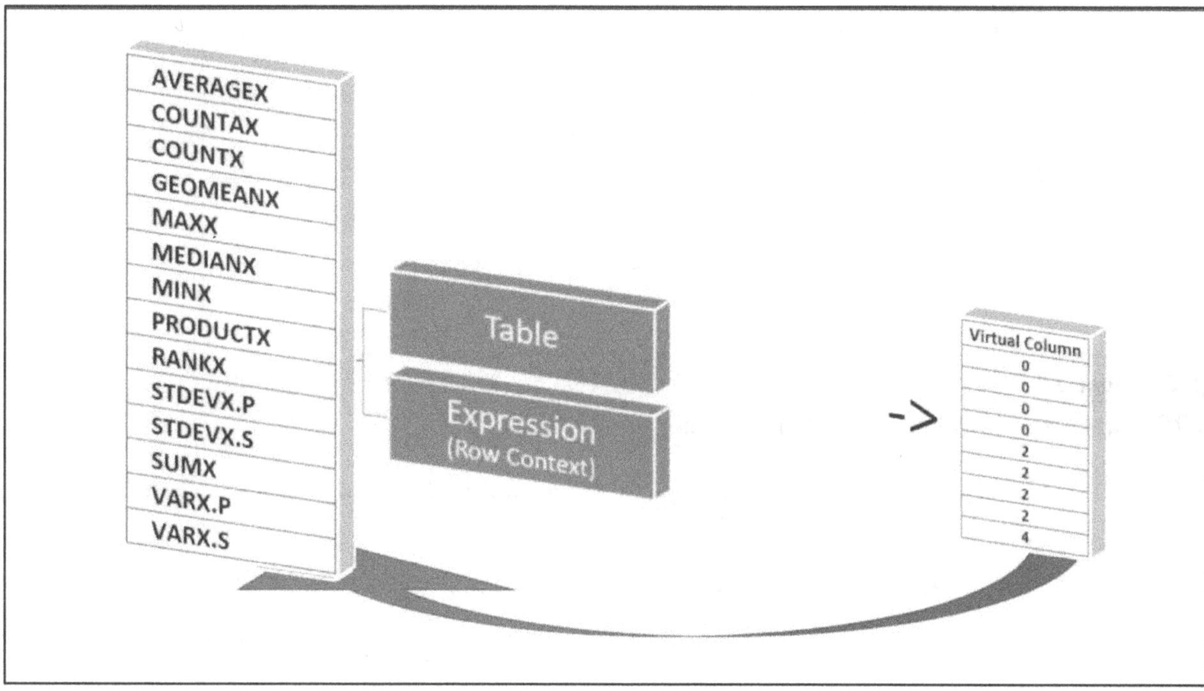

This is particularly useful in scenarios where the data we need to work with isn't represented directly in a single column, but must instead be derived from other values on a per-row basis. As we'll see, iterator functions are more flexible, often more efficient, and essential for crafting high-performance DAX measures.

Calculating Average Lunch Break with AVERAGEX

Let's begin by exploring the AVERAGEX function. Our goal here is to calculate the average lunch break duration for staff. If we examine the Attendance table, we'll see that it includes two relevant columns: Start Lunch and End Lunch. However, there's no column that tells us how long the lunch break actually lasted.

We can't simply average either of these columns—they are timestamps, not durations. What we really want is to compute the time difference between Start Lunch and End Lunch for each row, and then average those differences.

This type of calculation depends on something called row context. In DAX, row context means evaluating an expression for each row in a table individually, and then aggregating the results. To illustrate this, we'll start by creating a calculated column that explicitly performs the row-by-row operation.

The function we'll use to calculate the time difference is DATEDIFF. This versatile function allows us to calculate the difference between two date or time values in a unit of our choice—years, days, hours, minutes, or seconds.

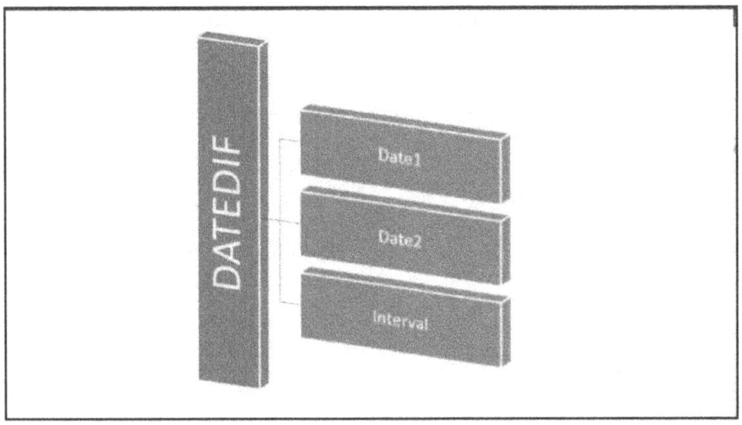

Lunch Duration =
DATEDIFF(Attendance[Start Lunch], Attendance[End Lunch], MINUTE)

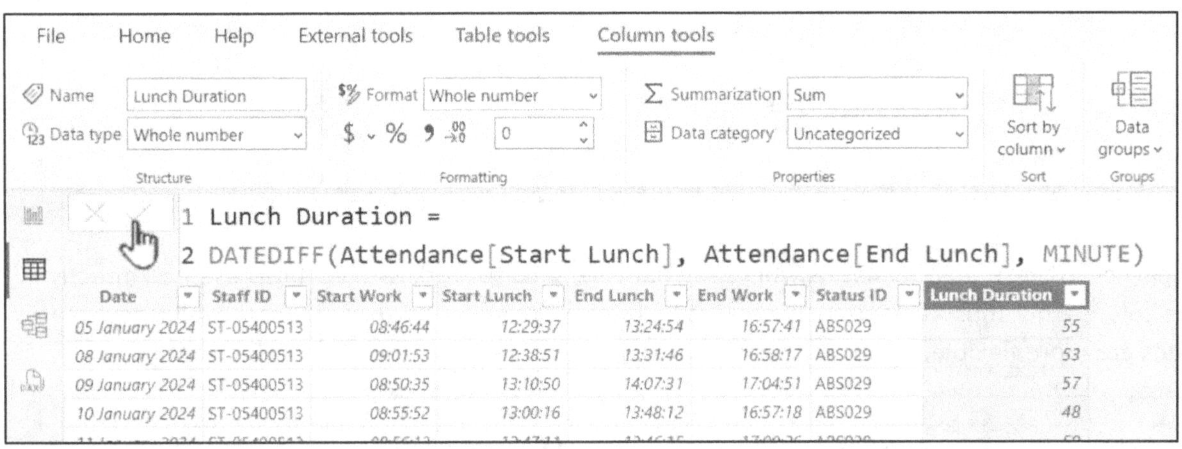

Although this calculated column works, it adds permanent weight to the data model. Every extra column increases memory usage, file size, and the chance of performance bottlenecks—especially when working with large datasets.

Instead of storing the calculated result for every row, we can use AVERAGEX to calculate the same values on the fly, in memory, as part of a measure. This avoids creating additional columns and keeps our model lean.

So, let's delete the calculated column and replace it with an equivalent measure.

```
Average Lunch Break =
AVERAGEX(
    Attendance,
    DATEDIFF(Attendance[Start Lunch], Attendance[End Lunch], MINUTE)
)
```

Here's what's happening: AVERAGEX takes two arguments. The first is the table to iterate over—Attendance. The second is the expression to evaluate for each row—in this case, the DATEDIFF between Start Lunch and End Lunch in minutes.

DAX evaluates this expression one row at a time, creating a virtual column of results. It then calculates the average of these values—all in memory, with no need to persist the intermediate results.

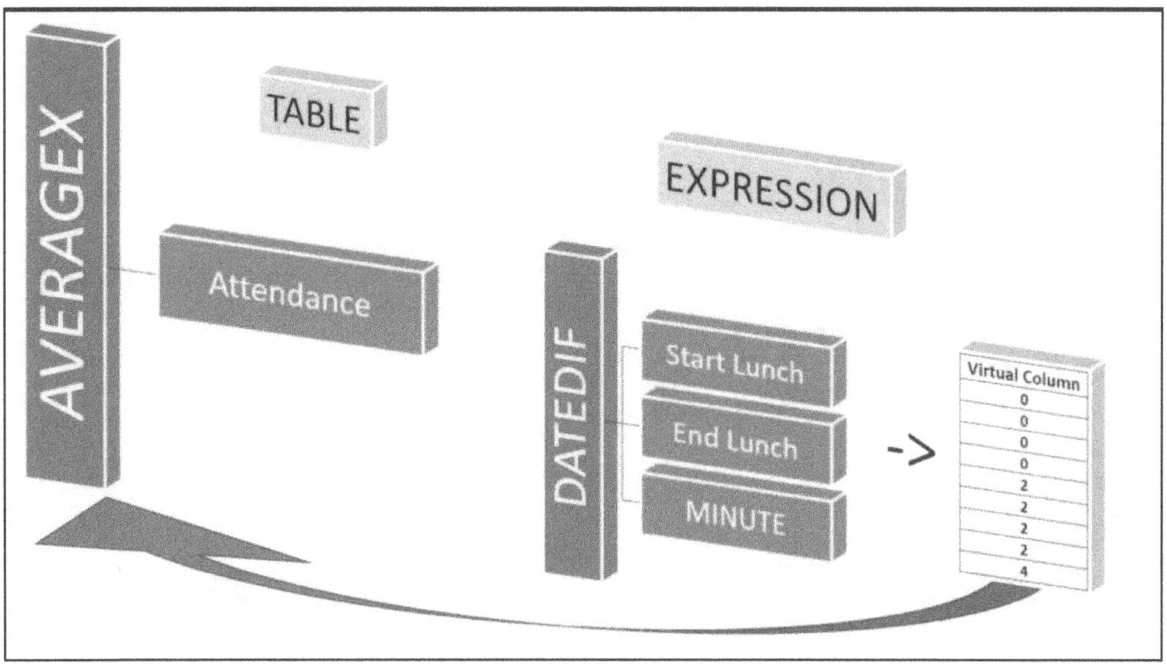

This approach is clean, efficient, and very typical of how we use iterator functions to extend the capabilities of our models.

Calculating Total Sickness Cost with SUMX

Next, we turn our attention to the SUMX function to calculate the total cost of sickness absences. At first glance, this might seem straightforward if we had a column listing the cost for each absence. But we don't.

The Staff table contains a field called Sickness Cost, representing the cost of one sickness absence for each staff member. The Attendance table holds the actual absence records. So, what we need is a measure that sums the sickness cost, but only for those rows in Attendance that actually record an absence.

To do this, we'll use SUMX to iterate over the Attendance table. For each row, we'll pull the sickness cost of the relevant staff member from the Staff table using the RELATED function.

The RELATED function is DAX's way of navigating from a row in a "many-side" table (like Attendance) to the corresponding value in a "one-side" table (like Staff), assuming a relationship exists. It's much more efficient than alternatives like LOOKUPVALUE, and it's perfect for this kind of row-wise association.

```
Total Sickness Cost =
SUMX(
    Attendance,
    RELATED(Staff[Sickness Cost])
)
```

Let's break that down. The first argument to SUMX is again the table to iterate—Attendance. For each row, DAX uses the RELATED function to fetch the sickness cost of the staff member linked to that row. These individual costs are then summed across all relevant rows.

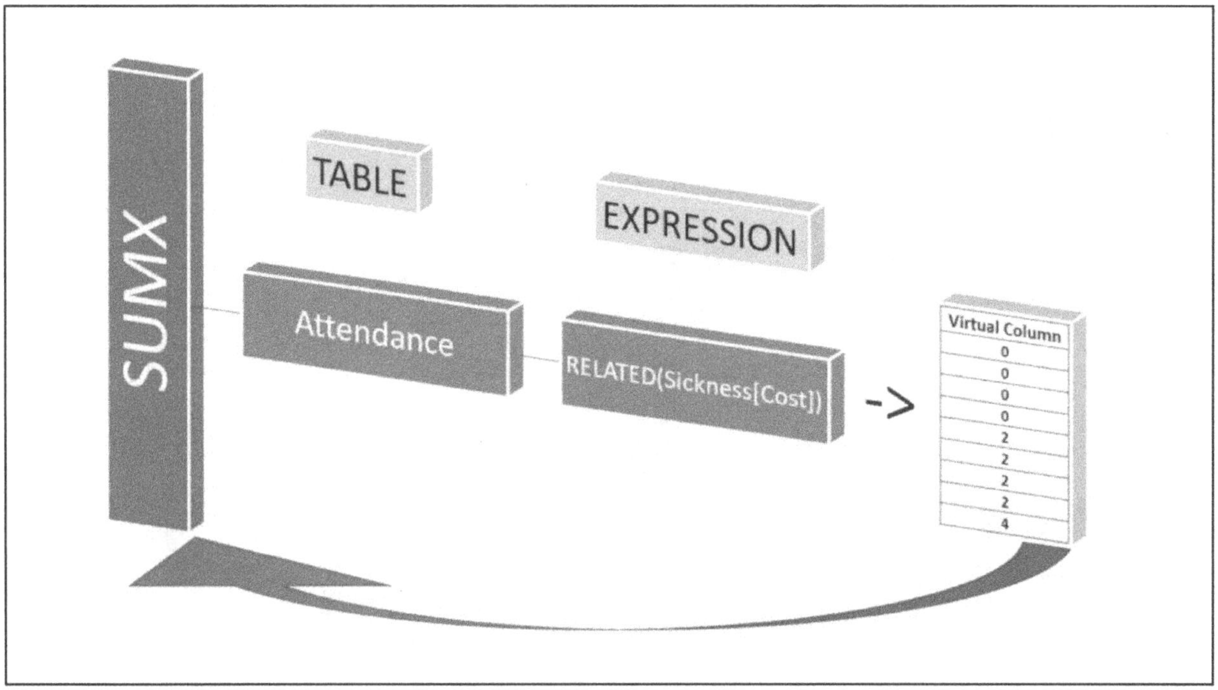

In effect, we are generating a virtual column where each row contains the sickness cost from the related staff member, and SUMX then totals that virtual column. Again, no physical column is created, and the calculation is both dynamic and memory-efficient.

Recap: Iteration and Efficiency

Both AVERAGEX and SUMX follow a two-step logic: iterate over a table, and apply an expression to each row. These expressions can include functions like DATEDIFF or RELATED to bring in values from other columns or tables. What's powerful here is that the resulting intermediate values live only for the duration of the calculation—they are not stored in your model, which keeps everything tidy and performant.

To summarise:

- Use AVERAGEX when you need to calculate an average based on a derived value per row.
- Use SUMX when summing values that are either calculated on the fly or pulled from another table using a relationship.
- Avoid creating extra columns unless they're absolutely needed for modelling logic or user interactivity.

With these two iterator functions in our toolkit, we've now completed our set of base measures. These foundational elements will prove essential in the next stage of development, where we begin building more targeted, filter-sensitive measures using DAX's most powerful function: CALCULATE.

Let's save our work here, and when ready, move on to the next section, where we shift focus from base aggregations to tailored, context-aware calculations.

5.3: Using the DAX CALCULATE Function

In this section, we turn our attention to CALCULATE, which is arguably the most powerful and most widely used function in all of DAX. This function forms the backbone of countless analytical expressions and is central to how data is manipulated in Power BI. Once mastered, CALCULATE will underpin almost every measure we create in our reports.

The purpose of CALCULATE is to take an existing measure and recalculate it in a different context. This is done by applying one or more filters which can come from any table in the model. The function is deceptively simple in appearance—on the surface, it just looks like it wraps a measure and applies a few filters. But under the hood, it completely rewrites the context in which your DAX expression runs. That shift in context fundamentally changes how your data is evaluated and the results it produces.

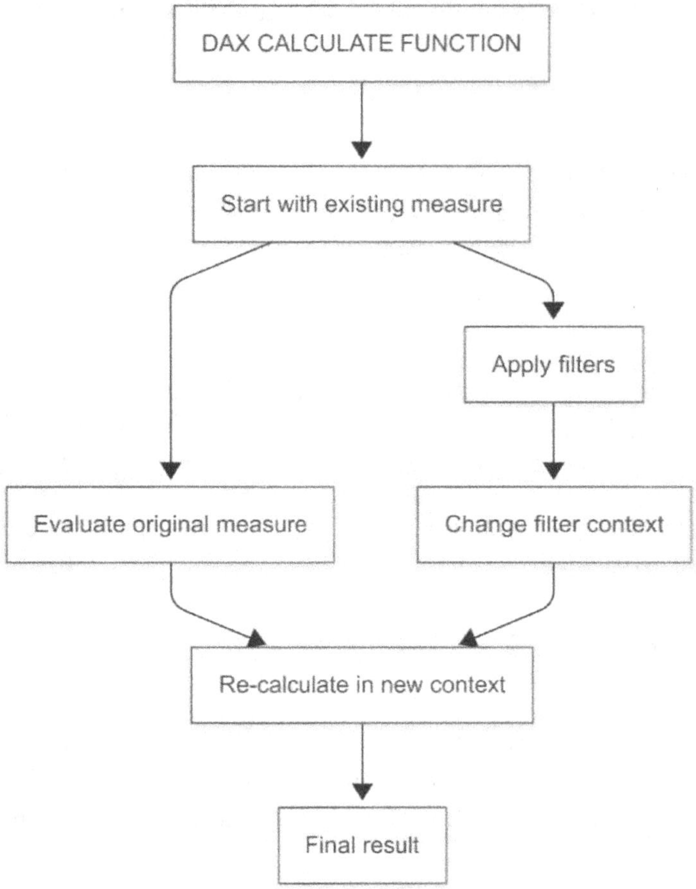

The CALCULATE function takes two types of arguments. First, the expression you want to evaluate—most often, this will be one of your existing measures, such as the base measures we've already created. Second, one or more filters that tell CALCULATE how to narrow down the dataset before performing the calculation.

The simplest kind of filter argument is a Boolean expression—any statement that can only result in TRUE or FALSE. This might be a column comparison such as "Is [Column A] greater than zero?" or "Does [Column B] equal a specific string?" As long as the condition returns true or false, it can be used to filter your calculation.

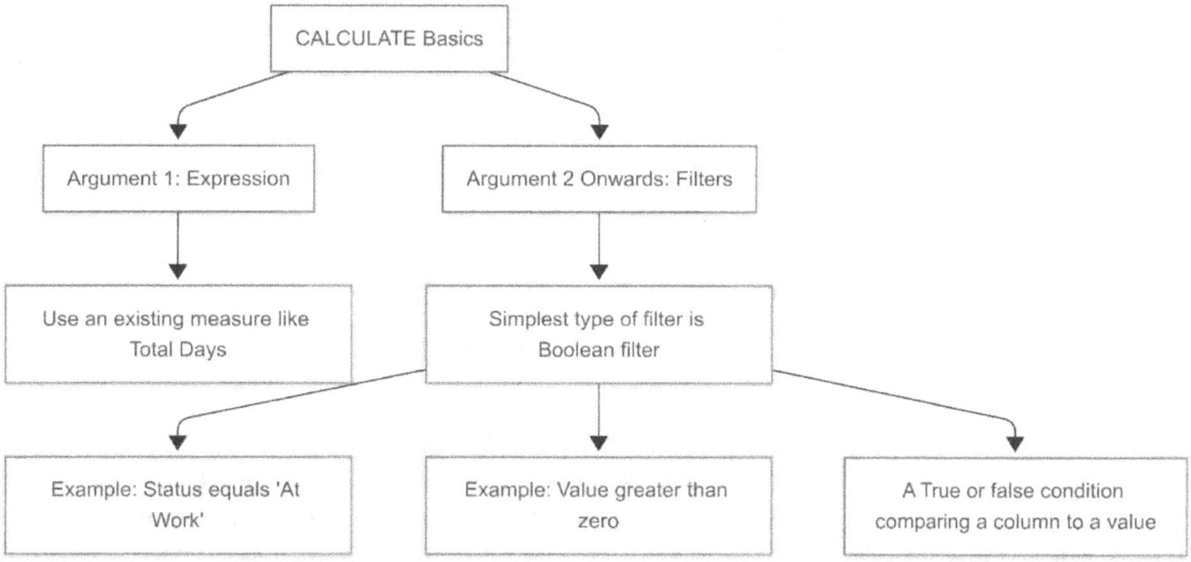

Total Working Days

Let's explore this with a practical example. We already have a measure called Total Attendance Days, which simply counts the rows in the Attendance table.

```
Total Attendance Days =
COUNTROWS(Attendance)
```

Now, we want a version of this that only counts days when someone was actually at work. To do this, we create a new measure using CALCULATE to apply a filter on the Attendance Status. Right-click on the Measures table and select New Measure. Then enter the following formula:

```
Total Working Days =
CALCULATE(
    [Total Attendance Days],
    'Attendance Status'[Status] = "At Work"
) + 0
```

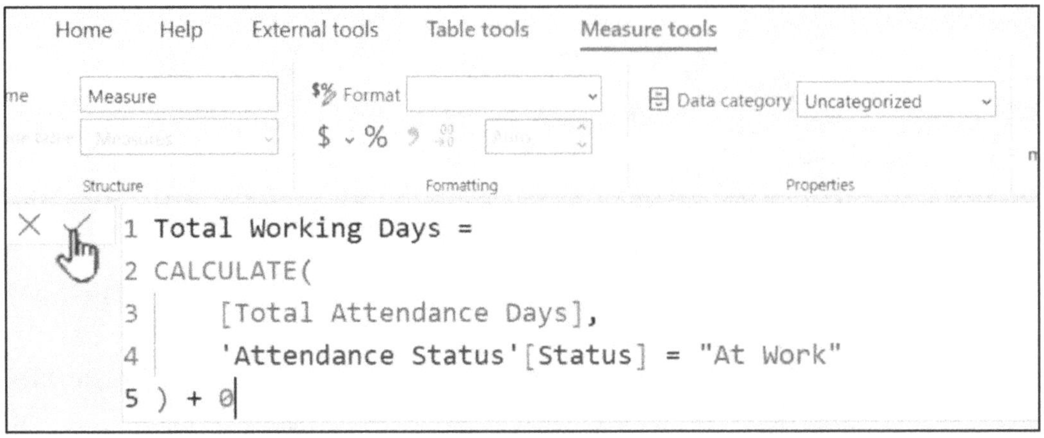

Here, we are recalculating the Total Attendance Days measure, but only for rows where the Attendance Status is "At Work". The + 0 at the end is a small trick to prevent blank values from being displayed. If no rows match the filter, the measure will return 0 instead of blank—this results in a cleaner output on visuals like cards and matrices.

Although the original count comes from the Attendance table, we are filtering a column from the Attendance Status table. This works because of the relationship between these two tables.

If we switch to Model View, we can see that the arrow on the relationship line flows from Attendance Status to Attendance. This means that filters applied to Attendance Status will automatically propagate to the Attendance table—an essential concept that allows CALCULATE to operate across related tables efficiently and with high performance.

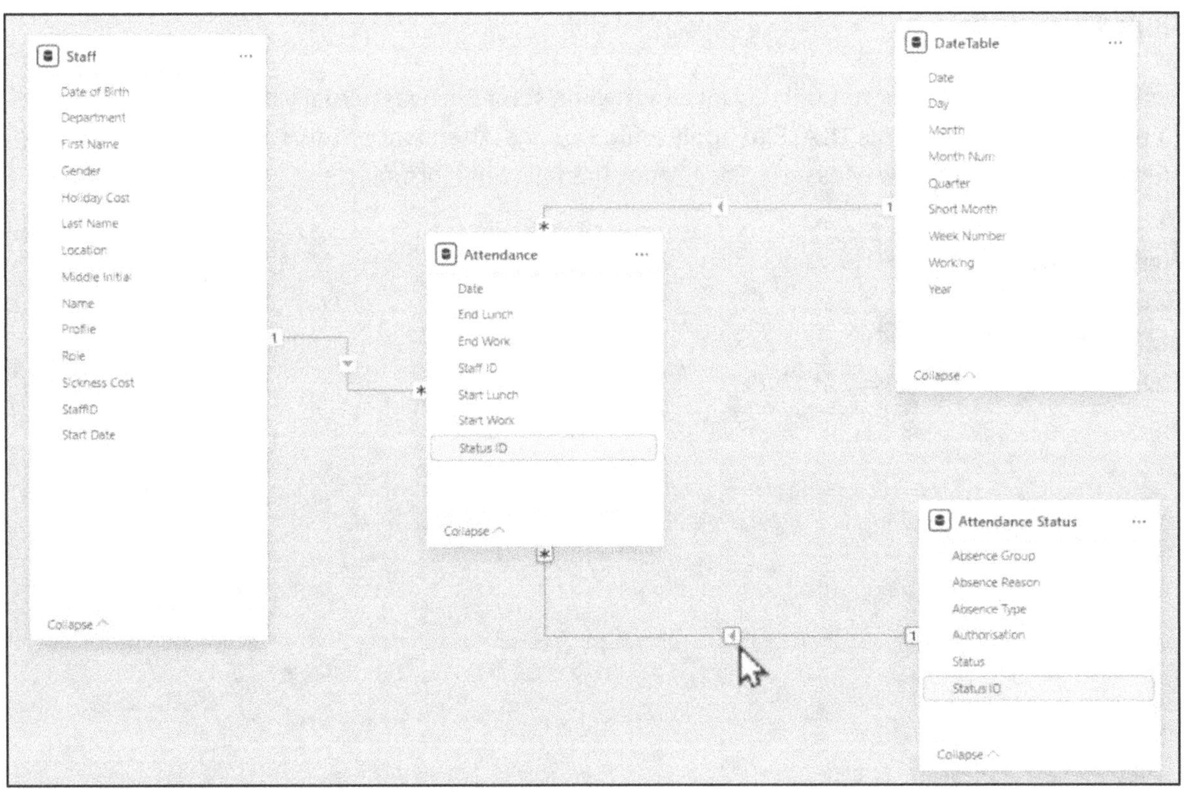

Before we create more measures using this technique, it's good practice to group them logically. So, as before, go to the Measures table, select the Total Working Days measure, open the Properties pane, and in the Display Folder field, type Context Measures.

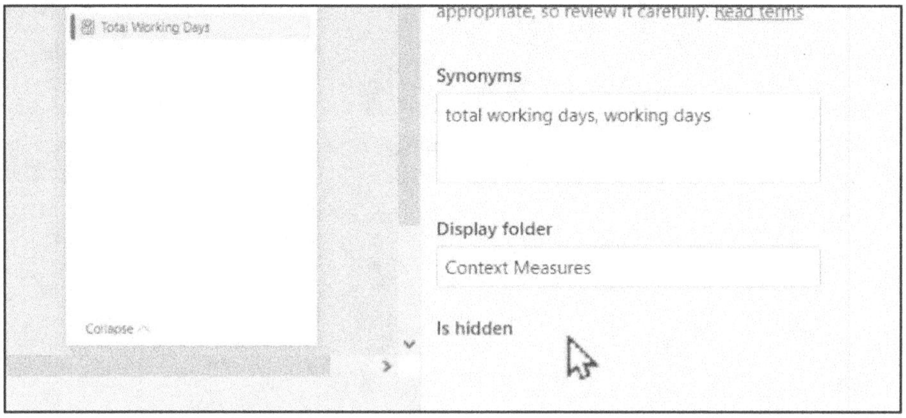

Total Vacation Days

Let's now create another measure using a similar pattern—this time to calculate the number of vacation days.

Switch to Table View to confirm the appropriate column. In this case, we'll use the Absence Type column from the Attendance Status table, and we want to include only rows where the absence type is "Holiday".

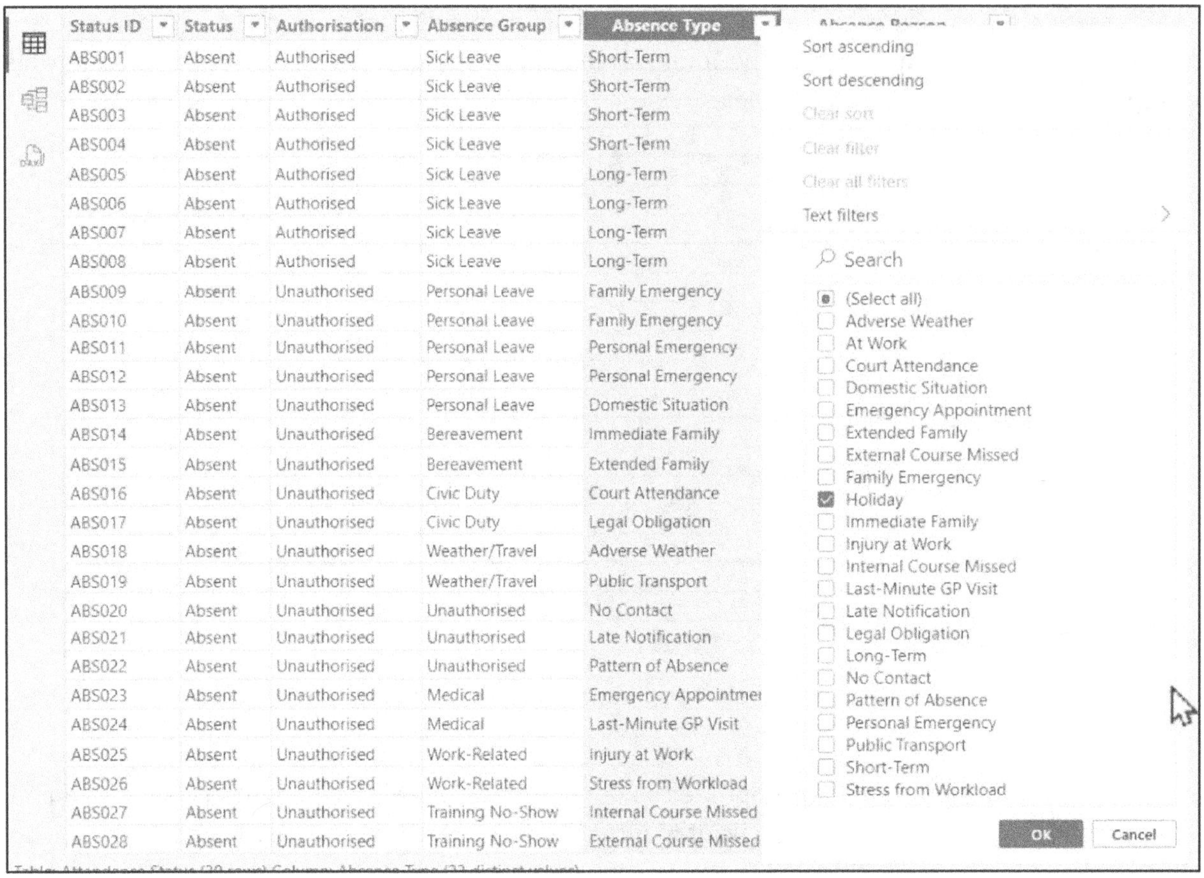

Status ID	Status	Authorisation	Absence Group	Absence Type
ABS001	Absent	Authorised	Sick Leave	Short-Term
ABS002	Absent	Authorised	Sick Leave	Short-Term
ABS003	Absent	Authorised	Sick Leave	Short-Term
ABS004	Absent	Authorised	Sick Leave	Short-Term
ABS005	Absent	Authorised	Sick Leave	Long-Term
ABS006	Absent	Authorised	Sick Leave	Long-Term
ABS007	Absent	Authorised	Sick Leave	Long-Term
ABS008	Absent	Authorised	Sick Leave	Long-Term
ABS009	Absent	Unauthorised	Personal Leave	Family Emergency
ABS010	Absent	Unauthorised	Personal Leave	Family Emergency
ABS011	Absent	Unauthorised	Personal Leave	Personal Emergency
ABS012	Absent	Unauthorised	Personal Leave	Personal Emergency
ABS013	Absent	Unauthorised	Personal Leave	Domestic Situation
ABS014	Absent	Unauthorised	Bereavement	Immediate Family
ABS015	Absent	Unauthorised	Bereavement	Extended Family
ABS016	Absent	Unauthorised	Civic Duty	Court Attendance
ABS017	Absent	Unauthorised	Civic Duty	Legal Obligation
ABS018	Absent	Unauthorised	Weather/Travel	Adverse Weather
ABS019	Absent	Unauthorised	Weather/Travel	Public Transport
ABS020	Absent	Unauthorised	Unauthorised	No Contact
ABS021	Absent	Unauthorised	Unauthorised	Late Notification
ABS022	Absent	Unauthorised	Unauthorised	Pattern of Absence
ABS023	Absent	Unauthorised	Medical	Emergency Appointme
ABS024	Absent	Unauthorised	Medical	Last-Minute GP Visit
ABS025	Absent	Unauthorised	Work-Related	Injury at Work
ABS026	Absent	Unauthorised	Work-Related	Stress from Workload
ABS027	Absent	Unauthorised	Training No-Show	Internal Course Missed
ABS028	Absent	Unauthorised	Training No-Show	External Course Missed

Right-click on the Context Measures table and choose New Measure, then enter the following formula:

```
Total Vacation Days =
CALCULATE(
    [Total Attendance Days],
    'Attendance Status'[Absence Type] = "Holiday"
) + 0
```

Total Absence Days

Next, we'll create a measure that calculates Total Absence Days, but this one will use a composite condition—meaning we'll filter using more than one clause.

We want to count only those rows where the person was absent for reasons other than "Paid Leave" or "At Work". That means excluding both of those categories using two NOT EQUAL TO filters.

Right-click on Context Measures, select New Measure, and enter:

```
Total Absence Days =
CALCULATE(
    [Total Attendance Days],
    'Attendance Status'[Absence Group] < > "Paid Leave" &&
    'Attendance Status'[Absence Group] < > "At Work"
) + 0
```

```
CALCULATE(
    [Total Sickness Cost],
    'Attendance Status'[Absence Group] <> "Paid Leave" && 'Attendance Status'[Absence Group] <> "At Work"
)
```

You might be wondering why we're not using the AND() function like you would in Excel. In DAX, the AND() function is more limited. It only works on logical values, and it doesn't support chaining multiple conditions as neatly as && does. That's why the double ampersand operator is the preferred method—it's cleaner, simpler, and often more efficient.

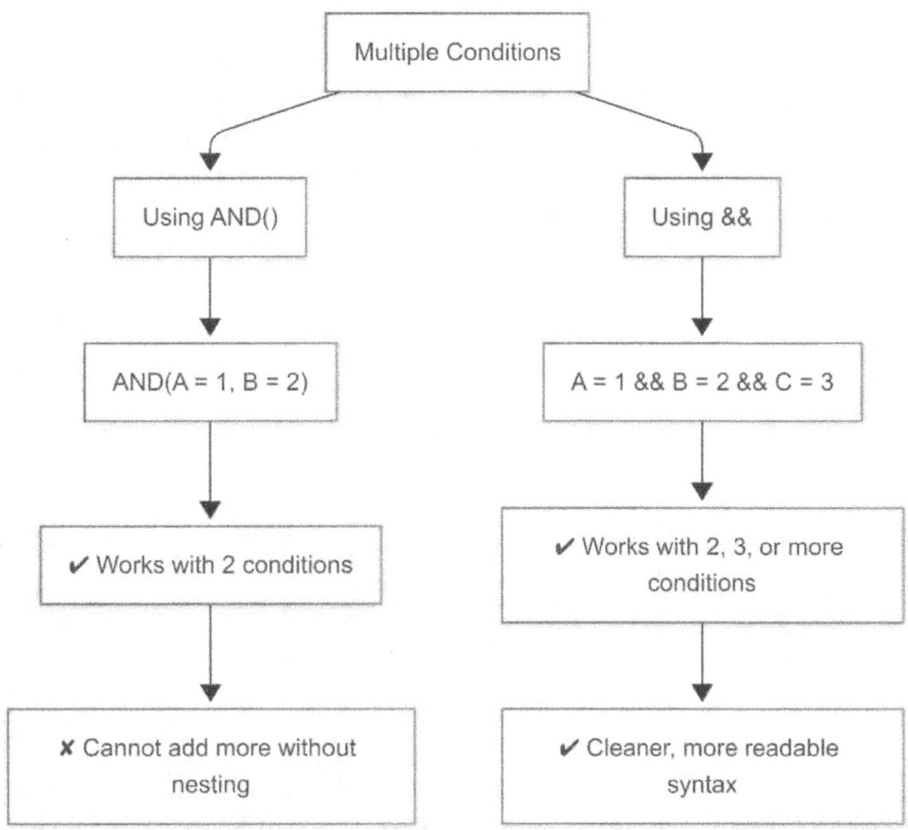

Total Absence Cost

Our next measure is Total Absence Cost. Since it uses the same filtering logic as Total Absence Days, we can simply duplicate the previous formula and make small adjustments.

Right-click Context Measures, choose New Measure, and paste the formula, then adjust as follows:

Total Absence Cost =
CALCULATE(
[Total Sickness Cost],
'Attendance Status'[Absence Group] < > "Paid Leave" &&
'Attendance Status'[Absence Group] < > "At Work"
)

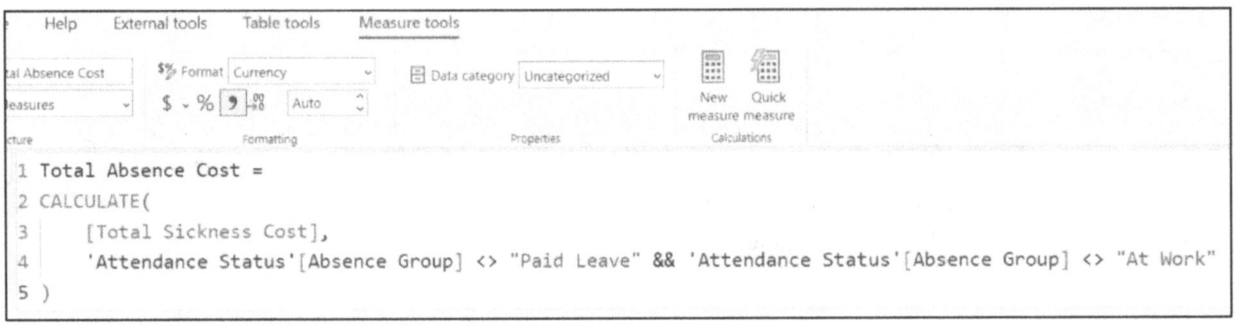

Notice we've removed the + 0 at the end. That's intentional. This measure will be used in a line chart showing absence cost over time. When there's no data, we prefer the measure to return blank rather than zero (since blanks are not plotted while zeros are)—this prevents the chart from showing flat lines on days with no activity, giving a smoother trend.

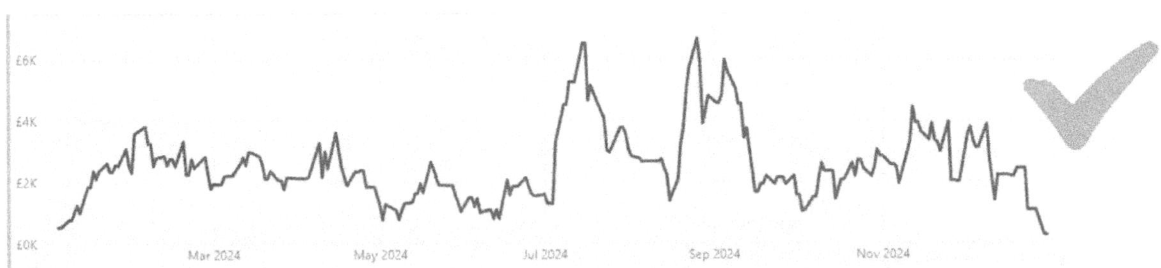

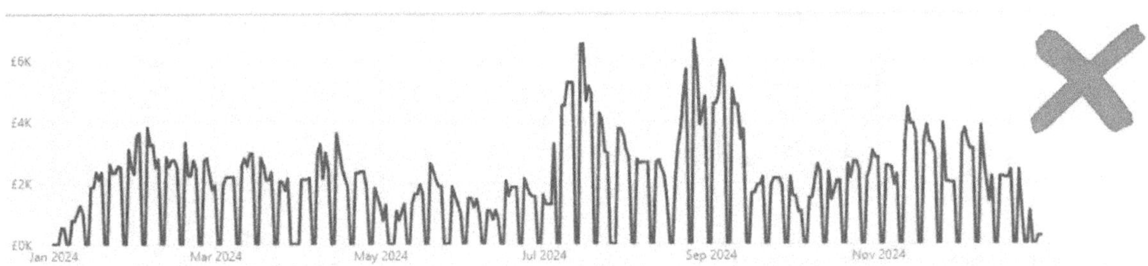

Late Arrival Count

The final measure we'll create in this group is Late Arrival Count. This time, we're filtering based on time. Specifically, we want to count how many times someone started work after 9:05 AM.

Right-click on the Context Measures folder and select New Measure, then enter the following:

```
Late Arrival Count =
CALCULATE(
    [Total Attendance Days],
    'Attendance'[Start Work] > TIME(9,5,0)
) + 0
```

Here, we're using the TIME function to create a specific time value—9:05 AM in this case. The filter then checks whether the Start Work time is later than that. Again, we end with + 0 to replace blanks with zero.

Early Leaving Count

We also need a measure for early leaving count.

Let's create it now by copying the formula from Late Arrival Count and modifying the logic.

In Late Arrival Count, we filtered for rows where StartWork was after 9:05 AM. For early leaving, we want rows where EndWork is before 4:55 PM.

So, we create a new measure in the Context Measures folder and update it accordingly.

```
Early Leaving Count =
CALCULATE(
    COUNTROWS('Attendance'),
    'Attendance'[EndWork] < TIME(16, 55, 0)
)
```

With that, we've completed our suite of context-sensitive measures using the CALCULATE function. These measures form a key part of any analytical model in Power BI, allowing you to slice and re-evaluate data dynamically, depending on the logic you need.

Save your changes, and in the next section, we'll look at rate-based measures—turning raw counts into meaningful percentages and ratios.

5.4: Creating Rate-Based Measures

In this section, we're going to create a set of rate-based measures such as absence rate, attendance rate, late arrival percentage, and early leaving percentage. These measures are essential for any HR or workforce report and will typically be displayed as percentages. They are derived by dividing one measure by another—leveraging the base and context measures we've already built. That's why these are saved until now: they don't introduce new logic but instead combine existing components.

All the measures in this section will be formatted as percentages, but remember—they're fundamentally ratios: one value divided by another. To do this safely and cleanly, we'll use the DIVIDE function. This function not only performs division but also avoids awkward visual errors when the denominator is zero or missing.

Using the DIVIDE Function

The DIVIDE function takes up to three arguments:

1. Numerator – the value to divide (the top of the fraction).
2. Denominator – the value to divide by (the bottom of the fraction).
3. Alternate result – an optional value returned if division isn't possible (e.g., division by zero).

If you leave out the third argument, Power BI will return a blank instead of throwing an error. But if you want to be explicit, you can supply a fallback value like zero.

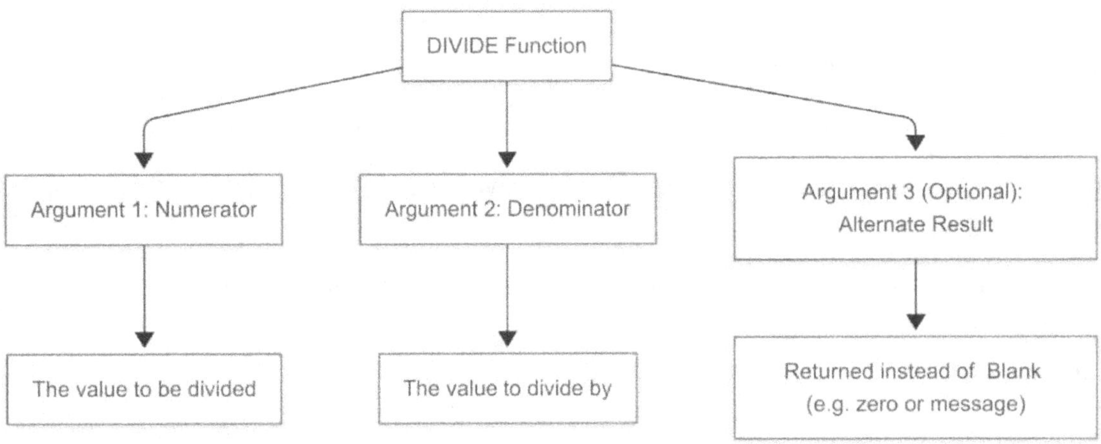

Late Arrival Percentage

Our first rate-based measure is the Late Arrival Percentage. This will appear in a card visual on the Executive Summary page.

We already have the components needed:

- A measure called Late Arrival Count (in the Context Measures folder), which counts days when someone clocked in late.
- A measure called Total Attendance Days (in the Base Measures folder), which is a total count of attendance records—one row per person per day.

We simply divide late arrivals by total attendance days.

```
Late Arrival Percentage =
DIVIDE(
    [Late Arrival Count],
     [Total Attendance Days],
    0
)
```

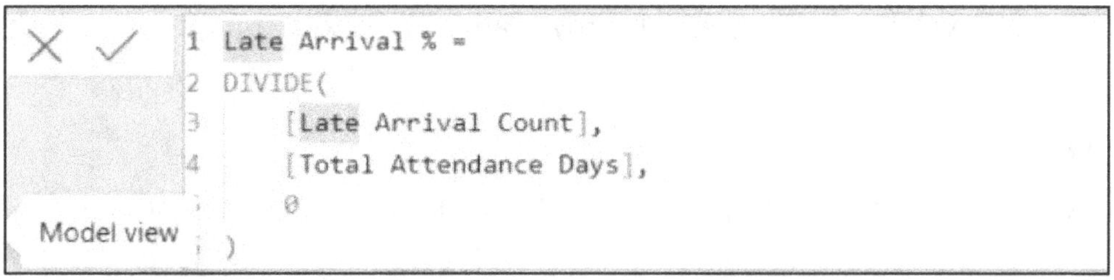

Create this measure by right-clicking on your main Measures table, selecting New Measure, and entering the formula above.

Then, in the Model View, with the new measure selected, look over to the Properties pane. In the Display Folder box, type: Rate Based Measures. This helps us group all similar measures together.

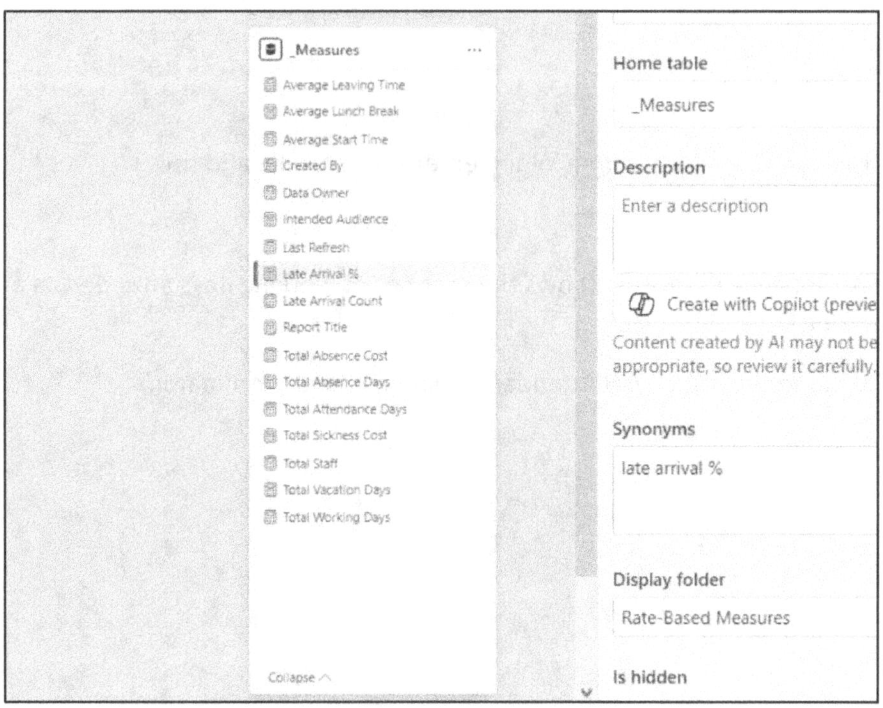

Early Leaving Percentage

Once created, we can now define the Early Leaving percentage measure.

```
Early Leaving Percentage =
DIVIDE(
    [Early Leaving Count],
    [Total Working Days],
 0
)
```

This will show the proportion of days where employees left early relative to the total number of working days.

Absence Rate (%)

Our next metric is the Absence Rate. This one will appear in a matrix visual on the Staff Absence report page.

This is calculated by dividing Total Absence Days by Total Attendance Days.

```
Absence Rate (%) =
DIVIDE(
 [Total Absence Days],
 [Total Attendance Days],
 0
)
```

Again, use New Measure within the Rate Based Measures folder, enter the formula, and save.

Attendance Rate (%)

Lastly, let's create a measure for Attendance Rate. This shows the number of working days attended as a proportion of total scheduled working days.

We use Total Working Days as the numerator and Total Attendance Days as the denominator.

```
Attendance Rate (%) =
DIVIDE(
 [Total Working Days],
 [Total Attendance Days],
 0
)
```

As with the others, create this using New Measure, and place it in the Rate Based Measures folder.

Formatting the Measures as Percentages

Once all the rate-based measures are created, we need to ensure they are properly formatted as percentages. The most efficient way is to format them all at once in Model View.

Hold down the Control key and select each of the new percentage measures in the fields pane. Then, in the Properties pane:

1. Set the Format to Percentage.
2. Set Decimal Places to 1 for a clean and consistent appearance.

This ensures all measures appear correctly in visuals—crisp, meaningful, and easy to interpret.

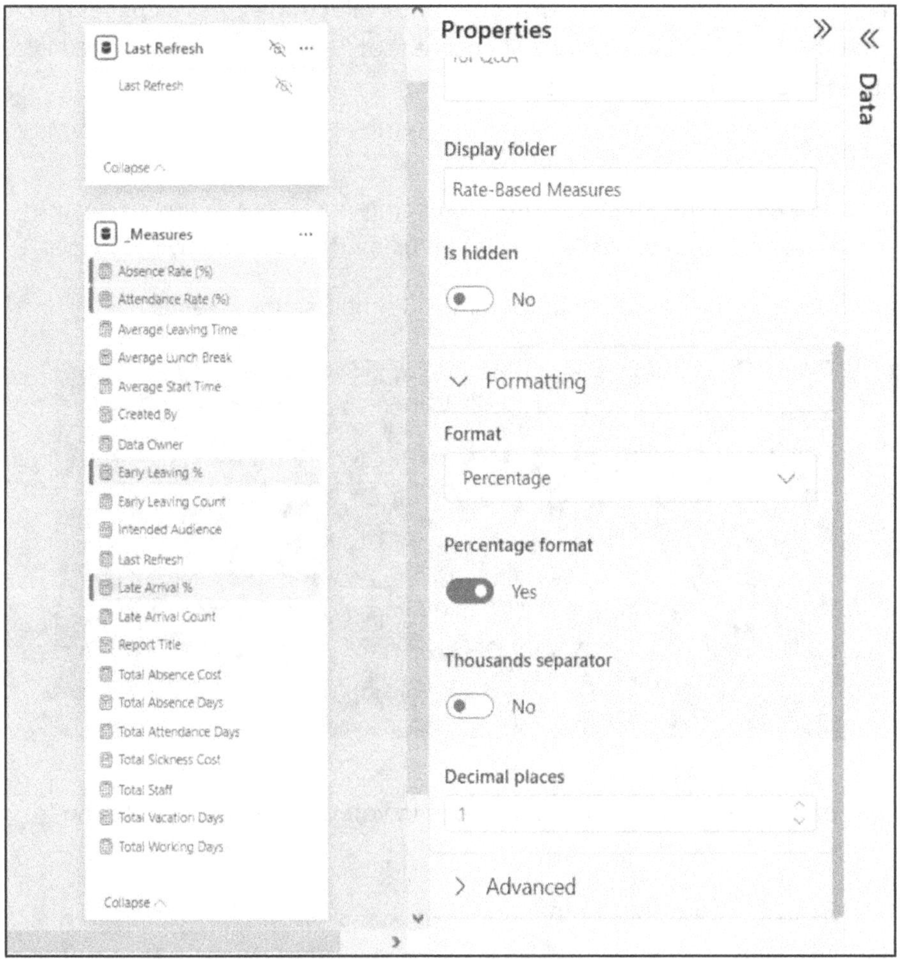

With these calculations in place, we now have a strong set of rate-based performance indicators. These can be reused across pages, visuals, and filtered contexts without any additional logic or rewriting.

Let's save our changes, and in the next part of the report build, we'll move on to visualisation—starting with creating a date slicer that synchronises across all five report pages.

Chapter 6: Attendance and Absence Report - Visualization

6.1: Creating a Synchronized Date Slicer

In this chapter, we'll build a synchronized month slicer using Power BI's button slicer visual. This slicer will appear at the top of each report page and reflect a consistent month selection across all pages. For example, selecting "April" while on the Executive Summary will ensure that "April" remains selected when navigating to pages like Absence Cost or Staff Attendance.

Renaming Pages for Clarity

Before building the slicer, it's helpful to assign meaningful names to each report page. Doing so ensures clearer navigation and improves the user experience, especially when using the built-in navigation bar.

You'll find a suggested list of page names in the "Assets" subfolder inside the Section 4 folder.

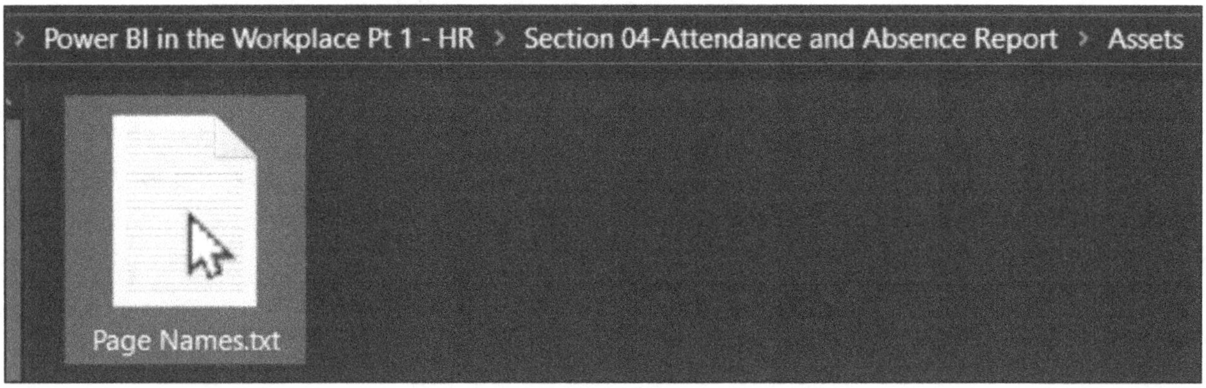

Open that file and copy the names one by one. Then, go to each page in your report and update the name using these steps:

1. Double-click the tab of the report page you want to rename.
2. Press Ctrl + A to select the current name.
3. Press Ctrl + V to paste the new name.
4. Press Enter to confirm.

Apply these names:

- Executive Summary
- Staff Absence
- Staff Attendance
- Absence Types
- Absence Cost

As you rename each page, you'll notice the updated names appear instantly in the navigation bar across all pages, reflecting the new structure.

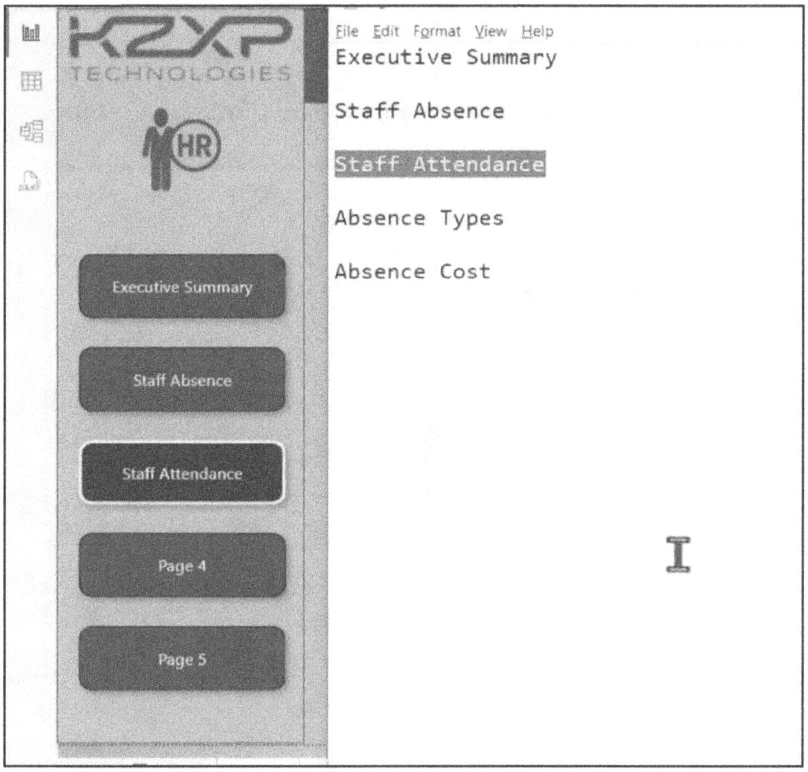

Creating the Button Slicer on the Executive Summary Page

Navigate back to the Executive Summary page to create the date slicer. For this implementation, we'll use the button slicer visual, not the standard slicer.

The button slicer offers superior aesthetics and interaction by supporting four visual states—Default, Hover, Pressed, and Selected—which gives your report a polished look.

We will base the slicer on the "Short Month" field from the Date table. This field displays months using their three-letter abbreviation (Jan, Feb, etc.).

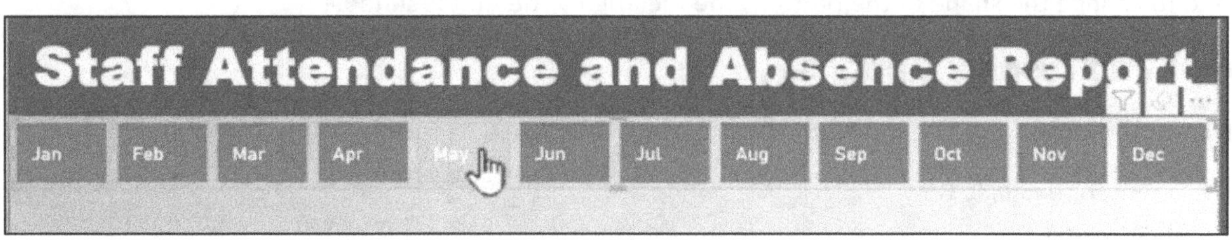

Correcting the Sort Order of Months

By default, Power BI sorts text fields alphabetically. That's not suitable for months, as "Apr" might come before "Feb". To apply a custom order:

Our Date table contains a numeric column representing the month's order, called Month Num.

1. Select the "Short Month" column.
2. Go to the Column tools tab on the ribbon.
3. Click Sort by Column and choose the Month Num column.

This ensures that months display in their correct chronological order from January through December.

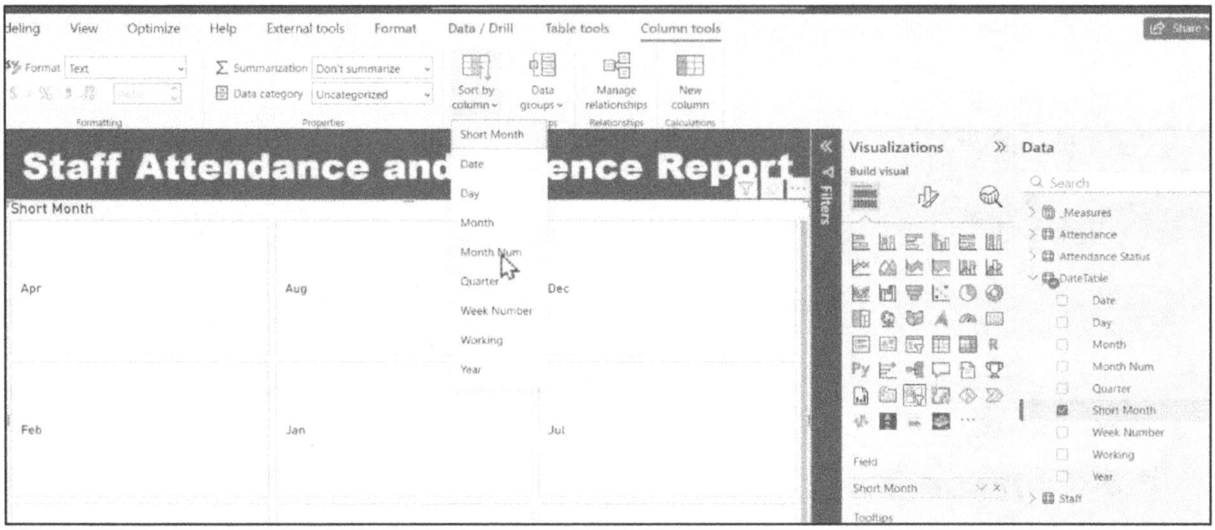

Formatting the Button Slicer

Now that the slicer displays months correctly, let's format it. Select the slicer visual and click the Format tab (paintbrush icon) in the Visualizations pane.

General Formatting

Under the General section:

- Turn off the Title—it's not necessary.
- Turn off the Background—this will allow the buttons to appear seamlessly over the report background.

No need to change the shape of the buttons; the rectangular default is suitable.

Layout and Display Options

Navigate to the Layout section and apply the following settings:

- Orientation: Single Row
- Style: Cards
- Maximum Buttons: 12 (to represent each month)

- You can now resize the height of the visual to fit a single row. The slicer will display all 12 months in button format.

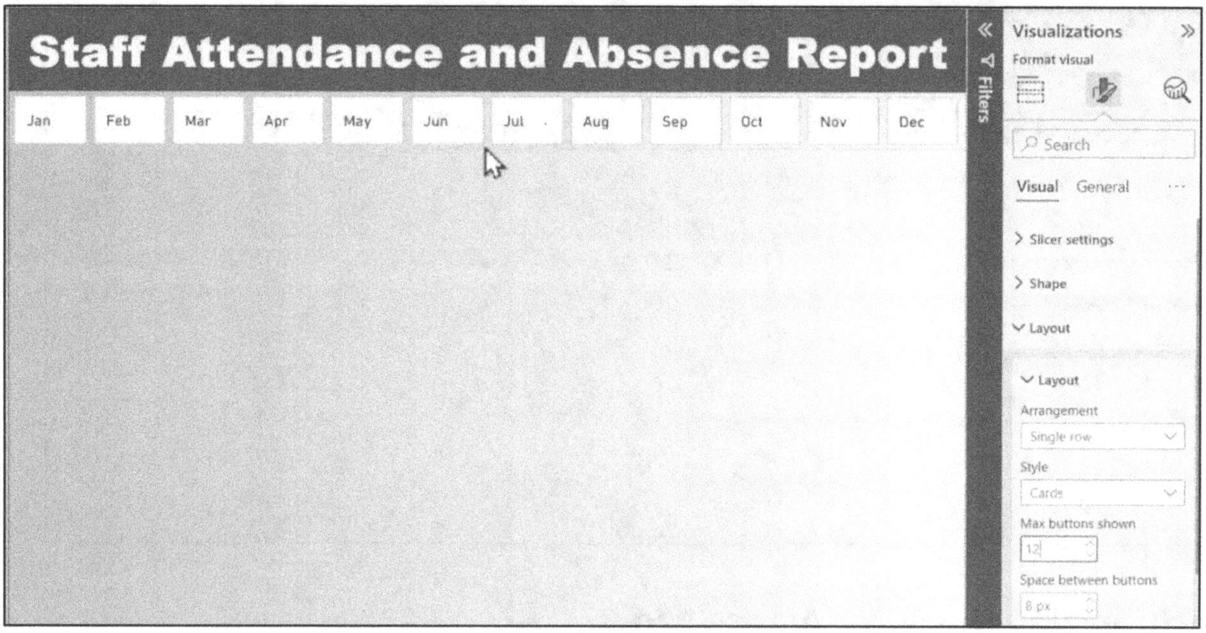

Styling the Button States

Let's now improve the aesthetics of the buttons to better match your report theme.

Under Callout Values, which controls the text on the buttons:

1. For the Default state: set text colour to white.
2. Under Buttons, for the Default state: set fill colour to your theme's blue.

For the Hover state:

1. Under Callout Values: set text colour to a dark theme blue.
2. Under Buttons: verify that the hover fill becomes white for contrast.

For the Pressed state:

1. Under Callout Values: leave the text colour unchanged.
2. Under Buttons: change the fill colour from grey to a light theme blue.

Finally, for the Selected state, the default is white text on a black background. This is visually strong and does not require changes.

With all four button states styled, your slicer now has both functionality and visual appeal.

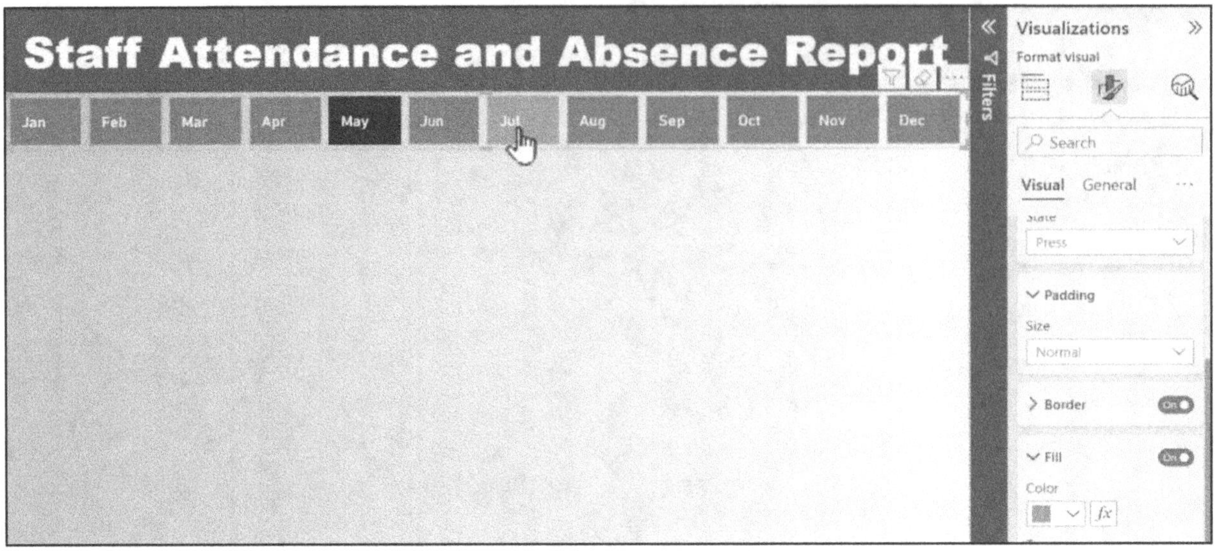

Synchronizing the Slicer Across Pages

With the slicer created and formatted on the Executive Summary page, the final step is to synchronize it across all report pages. This ensures that the selected month remains consistent as users navigate the report.

Method 1: Copy and Paste

This is the simplest method.

1. Click the slicer on the Executive Summary page.
2. Go to the Home tab and select Copy.
3. Navigate to another page, e.g., Staff Absence, and paste the slicer.
4. Power BI will display a prompt asking if you want to sync the slicer—click Sync.

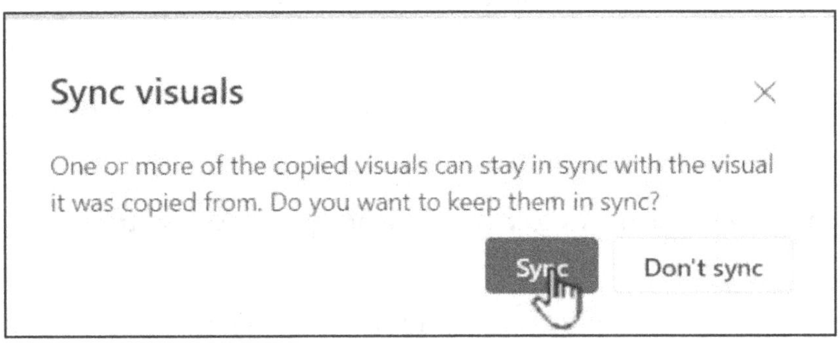

Method 2: Sync Slicers Pane (Recommended)

This method offers more control and allows you to configure synchronization settings:

1. Go to the View tab and click Sync slicers.
2. This opens the Sync Slicers pane. (Note: the pane appears blank unless a slicer is selected.)
3. Click on your slicer to activate it in the pane.
4. You'll see each page listed with checkboxes for Sync and Visible.

5. Ensure both boxes are ticked for all report pages except the Start page.

Once done, the slicer will remain visible and synchronized across your report.

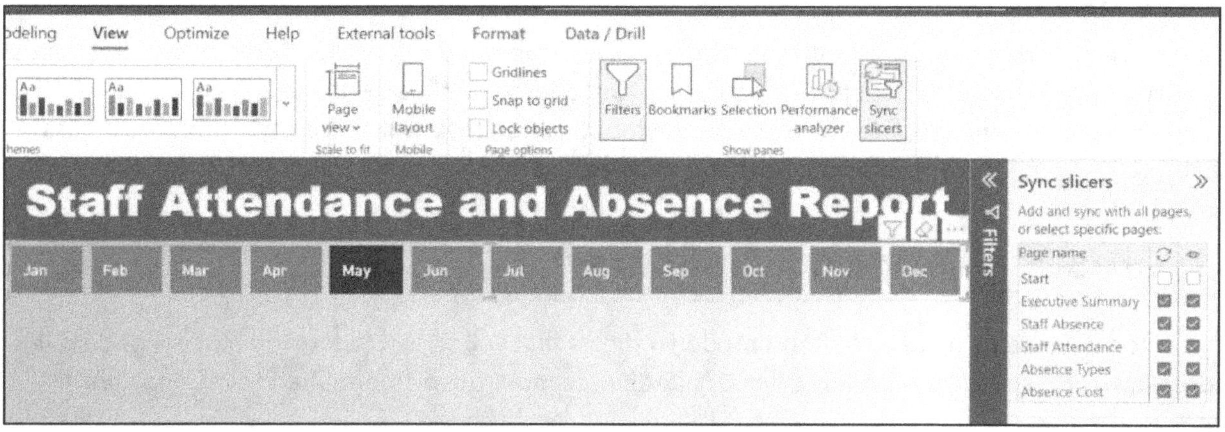

Testing the Synchronization

To confirm the setup works:

1. Select a month, e.g., May, on the slicer.
2. Navigate between pages.
3. You'll notice that "May" remains selected on each page.

Note: while interacting with regular buttons in Power BI Desktop (such as navigation buttons), you must hold down the Control (Ctrl) key when clicking. However, this is not required for slicers.

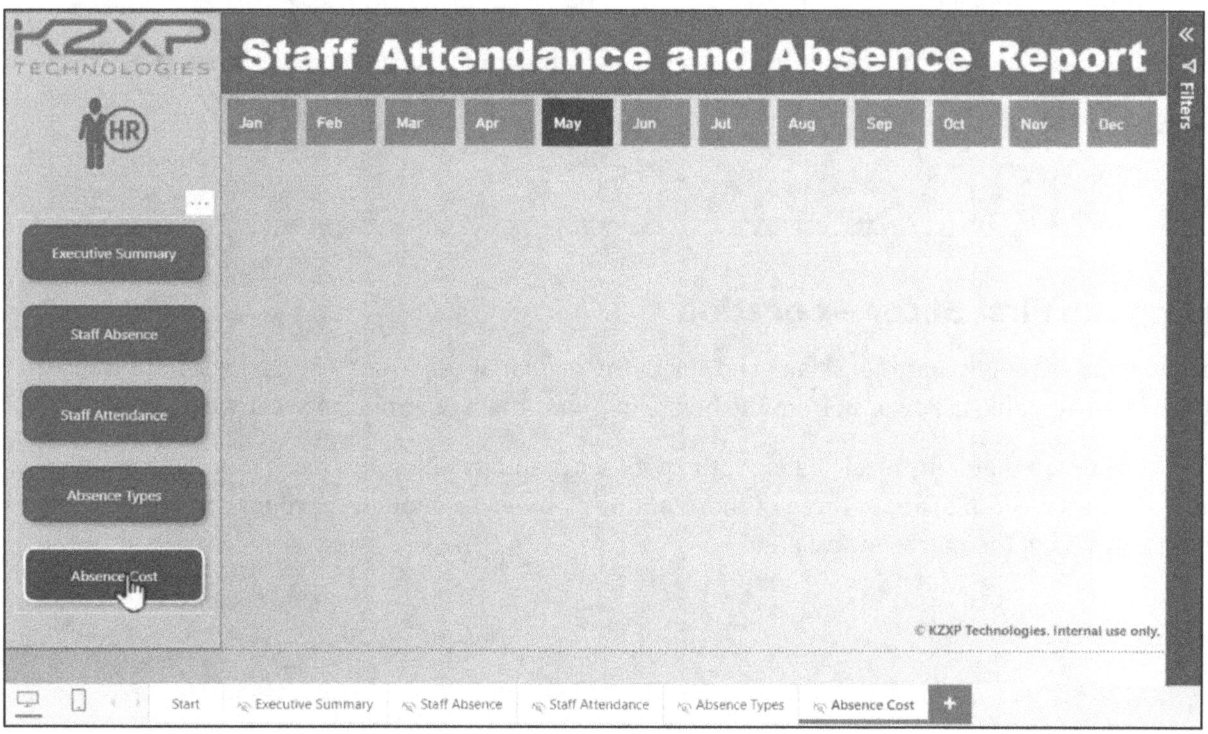

Once you've confirmed everything works as expected, clear the May selection by clicking it again. Then save your report.

What's Next

With the synchronized month slicer now in place, you've established a consistent time-based filter across all report pages. In the next section, we'll introduce four additional slicers—these will sit beneath the month slicer and use the drop-down style. Like the month slicer, they will also be synchronized across all pages.

6.2: Creating Dropdown Slicers

In this tutorial, we're going to build four dropdown slicers that will sit just below the date slicer on our report canvas. These slicers will allow users to filter by Location, Department, Staff Level, and Staff Name.

The dropdown format is particularly useful when you're dealing with large lists—like a long list of staff names or departments—because it allows you to present many options in a compact space. To improve usability, we'll also configure these slicers to remain synchronized across all report pages. That means if a user selects "Cardiff" as the location on one page, that selection will persist when they switch to another page, such as the Staff Absence report.

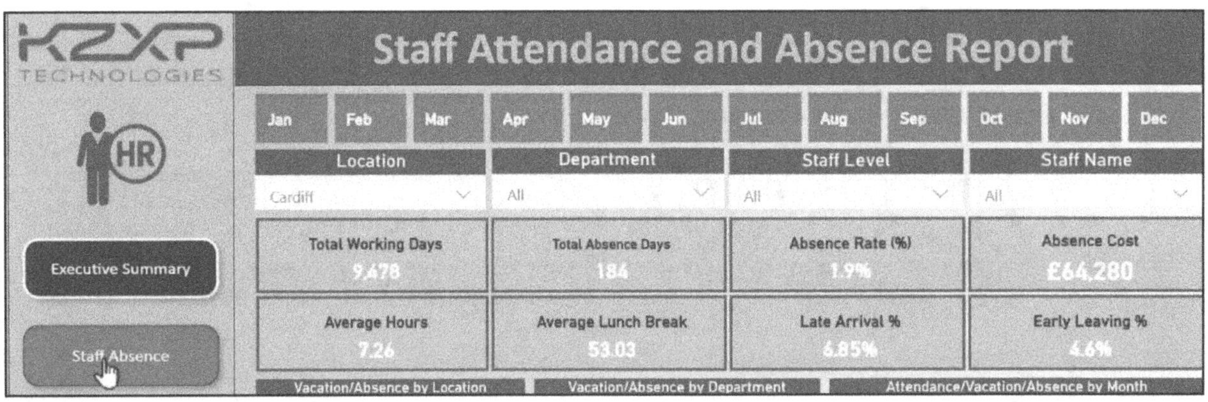

Adding the First Slicer – Location

To begin, head to the Visualizations pane and select the regular Slicer visual. This is the standard slicer that has been available in Power BI from the beginning—not the newer button slicer we used earlier.

Resize the slicer so that it fits nicely beneath the date slicer and its 12-month navigation buttons. Ideally, it should span the width of about three of those buttons. This gives enough space for dropdown content without consuming too much vertical area.

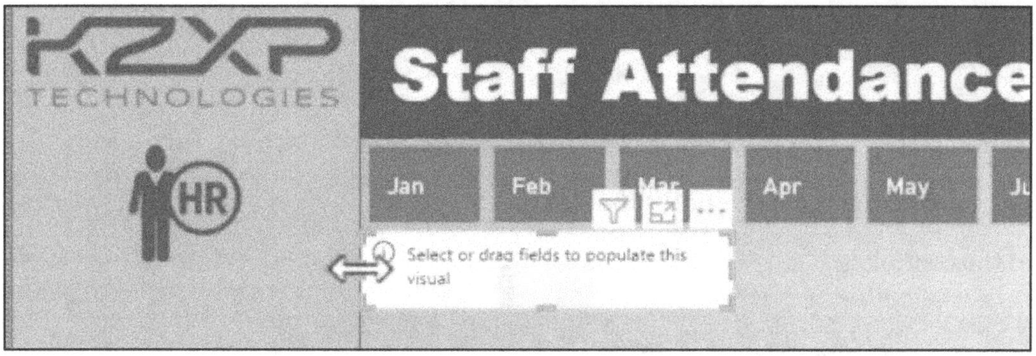

Next, go to the Fields pane, locate the Staff table, and drag the Location field into the new slicer visual.

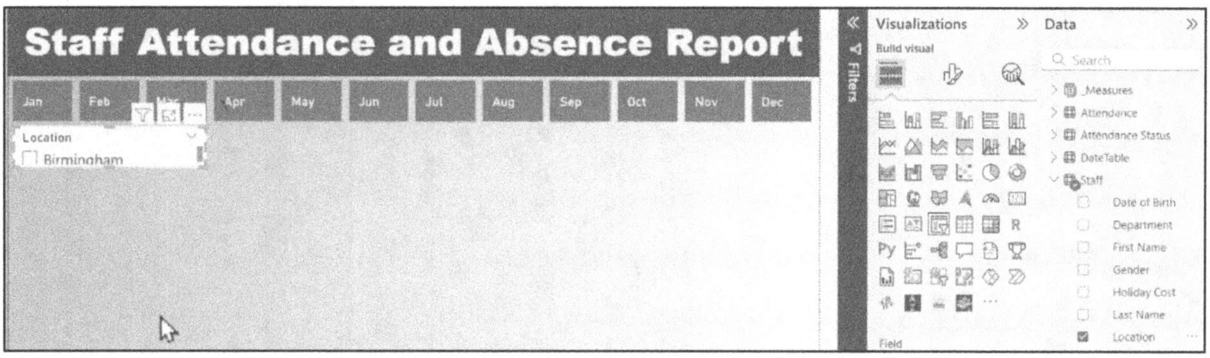

Formatting the Location Slicer

Click on the Format icon (the paintbrush) in the visualizations pane to begin formatting the slicer. The first thing we'll do is switch off the slicer header, since we're going to use the title bar for that purpose instead.

Now let's convert this slicer into a dropdown format. Under Slicer settings, change the style from the default Vertical List to Dropdown.

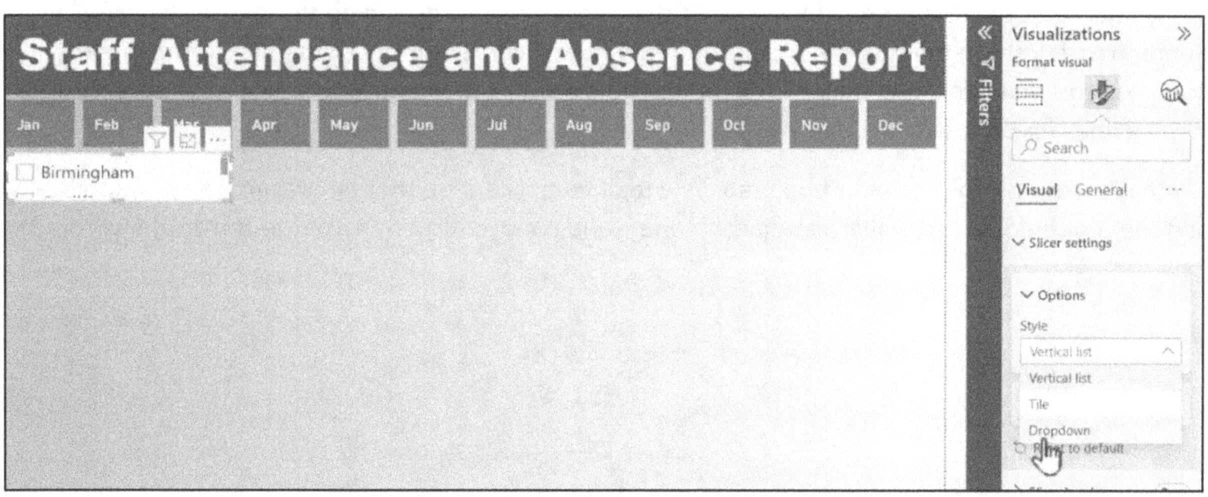

Then, turn on the Title toggle under the General section. In the title box, type the static label: Location.

For styling:

Set the title text colour to white.

Change the title background to match your report's theme blue.

Align the title text to the centre.

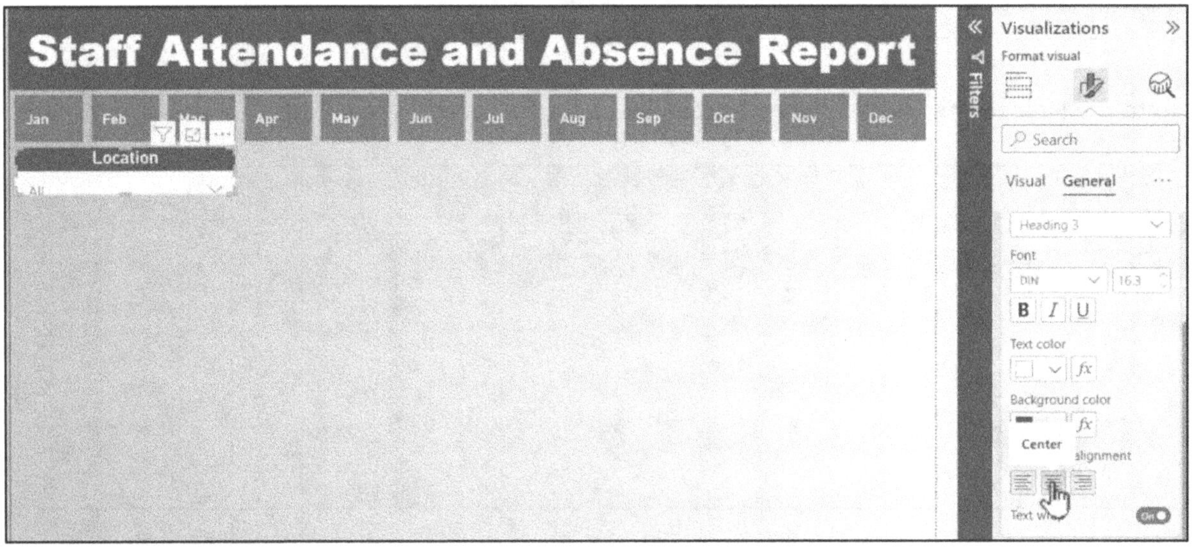

Now adjust the height of the visual to ensure it's compact but still usable. This completes the first slicer.

Creating and Reusing the Other Slicers

Since we'll need three more slicers with the same formatting, now is the time to duplicate the first one. In Power BI, a common practice is to fully format one visual and then duplicate it, modifying only the field it displays.

Use copy and paste to create three duplicates of the original slicer. You can do this quickly by pressing Ctrl+C, then Ctrl+V three times. Drag and position the new slicers underneath the first, arranging them vertically. As you move them, helpful red alignment guides will appear, making it easy to ensure everything lines up perfectly.

To tidy the layout, use the Format ribbon tab. Select all four slicers—either by dragging a selection box around them or holding Ctrl while clicking each one—and choose Align > Distribute Horizontally from the ribbon.

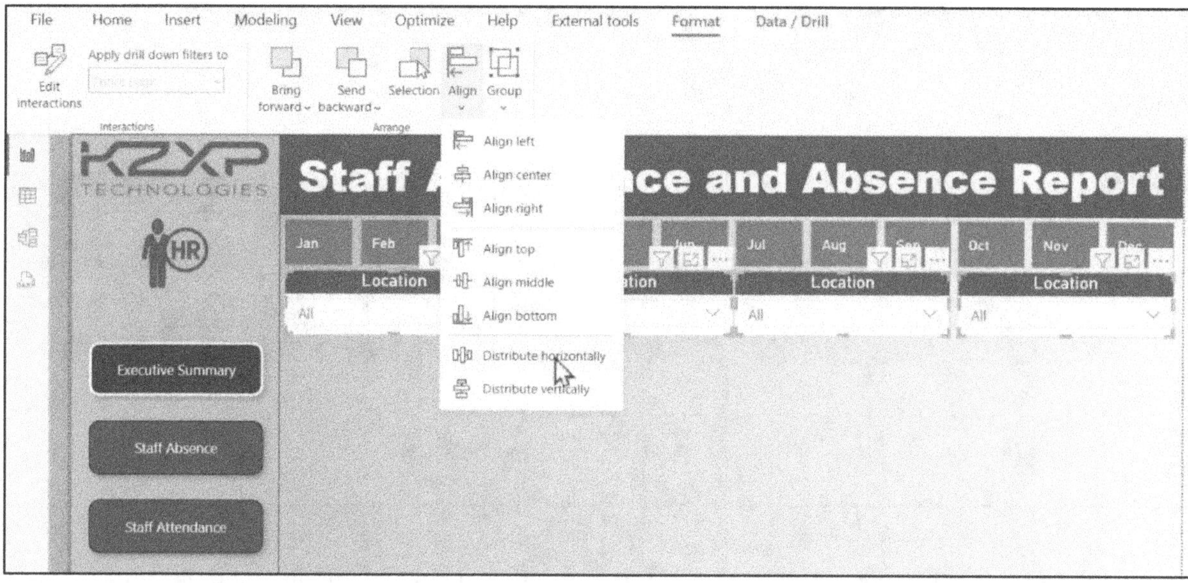

Assigning Fields to the Other Slicers

Now it's time to update each slicer to display the correct field.

1. On the second slicer:

    - Switch off the Location field.
    - Switch on the Department field.
    - Update the title to Department.

2. On the third slicer:

    - Switch off Department.
    - Enable the field that represents the Role of the person.
    - Change the title to Staff Level.

3. On the fourth slicer:

    - Switch off Role.
    - Enable the Staff Name field.
    - Set the title to Staff Name.

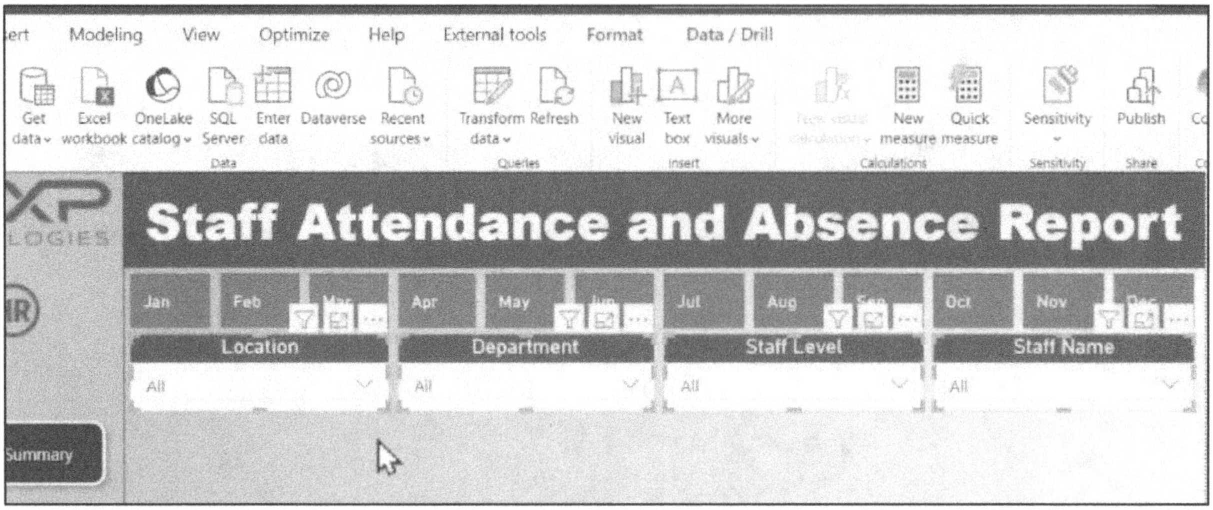

Once done, take a moment to verify that each slicer is correctly configured and labelled: Location, Department, Staff Level, and Staff Name.

Synchronizing Slicers Across Pages

Now that your slicers are correctly set up on one page, you'll want to synchronize them across all report pages. This allows users to make a selection once and have it persist throughout the report experience.

In Power BI, there are two methods for synchronizing slicers:

  - Using the Sync Slicers pane, or
  - Using Copy and Paste.
- Because we're working with four slicers at once, the Copy and Paste method is much faster in this scenario.
- Start by selecting all four slicers. Then press Ctrl+C to copy them. Now, go to each of the other report pages and press Ctrl+V to paste them in. You'll see a prompt:
- "Sync visuals – One or more of the copied visuals can stay in sync with the visual it was copied from. Do you want to keep them in sync?"
- Click Sync to confirm.
- Repeat the paste and sync process on the remaining report pages. Once done, all four slicers will remain synchronized across all five pages in your report.

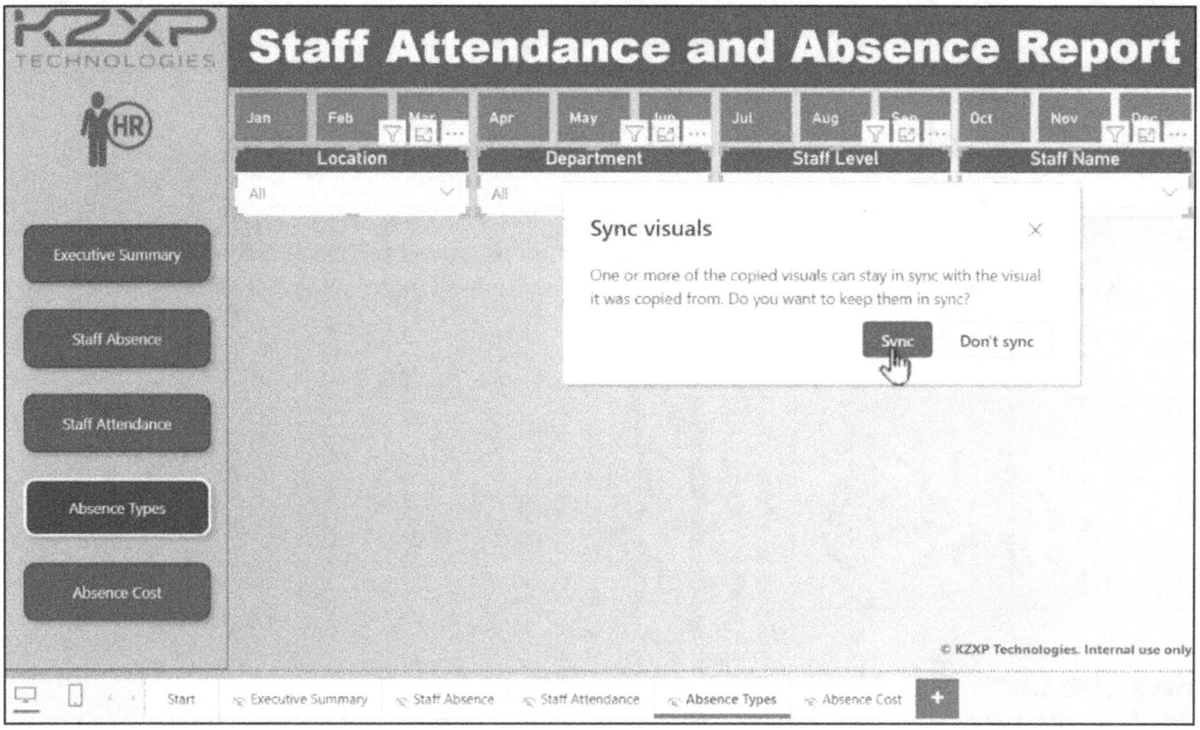

Final Checks

Before moving on, double-check that each slicer is functioning as expected and that selections persist across pages. If everything looks good, save your report.

In the next section, we'll explore how to build a grid of metric cards using the latest Card visual, allowing us to present multiple KPIs in a single visual layout.

6.3: Creating a Grid of Cards

One of the most effective ways to present high-level summary information in a Power BI report is to use cards. Cards provide a simple yet visually strong way to showcase KPIs and headline figures. In this section, we'll create a grid of eight cards to display executive-level summary metrics in a clean and manageable format, all within a single visual using the new card visual.

This new card visual can be identified by a lightning bolt icon in its top left corner. Unlike the classic card, which could only display one metric at a time, the new visual supports a grid layout, allowing you to display multiple cards inside a single visual object.

Adding the Card Visual

Start by inserting a new card visual onto your report canvas. Resize it to roughly the shape and space you expect it to occupy on the final layout.

Before we can access any of the formatting options, we need to add some fields to the card visual. If there are no fields selected, the Format pane remains inactive.

Populating the First Row of Cards

Let's begin by adding four headline metrics to the card visual. These will form the first row of our grid. From your measures, select the following:

- Total Working Days
- Total Absence Days
- Absence Rate
- Total Absence Cost

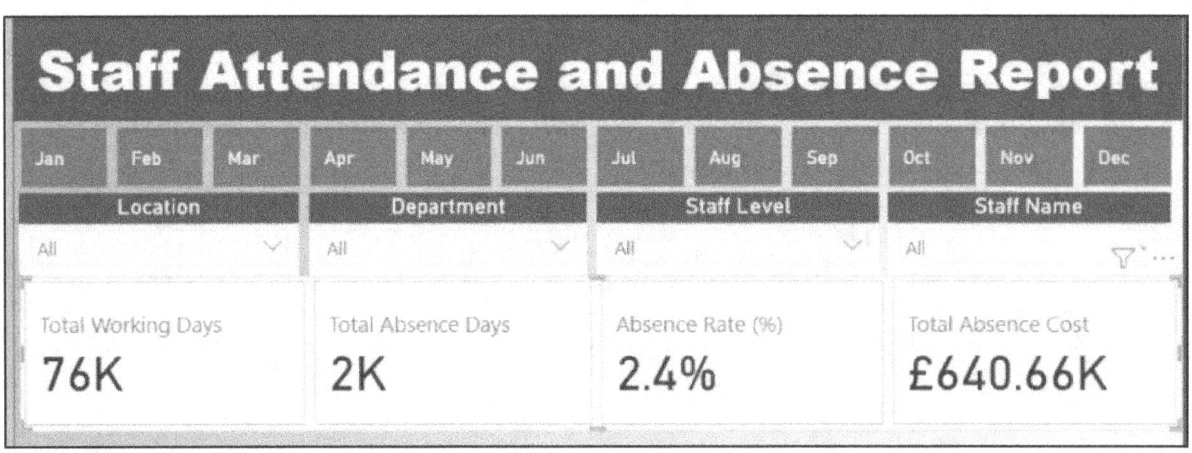

Once these measures have been added, the visual will automatically generate four cards, each displaying the selected metric.

Configuring the Grid Layout

To switch the card visual into grid mode, go to the Format tab, then expand the Layout section. Change the Arrangement setting to "Grid".

Set the layout Style to "Cards".

Then specify the following settings:

- Max Rows: 2
- Columns: 4
- Spacing between cards: leave at default

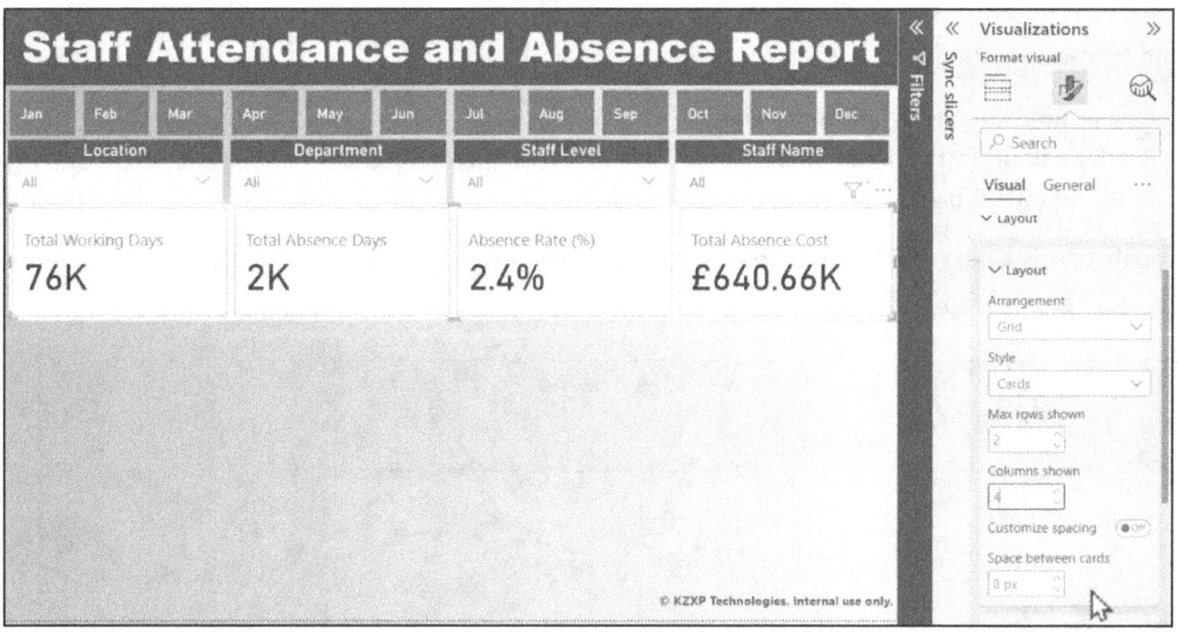

Formatting the Card Text

Next, we'll configure the text that appears in the cards—both the metric values and the labels. Expand the Callout values section in the Format pane.

Ensure that the setting is applied globally by confirming that Series is set to "All".

Then apply the following formatting changes:

- Font size: 18pt
- Font weight: Bold
- Horizontal alignment: Center

Now move down to the Label section.

Set the font size for the label to 14pt and turn on Bold formatting. This keeps the label text legible and prominent without overpowering the metric.

For colour styling, choose:

- Label font colour: Dark Theme Blue
- Value font colour: White

The white text may briefly disappear depending on your background, but we'll resolve that shortly.

Card Background and Border Styling

With the text styling in place, now let's set up the card backgrounds and borders.

Still in the Format pane, expand the Cards section.

Again, ensure Series is set to "All" so that all cards are formatted at once.

Apply the following settings:

- Background colour: Light Theme Blue
- Border colour: Dark Theme Blue
- Border width: 3 pixels

This gives the cards a neat, bold frame that stands out nicely on a light or dark background.

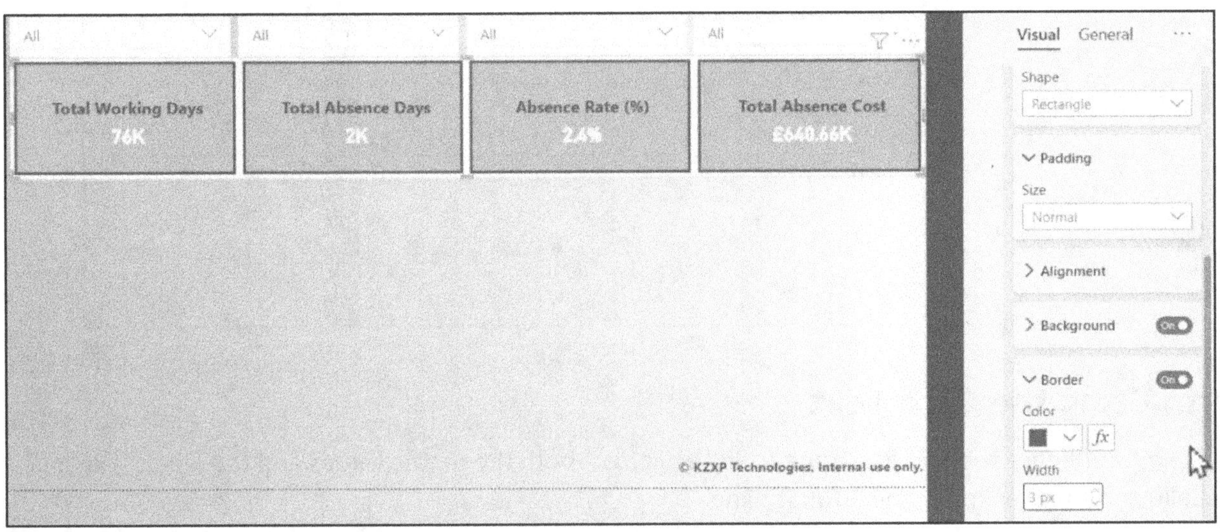

Adding the Second Row of Cards

Now return to the Data tab within the Visualizations pane. Let's add the remaining four measures to complete our second row. Make sure the height of the visual is increased to accommodate two rows of cards.

From the Base Measures folder, add:

- Average Hours Worked

- Average Lunch Break

Then, from the Rate-Based Measures folder, add:

- Late Arrival Percentage
- Early Leaving Percentage

At this point, adjust the height of the card visual to the minimum you can use without compromising readability. The entire grid of eight cards now exists within a single, unified object—making layout and future maintenance much simpler.

Final Touch – Removing the Visual Background

To complete the visual, remove the default white background of the entire card grid so that the individual cards appear to float on the report's blue background.

To do this:

- Go back to the Format tab.
- Open the General section.
- Expand Effects.
- Switch off the Background toggle.

Your grid of cards is now complete—neatly arranged, styled consistently, and occupying only a single visual element on the page. This approach streamlines your layout and ensures better consistency in your executive summary presentation.

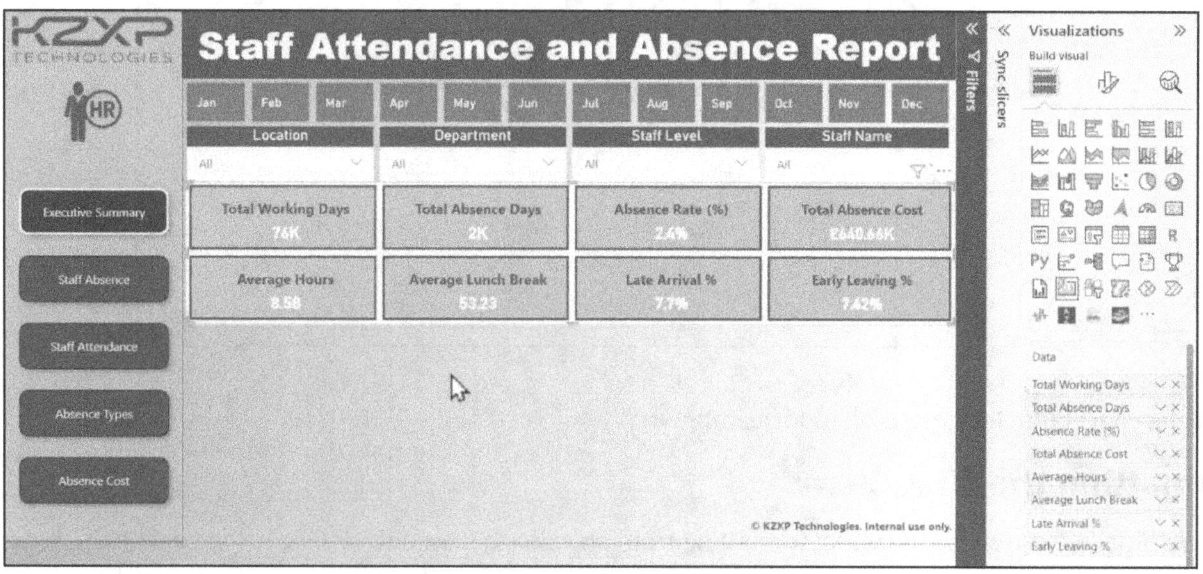

6.4: Creating Stacked Bar Charts

In this tutorial, we will build a set of stacked bar and column charts that appear at the bottom of the Executive Summary page. These visuals provide a clear view of staff absences, broken down into vacation and sickness, and allow for quick comparison across different categories such as location, department, and time.

We begin with two stacked bar charts. One chart shows absences broken down by location, and the second by department. Both display vacation and sickness data side-by-side within each category. A third visual, a stacked column chart, displays the same absence types across months, alongside a contrasting measure: total working days. The vertical layout of this column chart provides a natural view for trends over time.

Creating the First Stacked Bar Chart

Open Power BI Desktop and insert a Stacked Bar Chart, which is the first option in the Visualizations pane.

Reduce the width of the visual slightly to make room for others later. To populate the visual:

1. Drag Location from the Staff table into the Y axis.
2. From the Context Measures folder, add both Total Vacation Days and Total Absence Days to the X axis values.

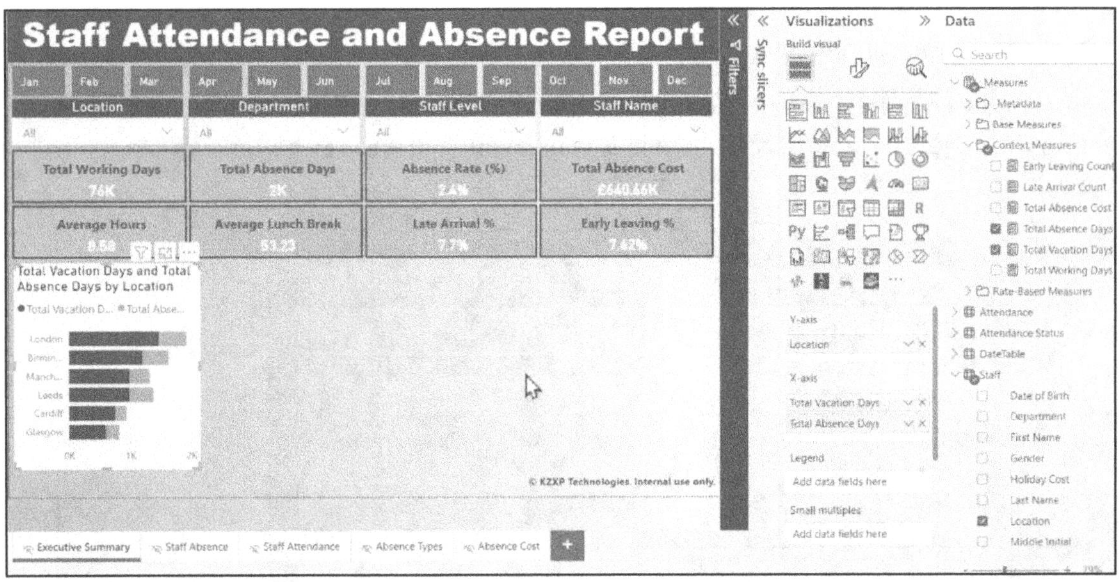

With the chart built, let's move on to formatting.

Formatting the First Chart

To save time, we can reuse the visual formatting from an existing element. Highlight the Location slicer on the page, click the Format Painter, and then click on the new bar chart visual to apply its styling.

Next, go to the Format pane, and under the General section, expand the title settings. Shorten the title to "Vacation / Absence by Location".

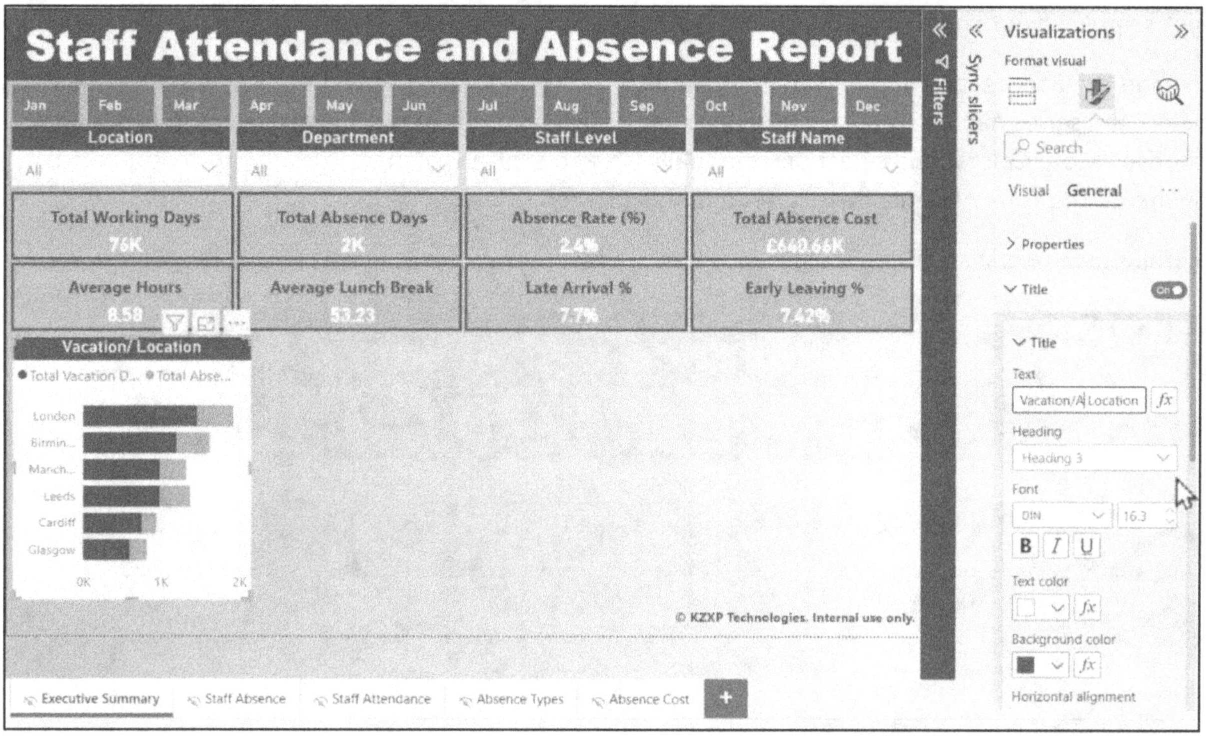

Switch to the Visual section in the formatting pane. You may notice the legend is being truncated due to oversized text. Expand the Legend section and reduce the text size to 10pt. You might still need to widen the visual slightly to make the entire legend readable.

Another issue is with the Y axis, where some location names might be cut off. Expand the Y axis section and adjust the Maximum Width setting. As you increase this—try up to 35%—you'll see the full names reappear.

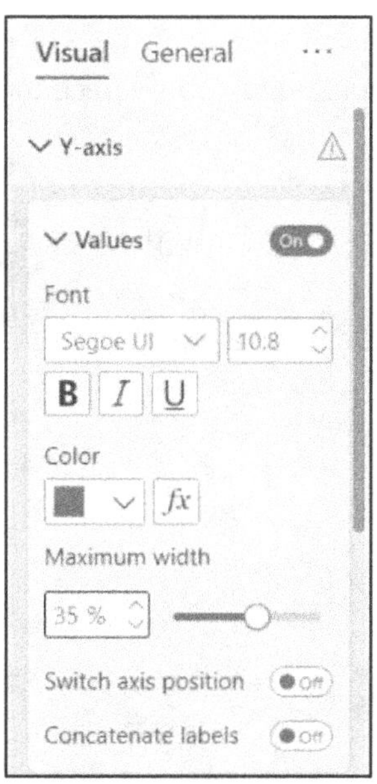

Now let's apply colour coding for easier distinction:

1. Expand the Bars section in the formatting pane.
2. Select the series named Total Vacation Days and assign a green colour. If green is not in the palette, choose "More Colors" and select one manually.
3. Switch to the Total Absence Days series and assign a red colour.

This completes the first stacked bar chart.

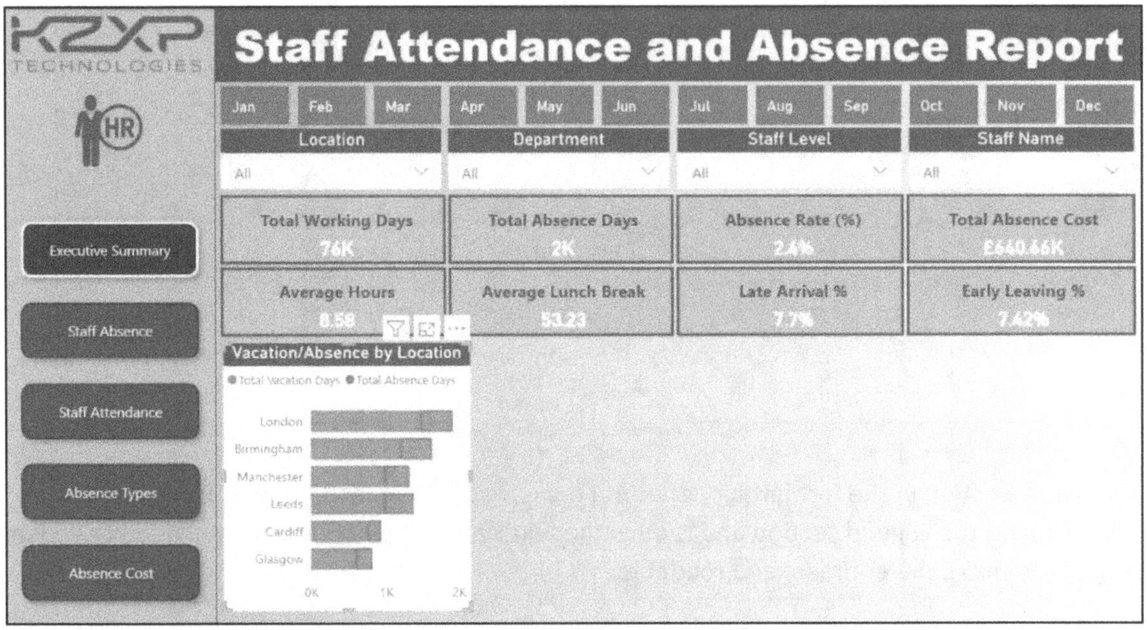

Creating the Second Bar Chart (by Department)

To build the second visual:

1. Copy the first bar chart (Ctrl+C and Ctrl+V) and move it to the right-hand side, leaving some space in between.
2. Widen the new visual slightly to accommodate more text.
3. In the Data section of the Visualizations pane, remove Location and drag Department into the Y axis instead.
4. Update the title by going to Format > General > Title and change it to "Vacation / Absence by Department".

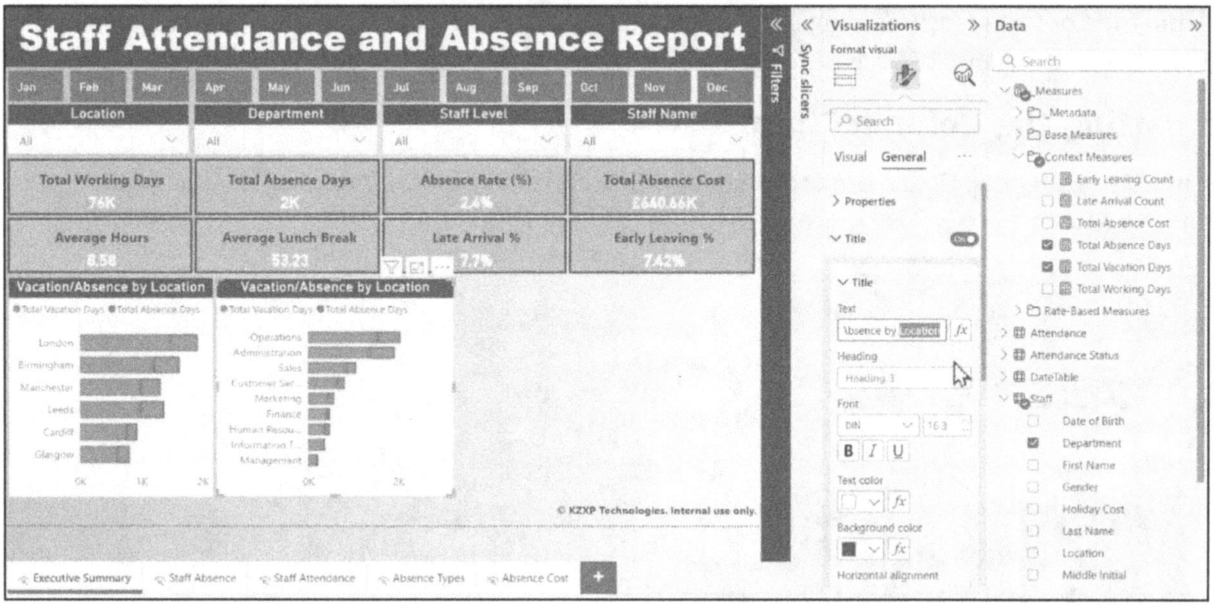

Since department names may be longer, go back into the Y axis section and increase the Maximum Width to its upper limit of 50%. This ensures names are no longer truncated.

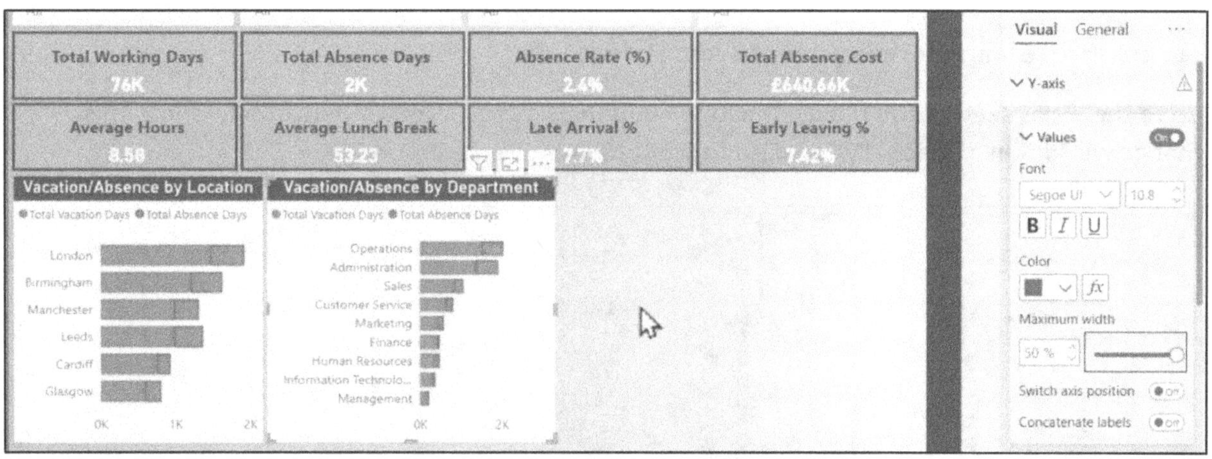

Creating the Stacked Column Chart (by Month)

Now we'll build a stacked column chart to visualise monthly trends. Instead of starting from scratch, copy one of the bar charts again (Ctrl+C and Ctrl+V), and resize the pasted visual to fit the right-hand column area of your page.

With the visual selected, change the chart type to Stacked Column Chart.

Next, we set up the axis and values:

1. Remove Department from the axis field.
2. From the Date Table, drag Short Month into the X axis.

3. From the Context Measures, drag in Total Working Days and place it above the other two values (vacation and absence). This ensures the bars for working days appear first in the chart.

Formatting the Column Chart

Start by editing the title. Go to Format > General > Title and change it to: "Attendance / Vacation / Absence by Month".

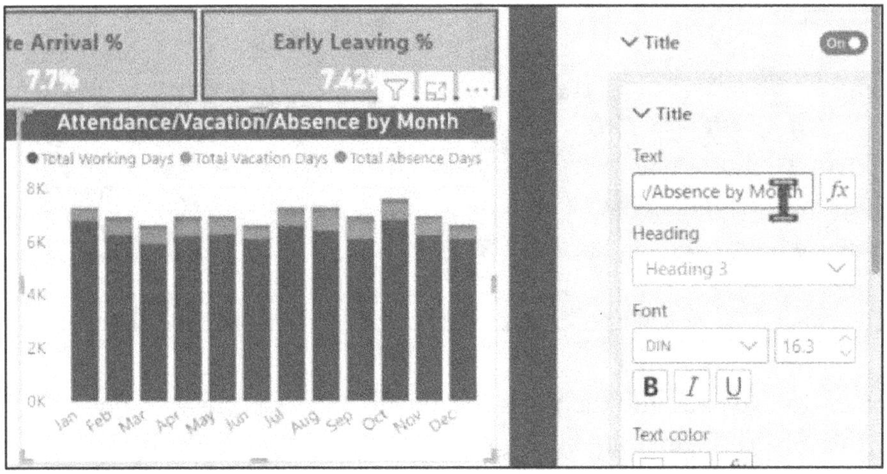

Now, to enhance readability, reduce the axis font sizes:

1. Go to the X axis section and reduce the font size until the text becomes horizontal. At 9pt, this change will kick in. (Optionally, increase to 9.5pt to improve clarity.)

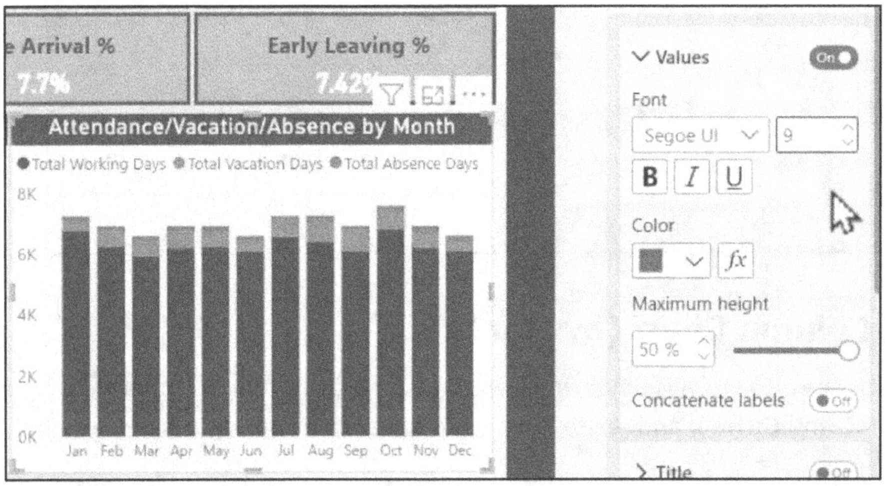

2. Repeat the same steps for the Y axis, setting it to 9.5pt as well.

This approach ensures that axis labels remain legible and neatly aligned, which is especially important on time-based charts where horizontal layout improves interpretation.

Finishing Up

We've now completed our three visuals: two stacked bar charts and one stacked column chart. Together, they offer a multi-angle view of absence across different organisational groupings and over time.

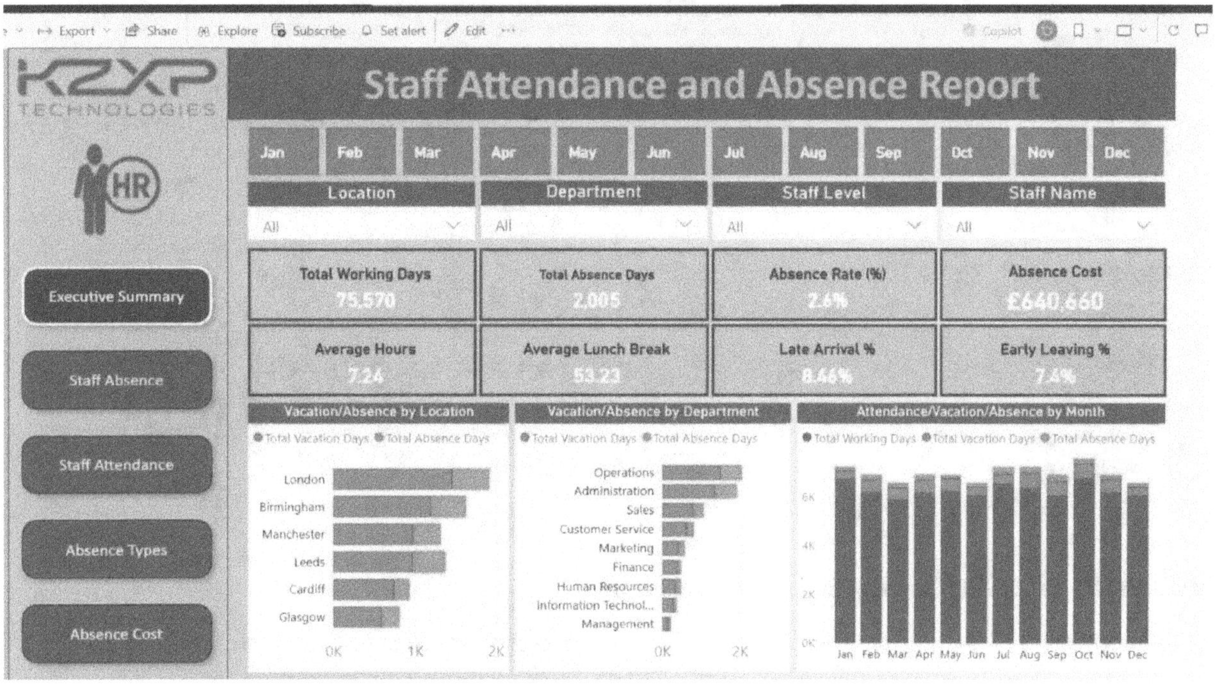

As a final step, don't forget to save your report to preserve your changes.

In the next section, we will enhance the report further by addressing how these visuals interact with one another—an essential aspect for improving the user experience when exploring the dashboard.

6.5: Editing Visual Interactions

When creating report pages in Power BI, one final but crucial step in user experience design is refining how visuals interact with each other. Visual interactions determine what happens to the other visuals on the page when a user makes a selection in a specific visual. This isn't just limited to slicers—chart visuals also participate in this interaction behaviour.

For instance, looking at the completed report, if a user clicks on a bar in a bar chart, the remaining visuals on the page may respond to that selection. This is known as cross-filtering or cross-highlighting, and while it can be useful, there are times when it makes more sense to turn it off. In this section, we'll go through each visual and decide whether it should influence the others—and adjust the interactions accordingly.

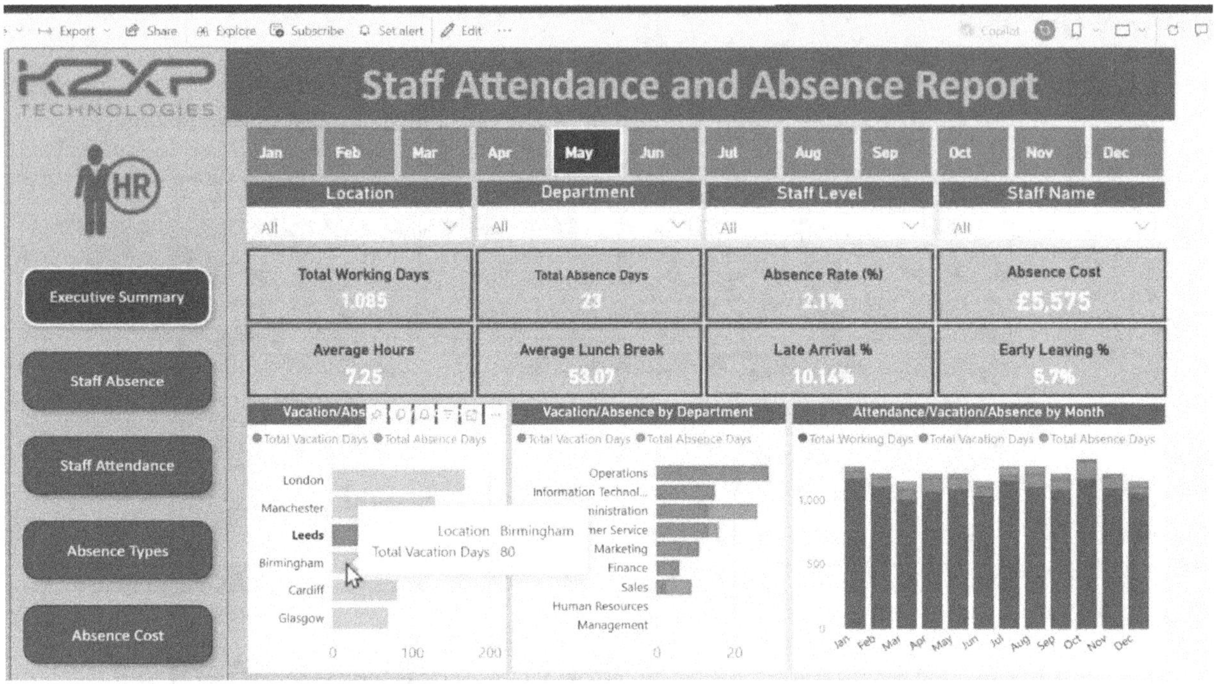

Reviewing the Date Slicer Interaction

Let's begin with the date slicer. To review its interaction with the rest of the visuals, simply make a selection in the slicer—say, choosing the month of May—and observe how the other visuals respond.

In our current layout, selecting May causes all visuals to update accordingly. This is generally good: users expect their selections to have a consistent effect. However, one visual does not respond in a helpful way—the column chart.

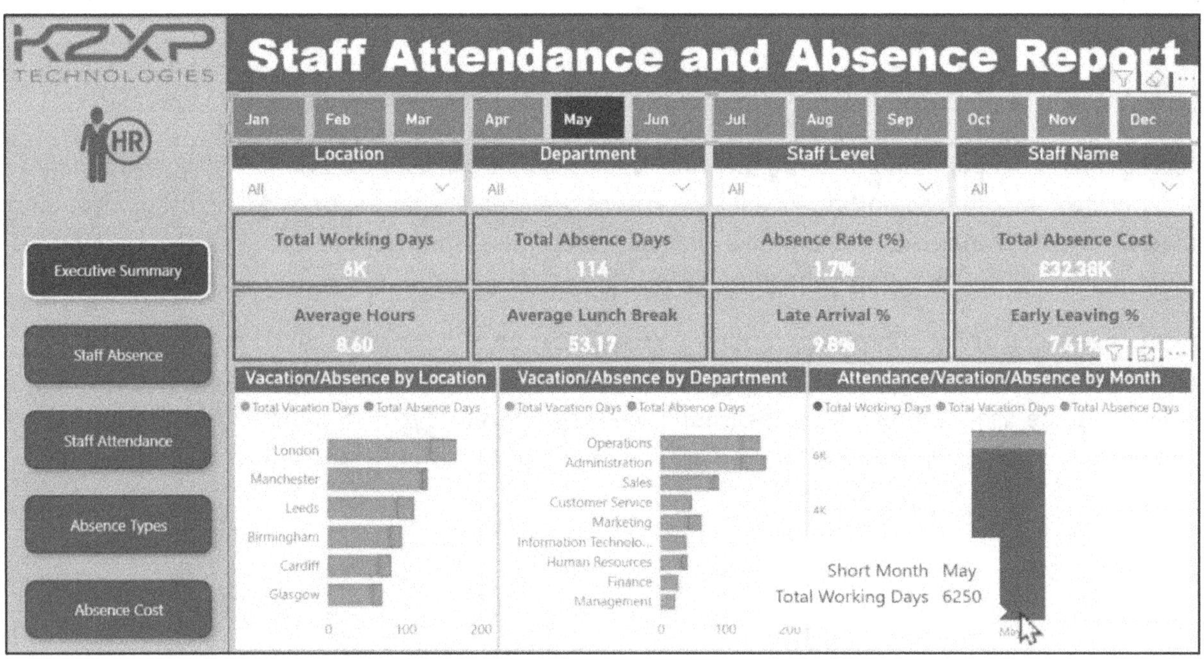

When May is selected, the column chart filters down to show only May. This isn't helpful because the value of that chart lies in seeing May in context, alongside the other months. So, this is a case where we want to decouple the date slicer from the column chart.

Changing Interaction from Filter to None

To do this, select the date slicer. Then, go to the Format tab on the ribbon and choose Edit interactions.

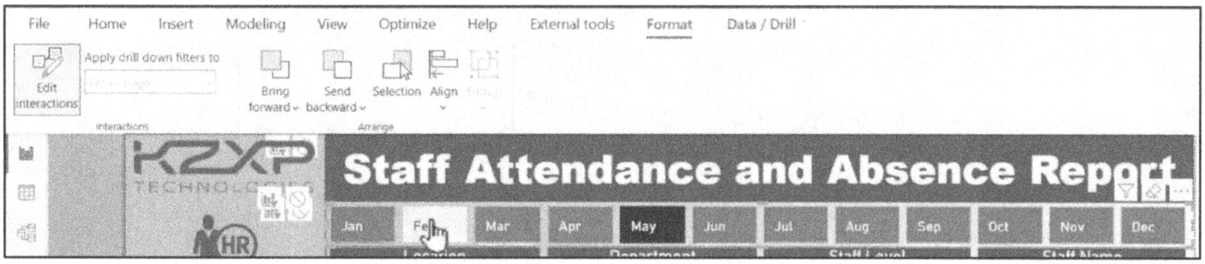

When Edit interactions is active, selecting a visual displays small icons on the top right of all other visuals. On the column chart, you'll see two icons: one for filter, which is currently selected, and another for none, meaning no interaction.

Click the none icon. Now, when May is selected, the column chart remains unchanged, allowing users to compare May with other months—an interaction that's both more helpful and more intuitive.

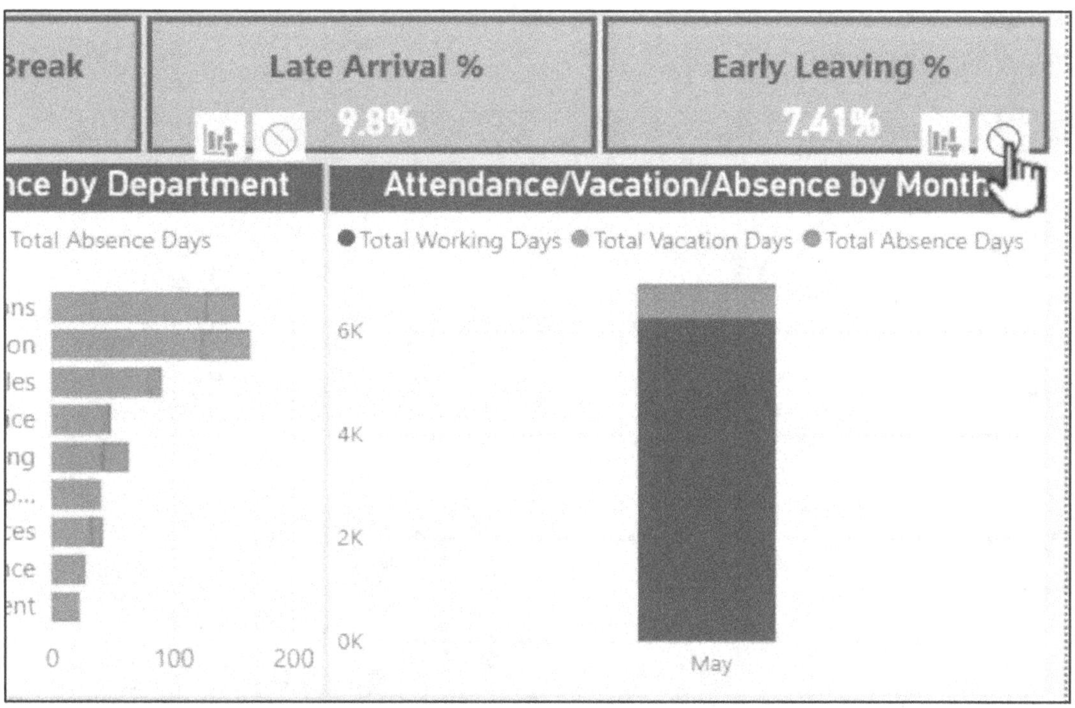

Configuring the Location Slicer

Next, let's review the interaction behaviour for the location slicer. This is similar to the previous situation.

Currently, when we choose a location, the bar chart displaying all locations filters to show just the selected one. This defeats the purpose of that visual, which is to compare across all locations.

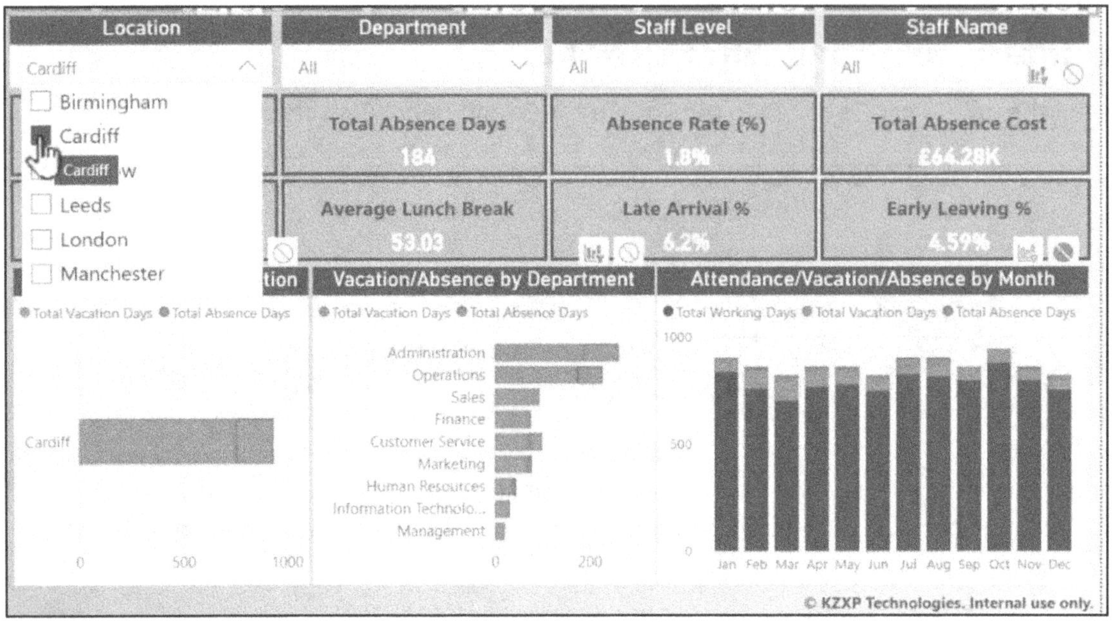

So again, we select the location slicer, switch on Edit interactions, and click the none icon on the location bar chart. Now, if a user selects a branch like Manchester, the rest of the page updates accordingly, but all branches remain visible on the bar chart.

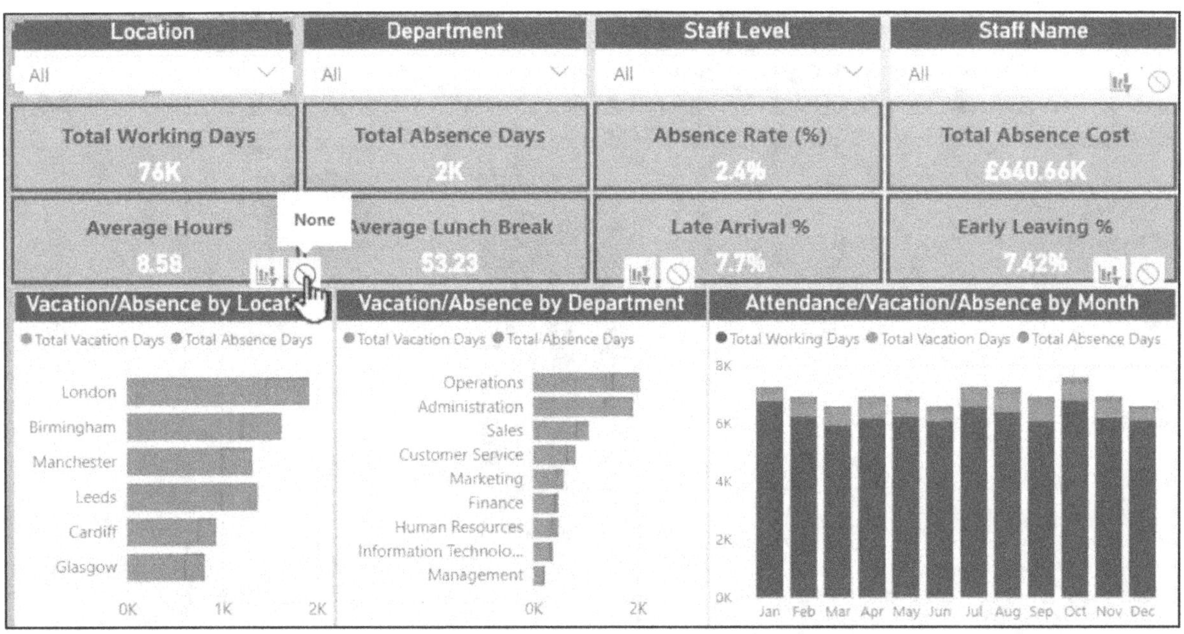

Adjusting the Department Slicer

We encounter a similar issue with the department slicer, which is tied to another bar chart.

When a department is selected, the bar chart that uses department on its y-axis currently filters down, which limits the comparison context.

To fix this, we highlight the department slicer, enable Edit interactions, and select the none icon on the top right of the department bar chart.

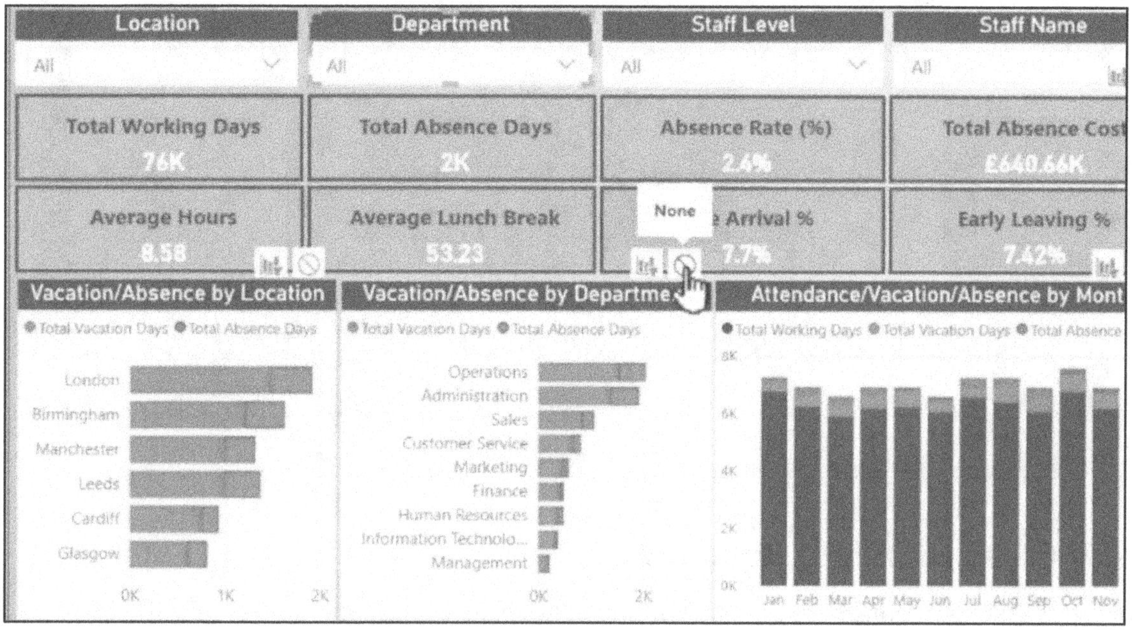

Now, selecting a department will still affect other visuals, but the department bar chart remains fully populated—allowing for meaningful comparison across departments.

Slicers We Leave As-Is

Not all slicers need to be decoupled. For example, the staff level and staff name slicers are working well with their default behaviour. Filtering by staff level or individual names produces sensible results across all visuals, so there's no need to change anything there.

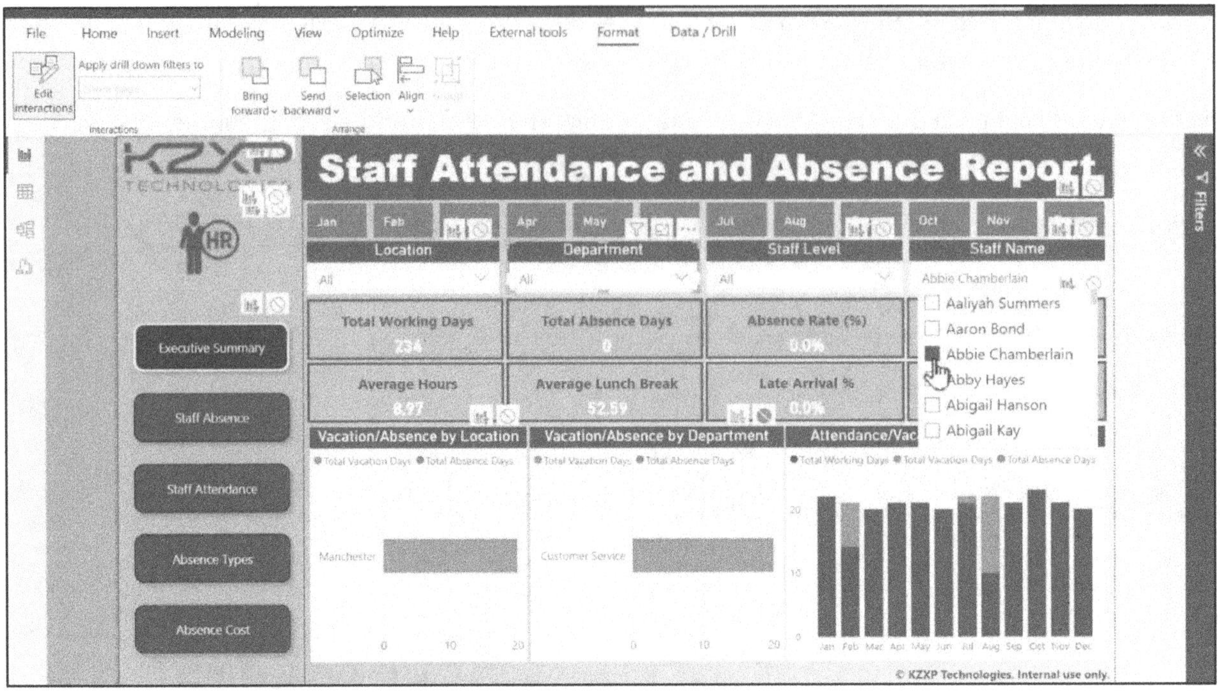

Improving Cross Highlight Behaviour

Now let's move on to interactions between the bar and column charts themselves. When clicking on a bar—for example, a location—Power BI's default behaviour is cross highlight.

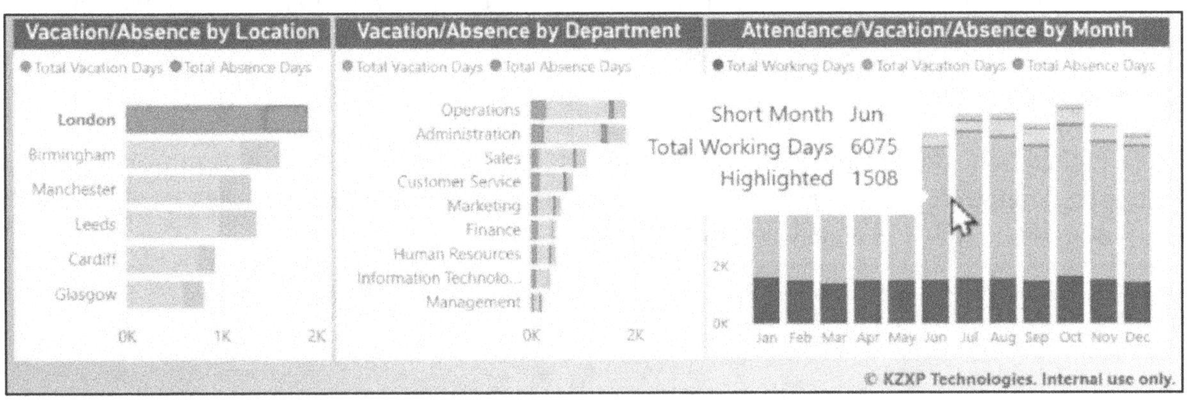

This means that instead of filtering the other visuals, it highlights only the relevant parts of each visual. For instance, clicking on London highlights the London values for vacation and absence, while still displaying other locations.

While this is sometimes helpful, it can also produce unclear visuals. In our case, the highlighted sections are subtle and hard to read. A cleaner experience would be to fully filter the other visuals based on the selected location.

To change this, select the location bar chart. Then, with Edit interactions enabled, look at the other two visuals—likely another bar chart and the column chart.

You'll see three icons: filter, highlight (the default), and none. Click the filter icon on both visuals. This will replace the cross highlighting with full filtering, making the visuals more readable and focused.

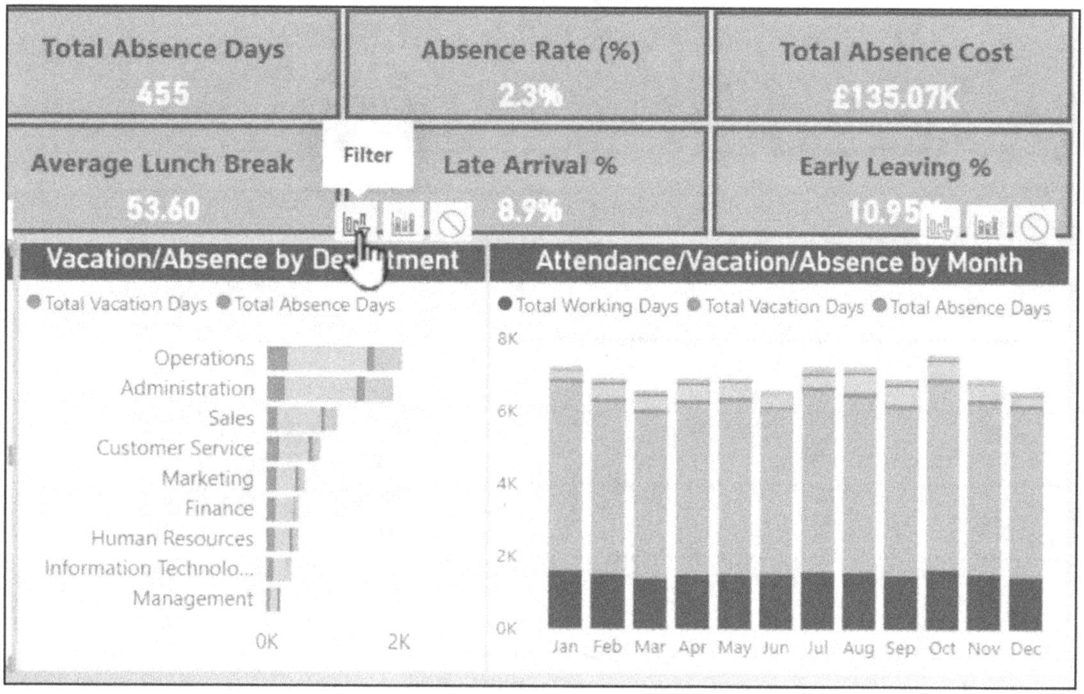

Applying the Same Changes to Other Charts

Repeat the same steps for the other bar charts.

First, select the department bar chart, then click the filter icon on the location bar chart and the column chart.

Next, select the column chart itself and switch its interaction mode from highlight to filter on both of the bar charts.

These changes ensure that any selection made on one chart results in a clear and consistent response from the others.

Exiting Edit Mode and Saving Changes

Once all the desired visual interactions are in place, simply click on Edit interactions again to exit the mode.

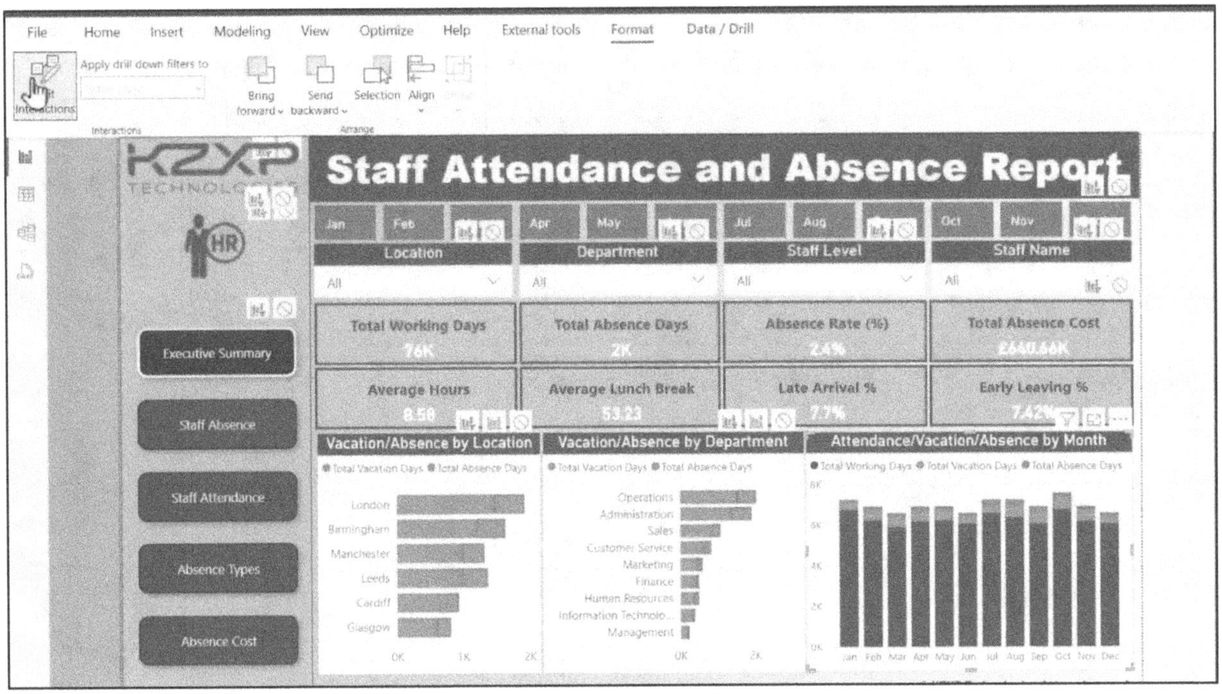

That completes the setup for this page. The Executive Summary page is now fully configured with interactions that serve the report's purpose and enhance usability.

Finally, save your work. In the following section, we'll move on to building the Staff Absence page, where we'll explore a powerful feature called Field parameters.

6.6: Staff Absence Field Parameters

In this section, we'll construct the Staff Absence page. The layout is intentionally simple yet highly functional. At its heart is a matrix visual—positioned on the right-hand side of the page—that displays staff names as rows and short month names as columns.

The innovation on this page will lie not in the visual layout, but in its interactivity. We will empower users to choose what metric appears in the Values area of the matrix. They'll be able to pick between four key measures: Total Absence Days, Absence Rate, Percent Absence Cost, and Total Vacation Days. This flexibility is made possible using a Power BI feature called Field Parameters.

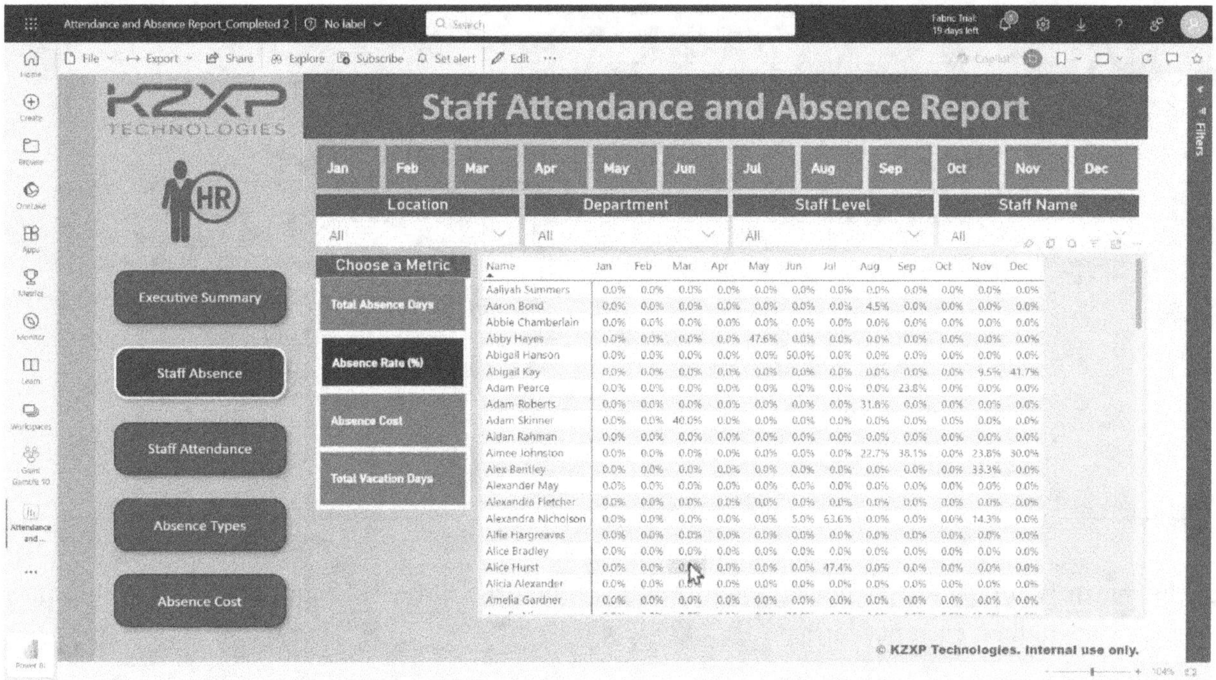

Field parameters allow a user to control what appears in a visual—whether it's the axis of a bar chart or, as in this case, the Values of a matrix. In effect, we're allowing the user to toggle between multiple measures using a clean and compact interface.

Building the Matrix Visual

To begin, we create a matrix visual and position it on the right-hand side of the page. This layout reserves space on the left-hand side for the interactive slicer we'll add later.

We then populate the matrix using the following fields:

- In the Rows area: Name from the Staff table
- In the Columns area: Short Month from the Date table
- In the Values area (temporarily): Total Absence Days (just to see the structure)

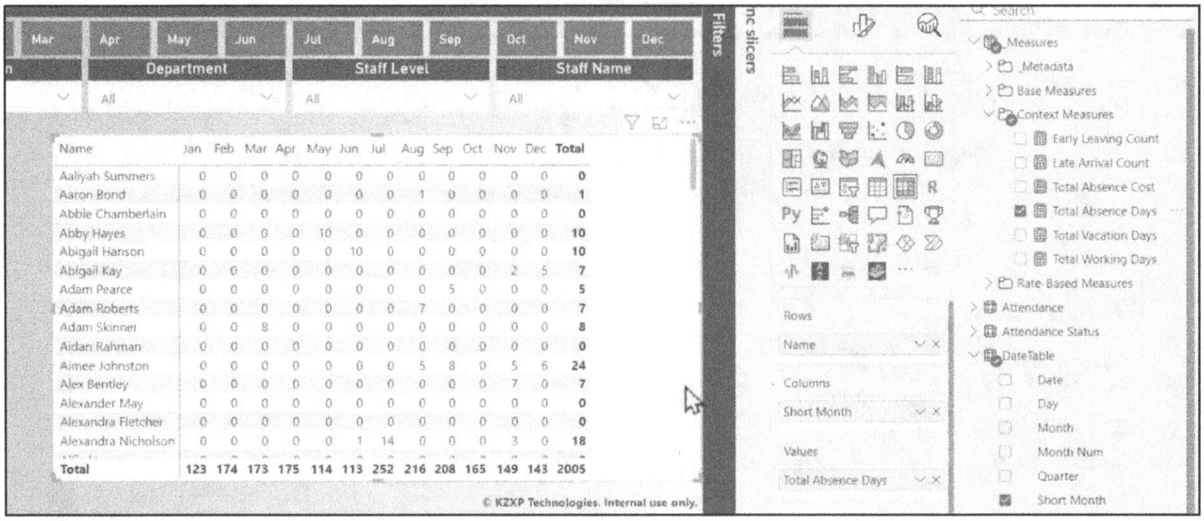

Once the matrix is populated, we tidy up the formatting. We turn off row subtotals and column subtotals and remove any default currency formatting.

Creating the Field Parameter

Now, let's introduce the functionality that lets users choose the displayed measure. From the Modeling tab in Power BI Desktop, we proceed as follows:

1. Click New Parameter, then choose Fields.
2. Name the parameter Absence Metric.
3. Add the following measures to the parameter list:

Total Absence Days

Absence Rate

Total Absence Cost

Total Vacation Days

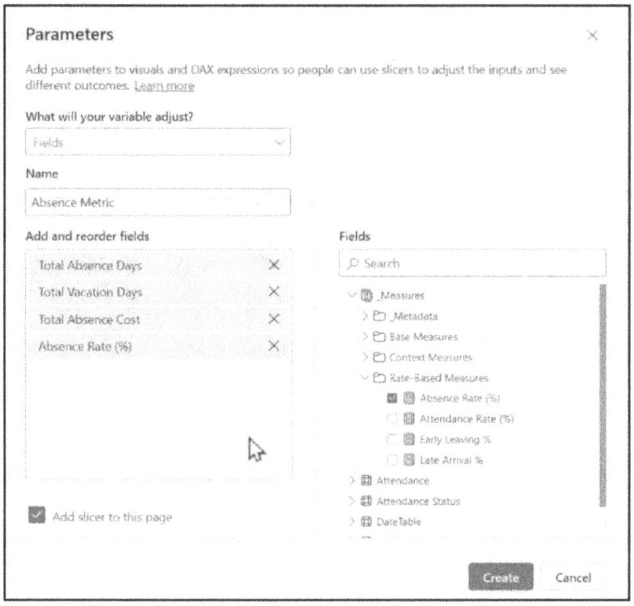

You can adjust the order by moving the measures up or down in the list. For example, place Absence Rate beneath Total Absence Days, and Total Vacation Days at the bottom.

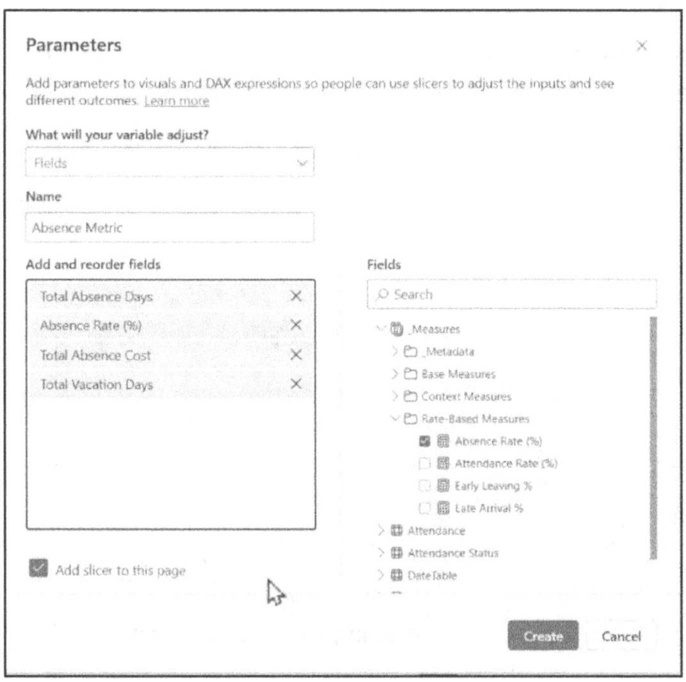

Ensure the checkbox “Add slicer to page” remains ticked. When you click Create, Power BI automatically generates a calculated table and displays the DAX used to define it.

Understanding the Calculated Table

The generated table is a manual definition written in DAX using curly braces. Each row consists of three elements:

- The label shown in the slicer (e.g., "Absence Rate")
- The actual measure reference to be returned
- The ordering index (which determines the sequence in the slicer)

If you inspect this new table in Table View, you'll find that the Absence Metric column is the one bound to the slicer. So, when a user picks an option, the underlying measure is swapped dynamically into the visual.

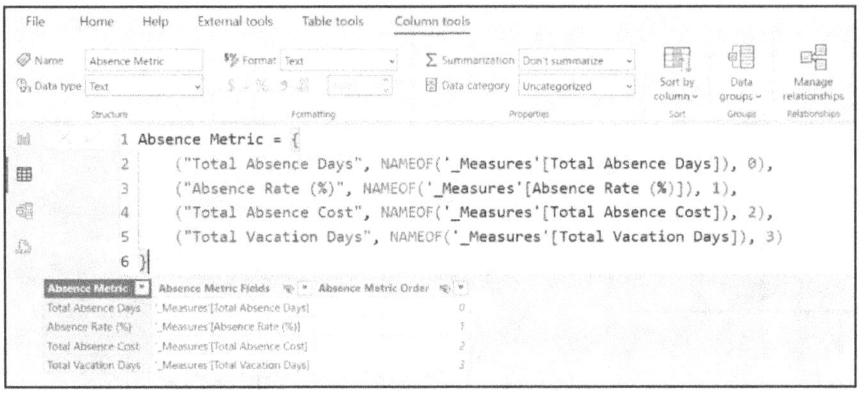

Wiring the Parameter into the Visual

Return to the matrix visual. Remove the placeholder measure (Total Absence Days) from the Values field, and replace it with the new Absence Metric field created by the parameter.

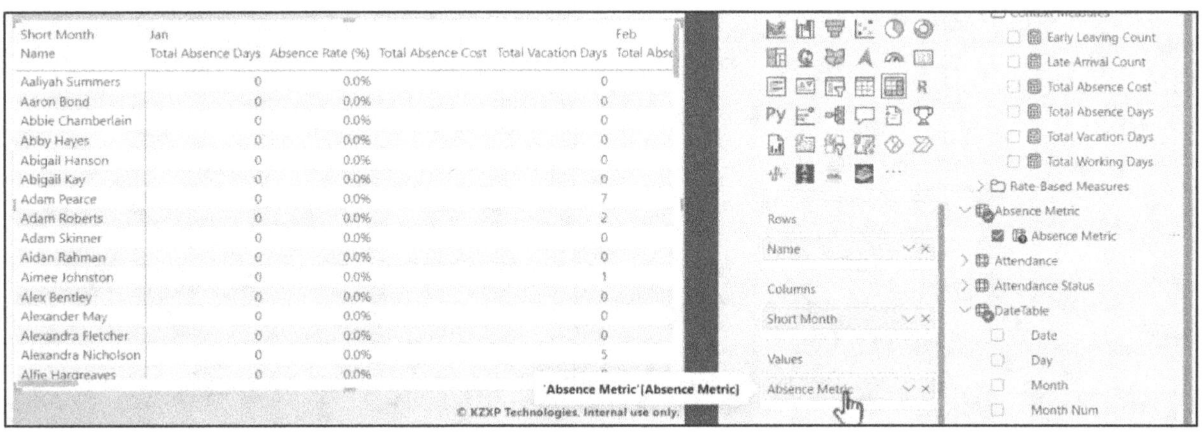

The matrix is now fully dynamic. When a user selects a metric from the slicer, that measure appears in the matrix. It's one visual, many uses.

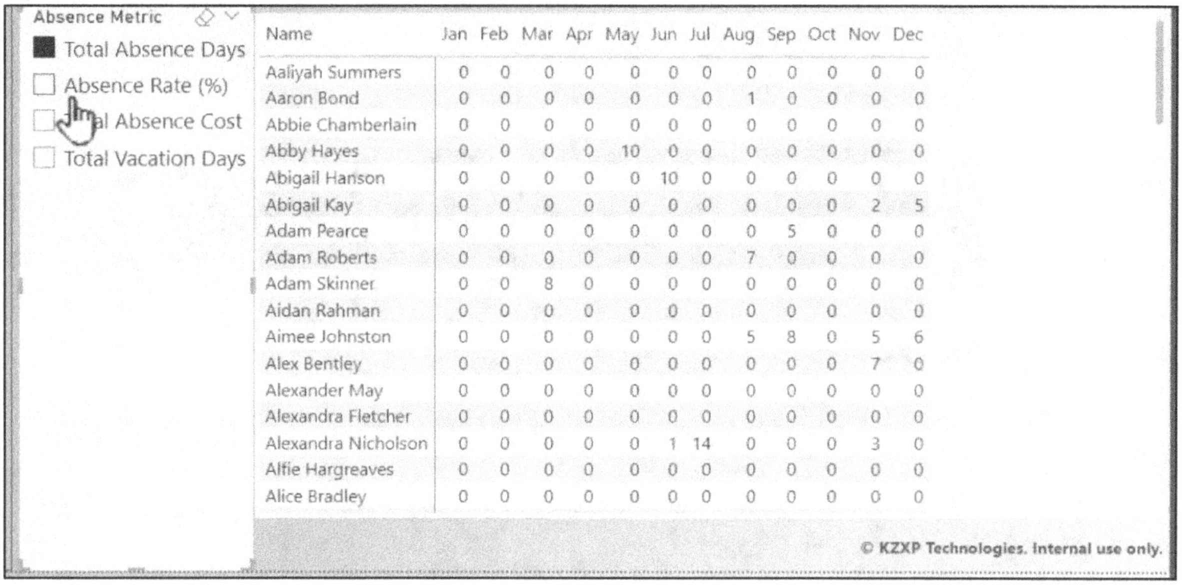

Name	Jan	Feb	Mar	Apr	May	Jun	Jul	Aug	Sep	Oct	Nov	Dec
Aaliyah Summers	0	0	0	0	0	0	0	0	0	0	0	0
Aaron Bond	0	0	0	0	0	0	0	1	0	0	0	0
Abbie Chamberlain	0	0	0	0	0	0	0	0	0	0	0	0
Abby Hayes	0	0	0	0	10	0	0	0	0	0	0	0
Abigail Hanson	0	0	0	0	0	10	0	0	0	0	0	0
Abigail Kay	0	0	0	0	0	0	0	0	0	0	2	5
Adam Pearce	0	0	0	0	0	0	0	0	5	0	0	0
Adam Roberts	0	0	0	0	0	0	0	7	0	0	0	0
Adam Skinner	0	0	8	0	0	0	0	0	0	0	0	0
Aidan Rahman	0	0	0	0	0	0	0	0	0	0	0	0
Aimee Johnston	0	0	0	0	0	0	0	5	8	0	5	6
Alex Bentley	0	0	0	0	0	0	0	0	0	0	7	0
Alexander May	0	0	0	0	0	0	0	0	0	0	0	0
Alexandra Fletcher	0	0	0	0	0	0	0	0	0	0	0	0
Alexandra Nicholson	0	0	0	0	0	1	14	0	0	0	3	0
Alfie Hargreaves	0	0	0	0	0	0	0	0	0	0	0	0
Alice Bradley	0	0	0	0	0	0	0	0	0	0	0	0

Slicer Styling and Configuration

The slicer needs to be made more intuitive and visually aligned with the rest of the page. Start by converting the default slicer into a button slicer.

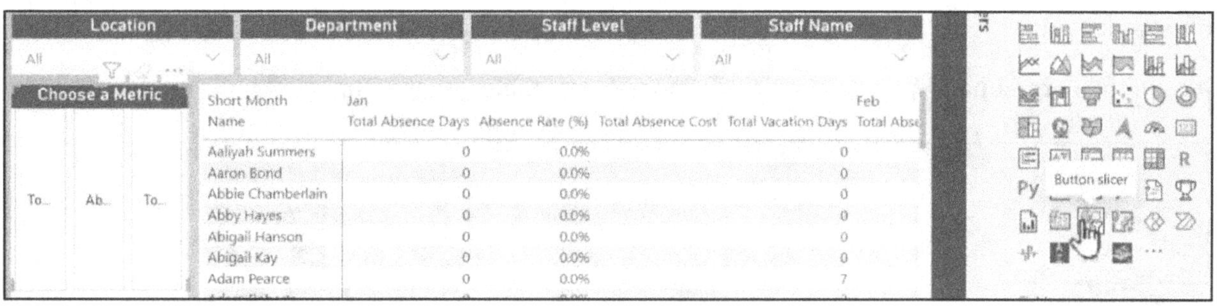

To ensure a consistent look, copy the formatting from an existing slicer—such as the one for month selection:

1. Select the existing month slicer.
2. Click Format Painter.
3. Then click inside the new Absence Metric slicer.

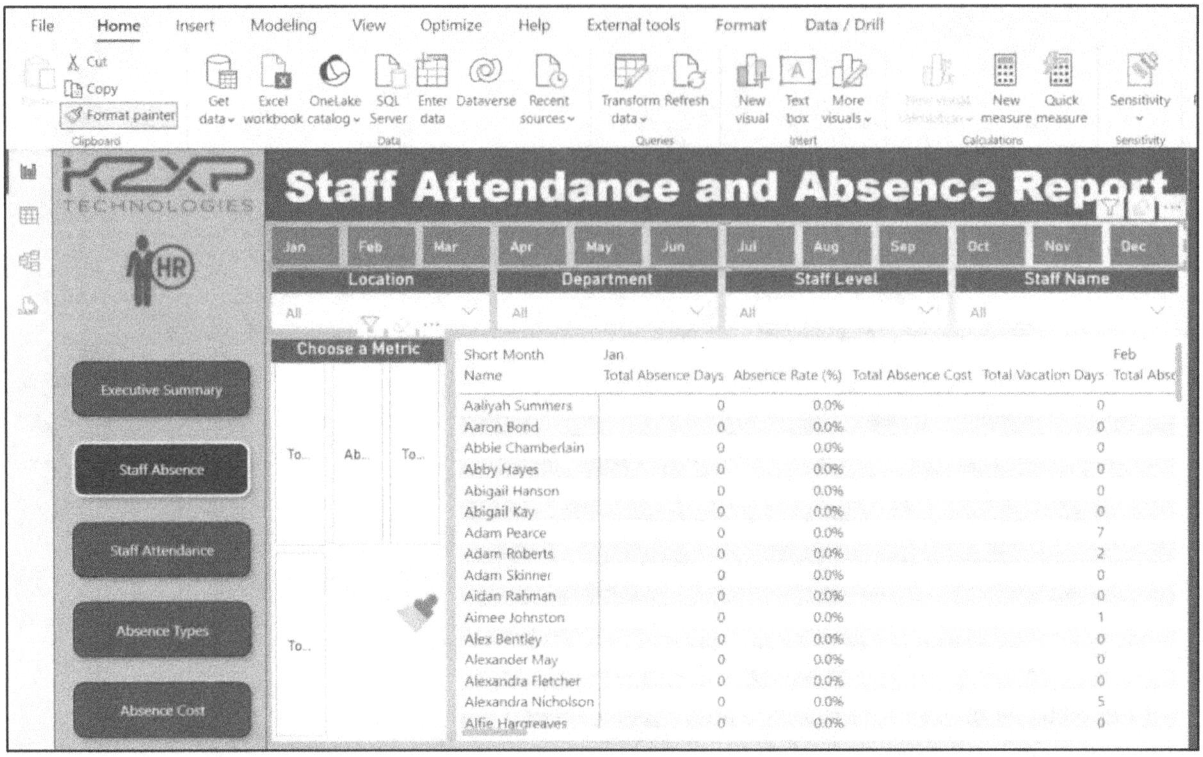

To improve layout:

- In the Format pane, go to Layout and change from Single Row to Single Column.

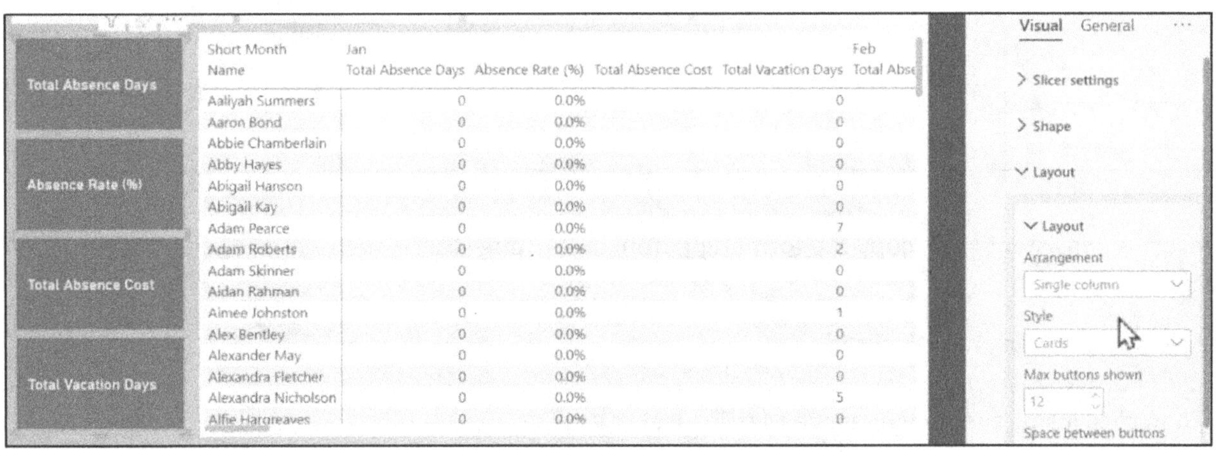

- Adjust the button height to match the visual proportions you want.
- In General > Title, toggle the title on, and type “Choose a metric”.

To complete the formatting:

- Use the Format Painter to copy the title style from another slicer (e.g., the Location slicer).
- Enable Single Select and Forced Selection in Slicer Settings. This ensures the user must select one—and only one—option at all times.

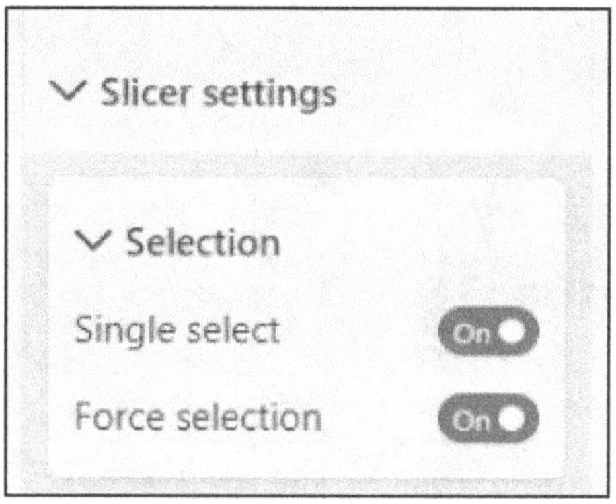

Finally, to maintain a clean design, go to General > Effects, and switch the background off for the slicer.

Conclusion

This Staff Absence page demonstrates the power and efficiency of field parameters. It allows for multiple insights within the same matrix visual, using a compact and user-friendly design. By combining a clean matrix layout with a dynamic metric selector, we empower users to explore data on their own terms—without clutter or complexity.

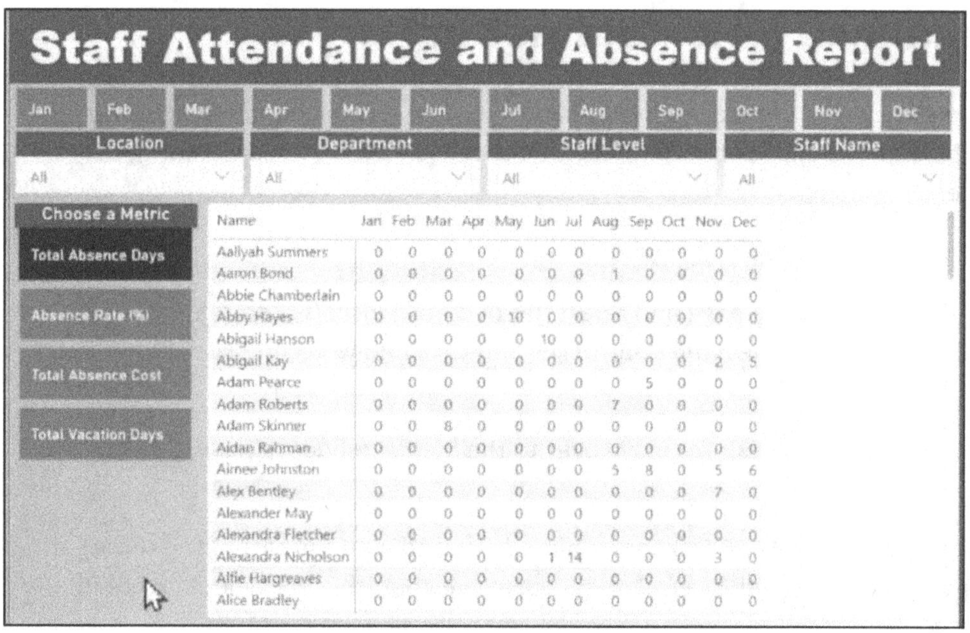

Let's save our changes here. In the next section, we'll apply a similar approach to build the Staff Attendance page.

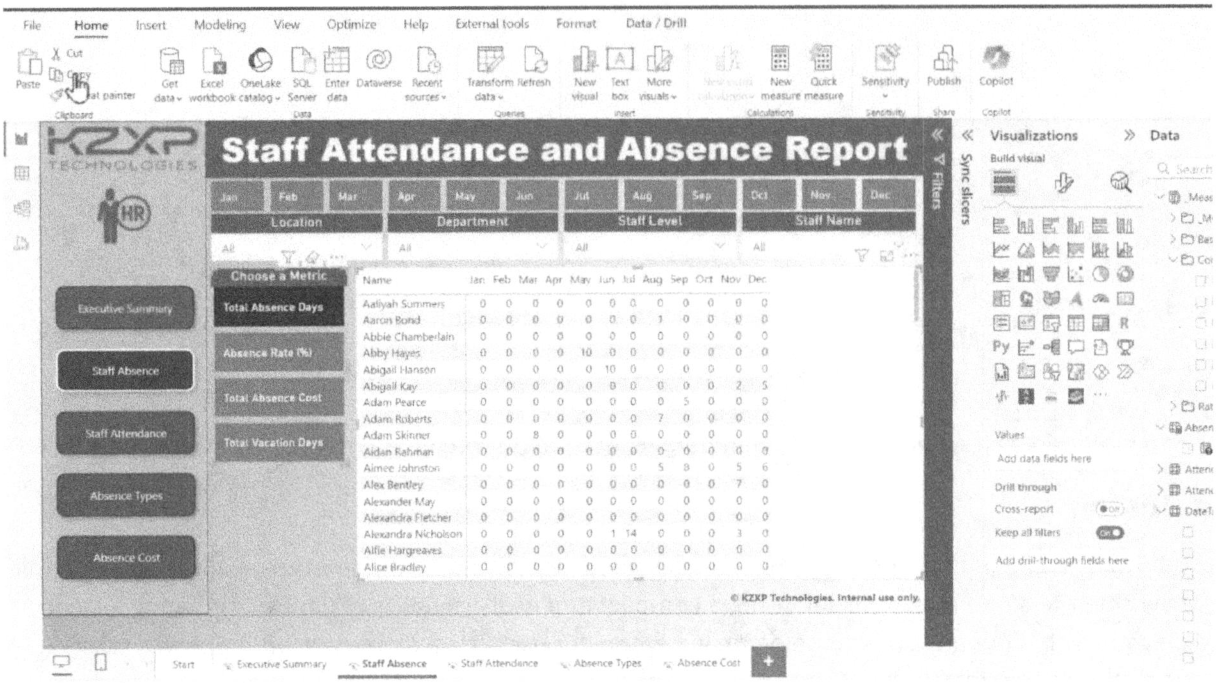

6.7: Staff Attendance Field Parameters

In this section, we complete the design of the Staff Attendance page by leveraging the structural similarity it shares with the Staff Absence page. This allows us to reuse existing visuals, making our development more efficient.

Copying the Visuals from Staff Absence

To begin, we navigate to the Staff Absence page and select the two main visuals used there. This is done by clicking the first visual, then holding down the Control key and clicking the second visual to select both.

Once both visuals are selected, we choose Copy, move over to the Staff Attendance page, and paste the visuals using Paste.

Because the visuals we're copying include a slicer that is already synced with the rest of the report, a dialog will appear asking whether to sync this visual. In this case, we choose Don't sync since we intend to change what the slicer controls.

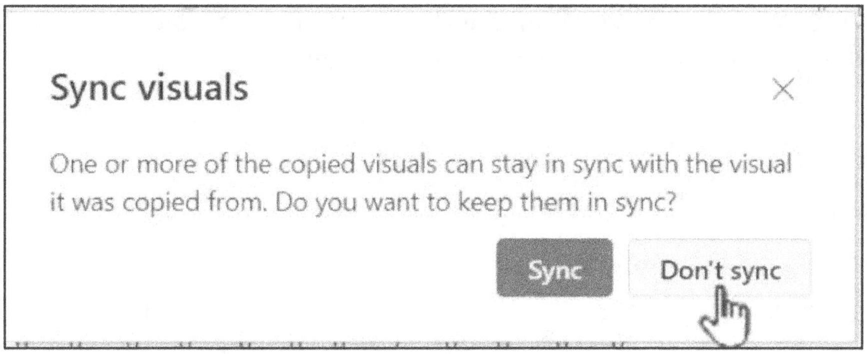

Creating the Attendance Field Parameter

Now we create a new field parameter to control which metrics are shown on this page. From the Modelling ribbon, we choose New parameter, then select our Fields.

We use the same naming convention adopted for the absence metric and name this one Attendance Metric.

Selecting Fields for the Parameter

Next, we browse through our measure folders to find relevant metrics related to attendance. The selected fields are:

From Base Measures:

- Average Hours Worked
- Average Lunch Break
- Total Hours Worked

From Context Measures:

- Total Working Days

From Rate-Based Measures:

- Attendance Rate
- Early Leaving Percent
- Late Arrival Percent

Refining the Parameter Contents

With the selections made, we now adjust the order to reflect a more logical flow:

1. Total Working Days
2. Attendance Rate
3. Late Arrival Percent
4. Early Leaving Percent
5. Average Hours Worked
6. Average Lunch Break

We also decide to remove Total Hours Worked because this measure does not offer meaningful insights when viewed at monthly granularity, which is the level used in our matrix visual.

Since we already copied a slicer onto this page, we do not need to add a new slicer during parameter creation. So, we turn off the option to "Add slicer to page" and click Create.

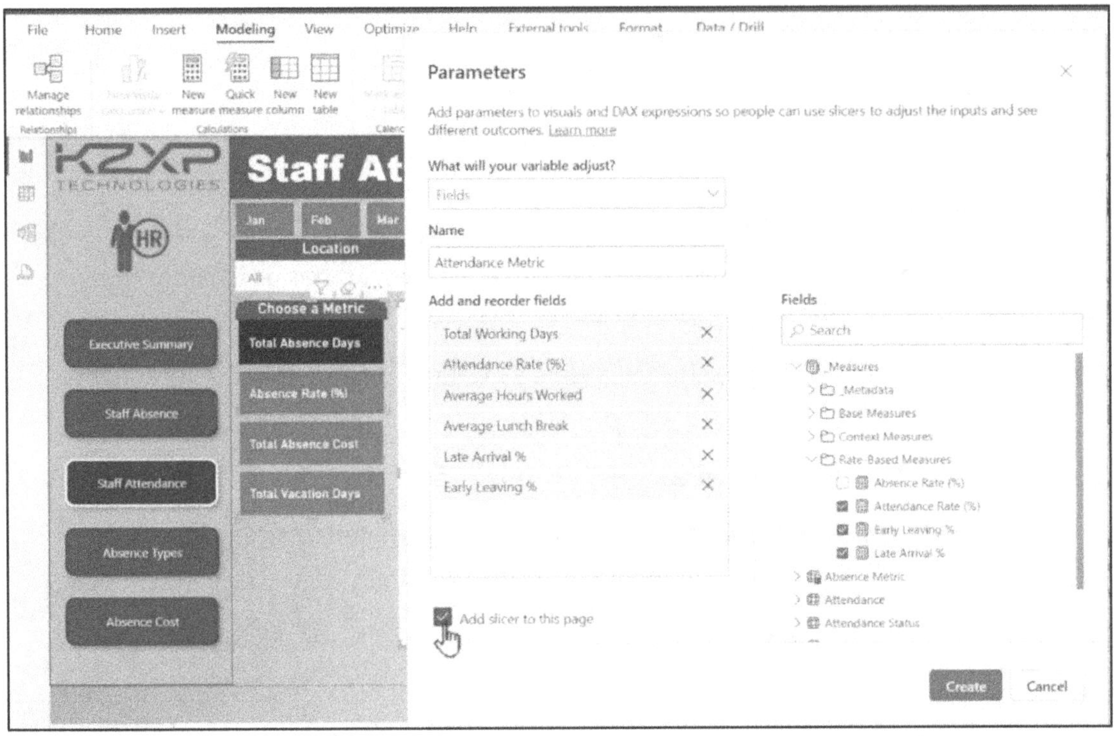

After creation, we close the formula bar to clean up the workspace.

Updating the Visuals to Use Attendance Metrics

Now, we switch the metric being used by both the matrix visual and the slicer. Starting with the matrix:

We select the matrix visual, then drag the new Attendance Metric field parameter into the Values field area.

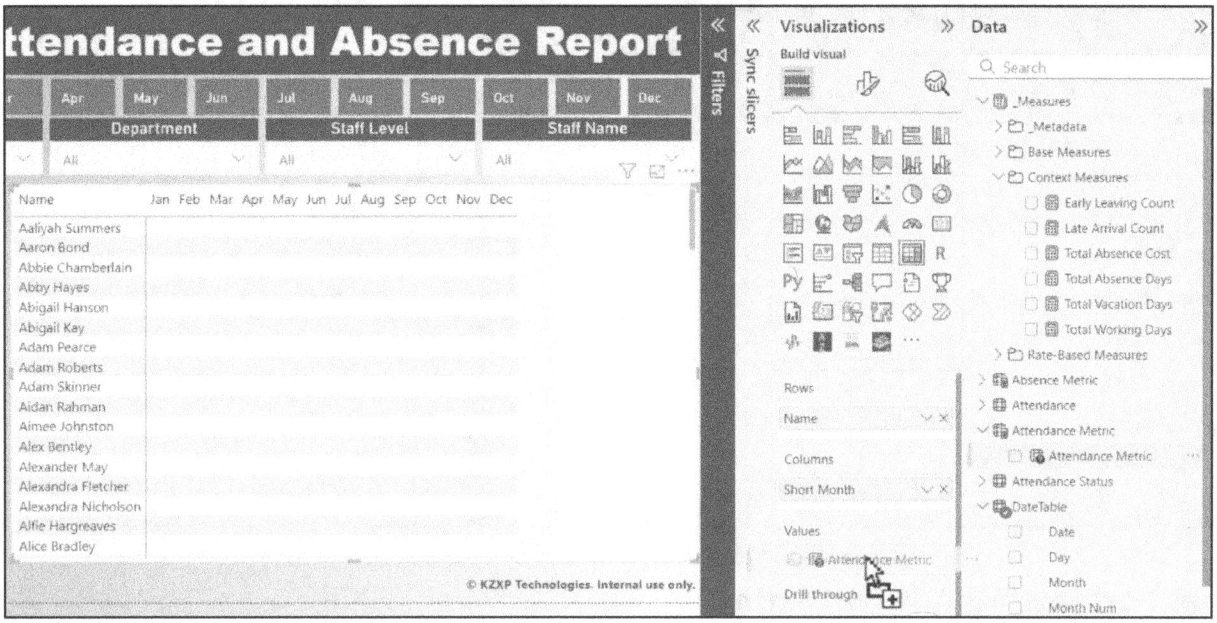

At first, the matrix appears misaligned. This is expected, as nothing is currently selected in the associated slicer, leaving the matrix unfiltered.

To resolve this, we turn our attention to the slicer:

We select the slicer visual, remove the previous Absence Metric parameter, and replace it with the new Attendance Metric parameter.

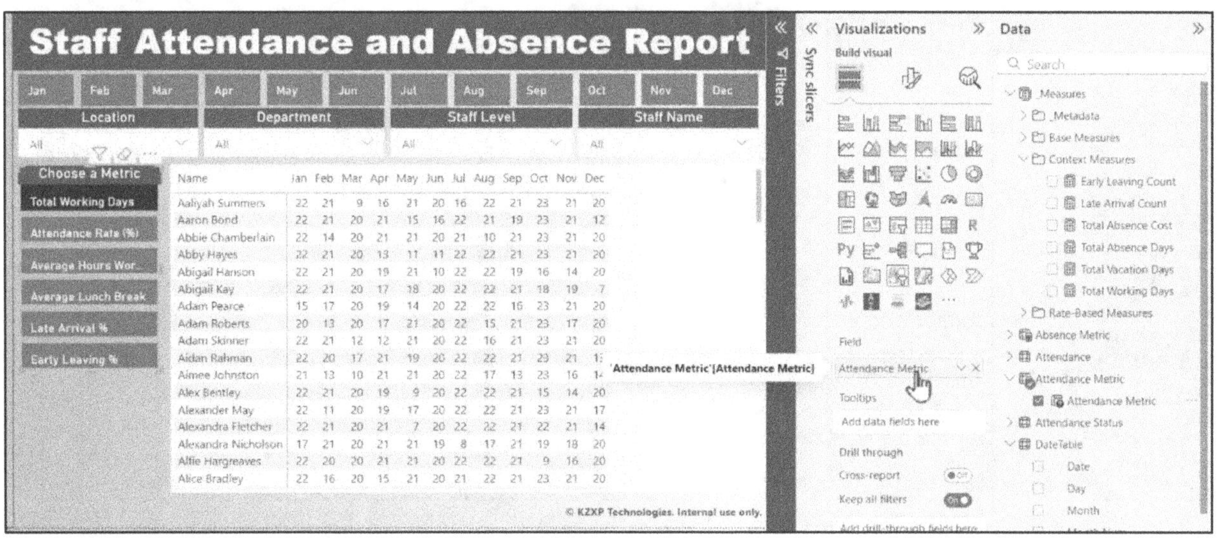

Because the slicer was copied from the absence page, it has inherited the single select behaviour. This means users can only choose one metric at a time, which is appropriate in this context.

Given that the attendance metric includes more options than the absence metric, we increase the height of the slicer visual to accommodate the extra buttons.

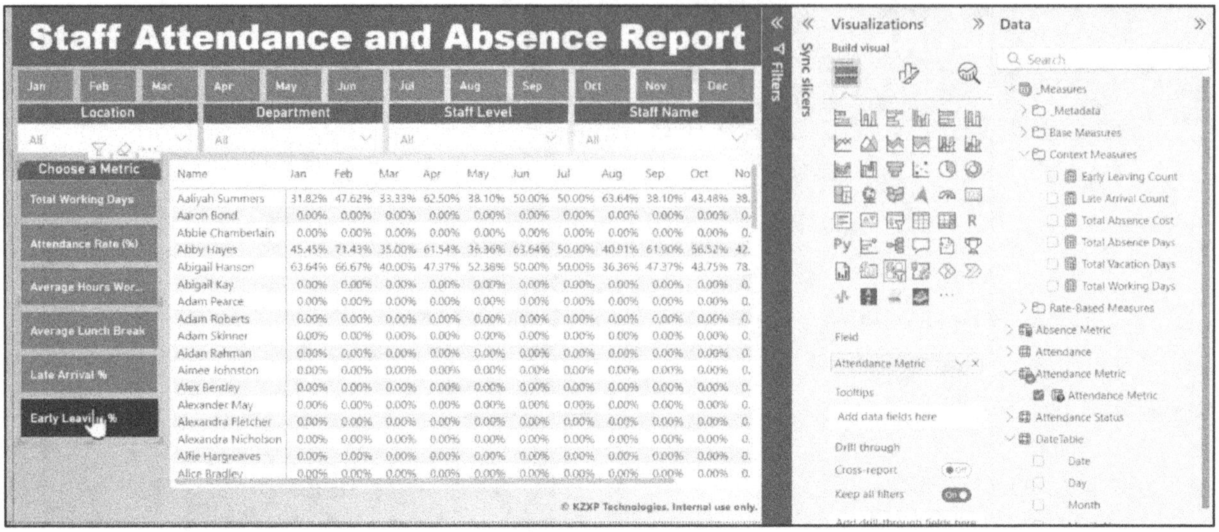

Final Formatting Adjustments

With the slicer now correctly connected, the matrix visual updates accordingly. You may notice that some metric selections cause the matrix to require horizontal scrolling.

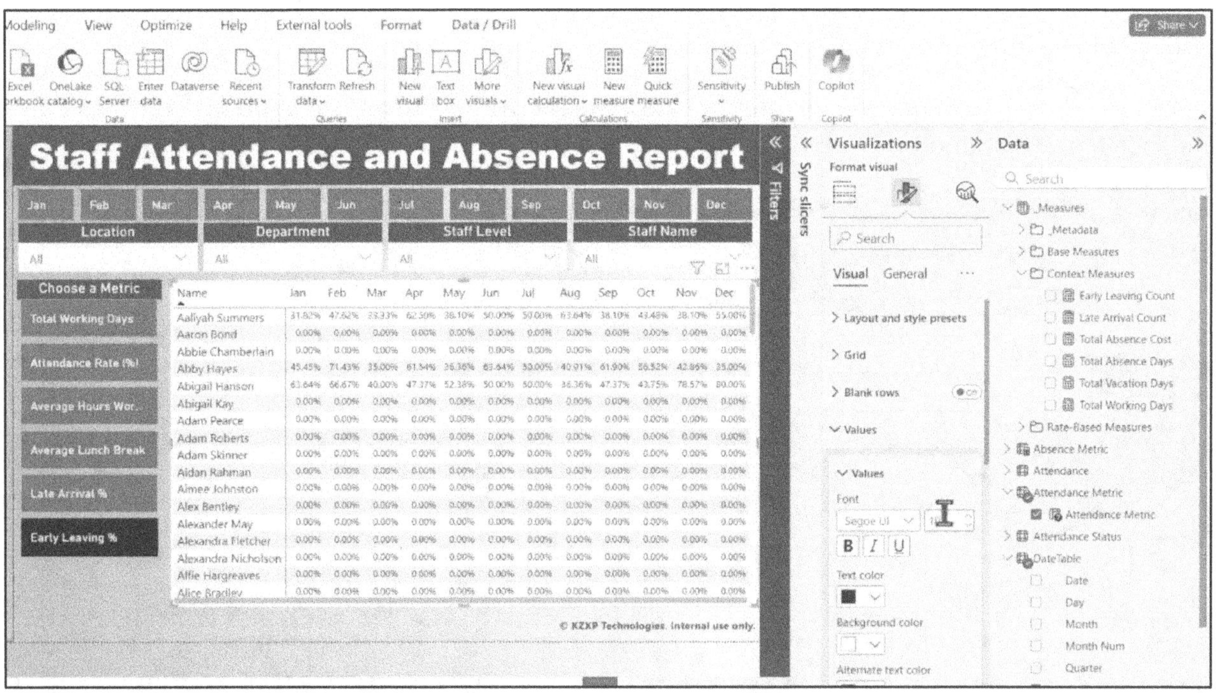

To fix this, you can make two formatting adjustments:

- Select the matrix, go to the Values formatting options, and reduce the font size to 10 or less if necessary.
- Slightly increase the width of the matrix visual to allow more columns to be visible.

These tweaks ensure all content is readable and conveniently displayed without scrolling.

With that, the Staff Attendance page is complete. The page is now dynamically controlled by a field parameter that includes multiple attendance-related metrics, presented in a clean and accessible format.

6.8: Creating a Drill-Down Hierarchy

In this section, we will complete the Absence Types page, which features a single visual—but that visual contains four separate fields working together. This is achieved using a feature in Power BI known as drill down, which works in conjunction with a data modelling construct called hierarchies.

A hierarchy in Power BI is a special object that contains multiple related fields, typically arranged in a parent-child relationship. For instance, when dealing with date fields, the classic example of a hierarchy consists of four levels: Year, Quarter, Month, and Day. Each year breaks down into quarters, each quarter into months, and each month into days. This is an intuitive, natural way to explore time-based data.

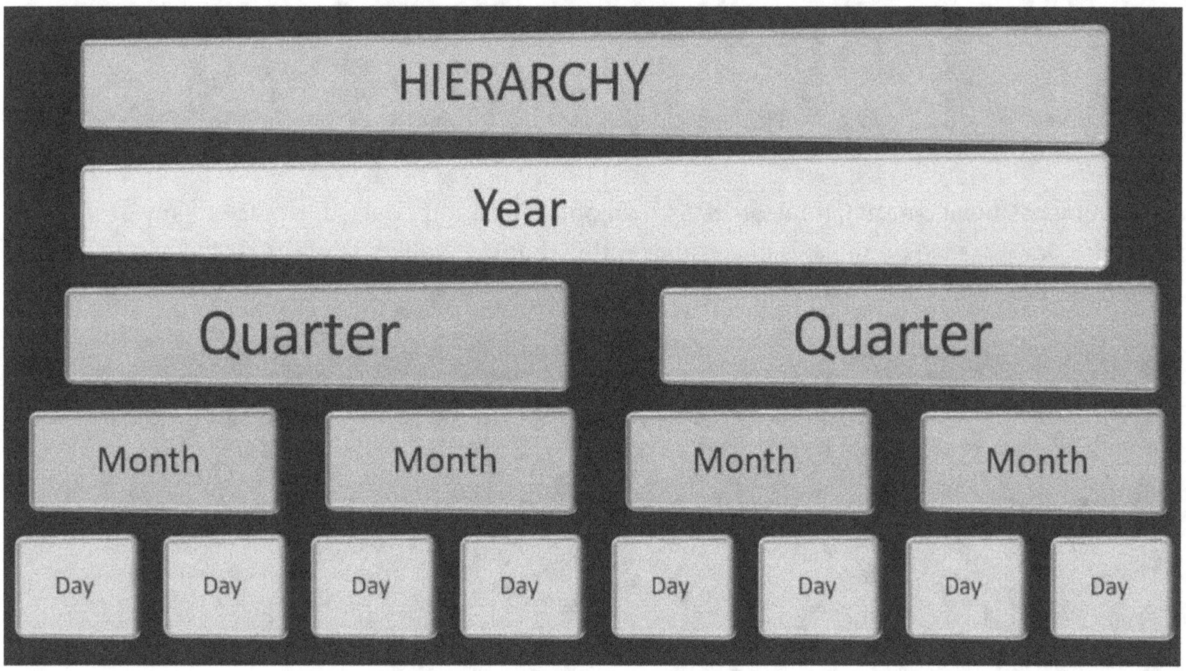

In our example, however, we're working with staff attendance data. We'll be using the Attendance Status table to construct our own hierarchy made up of four fields, all of which follow a clear parent-child relationship. At the top level, we have Authorization. Each Authorization category can then be broken down into an Absence Group. Each Absence Group in turn breaks down into Absence Type, and finally, each Absence Type can be broken down into a specific Absence Reason.

This structure is a textbook use case for Power BI's hierarchy feature:

1. Authorization – Level 1
2. Absence Group – Level 2
3. Absence Type – Level 3
4. Absence Reason – Level 4

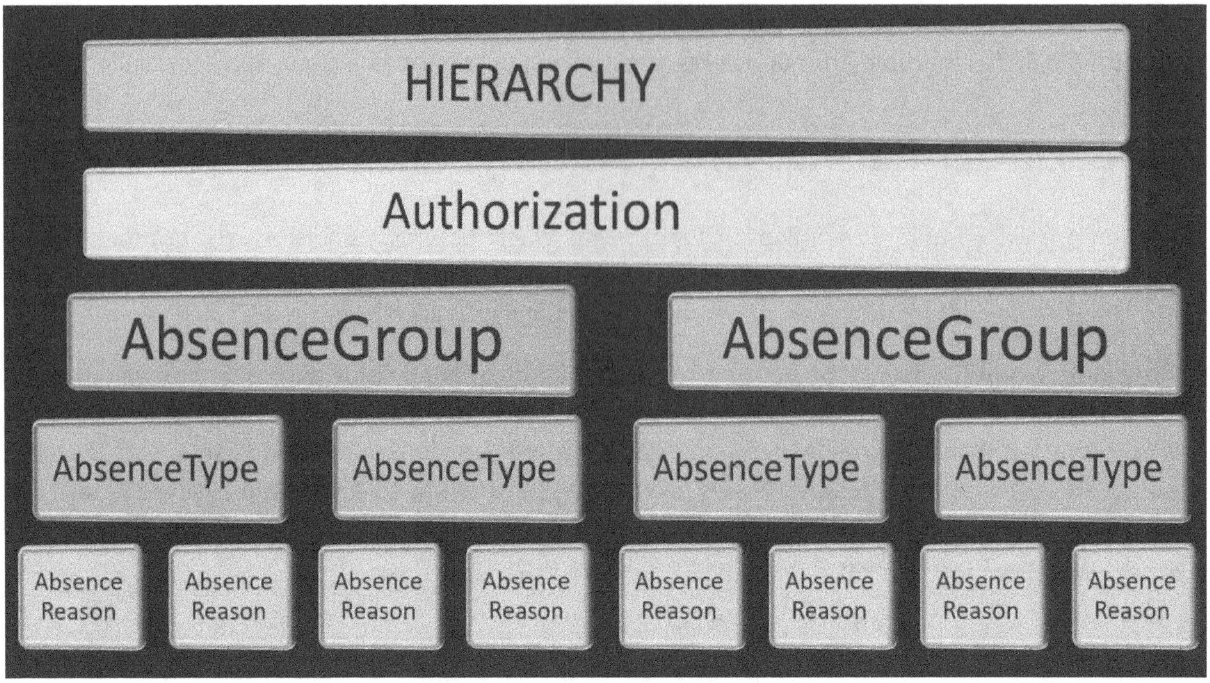

Once a hierarchy has been created, it becomes its own object and can be used in place of any of the individual fields, for instance on the axis of a visual. In this chapter, we'll create a TreeMap and use our new hierarchy as the categorical axis.

Placing a hierarchy in a visual's category field automatically enables drill down functionality.

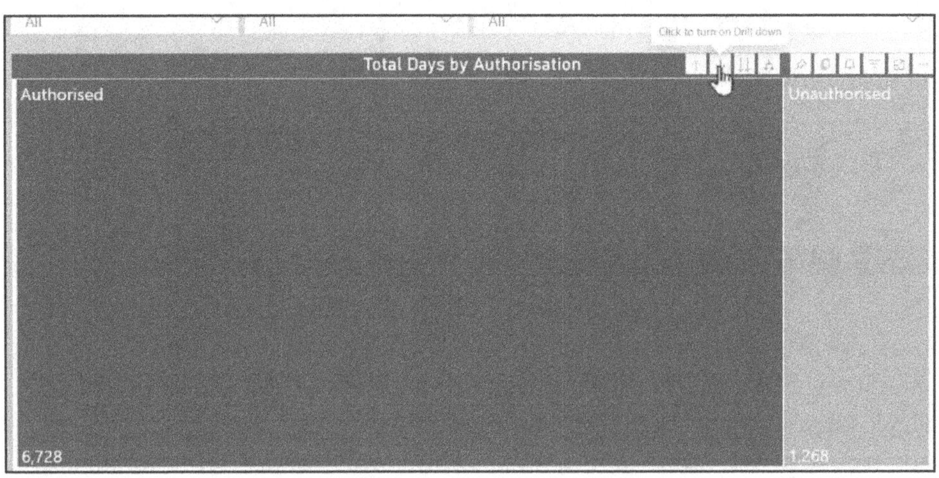

This allows users to interactively click into elements at any level of the hierarchy and drill deeper into the detail below. For example, clicking on "Unauthorized" at Level 1 will reveal the Absence Groups within that category. Clicking on "Personal Leave" within that group will expose the corresponding Absence Types and selecting "Family Emergency" within that will finally display the Absence Reasons associated with it.

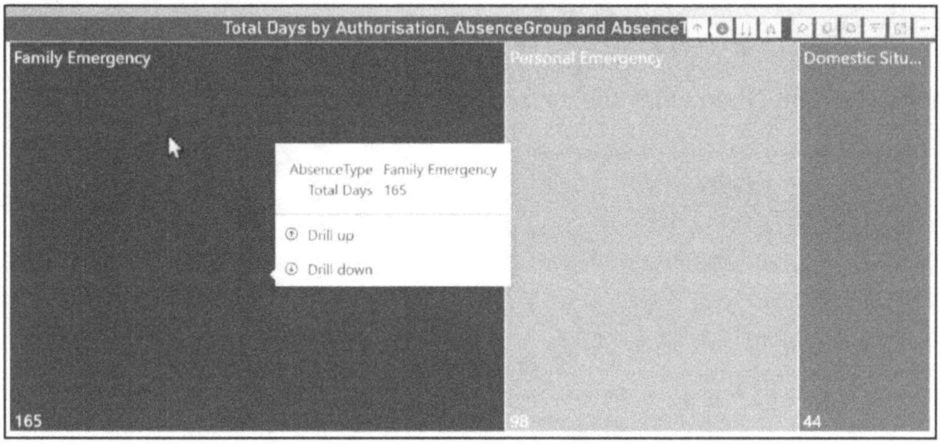

This drill-down functionality makes it easy for users to explore data with a nested or grouped structure, moving both down and back up through the hierarchy seamlessly.

Creating the Hierarchy

The first step is to create the hierarchy itself. Although this can be done in any view, we'll use Report View for ease of access. Open the Attendance Status table in the Fields pane.

To begin, right-click on the field that will serve as Level 1—in our case, that's Authorization—and choose Create hierarchy. This action creates a new hierarchy object named after the initial field, with Authorization as its only level.

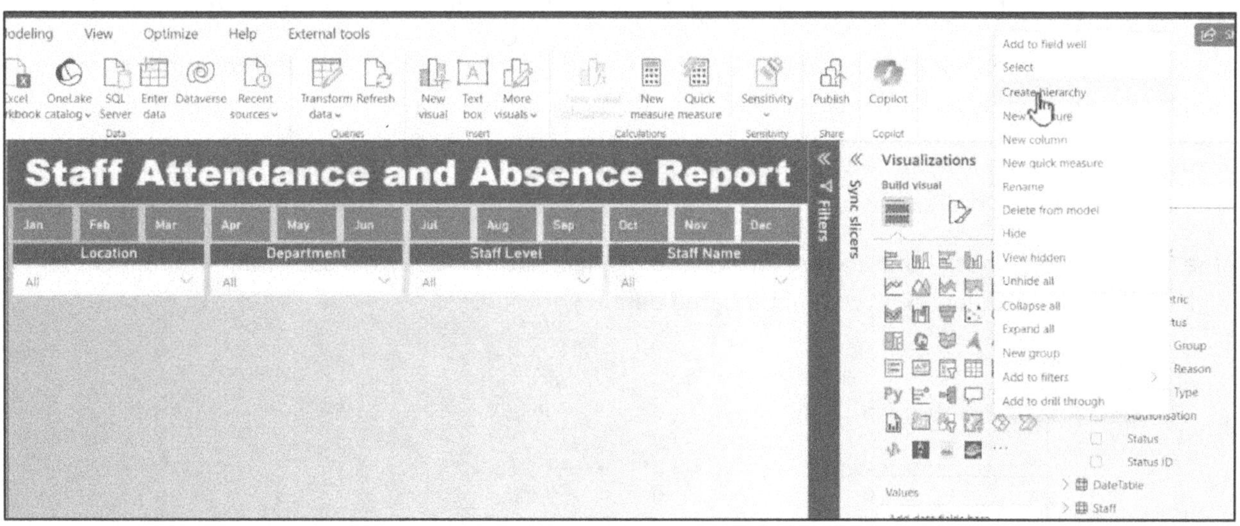

Next, we need to build the remainder of the hierarchy by adding each subsequent field in the correct order:

1. Right-click on Absence Group, and select Add to hierarchy → Authorization Hierarchy
2. Right-click on Absence Type, and again choose Add to hierarchy → Authorization Hierarchy
3. Right-click on Absence Reason, and choose Add to hierarchy → Authorization Hierarchy

At this point, you may wish to rename the hierarchy to reflect its broader contents. Since it now contains more than just Authorization, a name like Absence Hierarchy would be more appropriate. Right-click on the hierarchy object and choose Rename, then enter the new name.

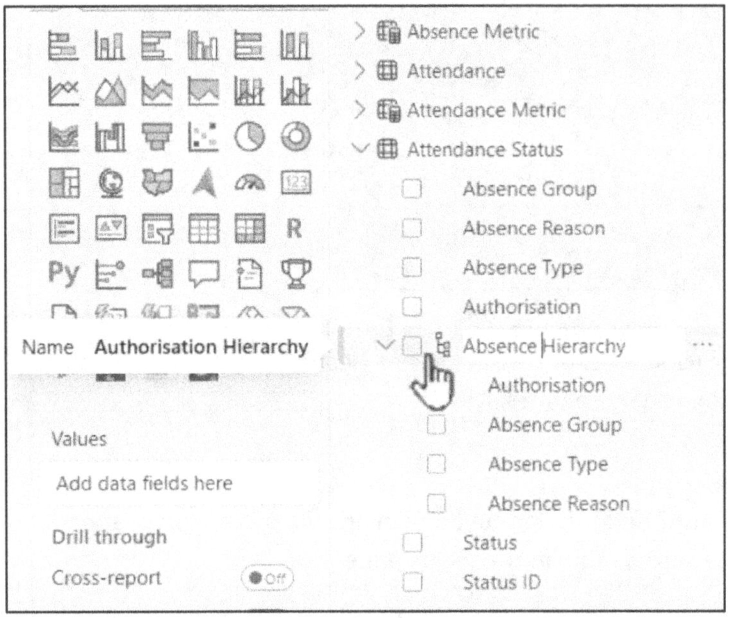

Adding the Hierarchy to a TreeMap Visual

Now that we've created the hierarchy, we'll use it in a TreeMap visual to allow drill-down exploration.

Start by adding a TreeMap to your report page. Resize and position it appropriately, ensuring there's enough room to display all interactive controls comfortably.

For the Category field, instead of selecting a single field, drag in the new Absence Hierarchy. This automatically enables drill-down mode.

In the Values area, choose the measure we wish to display. In this case, we'll use Total Attendance Days, which gives us a raw count of attendance-related data.

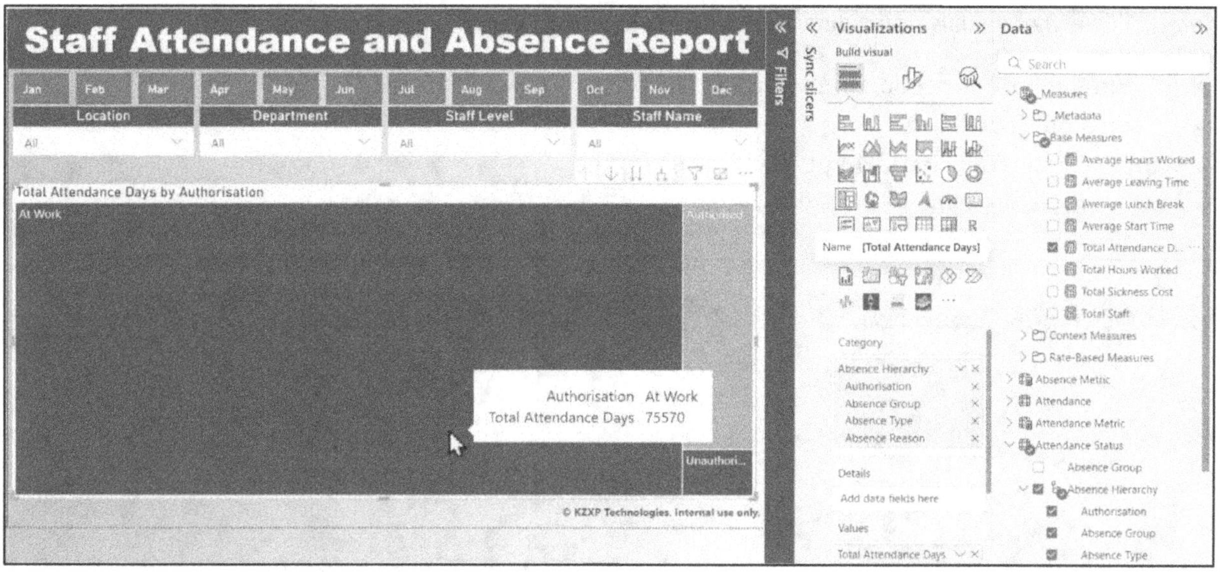

Filtering and Formatting

The TreeMap will initially show all top-level categories, including "At Work". Since our page is focusing specifically on absence-related data, we'll apply a filter to remove that category.

To do this, open the Filters pane, drag in the Authorization field, and filter it to exclude "At Work". Deselect it, leaving only the absence categories.

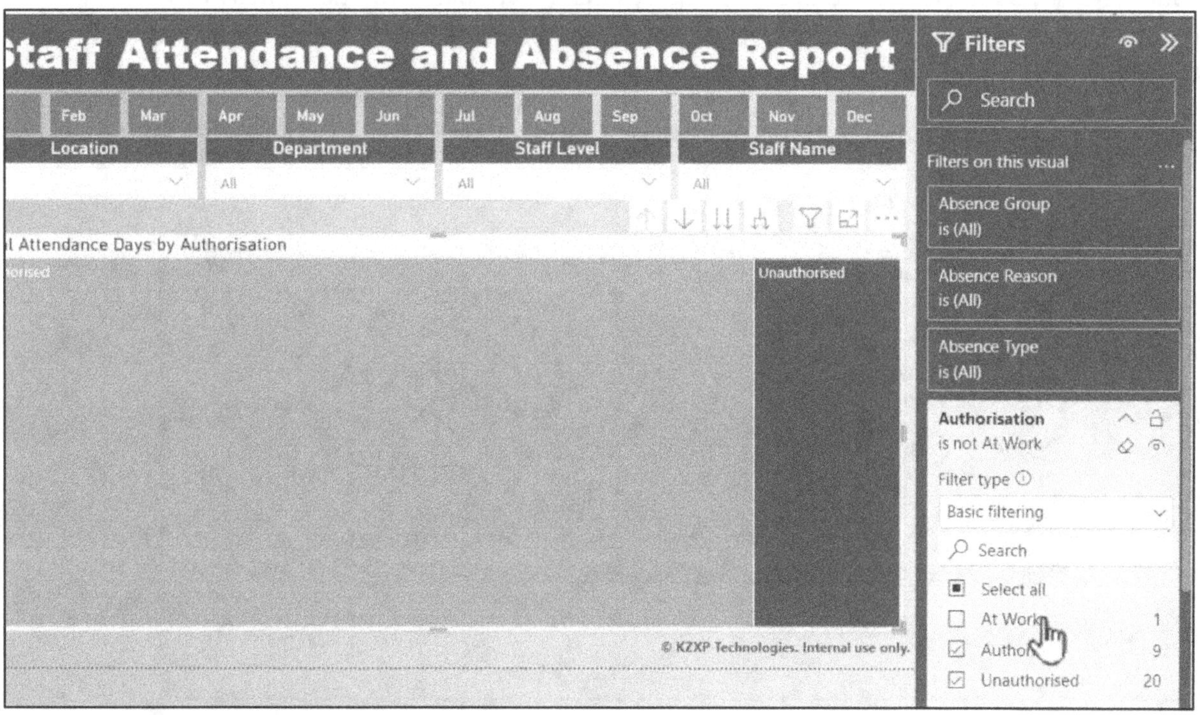

Next, let's improve the appearance. Start by copying the formatting from an existing slicer title. Select a slicer (e.g., Location), click the Format Painter, then click inside the TreeMap to apply the style.

By default, TreeMap visuals don't display numbers. To show figures clearly:

- Open the Format section in the Visualizations pane
- Switch on Data Labels
- Increase the font size to 14 pt
- Also adjust the Category Labels to match

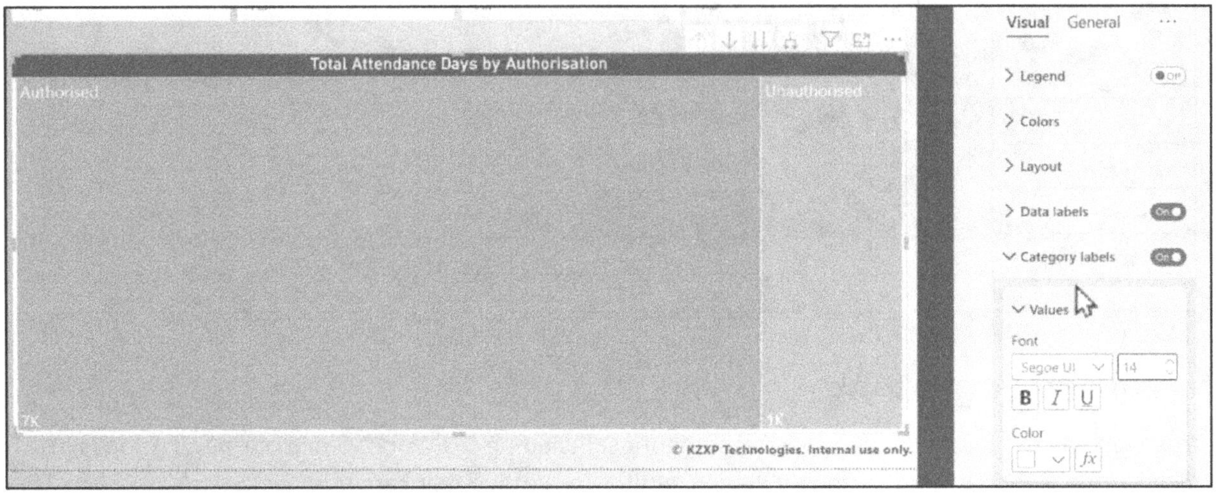

Interacting with the Drill-Down Feature

With our hierarchy added to the TreeMap's category field, Power BI automatically activates the drill-down icons in the top-right corner of the visual. You'll see four small icons—the second of which enables drill-down mode.

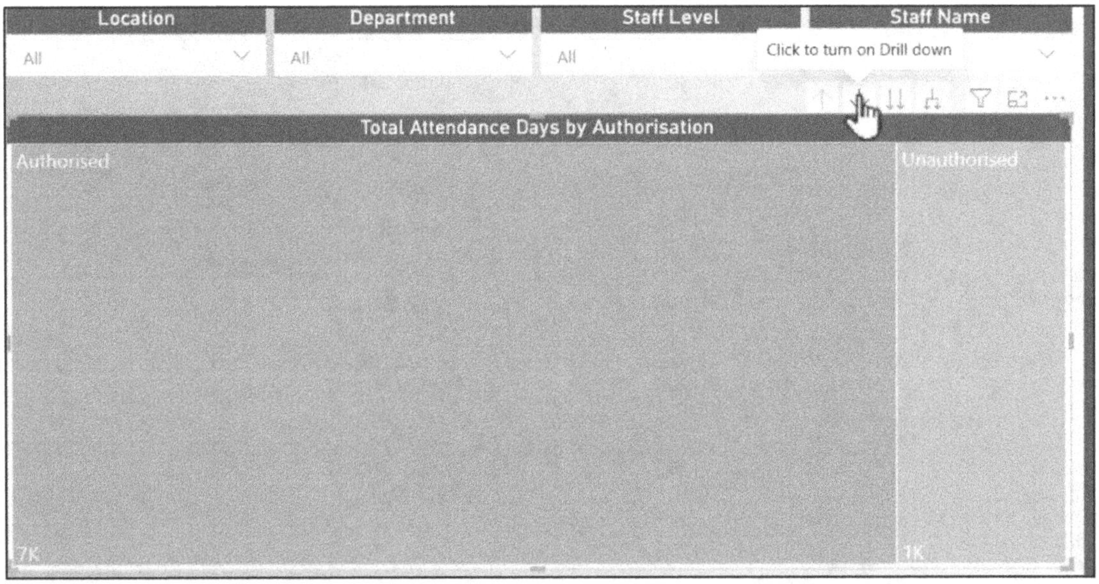

When a user clicks this icon, it toggles drill-down mode on. In this state, clicking on any item in the TreeMap drills one level deeper into the hierarchy.

For example, selecting "Unauthorized" will drill from Authorization into the corresponding Absence Groups. Clicking "Personal Leave" within that will show Absence Types. Selecting "Family Emergency" within Absence Type then displays the Absence Reasons tied to that path.

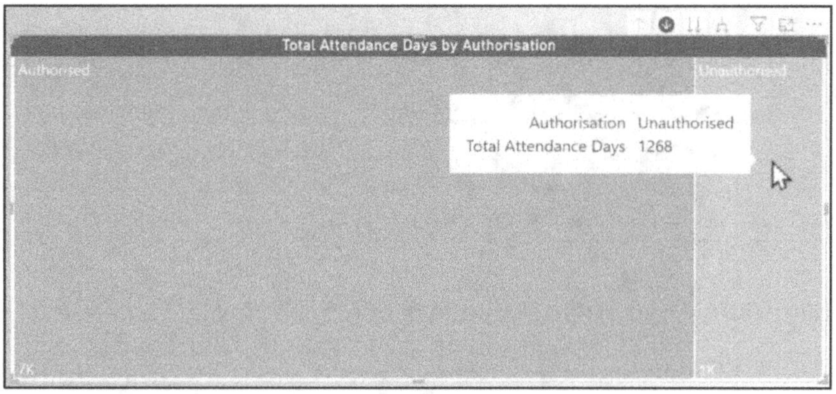

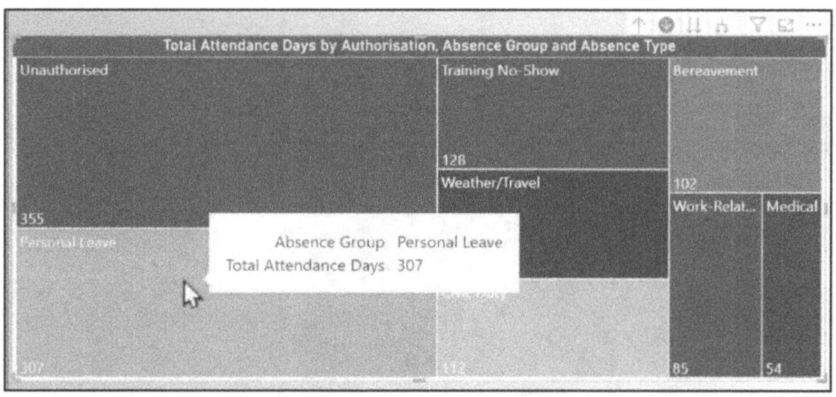

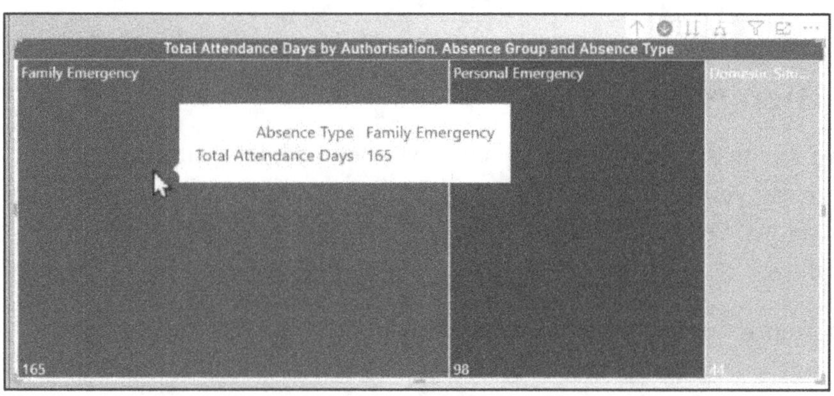

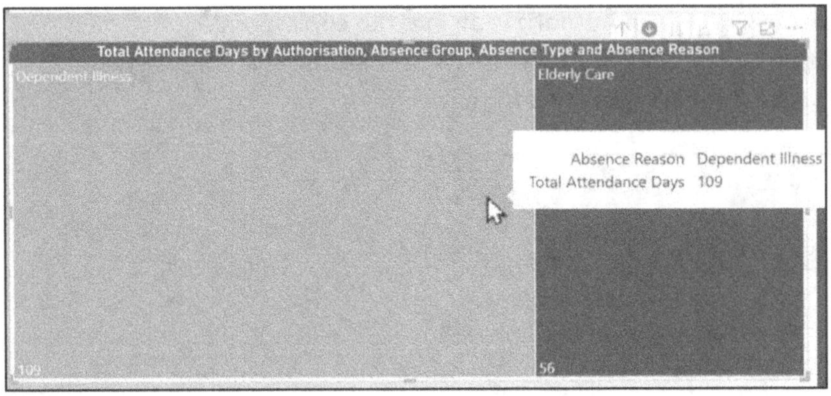

At any time, the user can click the drill-up arrow to move back up the hierarchy and explore a different path.

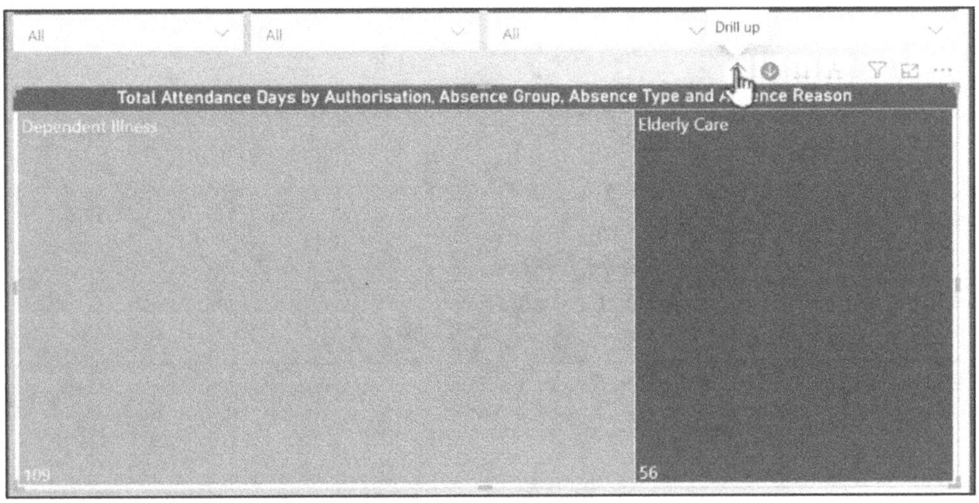

When to Use Drill-Down Hierarchies

This drill-down approach provides an intuitive way for users to explore structured data without overwhelming the visual space. Wherever you have fields that follow a logical parent-child relationship—especially in domains like HR, sales regions, product categories, or time—you might consider using hierarchies to expose those relationships.

They not only enhance the user experience but also keep your reports clean, dynamic, and interactive.

6.9: Visualizing Absence Cost

In this section, we will complete the Absence Cost page of the report by presenting the cost of staff absence in three clear and complementary ways: by location, by role, and as a trend over time. These visualisations offer different perspectives on the same underlying data, enabling clearer understanding and more informed decision-making.

As we add multiple visuals to a page in Power BI, it's important to understand how they interact with one another. By default, when you click on a data point in one visual—such as a pie chart—Power BI uses a behaviour called cross highlighting. This means other visuals on the page will show a highlighted subset of their data in response but will still display the full dataset.

In the example shown below, the treemap slice "Staff" has been selected in the treemap. This triggers cross-highlighting across the other visuals on the page, most clearly observed in the pie chart to the left.

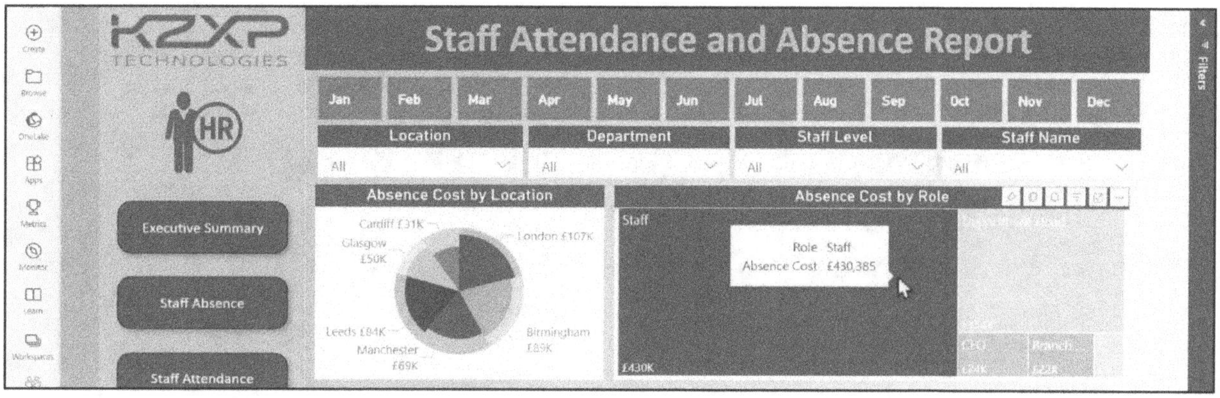

In some cases, especially when you're trying to simplify the user experience or create more focused filters, cross filtering is a better choice. Cross filtering replaces the current visual data entirely with a filtered version, making it easier to focus on one slice of information at a time.

If you're working on a report where you consistently prefer cross filtering over cross highlighting, you can change the default behaviour for your file. This ensures every new visual you add will use cross filtering without needing to adjust it manually.

Changing the Default Visual Interaction to Cross Filtering

To change the default interaction type from cross highlighting to cross filtering:

1. Go to the File menu in Power BI Desktop.
2. Select Options and settings, and then click Options.
3. Scroll down the list on the left and, under Current File, choose Report settings.
4. At the top of the Report settings pane, find the option labelled Change the default visual interaction from cross highlighting to cross filtering and enable it.

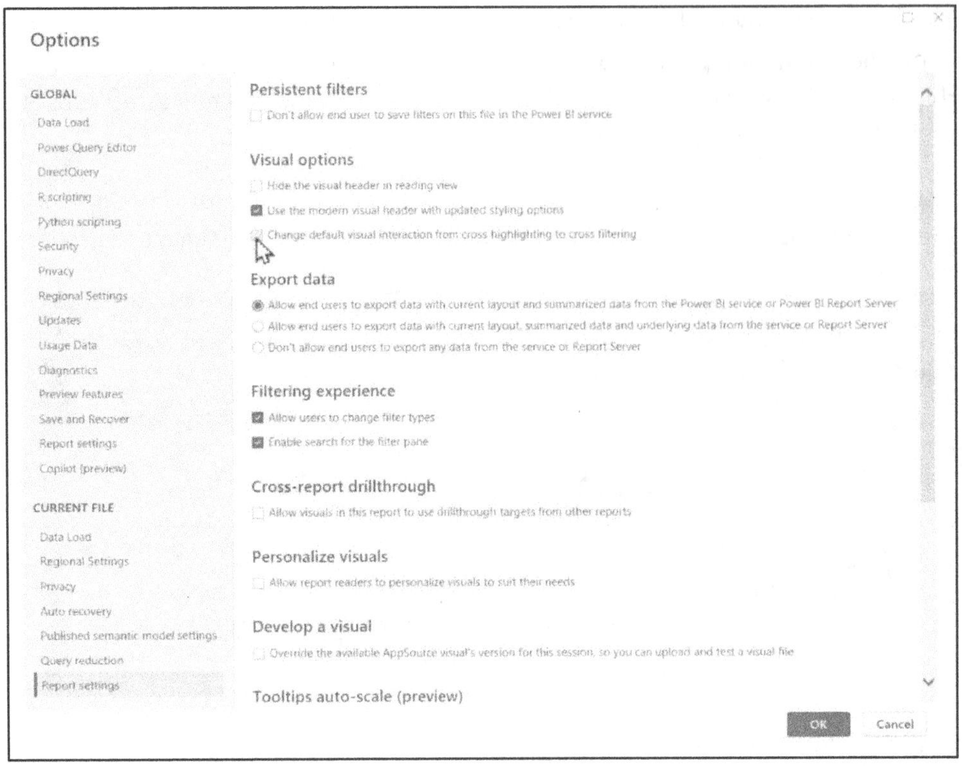

With this change made, any new visuals created in this report file will now use cross filtering by default.

Creating the Absence Cost by Location Pie Chart

Let's begin with a pie chart that displays absence cost by location. Position this visual in the top left of the report page.

1. Add a pie chart visual to the canvas.
2. In the Legend, add the field Staff Location.
3. In the Values, add the measure Total Absence Cost from your context measures table.

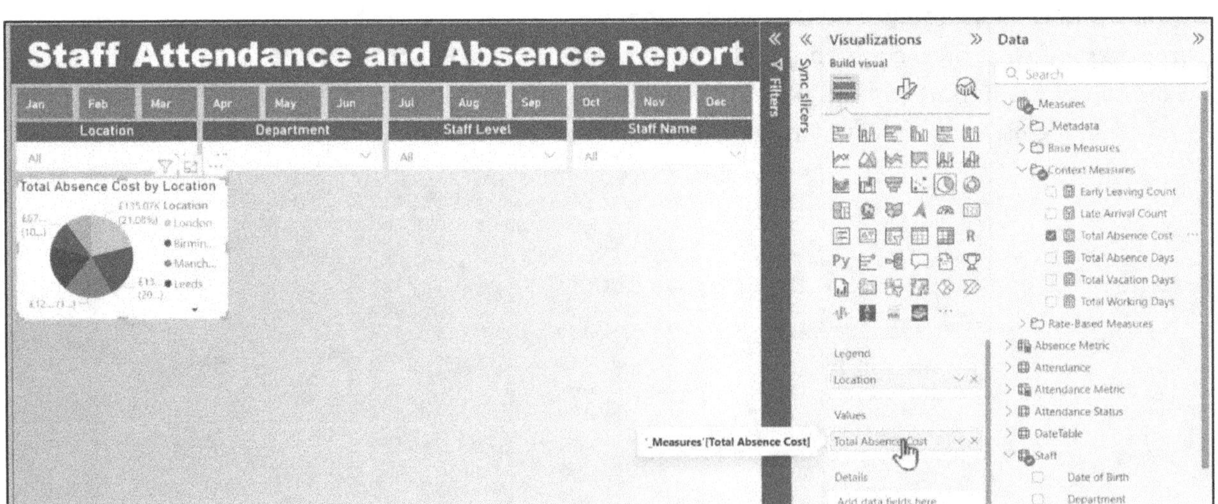

Next, we'll apply formatting for consistency.

1. Click on the existing location slicer, activate the Format Painter, and then click inside the pie chart to copy formatting.
2. Now, with the pie chart selected, open the Format pane in the Visualizations area.
3. If a selection has been made within the chart due to the click made during format painting, click elsewhere in the chart to cancel the selection and restore the full view and facilitate formatting.

Now make the following format changes:

1. Turn Legend off to save space.
2. Enable Detail Labels instead.
3. Set Label Contents to display both Category and Data Value.

- Change the title to read Absence Cost by Location, removing the word "Total".
- Resize the pie chart as needed to ensure no location names are cut off.

Creating the Absence Cost by Role Tree Map

To build the next visual, we'll use a copy of the pie chart and convert it into a tree map.

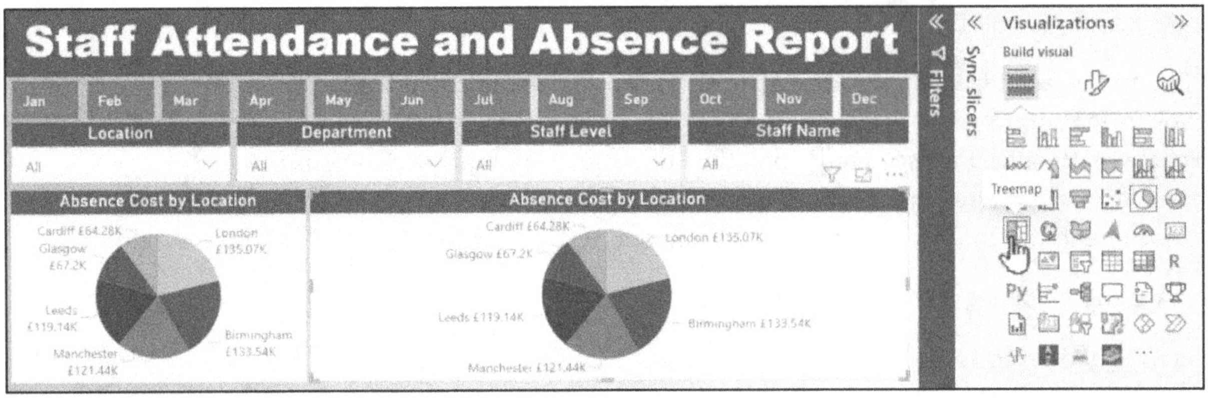

1. Select the pie chart and copy it.
2. Change the visual type from Pie to Tree Map.
3. Leave the Values as Total Absence Cost.
4. Replace the Legend/Category field with Staff Role.

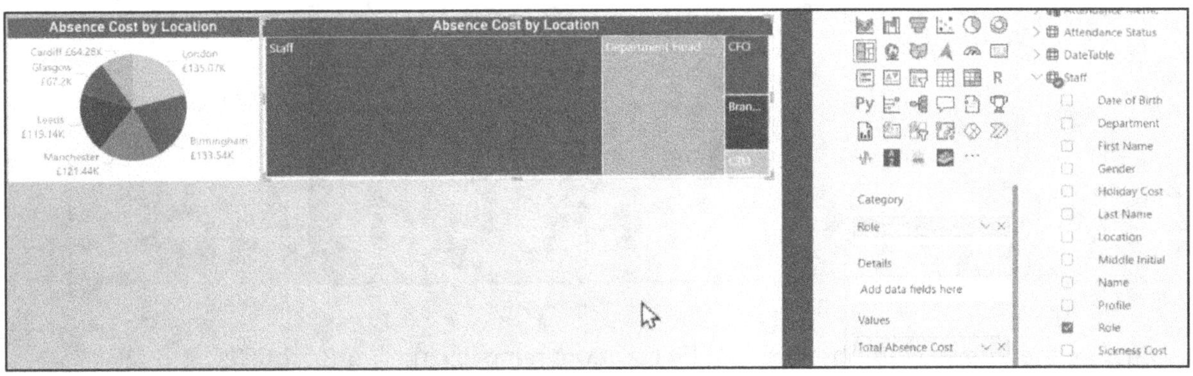

Now, test your cross-filtering setup:

- Click on a role, such as "Staff", and verify that the pie chart is now filtered accordingly.
- Click on a location in the pie chart, such as "London", and check that the tree map updates using cross filtering, not cross highlighting.

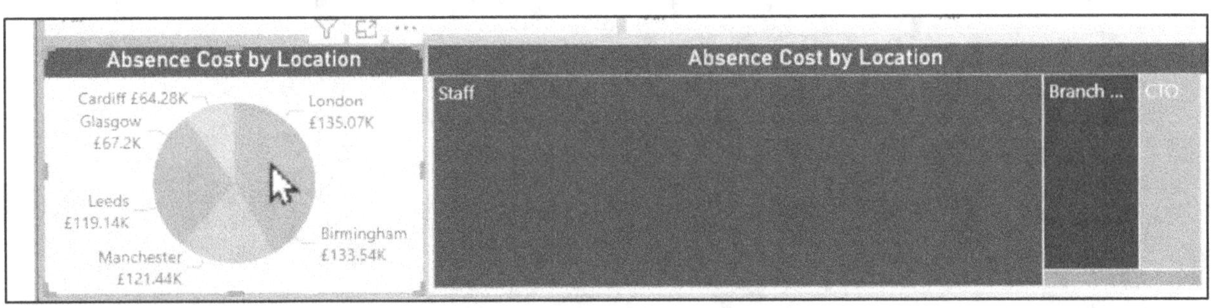

Visualising Absence Cost Over Time

To complete the page, we'll add a line chart to show how absence cost trends over the year.

1. Insert a Line Chart visual onto the canvas.
2. On the X-Axis, place Date Table[Date].
3. On the Y-Axis, place Total Absence Cost from your context measures.

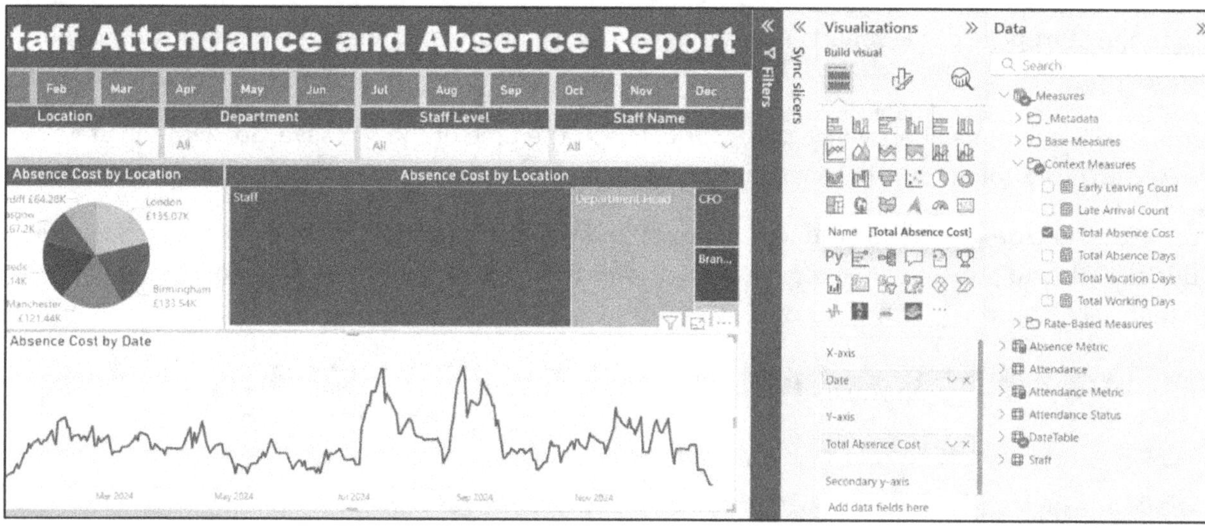

Now update the formatting:

- In the Format pane, under General, switch the Title off to reveal more of the chart area.

Finally, test cross filtering once more. Click on a specific data point in the line chart—in the following example, 15th July—and observe how both the pie chart and the tree map filter in response to that single date selection.

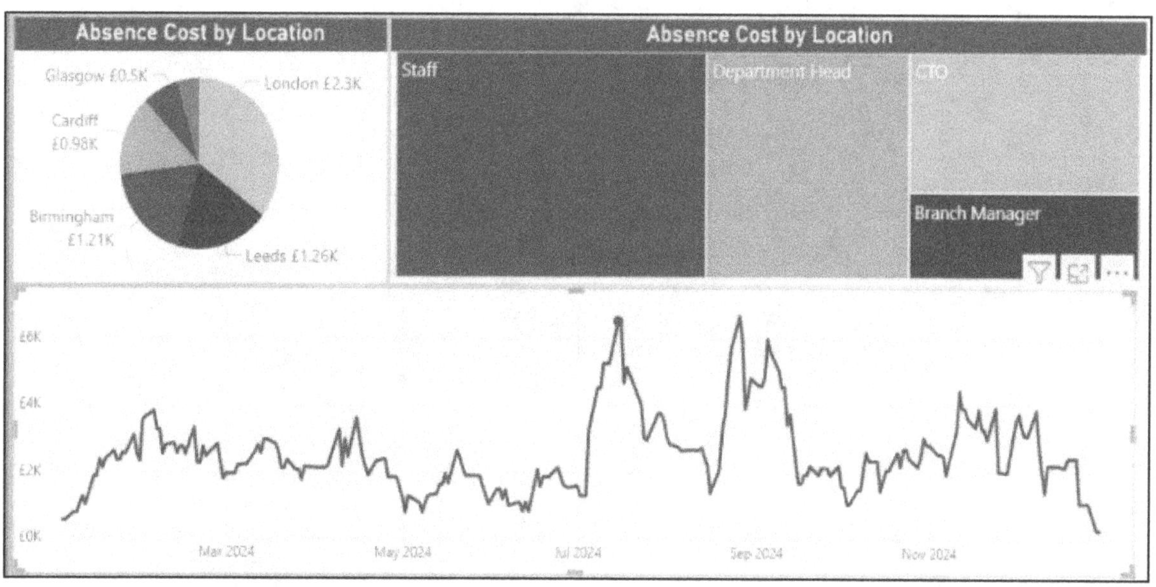

Final Save and Report Setup

With the Absence Cost page complete, we now conclude work on the report. As a final step, it's important to control which page the report opens to when viewed in Power BI.

Return to the Start page of the report. This is the page we want users to see first whenever they open the report.

Power BI, like Excel, remembers which page was active at the time of the last save. So, with the Start page selected, save your report to lock in this behaviour.

This completes the design of the Absence Cost page and the full report file. In the next chapter, we will turn our attention to publishing the report to the Power BI Service and begin building dashboards from its content.

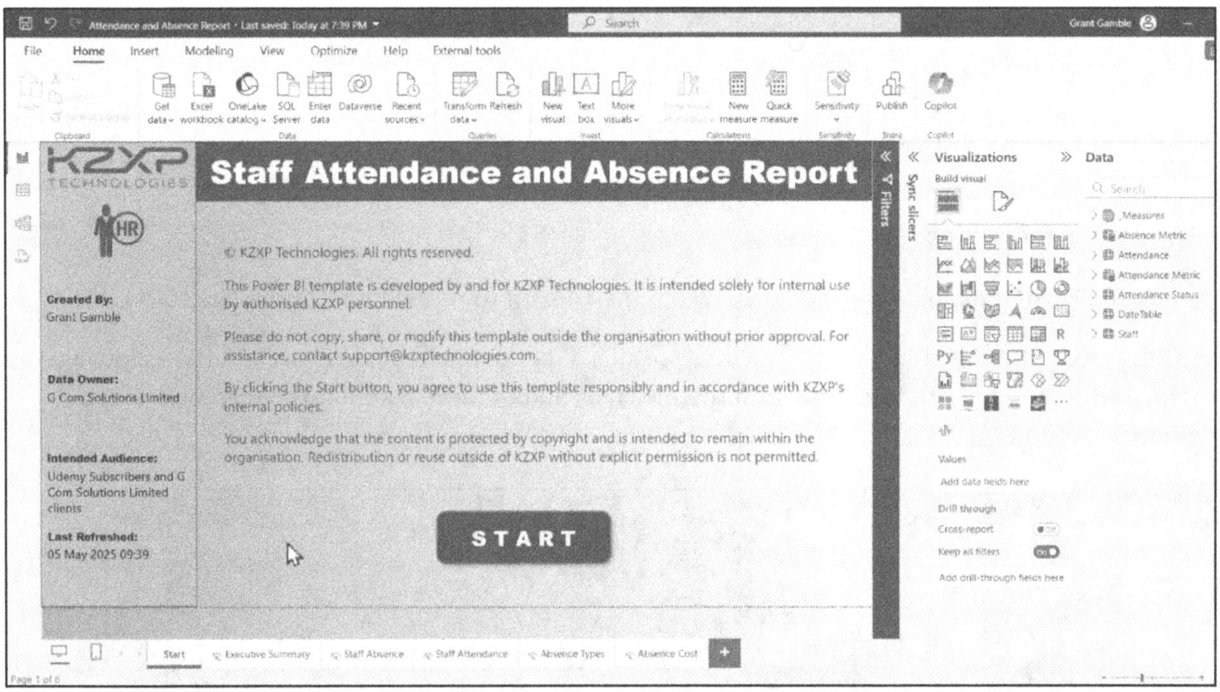

Chapter 7-Attendance and Absence Report- Sharing

7.1: Creating Dashboards

In this chapter, we explore how to publish your report into the Power BI Service and build dashboards from your existing reports. Dashboards are a powerful way to provide quick, high-level overviews of your business data and are distinct from the more interactive and detailed reports created in Power BI Desktop.

Publishing a Report to the Power BI Service

To begin, navigate to the Home tab in Power BI Desktop. From here, click the Publish button. Before the report can be published, Power BI prompts you to save any unsaved changes.

Once saved, a dialog appears where you can select a workspace. In this case, select the Human Resources workspace and click Select. Power BI will now publish the report to the chosen workspace in the Power BI Service.

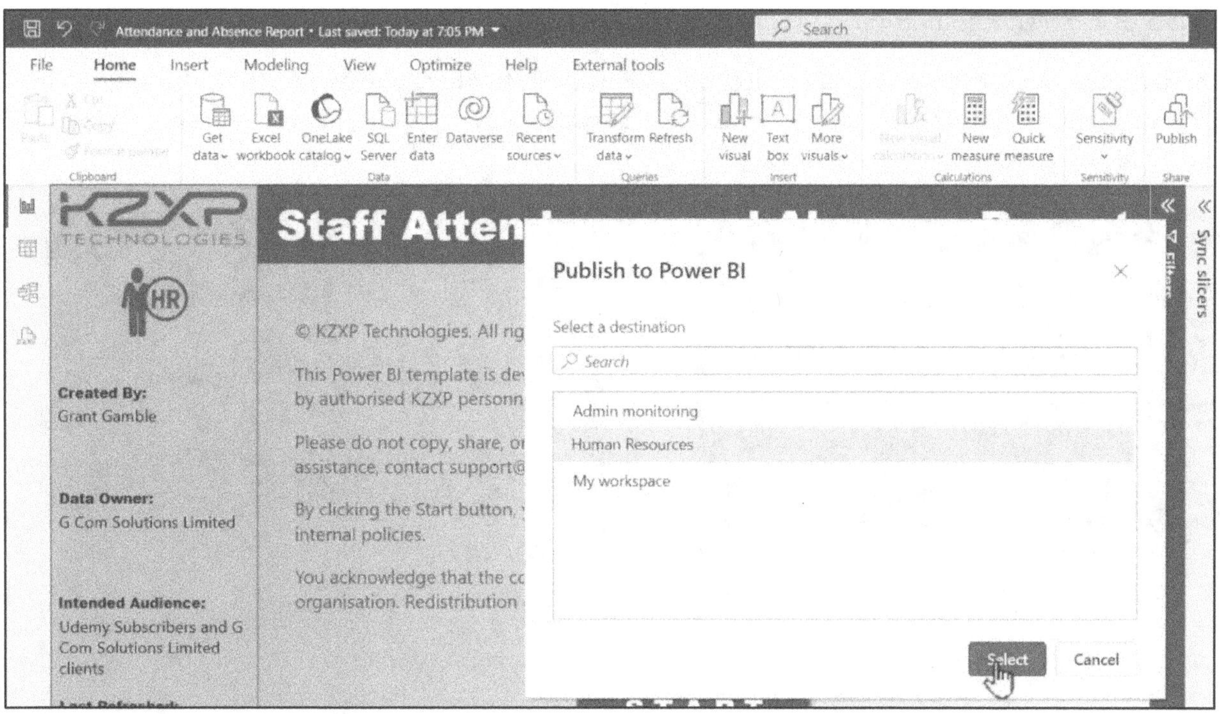

After publishing, open the Power BI Service and navigate to the Human Resources workspace. You should now see your newly published report listed, which in this scenario is an Attendance and Absence report.

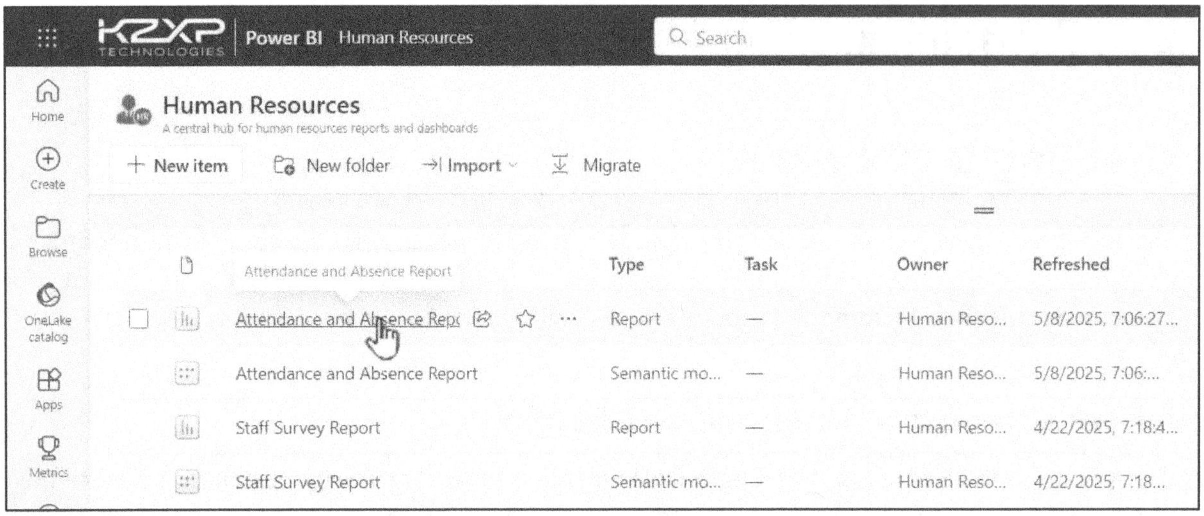

Understanding Dashboards in Power BI

Before creating dashboards, it's important to understand what a dashboard is in Power BI terms. A dashboard is a single-page canvas that combines visuals from one or more reports, offering a quick overview of key business metrics.

Dashboards are built in the Power BI Service, not in Power BI Desktop. While reports can be created in both environments, dashboards are exclusive to the Service. They are static, summary views, unlike reports which are interactive and multi-page.

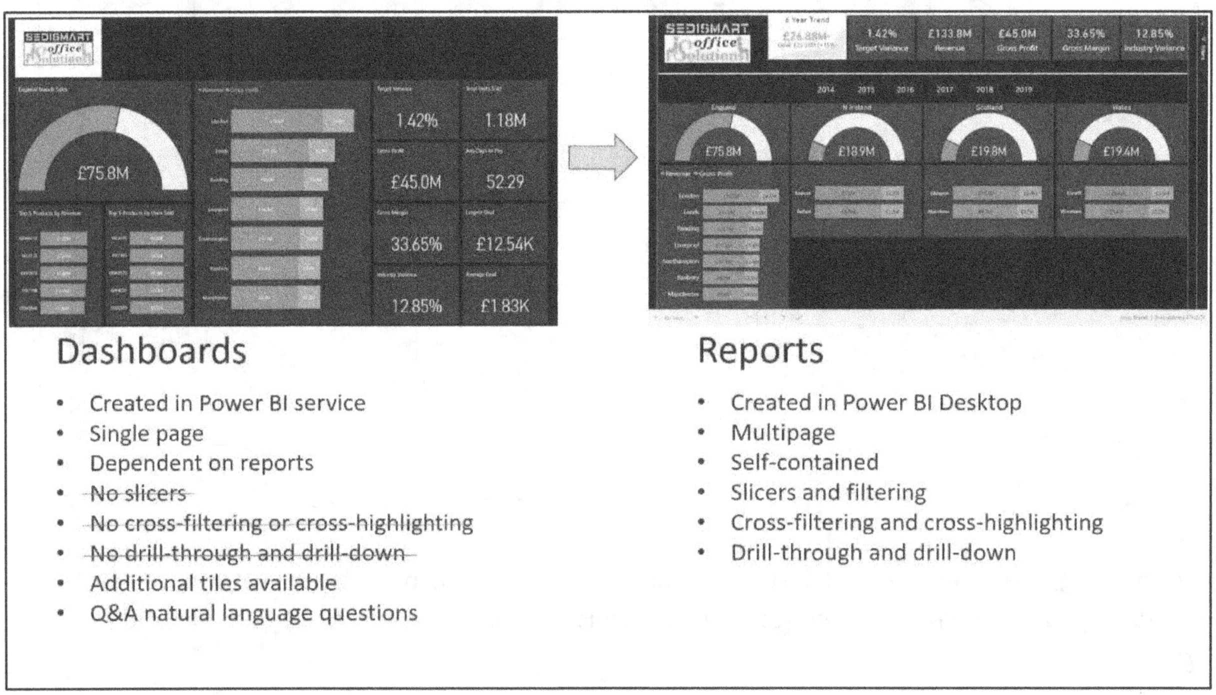

Here's a breakdown of key distinctions:

- Dashboards are always a single page, though you can scroll vertically if needed.
- Reports can contain multiple pages with detailed content.
- Dashboards are designed for overview consumption, while reports are for deep analysis.
- Dashboards offer no interactivity—no slicers, drill-downs, or cross-filtering.
- Clicking a visual on a dashboard takes the user directly to the report page the visual originated from.

Despite this lack of interactivity, dashboards can include extra elements called tiles, such as images, web content, or Q&A boxes. These make dashboards slightly more versatile than just being a static summary.

Creating a Dashboard Using Pinning

A common way to create dashboards is by pinning visuals from an existing report. In this example, we'll create an Absence Dashboard by pinning visuals from the Staff Absence report page.

Start by opening the Staff Absence page. Focus on a key metric like Total Absence Cost. Click on the visual and select Pin visual.

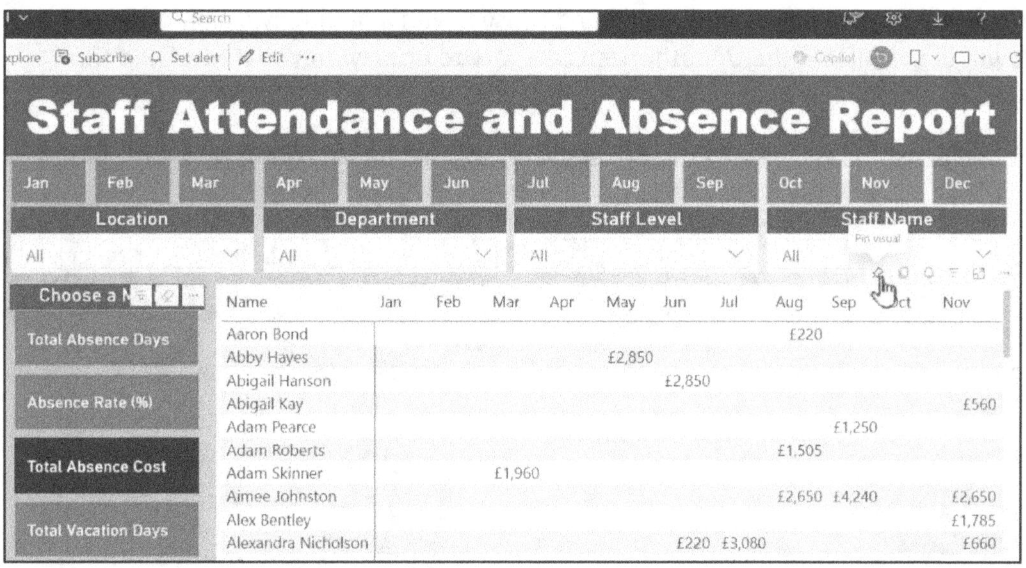

You'll be prompted to choose between pinning to an existing dashboard or creating a new one. Since there are no dashboards yet, the existing option is greyed out. Choose New dashboard, name it Absence, and click Pin.

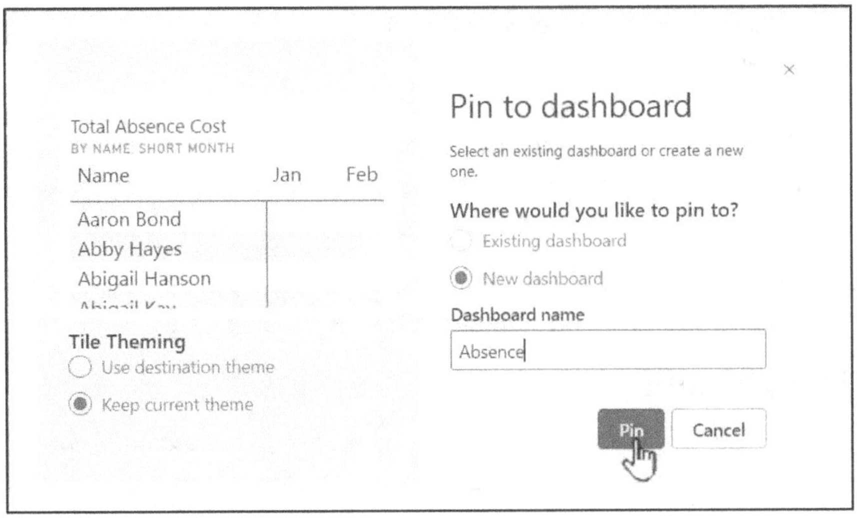

Power BI creates the dashboard and pins the visual.

Next, navigate to the Absence Types page. Here, you'll find a visual with a hierarchy on the categorical axis. Activate drill down, then drill into the Unauthorized category to display only that level. Pin this drilled visual to the Absence dashboard.

Note that what is pinned is a static view—only the drilled level, not the entire hierarchy, is included.

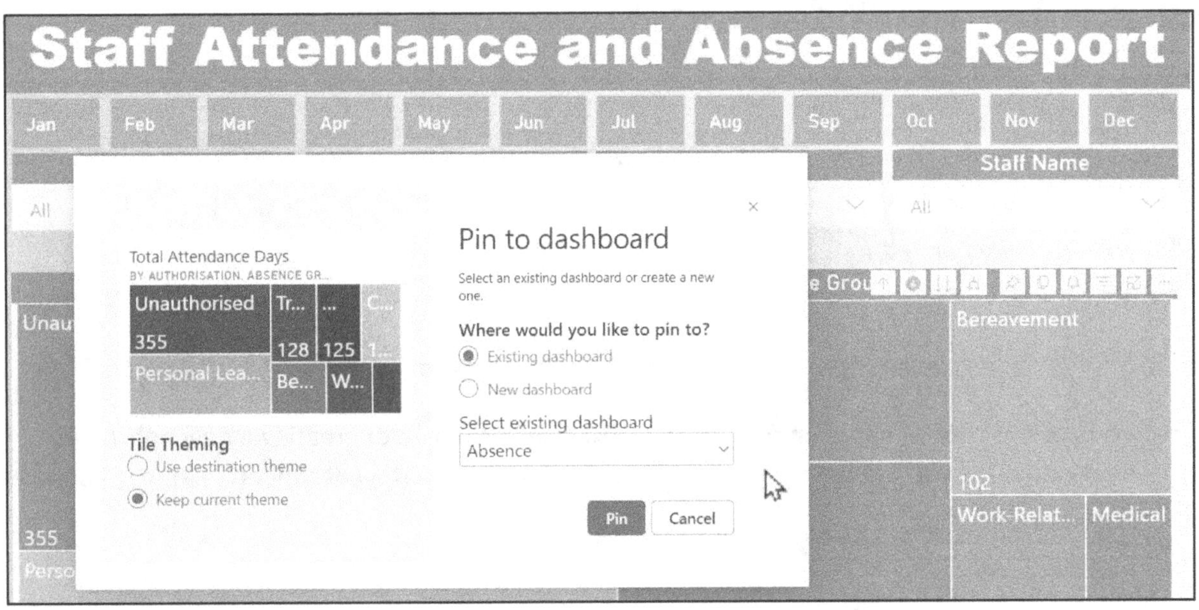

Finally, on the Absence Cost page, pin two more visuals—a tree map and a line chart—to the same dashboard. Then click Go to dashboard to view your result.

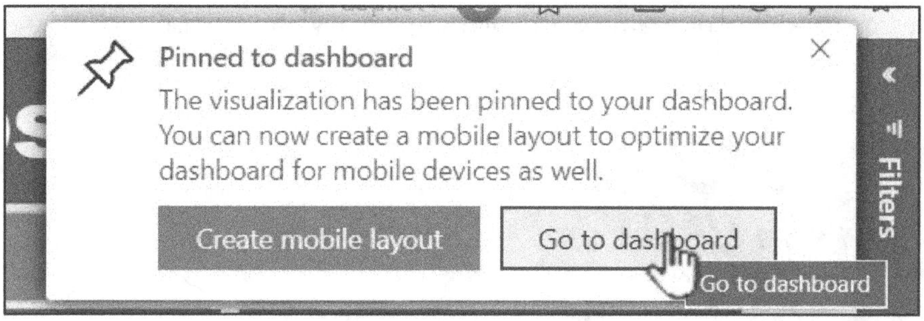

Exploring and Customizing the Dashboard Layout

The dashboard now contains all the pinned visuals, arranged in a grid layout. You can scroll to see them all. Clicking any visual on the dashboard opens the corresponding report page, not an interactive experience on the dashboard itself.

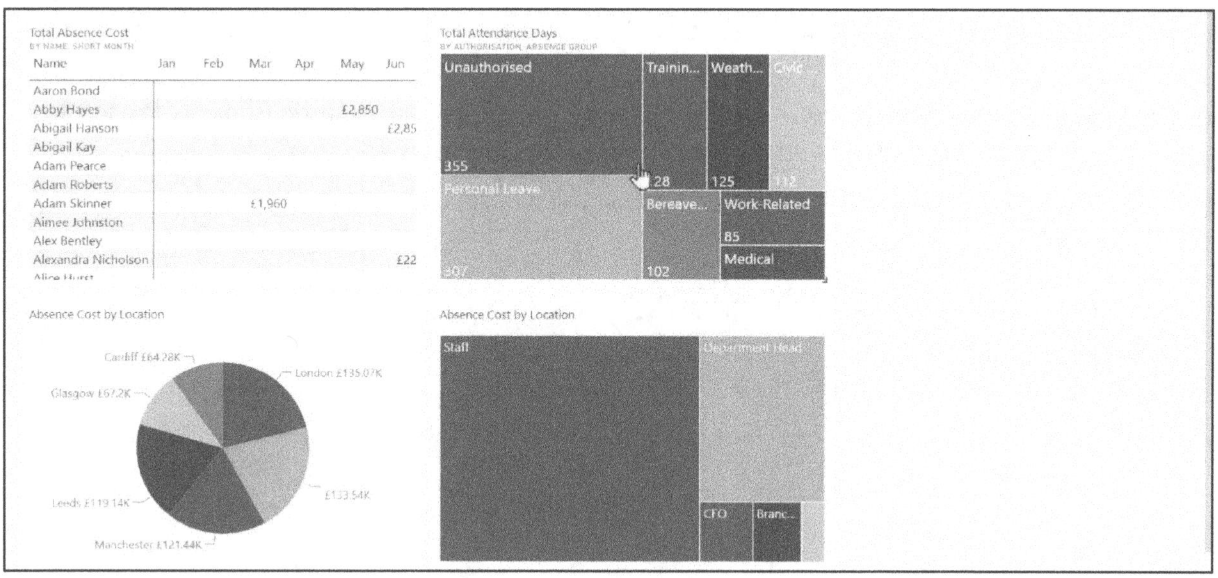

In the lower-left corner of the report page, users can use the Go Back button to return to the dashboard.

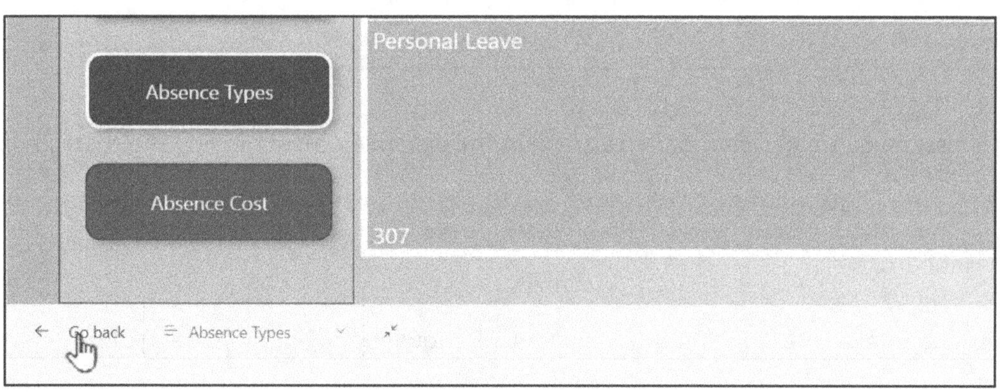

The dashboard layout is customizable. You can:

- Resize tiles—make the line chart wider, for example. (All tiles are initially one set size.)

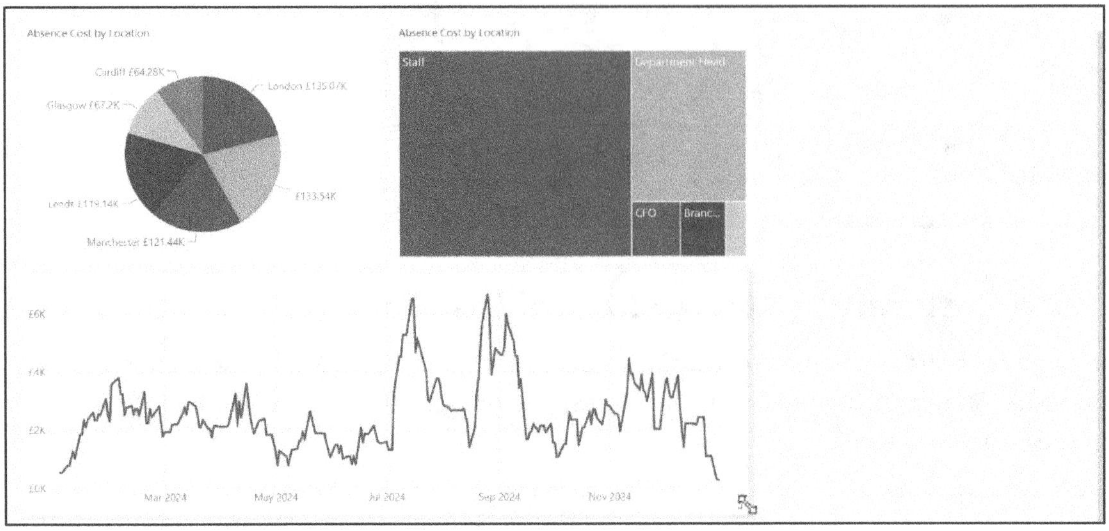

- Reposition tiles—for instance, in this example, we have moved the matrix from the top left to the bottom and aligned its width to match that of the line chart.

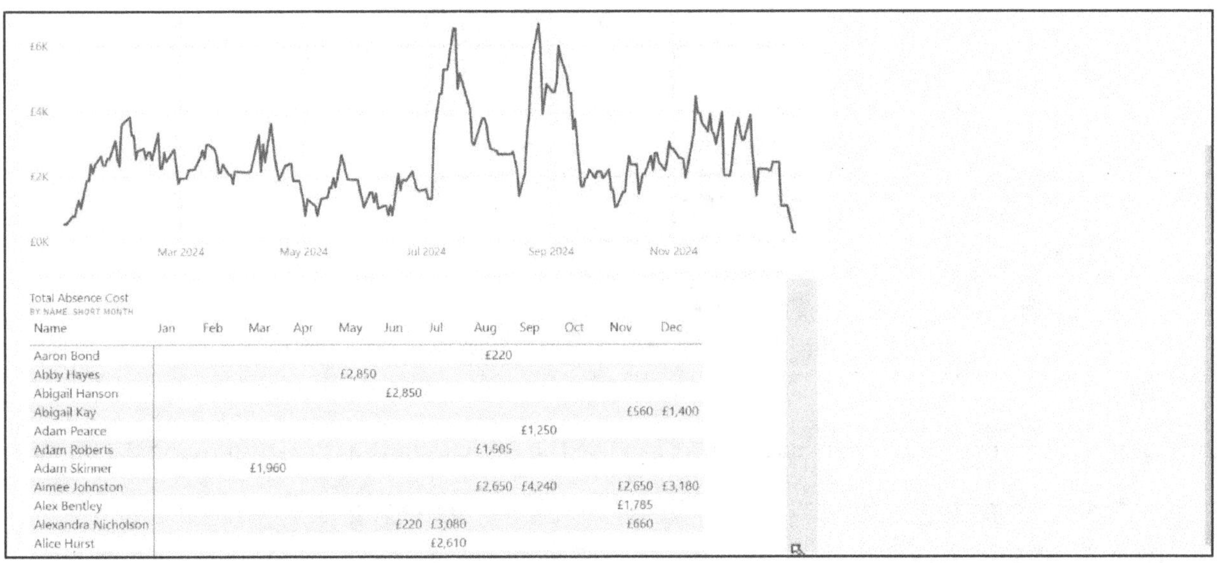

- Add branding—insert a company logo in the top left, in the space left after moving the matrix.

To add an image:

1. Click Edit on the dashboard.
2. Choose Add a tile > Image.
3. Click Next and paste the image URL (You'll find the image URL shown below in the assets folder).
4. Click Apply.

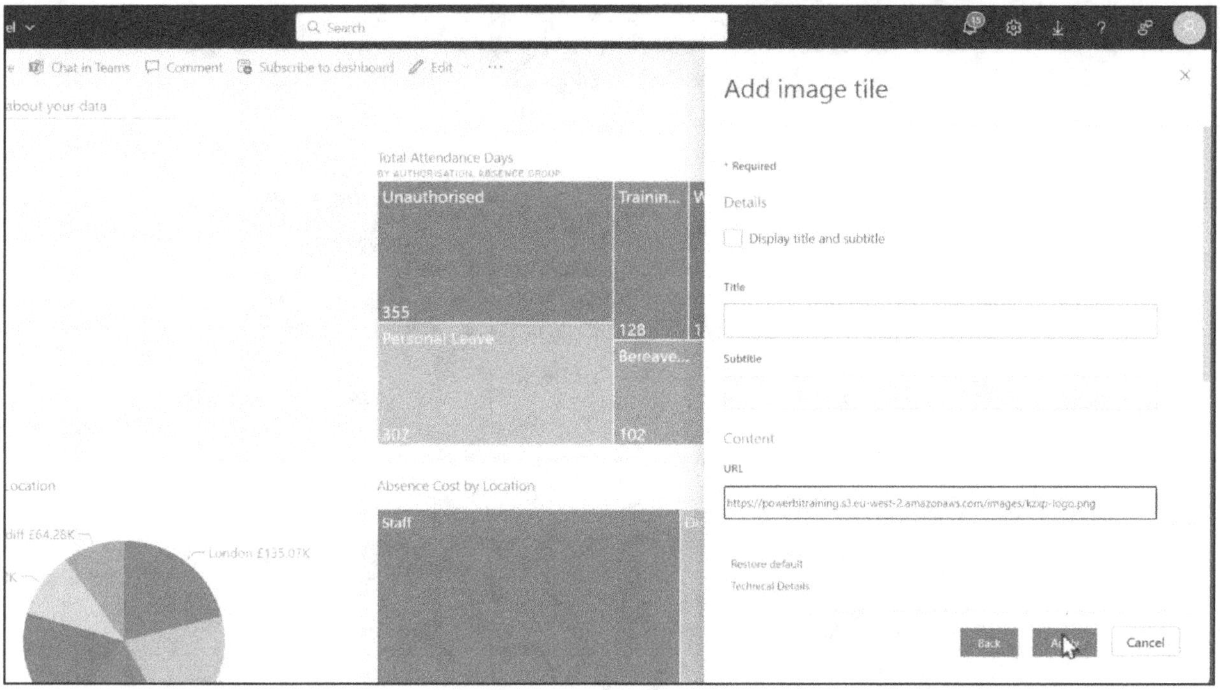

5. In this case, since the image is a logo, let's move the image tile to the top above the visuals.

This kind of dashboard design allows you to create audience-specific summaries, combining visuals and branding on one scrollable page.

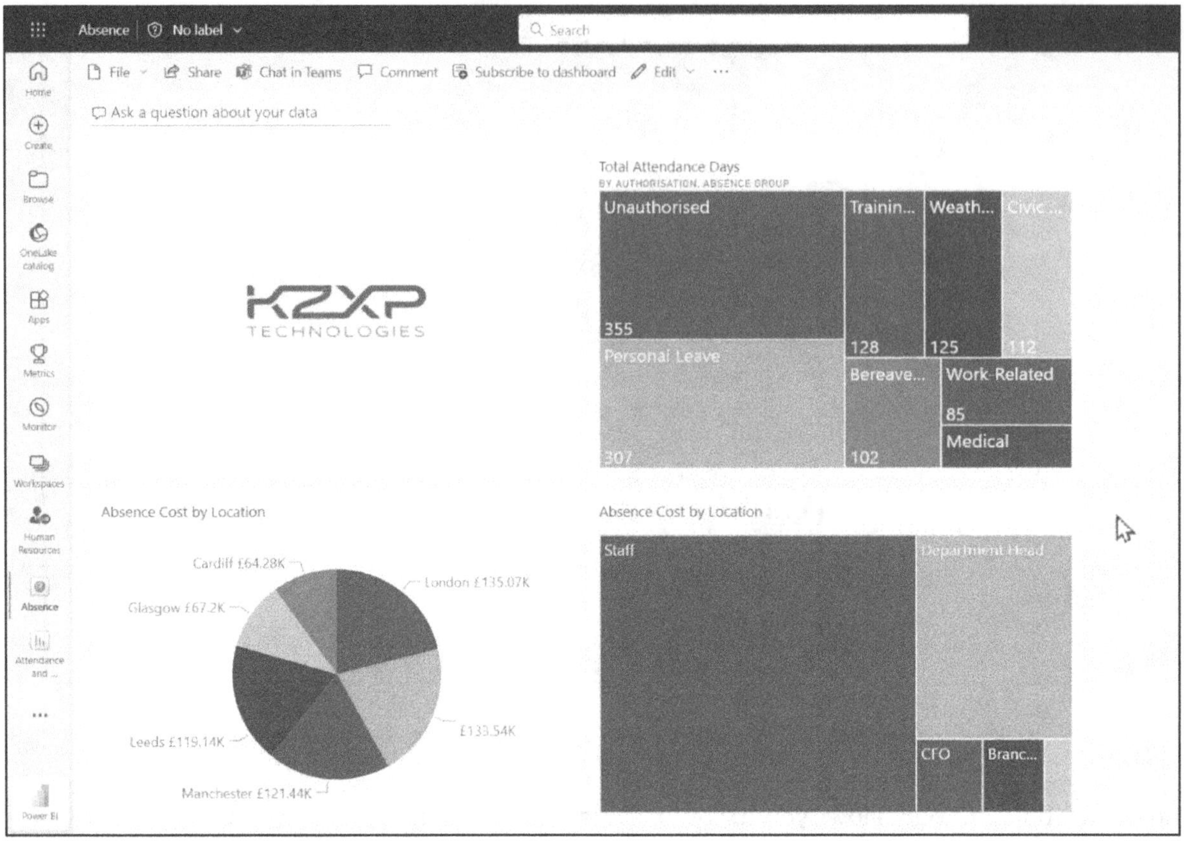

Click inside the Ask a question about your data box. Power BI will provide helpful examples to guide users. These suggestions demonstrate how to phrase questions using existing field and measure names.

Using Q&A in a Dashboard

Another interactive tile available on dashboards is the Q&A box. This enables users to type natural language questions directly into the dashboard and receive visual responses generated by Power BI.

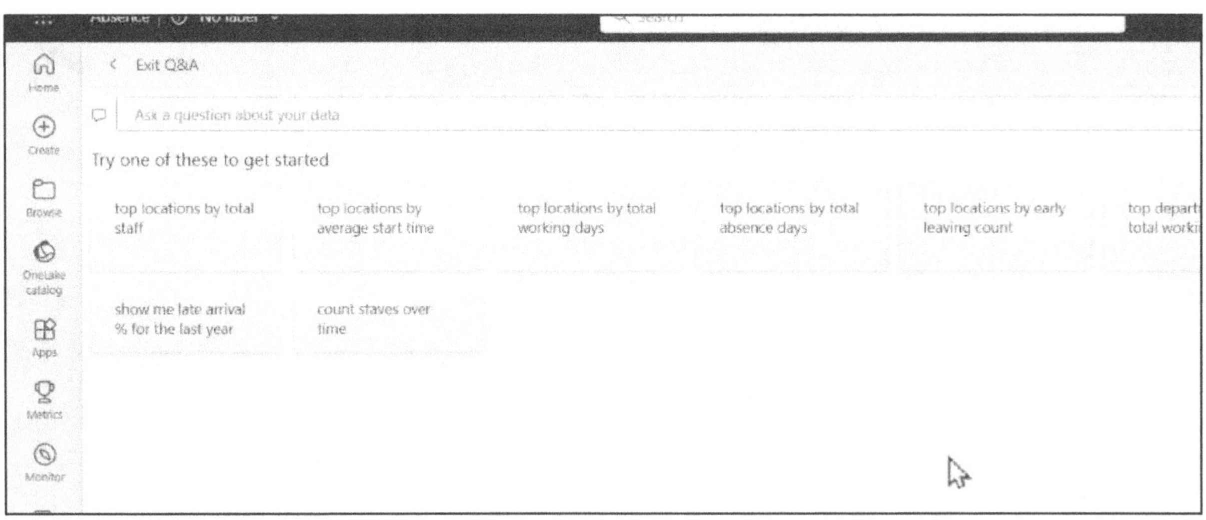

For example, to quickly break down absence rate by location, simply type:

absence rate by location

Press Enter, and Power BI will display a visual that best suits the query, in this case a bar chart. This makes the Q&A feature a useful self-service option for casual users.

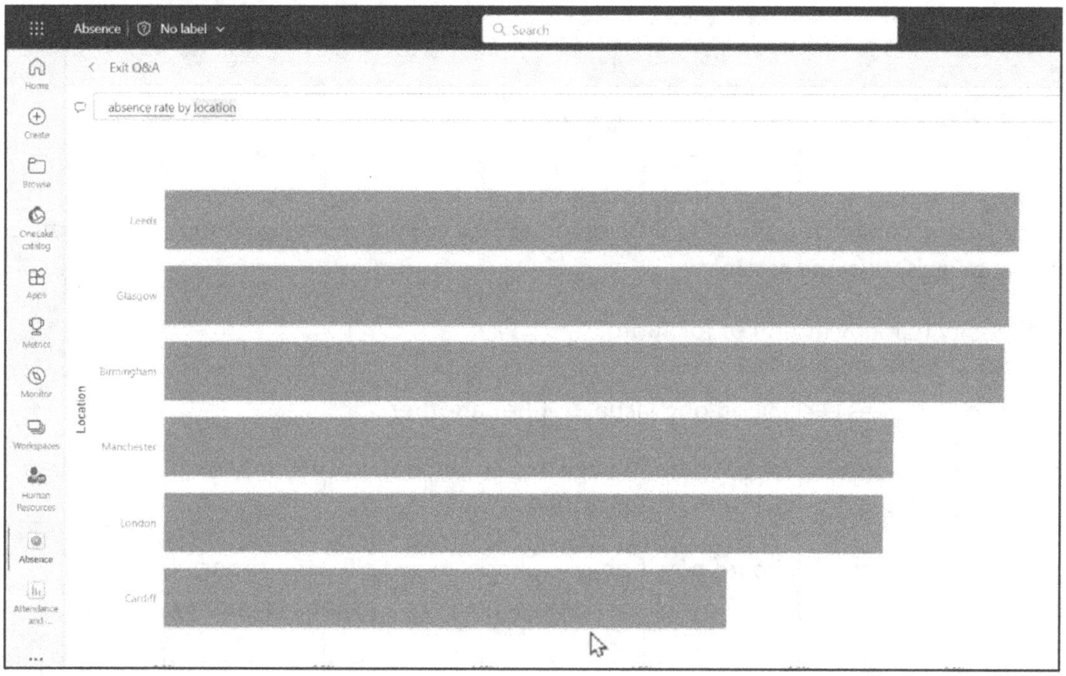

Pinning a Live Page

Another dashboard creation technique is using the Pin Live Page feature. Unlike pinning individual visuals, this option allows you to embed an entire report page—complete with all interactivity—onto a dashboard.

This is ideal for overview pages like our Executive Summary page.

To pin a live page:

1. Go to the desired report page.
2. Click the ellipsis (...) menu at the top right of the page.
3. Select Pin to a dashboard.

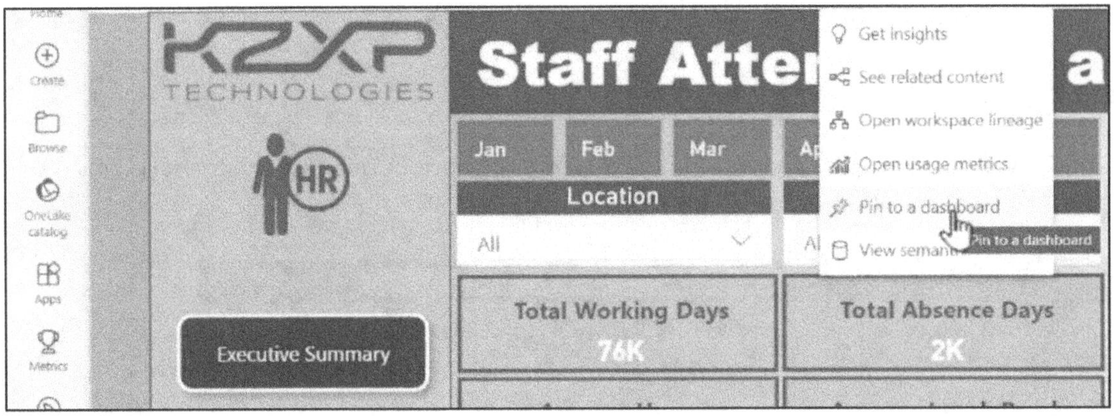

You'll be taken to the new dashboard. Switch to Full screen mode to view the page without distraction. Unlike traditional dashboards, this one retains:

- Slicer functionality (e.g., by month or location).
- Cross-filtering between visuals.
- Visual interactions such as clicking on one visual to filter another.

However, note that navigation buttons on the pinned page won't function as they rely on having access to other report pages—which are not part of the pinned view.

The key advantage here is that the dashboard now behaves almost exactly like the report, but it sits within the dashboard environment and can be included alongside other dashboard elements.

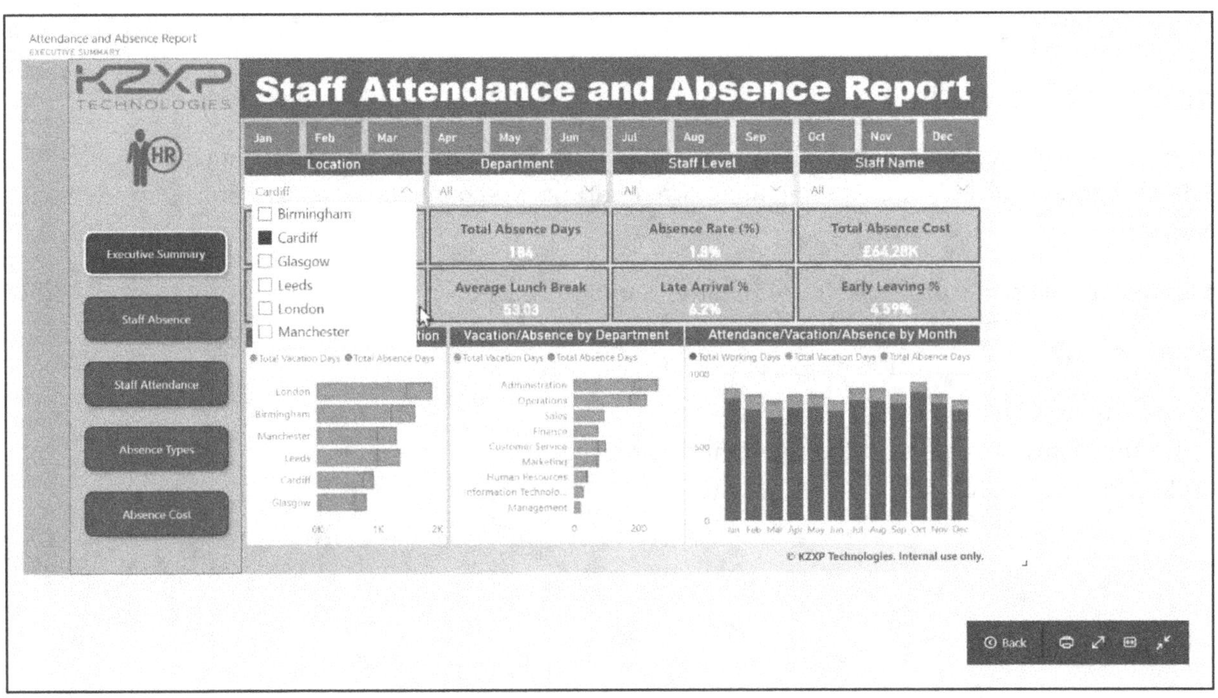

Summary

Dashboards in Power BI offer a way to summarise key insights on a single page, drawing content from reports or other data sources. They're intended for consumption, not exploration.

By pinning visuals or entire pages and incorporating additional tiles such as logos or Q&A features, you can craft audience-tailored dashboards that are both informative and visually aligned with your brand.

The choice between pinning static visuals and pinning a live page depends on the level of interactivity you want to preserve. Static dashboards are simple and clean, while live dashboards offer richer functionality at the cost of simplicity.

7.2: Creating an App

In a professional Power BI environment, sharing individual reports or dashboards is often sufficient for smaller audiences or short-term needs. However, as reporting grows more sophisticated and content increases, it becomes far more efficient to group and publish related items collectively. This is where the Power BI app functionality becomes invaluable.

An app in Power BI is essentially a packaged collection of dashboards and reports, grouped together from a workspace and presented as a unified, read-only experience for end users. It serves as a navigable portal—almost like a mini website—through which users can consume content in an organised and intuitive manner.

In our scenario, we've previously established a workspace for Human Resources and have already published two reports: the Staff Survey Report and the Attendance and Absence Report. Additionally, we've created two dashboards: Absence and Executive Summary. As the organisation grows, we can expect further HR-related reports and dashboards to be added to this workspace. Rather than sharing each item individually, we can now consolidate all of these into a single Power BI app.

To begin, we navigate to the top right corner of the workspace interface and select Create App. This opens a dialog box structured into three main tabs: Setup, Content, and Audience.

Setup Tab

The Setup tab is where we define the overarching metadata for the app. The app name is automatically inherited from the name of the workspace—in this case, Human Resources. We can leave this as-is or amend it if necessary.

We then add a short description. For example, "Human Resources: Reports and Dashboards". In a live environment, you would include a fuller summary detailing the types of insights and resources the app contains, and the departments or teams it supports.

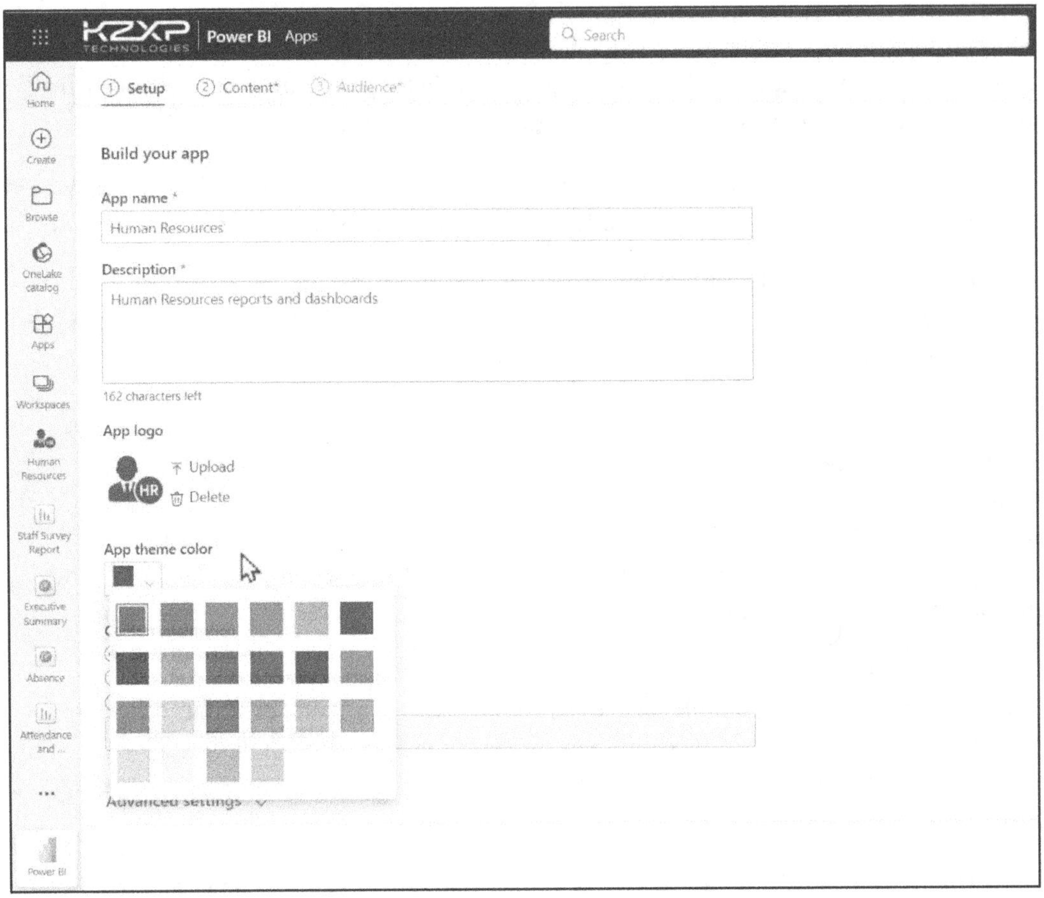

The logo for the app is also inherited from the workspace, though this can be changed if desired. You are also given the opportunity to choose from a limited set of theme colours. While these options are quite basic, you may find it useful to assign a consistent colour to apps for specific departments or business functions.

There is also an option labelled Show App Publisher, which will display the contact details of the person who published the app. This can be useful for users who may have questions or need support.

Content Tab

Moving on to the Content tab, this is where we decide exactly which items from the workspace will be included in the app.

Not all content needs to be shared. For example, you might have draft reports or dashboards in development, and these can be excluded. To select the items to include, we click Add Content. In our example, we have just four items, so we'll add them all.

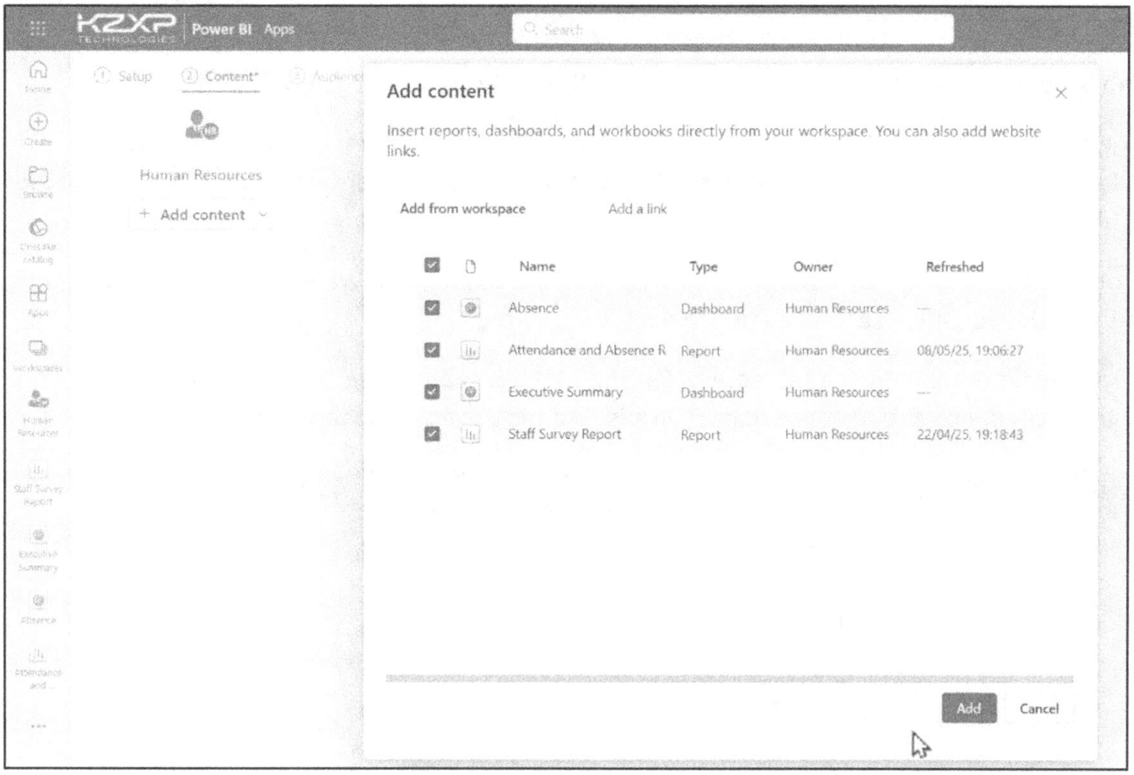

For workspaces with a larger number of items, we can create sections to organise content into logical groups. Sections help users navigate and find what they need more easily. You can also add external resources such as links to PDFs, policy documents, or intranet pages to supplement your reports.

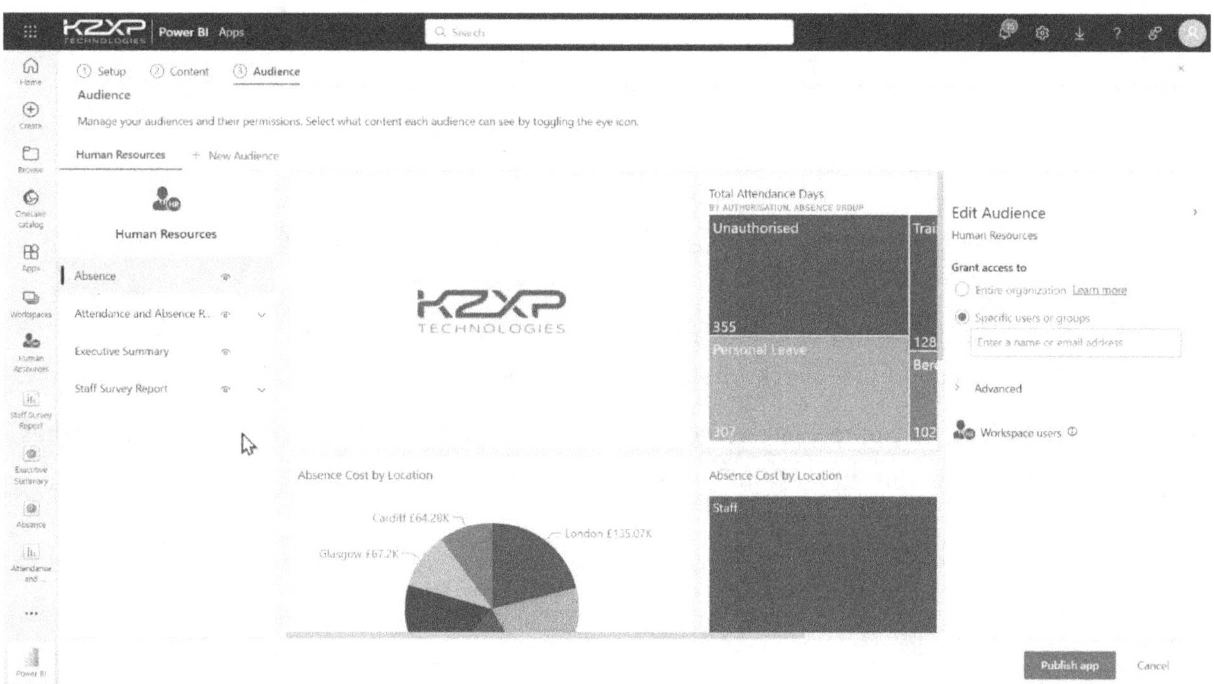

Audience Tab

The third tab is Audience, which is where the app's true flexibility comes into play.

This tab allows us to configure multiple audience groups, and for each group, we can define which content is visible. This enables targeted delivery of insights and tailored user experiences within a single app.

By default, one audience group is created with the same name as the app. We will rename this audience to Managers and then create a second audience named Directors.

Next, we decide what each audience can access. For the Managers audience, we make the Staff Survey Report and the Attendance and Absence Report visible. We hide the two dashboards.

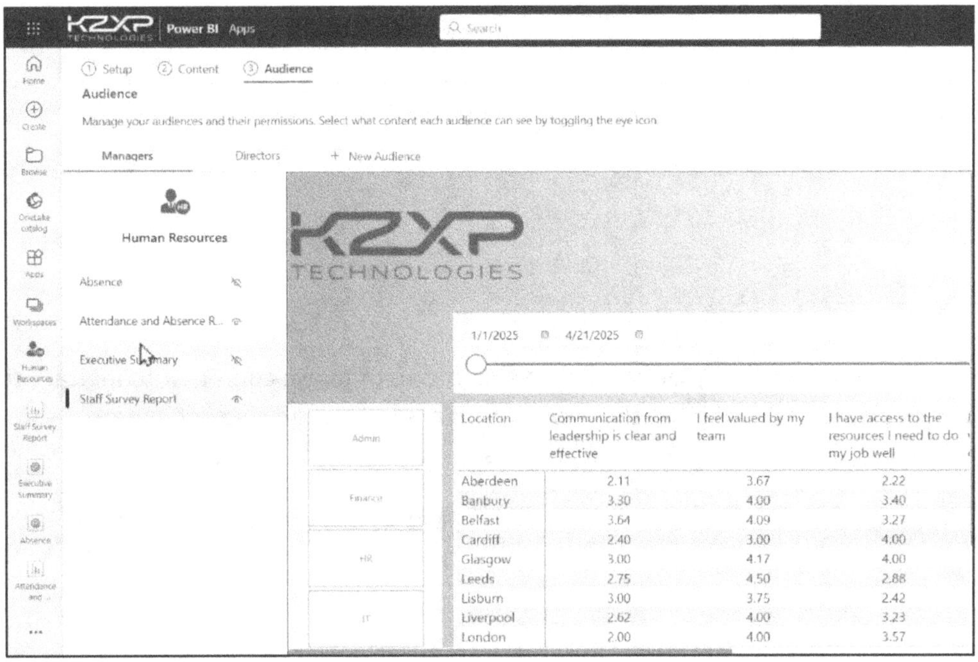

For the Directors audience, we reverse the setup—hiding the two reports and making only the Absence and Executive Summary dashboards visible.

You can preview how the app will appear for each audience by clicking on the visual thumbnails provided. This allows you to double-check what each group will see.

Finally, we assign users to the appropriate audience. This can be done by entering individual usernames or by referencing security groups in your organisation's Azure Active Directory.

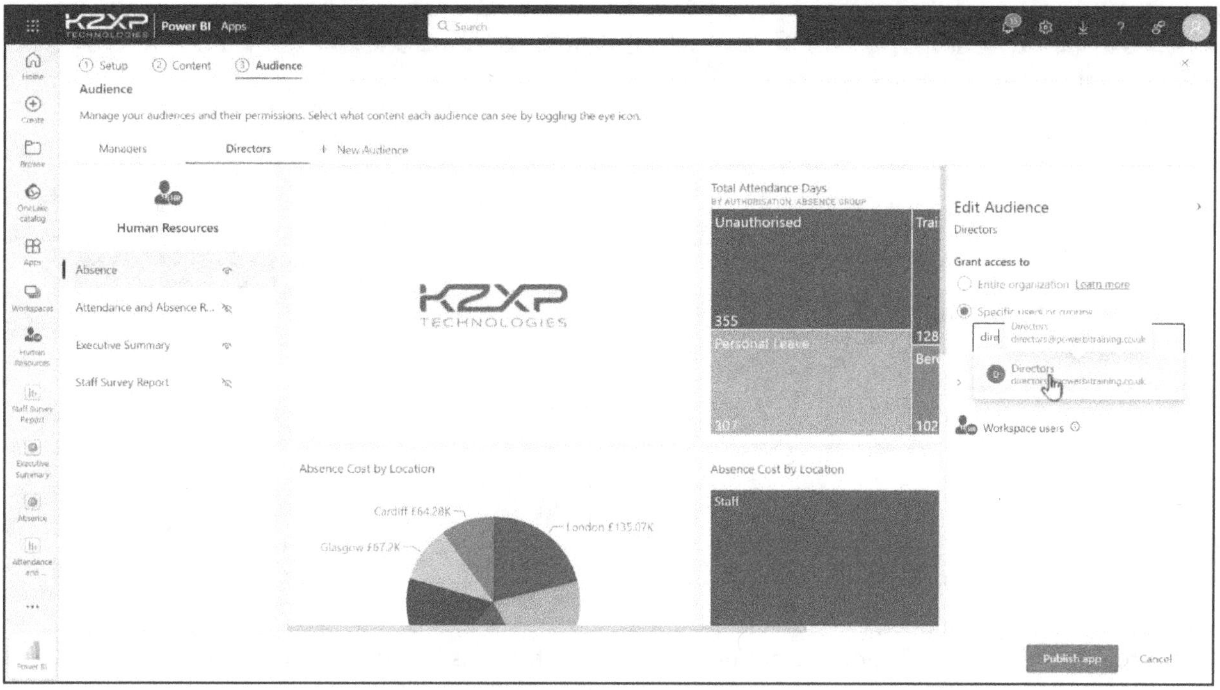

In our example, we've created two groups—managers and directors. We assign the appropriate group to each audience simply by typing the group name, selecting it from the suggestions, and confirming the selection.

Publishing and Access

Once all three tabs have been completed, we are ready to publish. Clicking the Publish App button confirms your choices, although a message may appear reminding you that the app might not be immediately available to end users.

Once published, you are given a direct link to the app. This link can be shared via email or added to documentation and internal communications, making it easy for users to access.

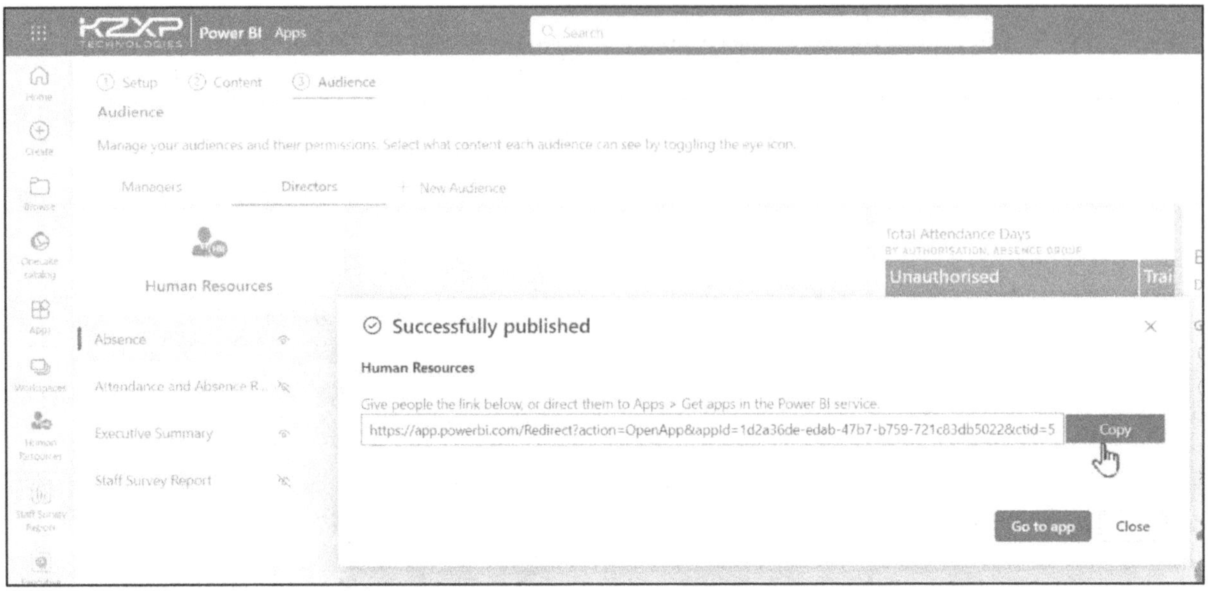

You can preview the app experience using the Go to App button. As the app publisher, you have full access and are not bound by the audience restrictions. This allows you to see all reports, dashboards, and pages, regardless of their visibility settings.

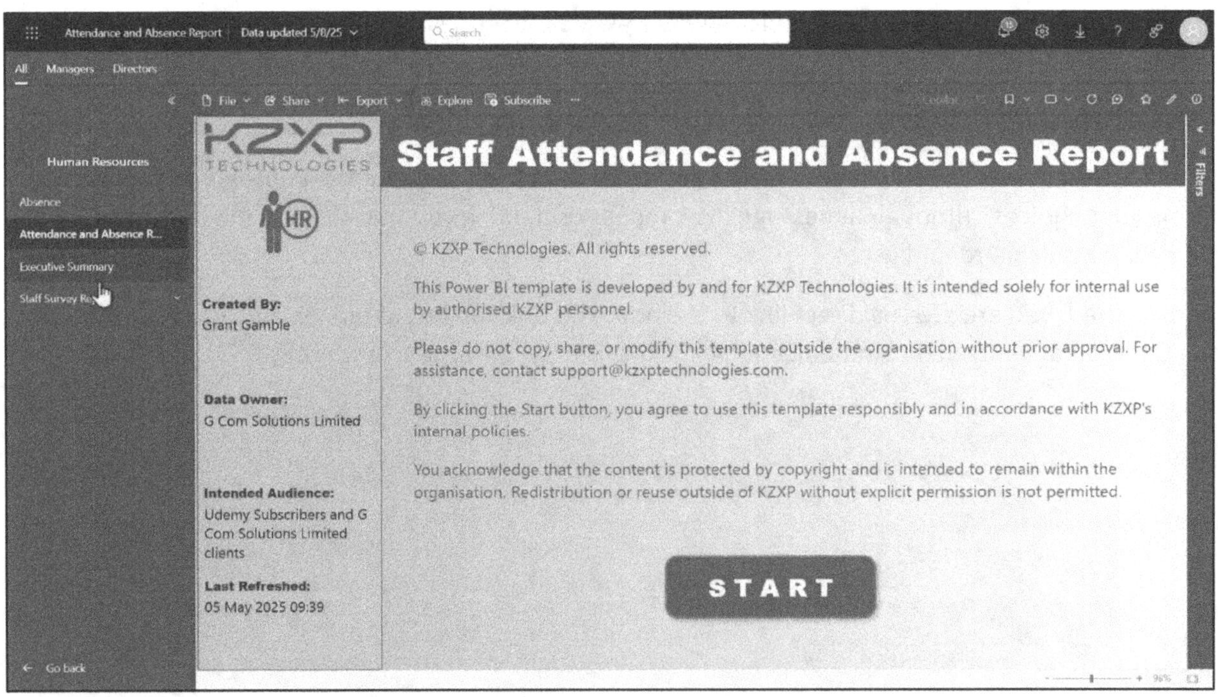

To test the end-user experience, we can log in as a user from one of the assigned groups. For example, logging in as a member of the managers group, we go to Apps and click Get App, then navigate to the Organisational Apps section. Here, the Human Resources app appears.

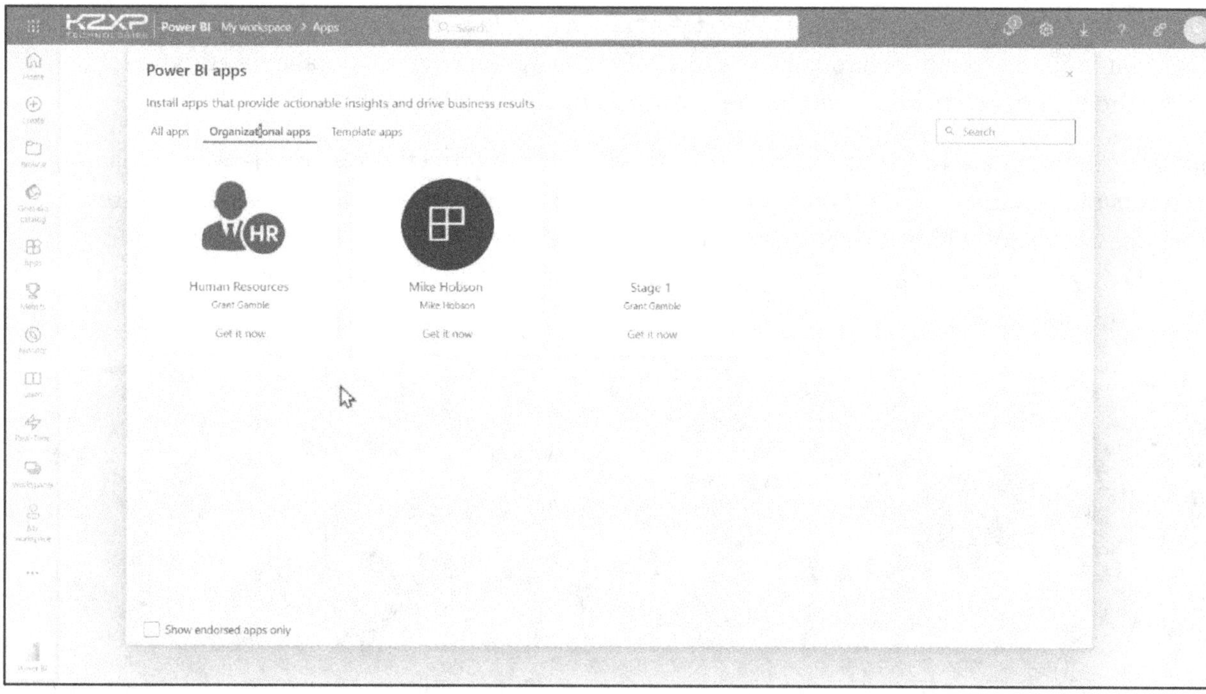

Opening the app as a manager reveals just the two visible reports—Staff Survey and Attendance and Absence. Since all pages of the Attendance report were hidden in this setup, users are presented with only the start page. If we had left the pages visible, Power BI would automatically have generated a navigation pane allowing users to click through each report page.

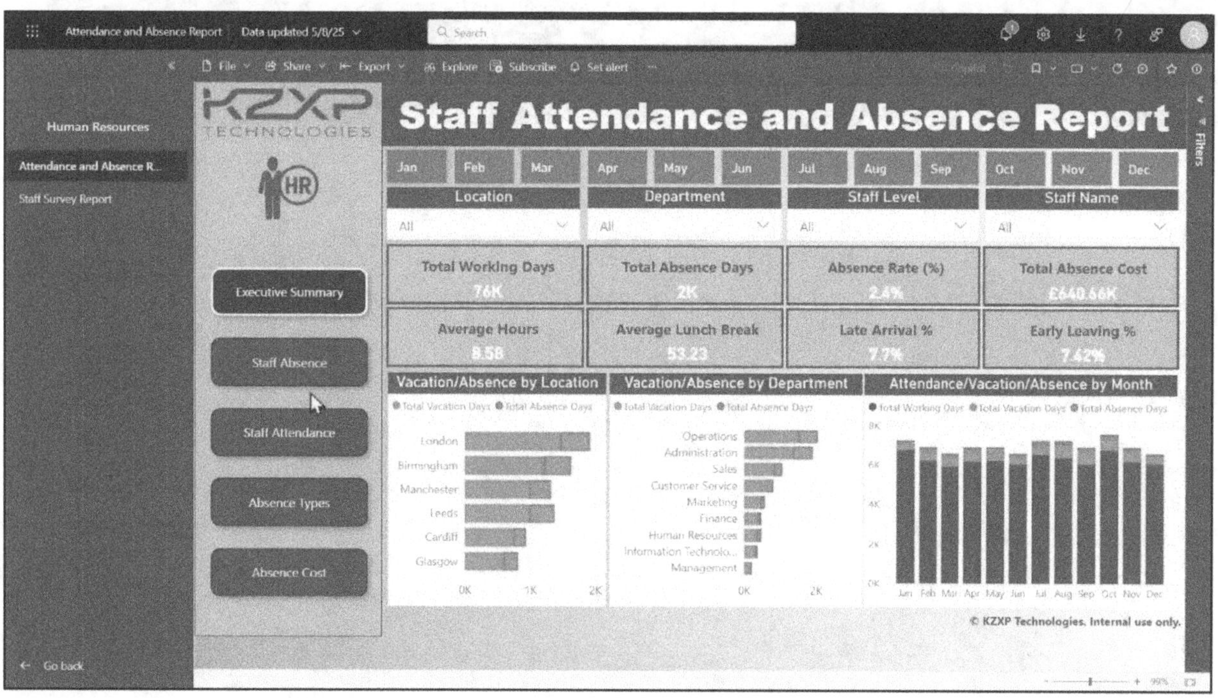

The beauty of the Power BI app model is that it remains available permanently to the assigned users. As new content is added to the workspace and included in the app, it becomes available automatically the next time the user opens the app—no further distribution or resending of links is needed.

In summary, publishing a Power BI app gives you a highly efficient and flexible mechanism for sharing curated sets of dashboards and reports. Rather than managing permissions for each individual report, you manage access through audience groups and share one single app URL. This approach scales effortlessly as your reporting estate grows and ensures your stakeholders have access to the right insights at the right time.

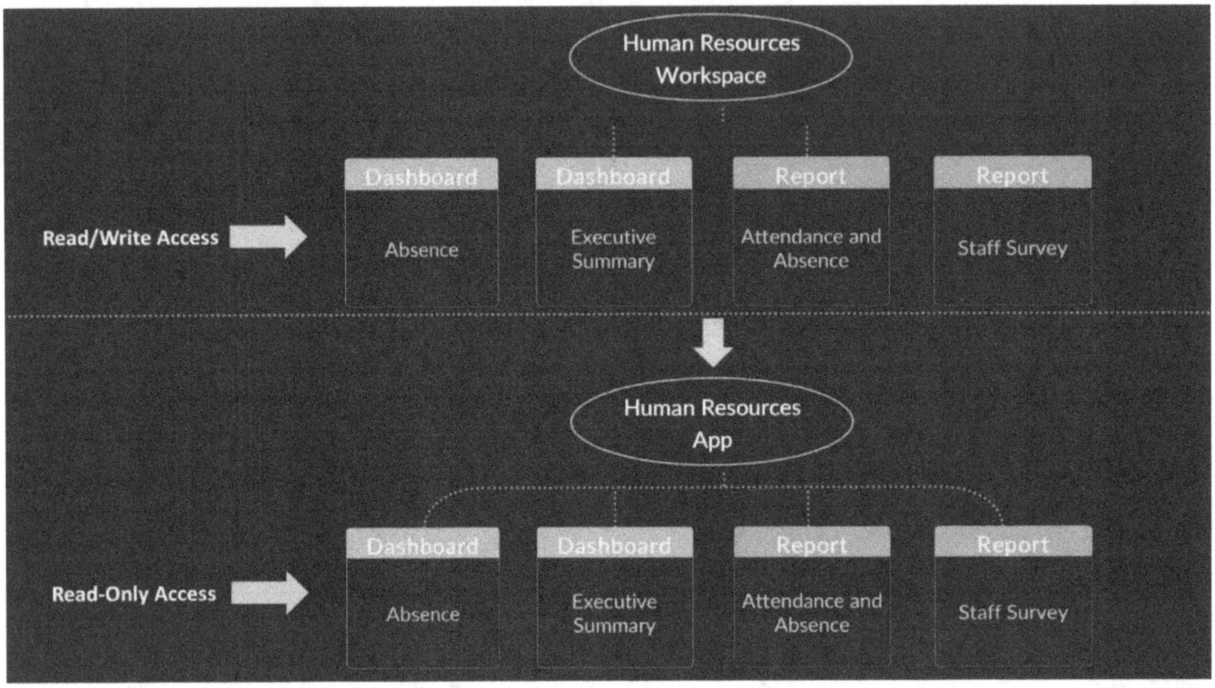

Conclusion

Congratulations on making it to the end of Power BI in the Workplace Part 1a HR Attendance and Absence Reporting. Over the course of this book, you've not just followed along with a series of Power BI exercises—you've built a fully-fledged HR reporting solution from the ground up.

You began with basic survey data and turned it into a branded, publishable report. From there, you expanded your skills into more advanced areas: data modelling, transforming data from SharePoint and Excel, writing meaningful DAX measures, and using field parameters and hierarchies to make your reports more dynamic and insightful.

But more than anything, what you've done is develop a way of thinking about Power BI that reflects how it's actually used in the workplace. You've gone beyond the sales dashboards and fictional demo datasets. You've tackled real-world challenges, with real-life datasets: inconsistent data sources, messy layouts, HR-specific metrics, and user expectations that evolve over time.

What You've Achieved

- You've learned to transform and shape HR data, including hidden and disorganised sheets, using Power Query.
- You've created a structured data model that supports accurate and flexible analysis.
- You've written custom DAX measures that go beyond sums and counts to deliver KPIs such as attendance rates, absence cost, and time lost.
- You've enhanced the user experience with thoughtful layout choices: dynamic titles, branded templates, and easy-to-use navigation.
- You've deployed your reports using Power BI Service, built dashboards, and created a Power BI app to deliver a polished end product.

These are not minor wins. In many organisations, what you've built in this book would represent a meaningful step forward in how HR data is understood, accessed, and used for decision-making.

Looking Ahead

While this book focuses on attendance and absence, the techniques you've learned apply far beyond this domain. HR departments rely on dozens of internal reports—from turnover to training, from engagement to equity—and every one of them needs clear visuals, structured data, and dependable metrics.

Future volumes in this series will help you continue that journey. You'll explore employee movement and turnover, compensation benchmarking, survey sentiment analysis, and other key HR topics. Each new dataset and reporting challenge will reinforce your understanding while introducing new tools and techniques.

But before moving on, consider how you can apply what you've built here in your own environment. Can your organisation benefit from a clearer absence report? Would a centralised HR dashboard save time across departments? Could your stakeholders make better decisions if they had access to insights like the ones you've just built?

Final Thoughts

Learning Power BI is not just about charts or queries—it's about becoming a better communicator of information. It's about taking raw data and shaping it into something that people understand and trust. And in the HR context, it's about giving teams the tools to support the people who make the organisation run.

As you close this volume, don't worry about remembering every detail. Instead, remember the principles: structure your reports thoughtfully, model your data clearly, write measures that answer real questions, and always keep the end user in mind.

This is what sets workplace reporting apart. This is what Power BI was made for.

Thank you for joining the journey—and we hope to see you again in the next volume.

www.ingramcontent.com/pod-product-compliance
Lightning Source LLC
LaVergne TN
LVHW080043210926
848481LV00011B/3267